Music in the
Restoration Theatre

Studies in Musicology, No. 4

Other Titles in This Series

Music in the Restoration Theatre

With a Catalogue of Instrumental Music
in the Plays 1665-1713

by
Curtis A. Price

RESEARCH PRESS

Library of Congress Cataloging in Publication Data

Price, Curtis A 1945-
 Music in the Restoration theatre.

 (Studies in musicology series ; no. 4)
 Includes indexes.
 "A catalogue of instrumental music in Restoration
plays, 1665-1713": p.
 "A list of sets of act music published by John Walsh,
1701-1713": p.
 1. Music, Incidental—History and criticism. 2. Music—
England—History and criticism. I. Title.

ML1731.P74   782.8'3'0942   79-11742
ISBN 0-8357-0998-1
ISBN 0-8357-0999-X pbk.

CONTENTS

v

CONTENTS

LIST OF PLATES

PLATE

NOTE ON ABBREVIATIONS

If any song mentioned in the following study is catalogued in Day and
Murrie's *English Song-Books*, the number of the song in this
bibliography is provided after the abbreviation "D&M." The names of
the composer and/or singer(s), when known, are also included, using
their system. For example, D&M 515, *m*H. Purcell *s*J. Boman means
that the song ("Celia, that I once was blest") was composed by Henry
Purcell and that at least one of its printed sources states that it was sung
by John Boman. The abbreviations devised by *Répertoire international
des sources musicales* (RISM) are used throughout to refer to libraries
and archives. The prefix "GB" (designating Great Britain) is omitted,
since most manuscripts cited below are found in that country. Given the
interdisciplinary nature of this study, I have not abbreviated the names of
periodicals, except those likely to be known by both musicians and
drama historians (*PMLA*, for instance).

PREFACE

This study of music in Restoration drama began in an attempt to locate as many of the sources of instrumental music originally associated with the plays as possible. I was encouraged in this project by Cyrus L. Day and Eleanore Boswell Murrie's *English Song-Books 1651-1702 A Bibliography* (London, 1940), a thorough and admirably accurate work which locates and identifies vast numbers of songs from hundreds of Restoration stage works. By combining their bibliography of songs with my catalogue of instrumental pieces (Appendix I), one may now assemble most of the music required by a large number of these plays. The following study of the musical practices of the Restoration theatre grew, then, from these two bibliographical works, and ultimately, it is hoped, from the surviving music itself.

To decide what editorial procedures to use in reproducing excerpts from late 17th-century English literature is difficult, for the language of Dryden and Congreve appears superficially very close to our own; yet 17th-century spelling, capitalization, italicization, and so forth, are inconsistent, and English usage has changed considerably in 300 years. I have adopted the following editorial policies. All quotations are exact, but I have not generally preserved italics in plays, with the following exceptions: the speaker's name in dialogue; titles of published works mentioned in quotations. The use of *sic* is avoided, except in a few instances. I have Anglicized two French surnames, Davenant and Durfey (rather than D'Avenant and D'Urfey), as one often finds them written in contemporary sources. Unless otherwise specified, all dates of plays are publication dates and not performance dates. The chief reference source for full titles, authors, dates of first performances, and so forth, is Allardyce Nicoll, *A History of English Drama 1660-1900* (Cambridge, 1967).

I owe a great debt to John Ward, who, as a man of the theatre, was an ideal advisor for this study. I should especially like to thank him for bringing to my attention G. F. Handel's incidental music for Jonson's *The Alchymist* (produced in London in 1710), which is probably this composer's first music to appear in England (see Appendix II). As he has graciously done for so many of his students and colleagues, Professor Ward would have us take credit for his best discoveries. I also owe much to Lowell Lindgren for many valuable suggestions. His knowledge of early 18th-century Italian opera, a dramatic form which was at once the nemesis and savior of the late 17th-century English play, is compendious, and his understanding of the theatre in general is profound.

PREFACE

Among other scholars, I should like to thank Margaret Laurie, Anthony Hicks, Hyatt King, Charles Cudworth, and particularly the late Thurston Dart. Special thanks go to Anice Joffray for her considerable help during the early stages of research and to Robert D. Hume, from whose close criticism and sound advice this study has greatly benefited; and to Lois Siegelbaum, for many suggestions and improvements concerning the whole of this work. Among the many librarians for whom I have been at times a source of irritation, I should like to thank Robert Latham of the Pepys Library at Magdalene College, Cambridge, D. Pepys Whiteley of the Magdalene College Library, Cambridge, and Mary Lou Little and Larry Mowers of the Eda Kuhn Loeb Library, Harvard University.

The initial research for this project was made possible by a Frank Knox Travelling Fellowship, awarded by Harvard University, and I am grateful to the Martha Baird Rockefeller Fund for Music, Maude E. Brogan, director, for a generous grant-in-aid enabling me to complete this study of Restoration plays in the most advantageous location: the still theatrically lively city of their origin.

ACKNOWLEDGEMENTS

The author gratefully acknowledges permission to use material in altered form from the following copyrighted works:

"The Critical Decade for English Music Drama, 1700-1710," *Harvard Library Bulletin*, XXVI (1978), 38-76; by kind permission of the editor.

"'. . . to make Amends for One ill Dance': Conventions for Dancing in Restoration Plays," *Dance Research Journal*, X (1977-78), 1-6; by kind permission of the Committee on Research in Dance.

"The Songs for Katherine Philips' *Pompey* (1663)," *Theatre Notebook*, forthcoming, by kind permission of the Society for Theatre Research.

INTRODUCTION

In the spring of 1660 the *H.M.S. Naseby*, soon to be renamed the *Charles II* in honor of its royal passenger, sailed the short distance across the Strait of Dover to return a long-exiled king to a country he knew mainly from childhood memories. With the return of Charles and hence the restoration of the monarchy to England, patents and monopolies were quickly granted to loyal subjects, and the London theatres reopened after being shut for 18 years during the Puritan rule of the Commonwealth. The 40 or 50 year period of prolific creation of stage works that followed is now known as the "Restoration," a term which writers of the time used to apply equally to the restoration of the theatre and to the restoration of the House of Stuart. Charles II vigorously encouraged the newly reinstated theatres, not only in his official capacities, somewhat diminished at the Restoration, but also in his unofficial capacities, which were rarely diminished.

The extravagant court masque, which had been an important part of his father's court and not insignificant in contributing to his downfall, was not encouraged in Charles II's reign. The stage play, presented by "his Majesty's servants" at the so-called public playhouses, was encouraged; and the expensive collaborative efforts necessary for court dramatic presentations were in part transferred to the theatre companies. In Charles's reign alone (1660-1685) nearly 250 new plays were staged.[1] And from 1685 until the ascension of Queen Anne in 1702, about 200 new stage works were presented by the licensed theatre companies. Although not all of these productions are comparable in magnificence of spectacle to the Jacobean court masques, a few certainly are; and the considerable number of stage works offered during the period is indicative of a voracious theatrical appetite of what was by present norms a very small audience.

The newly restored theatres of the 1660s were as much court playhouses as were their French counterparts in the same century. During these early years, the theatre became one of the fixed stations of aristocratic society, a place to congregate for the kind of formal entertainment previously provided by the masque. Since the audience was small and attendance at the theatre obligatory for those wishing to move in courtly circles, the theatre companies were forced to present new plays at what was at times a barely manageable rate. Dramatic offerings in the Restoration were as varied and constantly changing as during any other period of English drama. Yet London could hardly support even two repertory companies, and between 1682 and 1695, the heart of the period, only one house provided the court with theatrical entertainment. The London playhouses were supported and controlled by the aristocracy, wealthy patrons who determined what plays would be written and mounted; and a considerable number of Restoration plays were the product of the gentry itself.

The composition and character of the audience of the 1670s, 80s, and 90s has been hotly debated since Allardyce Nicoll described it as a "depraved and licentious" gathering of the privileged,[2] but during this period, the theatres began to be filled with a more representative assortment of the various strata of London society. Certainly by 1700 the cits (from the merchant classes) constituted a large segment of the audience.[3]

The Restoration produced a few dramatic masterpieces and fewer masterly dramatists. The very nature of the theatrical structure and the demand for great numbers of new entertainments by an audience whose tastes were often at best frivolous, produced a prodigious number of inferior plays, displaying the basest of morals, the most ludicrous of bombastic rants, and occasionally no purpose other than simply to amuse in a most ephemeral and unredeeming way. How these works could follow by a mere 40 years the most glorious era in English literary history has long troubled critics and drama scholars.

Though the scholarly efforts expended on the Restoration period are in no way comparable (in numbers at least) to those on the Elizabethan, the late 17th-century English theatre has not been neglected by students of the drama. Several important studies are now available,[4] and the stage works of many of the major poets have been given modern complete editions.[5] Unfortunately, these works have not devoted adequate study to an important constituent of the 17th-century English play: music. For this reason, this corpus of dramatic literature is still misunderstood even by some authorities.

I. THE SPECIAL PLACE OF MUSIC IN RESTORATION DRAMA

During no period in the history of English drama has the play been more infused with music, and never was music considered more essential to dramatic representation. Nearly all of the 600 or so stage works performed during the period, whether quasi-operas or grim tragedies, required music. Many plays included several songs, at least some of them with choruses and followed by dances; in tragedies one often finds full-blown masques, and music frequently accompanies religious processions or rituals and intensifies and foreshadows tragic events. In comedies, scenes are enhanced with a miscellany of musical entertainments, from miniature concerts to carefully choreographed entry dances. And in all types of plays, music is used for special effects, ranging from battle scenes to pantomimes. In addition to the music within the acts, plays were accompanied by "incidental" music heard before the drama began and between the acts, the tunes often chosen to heighten the dramatic effect. In fact, the intrusion of music into all genres of late 17th-century English drama, even into those one might expect to be devoid of music--the farce and the tragedy--distinguishes the Restoration from all other ages of English drama.

Yet what Restoration musical practice is not also found in the modern theatre? The overture and act music still come to us (albeit recorded and through loud-speakers and usually written or arranged by anonymous musicians) as the house lights dim and the curtain is about to rise, and the instrumental music which so often accompanies or foreshadows horrid events in late 17th-century English drama has found its place on the sound tracks of modern films as a repertoire of musical clichés that fit stereotyped dramatic situations. Entry dances and masques, too, hold the stage as firmly as ever as the elaborate production numbers which are obligatory for any variety show or Broadway musical.

The Restoration theatre derived almost all of its musical practices from earlier ages. Even the more "innovative" of these have antecedents. One, for example, is the convention that requires some principal characters to sing their own songs; music thus becomes an extension of their personalities. This contrasts with the usual Elizabethan practice of relegating songs to an attendant or to some lesser character; such songs are usually static commentaries on a situation, no more than atmospheric interludes in the drama. But even in earlier plays one finds examples of this practice which is common in Restoration drama, Desdemona's and Ophelia's songs being perhaps the best known. Likewise in George Peele's *David and Bethsabe* (c. 1594), the heroine sings; and in Marston's *Sophonisba* (1606), in Act III, the protagonist possibly sings her own song.

Also the integration of masque and play, which several Restoration playwrights took great care to accomplish despite the better known examples to the contrary (e.g., *The Fairy Queen*), is already seen in Jonsonian tragedy. In fact, the remarkable masque in Act IV of Elkanah Settle's *The Empress of Morocco* (1673), which artfully advances the bloody plot, closely resembles the similarly murderous masque in V.iii of *The Revenger's Tragedy* (1607) (probably by Cyril Tourneur). Most other Restoration musical conventions also have their roots in earlier dramatic traditions.

But *David and Bethsabe* and *The Revenger's Tragedy* are exceptional. What is so striking about Restoration drama is the large number of plays in which music actually furthers the dramatic action rather than simply supplements it. Perhaps Edward J. Dent best expressed the musical "limitations" of Elizabethan drama: "Shakespeare and his contemporaries never show us speech intensified into song under stress of emotion, but only the emotional effect produced by music on the characters represented."[6] In late 17th-century plays, however, the protagonist may express himself musically; he is able to change his actions in the course of a song. In a vision or dream, a character might see the future foretold in ballet and as a result alter his behavior to avoid unpleasant consequences. Moments of intense emotion may be punctuated by instrumental music. Perhaps none of these musical conventions is wholly unique to the Restoration, but the extent to which they were employed (and often exploited) represents a departure from earlier practice.

Dramatic music in Restoration plays (that is, the music *within* the acts) can be divided into two fragile categories. The first, considered at length in Chapter One of this study, produces a dramatic effect. At one extreme it is integral to plot and meaning, growing directly from the dramatic situation--to paraphrase Professor Dent, drama intensified into music under stress of emotion; at the other extreme it is simply diverting musical entertainment, however incidental, which nevertheless grows from and is still a part of the dramatic situation, and as such, enhances the flow of the play, though perhaps only atmospherically. The second type of music employed on the Restoration stage is more difficult to justify dramatically but is used in equal if not greater amounts than the first: this is the music performed within the act and often ostensibly as a part of the drama, which is present simply because the playhouse was a convenient and profitable forum for the display of musical and Terpsichorean vogues. This use of music, discussed at length in Chapter Four below, was consistently and vehemently damned throughout the period by both actor and playwright and occasionally by an enlightened critic. Since it occurs during the acts and not between them, it is not, strictly speaking, incidental, being accommodated, however irrationally, by the dramatic action. If not for the actors' sitting at the sides of the stage "hearkening to the Musick," the audience could just as well be at a concert. Throughout this study, I have taken the liberty to refer to this kind of music as "para-dramatic."

II. THE PLAY-BOOKS AND MUSICAL CONVENTIONS

As the drama historian has labored to achieve a better understanding of Restoration plays as literature by explaining allusions, defining words, locating sources, researching biographies--all preparatory to editing the plays themselves--the music historian has in turn devoted most of his 17th-century studies to locating and editing the sources of the music of some composers (and, of course, researching biographies), examining certain technical aspects in relation to earlier and later music and the works of contemporary continental composers, and has made a few tentative attempts to integrate theatre music with its corresponding stage works.[7] The musical practices and conventions of late 17th-century English plays have scarcely been touched.[8]

The plays themselves represent a large and as yet not thoroughly examined body of documents which reflect not only the musical life of Restoration London, but also, of course, provide the best evidence of how music was used on the stage, how important the poets and the audience considered music to be in the drama, and what effect music had on the development of the play itself. Although it would be unwise to accept as documentary evidence any single remark about musical practices made by a character in a play, the cumulative effect of many such remarks cannot be dismissed as mere fiction from the pen of a poet struggling to tickle the jaded tastes of an immoral audience. For of all the recorded remains of this period--essays, diaries, letters, criticism--only in the dialogue of the play does that society live again. Sir Harry is actually conversing with Lady Modish about the songs in the last new play or Baptiste Lully's latest tune to reach the town. In his spoken address to the fops and beaux in the pit, the prologue is actually berating their deplorable taste for foreign singers and dancers which is spoiling good English plays. And in his laconic stage directions, the playwright is confiding to the reader of the play-book the secrets of how the spectacular musical effects were executed during the ringing up of the curtain, or who sang from beneath the mask of Pluto in the masque in the fourth act.

For the following study all comedies, tragedies, tragi-comedies, farces, masques, and dramatic operas[9] published between 1660 and 1709, as well as plays in manuscript from the same period, were read,[10] and all allusions to music in prefaces, epistles dedicatory, prologues and epilogues, and in the acts proper, in addition to all stage directions for music and dance were recorded. Of the several available studies of the musical practices of the Restoration stage, all have certain deficiencies. Some are intentionally self-limited by the restricted scope of their enquiry,[11] and others, unfortunately, are limited by the expediency of their approach. In the latter category are those studies which attempt to make generalizations about and to draw conclusions from a small sampling of what is unquestionably a large and unwieldy body of literature.[12] The danger in this approach is that only a small proportion of these plays is available in modern editions. As a result, a pitfall is created by the scholar who attempts to apply the musical practices of the plays of the particular playwright with whom he is concerned to other poets active at different times in the 50-year period. Perhaps the most serious defect of this procedure is the assumption that the best plays display the most characteristic dramatic and/or musical practices.

INTRODUCTION

The literary quality of an individual stage work has rarely had any direct effect on the conventions which characterize the genre to which it belongs. That is, the musical practices displayed by the most undistinguished (from our viewpoint, at least) Restoration comedy are just as important to an overall understanding of the musical practices of the era as those found in *The Way of the World* or *The Man of Mode*. Each stage work, regardless of what modern critics deem its worth to be, was an equal contributor in producing a convention or practice. The reluctance of modern scholars to examine the works of what they consider to be worthless poets (even though their plays may have been among the most popular of the day) has left many extraordinary musical practices undiscovered.

As the following study of music in Restoration plays draws heavily from the plays themselves, a warning is offered both with regard to the "original" authorial version of any play discussed or, as in most of the plays considered here, the first printed edition, and to how these extant remains relate to the musical practices of the 17th-century London theatre. Except for a few instances, the plays under discussion exist only in printed form; these play-books were almost always made up shortly after the play was first presented, either from prompt copies or at least versions that incorporate revisions to which a play may have been subjected during initial production. For these reasons it should be stressed that the musical practices outlined below are just as attributable to printers, publishers, producers, directors, actors, and musicians, as to any "original intentions" of the author. Any stage work, whether play, opera, ballet, musical comedy, etc., is always a collaborative effort by playwright, lyricist, producer, director, actor, musician, dancer, etc., through careful design, last minute expedient, or gradual practical evolution of the dialogue, stage directions, and prompt notes, resulting from the lessons of experience.[13]   The musical practices of the Restoration stage were shaped by all these ingredients, and though the following study attempts to assess the importance of each aspect, it is never possible to determine precisely whether the playwright had any more or any less to do with the amount of music in a play and how it was employed than the theatre company, charged with the task of realizing the poet's dramatic muse. Michael Shapiro's admonition to students of Shakespeare which cautions "against speaking too confidently of 'Shakespeare's use of music'" is equally applicable to Restoration plays.[14]

If it is untenable to attribute musical practices of the stage (as recorded in the play-books) solely to the poet/playwright, then to assume that the play-books fully reflect these practices is similarly untenable. The ephemeral nature of stage works precludes this possibility, and even a play-book with voluminous stage directions for music may sometimes misrepresent the actual amount of music heard within the acts of a play. It is striking just how little control an author had over the musical aspects of his plays. For example, in the preface to his comedy *Love Betray'd* (1703), William Burnaby, probably with full cognizance of Jeremy Collier's and others' attacks upon the quality of plays of the time, writes in his own defence that ". . . the conduct of the Drama I broke by design, to make room for a Mask that is mention'd in the last Act. . . ." As he indicates, in V.i, Moreno, after summing up the happy conclusion of a tangled plot, calls for music in the usual manner: "Let the Mask begin." The stage direction, "After the Mask," follows. But in the preface Burnaby admits that the theatre company neglected to have his masque set to music, and therefore his play "came on like a change of Government, the weight of the Calamity fell among the Poor." The management of the Lincoln's Inn Fields Theatre, where this play was first performed, apparently deleted Burnaby's masque against his will, doubtless substituting an already existing entertainment or some less ambitious musical episode so as to risk as little expenditure as possible on this play from a mediocre pen.

The alteration of a minor playwright's original design for the music in his play was often drastic and in some cases considerably changed the shape of the drama. Charles Goring in the dedication to his tragedy *Irene; or, the Fair Greek* (1708) is almost bitter:

> I am sensible, My Lord, that IRENE appear'd to the greatest Disadvantage on the Stage, strip'd of Her Ornaments of Musick by a Superior Order; and in many of Her Characters suffering very much in the Action.[15]

But the drama was probably not structurally damaged by this action, for Goring refers to the music of his plays as only "Her Ornaments." What most concerns him is that "the Town was depriv'd of one of the more agreeable Parts of the Entertainment. . . ." But as will be shown later, the "entertainment" could outgrow the drama itself (so as not to deprive the town of what was to become more and more agreeable).

Even more important authors probably had little to do with the setting of music. For instance, in the preface to Roger Boyle's posthumously published play *The Tragedy of King Saul* (1703), an anonymous writer states:

> . . . To give an advantage and adopt it in some measure to the air of the times, the reader is here and there entertained with poetical interludes of Ghosts, Furies, etc. which the publisher has taken care be set to Musick by the best hands, which may recommend it to be

acted in Schools and Universities as a proper entertainment for those
that have ingenious and liberal education on Solemn Occasion. . . .[16]

That a publisher rather than the theatre company arranged for the music
indicates either contempt or indifference for musical concerns on the part
of persons closely associated with the production of a play, or, more
likely, suggests a more important role taken by the publisher in such
matters than has hitherto been recorded.[17]

In a rather baffling comment in the preface to his comedy *The
Wary Widdow: or, Sir Noisy Parrat* (1693), Henry Higden states that one
reason the play was not well received is that "The Songs designed were
never Set by omission or combination."[18] This is further evidence that
the arrangements for having music composed, compiled, or performed
were the responsibility of someone other than the playwright, especially
if the playwright were unknown.

In contrast to the plaints of poets that their requirements for
music were ignored or at least scaled down are a few instances in which
authors were prevailed upon "by a Superior Order" to insert more music
and dancing into their dramas than they had originally designed. One
such instance is discussed in the preface to Peter Motteux's masque *The
Loves of Mars and Venus* (1696), in which this Anglicized Frenchman,
rather than risk condemning the powers that be, attempts to rationalize
the dictates of his superiors with an "everbody's doing it" argument: "I
was prevailed [upon] to bring in a Song and Dance of Cyclopes, tho I
knew there is one in Psyche, borrowed almost verbatim from Molière's,
as he borrow'd his from an old Italian Opera called Le Nozze de gli
Dei. . . ."

In light of this evidence, the theatre company, probably
specifically the manager or person in charge of a particular production,
after budgetary considerations were weighed against the tastes of the
audience and the current successful dramatic offerings of the other house,
commissioned the music piece by piece.[19] The original stage directions
suggested by the author, unless they were those of a Dryden or perhaps
of a lesser poet charged specifically with producing a quasi-libretto for a
stage work whose end was to be musical entertainment, were
undoubtedly largely the domain of the theatre company.

Thus, the following study of music in late 17th-century English
plays is really about the theatre itself, the actors, musicians, managers,
audiences, and poets, all of whom were responsible for bringing to the
stage the music of the best composers of the age. Although Restoration
musical practices may differ little from those of the Elizabethan and
Jacobean ages, or, for that matter, our own, the play has never been
more dependent on musical spectacle than it was between 1660 and 1700.

Furthermore, this is the earliest body of English drama for which a significant amount of art music survives: songs, dances, choruses, overtures, curtain tunes, act tunes, symphonies, masques, and so forth, all composed for the first productions of specific plays. Understanding how this music complements these plays is requisite to understanding Restoration drama itself. And learning how the play was stripped of most of its music during the first decade of the 18th century helps to explain why England did not evolve a native operatic tradition during the baroque era.

CHAPTER ONE

MUSIC WITHIN THE DRAMA

Music in plays is most closely bound to drama when it contributes organically to the development of the plot and when its absence would weaken the structural fabric of the play. This interdependent relationship is most apparent between songs and the dramatic situations which they enhance or, occasionally, whose development they further. But the Restoration playwright rarely limited himself to songs in creating dramatic effects. Often instrumental music and dances are as tightly bound to the songs as the songs to the dramatic situation. The foreshadowing of death, for example, might be accomplished at one time in a song, at another in a dance, and at yet another time with instrumental music. Or perhaps all three media might be used simultaneously to produce the desired effect. To separate the musical conventions of the late 17th-century London stage into three neat categories--song, dance, and instrumental music (without dance or pantomime)--is impossible, as all three flow together in the hands of a masterful dramatist. One can speak of a "convention of song" or a "convention of dance" only in those instances where a musical type functions singly, without the aid of other music.[1]

I. INDEPENDENT SONGS AND INSTRUMENTAL MUSIC FOR DRAMATIC EFFECT

Often the dramatic effect of instrumental music can be assessed only subjectively, except, of course, when its function is obvious (battle music, for example). And dances are the most ephemeral of all stage representations. Only rarely is one described in detail in stage directions; "Here follows a Dance" is usually the sole remnant of a stage spectacle the dramatic effect of which would be folly to interpret in detail. The song (and its more extended forms, the masque, entry, etc.), however, may readily be seen to have, for example, an atmospheric effect on a scene or perhaps even an influence on subsequent developments of plot. But in numerous cases a lyric is coupled to other non-vocal music or dance, and the musical conglomerate may have a different effect than that produced by the song itself; that is, a lyric which on first reading appears pertinent to the business of a scene may be made quite incidental by its musical surroundings (a melancholy song followed by an antic dance, for instance). On the other hand, a song which appears simply atmospheric may have provided the music for a dance whose dramatic purpose was most explicitly related to the action. The song must never be considered as the only musical aspect of a play capable of dramatic expression.

As intimated in the Introduction, to distinguish between para-dramatic music (that is, music introduced for its own sake) and that whose absence would cause a structural hiatus in the play is often difficult. The Restoration practice which requires main or secondary characters to sing their own songs makes distinction particularly vexing. A song may be injected into a scene purely for diversion; the lyric may have no connection with the plot and therefore is awkwardly rationalized by incongruous dialogue. But if it is sung by a main character or by any character whose personality is developed elsewhere in the play by other than musical means, then the song must be considered organic to the plot; to omit it would create a gap in our knowledge of the person represented.

In Motteux's comedy, *Love's a Jest* (1696), IV.i, for instance, Airy and his coquettish lover, Christina, important though not major characters, squeeze a song into a play already quite resplendent with extraneous music. Although their song displays the commonest theme of duets of the period (a rake in pursuit of an innocent Phyllis) and is only broadly apropos to the dramatic situation, it is germane to the development of these lively characters. Christina and Airy are accusing each other of being immodest about their vocal abilities:

> *Christina.* What, I suppose you've a mind I should ask you to sing?
> *Airy.* Why don't you then? Gad, I fancy you are as fond of being
> asked as I. Why, you sing almost as well as I do. Come, let's
> sing the last Dialogue our Master set.[2]

Although the song itself tells us little of the happy couple (it is, after all, just a duet that their singing teacher has had them learn), their reason for singing it clearly reveals a pair of spirited egos which must be reconciled before the wedding bells peal.[3] But a further complication surrounds this scene, one which does not bode well for the dramatic effectiveness of the song. Airy and Christina were played by John Boman and Anne Bracegirdle, the most popular of the actor-singers.[4] When Airy says ". . . you are as fond of being asked as I," the allusion is clearly to the players as well as to the characters they represent. The audience probably anxiously awaited the moment when these famous musicians, cast here as lovers, would sing their first duet on the London stage.[5] No song in a Restoration play should be examined in the vacuum of its dramaturgical context, for extra-dramatic circumstances may have caused it to be included in a play.

The dramatic music in Restoration plays is so varied that categorization is difficult. The differences between the two main types of plays, tragedy and comedy, is vast. Comedy scarcely slackens its wit for a serious moment and, indeed, rarely indulges even in melodrama. And Restoration tragedy, unlike its Elizabethan counterpart, does not often allow indecorous humor to intrude, even in minor subplots. One hardly ever finds a gravedigger in these grim affairs. Yet the way in which music is used in the two radically dissimilar dramatic types is not so categorically restrictive. A comedy is not likely to have a funeral march, but melancholy songs (a musical staple of the tragedy) find their way into the lighter forms. Nor is a sexy dialogue apt to appear independently in a tragedy, though one occasionally finds such songs in masques or entertainments inserted into the heavier type. Comedy and tragedy share many musical practices. Instrumental music and dance are particularly difficult to separate into tragic and comic functions. Hence, the only possible categorization of musical practices in plays must cut across dramatic and musical types. At the most general level, music within the acts of plays may be divided into that which is dramatic and that which is para-dramatic; and dramatic music is best subdivided into that which is atmospheric to the drama and that which is organic to the action of the play.[6]

Even a Restoration play that contains more music than spoken dialogue is not opera; only in opera is music used exclusively in the development of drama. Since the Restoration playwrights and their audiences never fully accepted the conventions of opera in the context of the spoken English play, the structural use of music, while frequently encountered in the plays, is restricted to certain situations (to be described presently). Far more prevalent is that music which enhances rather than participates in the dramatic development of plots.

Melancholy Music

Music used atmospherically, although quite effective in intensifying a dramatic situation, often appears to have only a tangential connection with the scene it accompanies; in many instances it is introduced to entertain the play-going courtiers rather than to deepen the effect of the drama. Robert Noyes observes, for instance, that "it is impossible to make clear distinction between songs used to intensify a sad scene and those used to comfort and divert the dumps."[7] While the text of an atmospheric song might not pertain exactly to the situation in which it is used, playwrights usually make the purpose of a song clear to the audience. In Thomas Otway's tragedy *The Orphan: or, the Unhappy Marriage* (1680), III.i, Polydor, who has been wronged in love, is explicit in the extreme about the kind of song he would like his page to sing:

Go to your Chamber and prepare your Lute;
Find out some Song to please me, that discribes
Womans Hypocrises, their subtle wiles,
Betraying smiles, feign'd tears, inconstancies,
Their painted outsides, and corrupted minds,
The sum of all their follies, and their falshoods.

This is quite an order, but the page is spared from having to fulfill it when another servant announces the sudden illness of Acasto, Polydor's father. Although Polydor's wish is not granted, the dramatic situation which prompts him to call for song is the most common of those which demand atmospheric music: a brooding, melancholy protagonist, having done evil or had evil done to him, is unable to talk, sleep, eat, or move to action until he is consoled or revived by the soothing strains of melody, usually a song sung by a servant on the stage or by an unspecified singer from behind the scenes.

Because the melancholy song accompanied an essentially static situation (for example, a character sitting in a "melancholy Posture"), the skillful playwright ensures that these scenes in which little happens on stage (indeed, the scene is often bare, save for the wretched king or queen hearkening to the song) are placed at the beginning so as not to disrupt the action.[8] In Mary Pix's tragedy *Ibrahim, The Thirteenth Emperour of the Turks* (1696), the second scene of Act III opens with two songs to help divert the sultan's bad dreams. As he settles down on a couch, the music is performed "to Chase these Melancholy Fumes away." He is told that it has been "Prepar'd by the Italian Masters," who must have been as popular in Ibrahim's day as they were in 1696.[9] Nathaniel Lee chose to give the audience somewhat more to behold in the first scene of his *Gloriana, or the Court of Augustus Caesar* (1676), which opens with a banquet; but the emperor, who is musing on the licentiousness of his daughter, "sits melancholy," listening to a song that fails to cheer him.[10] In Henry Nevil Payne's tragedy *Fatal Jealousie* (1673), the song that opens Act III is more appropriate for its auditor, as Don Gerardo "with a Book in his Hand" and Faustian thoughts of death in his head, hears a lyric which speculates about the rewards of heaven.[11] Such songs as these are very effective in setting a mood of gloom for the scenes to follow with their lyrics alone; many other examples are found in Restoration tragedies.[12] Instrumental music, devoid of poetic elucidation, is also used to achieve a somber mood at the outset of a scene.

The first act of Aphra Behn's tragedy *Abdelazer, or the Moor's Revenge* (1677) opens with a sad scene: "A Table with Lights, Abdelazer sullenly leaning his Head on his Hands;--after a little while, still Musick [probably recorders] plays." This is furnished by Queen Isabella who hopes to rekindle Abdelazer's love. After the instrumental prelude, a song ("Love in Phantastique triumph sat") rouses him but to no avail: "On me this Musick lost?" The queen then commands the musicians to "Play all your sweetest notes, such as inspire / The active Soul with new & soft desire." They play but the king remains sullen. In Powell's *Alphonso King of Naples* (1691), a song near the beginning of Act I to comfort Urania is also preceded by instrumental music, and she is similarly displeased with the prelude, having been told that it comes from an out-of-favor suitor: "Musick from Ferdinand! / The Groans of tortur'd Ghosts were Airs more pleasing." But the song to follow softens her ire ("When Silvia is kind, and Love plays in her Eyes," D&M 3793 *m*Eccles).[13]

Occasionally a lute alone provides the melancholy music, and if no song follows, the distressed king or prince may express the effect the music has on him. In Behn's tragi-comedy *The Young King: or, The Mistake* (1683), the opening of the second act, "After a little playing on the Lute," finds Orfames in a castle by the sea, "looking melancholy, followed by Geron with a Lute in his hand."

> *Orfames.* I do not like this Musick;
> It pleases me at first,
> But every touch thou givest that is soft and low
> Makes such impressions here,
> As puzzles me beyond Philosophy
> To find the meaning of;
> Begets strange Notions I know not what
> And leaves a new and unknown thought behind it
> That does disturb my quietness within.

Music is apparently as new to Orfames as is the rest of the world, which, in *Tempest* fashion, he has never seen--not even so much as a woman. The protagonist of Sir William Killigrew's *The Imperial Tragedy* (1669) is not so innocent but is in deeper despair as his lutenist tries to brighten his black mood at the beginning of the second act:

> [The Scene, a black Room, and in it Longinus in black, and a
> Musician tuning his Lute at a Distance.]
> *Longinus.* . . . What strange noise doest thou make? and why so long?
> *Musician.* I tune my strings, Sir, that they may agree.
> *Long.* Pox of agreement, discords please me best;
> Thy jarring strings, my fancy will erect,
> And sute with the confusions, I design.
> *Music.* Would you to saddness, or to mirth be mov'd? [He plays a merry
> tune.]
> *Long.* Guess.
> Hold, if thou would'st not have thy brains beat out.
> *Music.* Pray Sir tell me, what you would have me play?

Longinus relates his rueful condition to his lutenist and asks that he

> now make thy Lute send forth
> Sounds, dismal as the work I have in hand;
> As black, and bloody, as my troubled mind:
> That with each touch, my heart may simpathize.

The musician "playes a sad tune: Longinus sits and keeps time with his head and feet," but gradually he falls asleep. As reality fades into fantasy, a song is sung ("The Sun, and Stars, with wholesome Rays") and then follows a masque-like entry depicting his dream. This beautifully formed scene, in which the dramatic motion gradually slows to a halt (albeit eventually enlivened by a masque) would be less effective in the middle of an act; and so static a situation as this would never occur at the end of a scene, where the Restoration poets habitually tighten the action with a rush of events--in tragedy, usually murder upon murder. However, one occasionally finds melancholy music within scenes, but these episodes are brief and seldom couple songs with instrumental preludes or concluding dances, unless, of course, these scenes expand into an entry, masque, or some other formal entertainment.[14]

One of the best examples of melancholy music used within a scene is found in Dryden's version of Antony and Cleopatra, *All for Love: or, The World well Lost* (1678), I.i. Antony has thrown himself onto the ground in a fit of melancholy. Hiding nearby is Ventidius, who is about to convince the wretched protagonist to leave Cleopatra and return to his troops in Syria. The music is not allowed to blunt the forward thrust of the scene, as it probably accompanied the dialogue, but is used to great effect to reinforce Dryden's image of Antony as a hermit in a pastoral setting.

> *Antony.* Give me some Musick; look that it be sad:
> I'll sooth my melancholy, till I swell,
> And burst my self with sighing.--
> [Soft Musick.]
> Stay, I fancy I'm turned wild, a commoner of Nature
>
> . . . .
>
> More of this image, more; it lulls my thoughts.
> [Soft Musick again.]

Perhaps Dryden forces the point somewhat, but this scene as a whole bears comparison with Shakespeare's original.[15]

A particularly poignant use of song within a scene occurs in Lee's *Theodosius: or, The Force of Love* (1680), V.i. Athenais is about to drink poison rather than marry the villainous protagonist. She dispatches her maid to fetch a lute and sing a verse which Athenais herself has prepared. It tells of a Phyllis who kills herself to be with her dead lover.[16] During the song, she takes the poison. Rarely does one encounter an atmospheric song in Restoration plays which pertains so closely to the dramatic situation and at the same time does not hinder the flow of the action. While Lee, perhaps the greatest of the Restoration tragedians, is careful to make a melancholy song fit the situation, other poets on occasion appear to have used an atmospheric lyric whether or not it was needed for a dramatic effect. For example, in W. Killigrew's tragedy *Selindra* (1666), II.i, Ordella is called away by the emperor from a happy reunion with her brother, Phillocles, but she commands Selindra to "entertaine him in my Chamber, with Cleonels last Melancholly Song, I like so well." There follows a sad enough song,[17] strangely out of place in this scene. But this para-dramatic use of an atmospheric song is not common, and most instances of this overworked musical convention are dramatically viable, if only because light moments are rare in Restoration tragedies, and any dreary verse would be appropriate on some level to an equally dreary scene.[18]

Music for Soliloquies

Closely allied to the music enhancing a melancholy scene is that to accompany soliloquies or, occasionally, dialogue, where the complete cessation of action in favor of music would detract from the expression of anguish, wonderment, frustration, and so forth, but where music (usually non-vocal) was thought necessary to intensify emotion. Longinus's reaction to his lutenist's tunes in Killigrew's *The Imperial Tragedy* (1669), II.i, and the musically induced image in Dryden's *All for Love* (1678), I.i (mentioned above) are certainly examples of this practice, although the former scene is eventually enveloped by music. A more striking example is found in Joshua Barnes's unpublished tragedy, "Englebert," n.d., V.i,[19] in which music almost assumes an organic function. Theo is reflecting on a murder he has committed. He defies his victim's ghost to appear: "Hee's dead but comes not, this confirms my . . ." But his words are broken off by "Soft Musick playing & stopping." Believing this to be the music of the spheres, he comments that "the raptures must procede from skills far higher than . . . of the Delphick lyre . . . But while I hear their heaven tempered string. . . ." The music begins to have its effect as Theo stumbles through his words of bewilderment. It slowly effects a change of heart; he desires to make peace and finally feels guilty for the murder. The other characters onstage apparently have not heard this "ghost" and are amazed at Theo's change. As the scene ends and when the stage is empty, there is "soft Musick as before." But music to accompany dialogue does not often produce such a definitive effect in other Restoration plays.

In Dryden's tragedy *Aureng-Zebe* (1676), IV.i, the protagonist considers death, which all too soon will overtake him:

> Distrust, and darkness, of a future state,
> Make poor Mankind so fearful of their Fate.
> Death, in it self, is nothing; but we fear
> To be we know not what, we know not where.

This soliloquy, pounding forth in heroic couplets, was accompanied by "Soft Musick." Since these instrumental strains do not appear to issue from a banquet within nor to have been requested by a Portia-like wife to soothe her troubled lord, here the effect would seem to be purely atmospheric: to intensify Aureng-Zebe's gloomy musings. The modern critic might accuse Dryden of milking the scene for the drama his poetry cannot provide (this soliloquy is not one of his better pieces) or of asking music to accomplish what the actor could not. Lesser poets certainly found the melancholy song, for instance, a reliable if rather hackneyed device to paint a black scene without having to tax their poetic skills. But instrumental music underscoring dialogue is not frequent in this body of plays. Dramatists usually took great care to ensure that the music prepared for their plays was clearly audible and did not encroach upon dramatic cohesiveness. The convention which governed Dryden's use of music in Aureng-Zebe's soliliquy, as will be seen below, is usually associated with the foreshadowing of death, and was seldom exploited for transitory effect. But this practice, like most of those involving music in Restoration plays, was abused. That is, a lofty character's morose musings were on occasion seen to be opportunistic moments into which music for the audience's sake (rather than for the drama's) could be inserted.

In *The Generous Conquerour: or, The Timely Discovery* (1702), III.ii, by Bevill Higgons, "Martial Loud Musick Plays, the King Listens." Later, when the scene has become somewhat less bright, "Soft Musick Plays, the King Listens." The most difficult task for the actor portraying the king in this scene was probably to keep his brow furrowed in a look of melancholy worry while the music played on and on. Oldmixon, in his dramatic opera *The Grove, or, Love's Paradice* (1700), IV.i, makes a more serious attempt to integrate the music which accompanies Phylante's grief. The music begins softly under a considerable amount of dialogue; finally she notices it:

> Ye fair companions of my better days!
> Come, minister your aid in my distress,
> And with your tuneful airs compose my mind.

"She lies on a Couch, Musick plays louder, Scene opens and discovers Nicias and Guards waiting on Adrastus. . . ." But this background music grows into a formal entertainment (earlier the stage direction "Soft Musick begins here, and continues till other is perform'd" appears) as two songs are performed.[20] Music at first had served Phylante's sadness, but now she must serve music as a patient auditor.

As has been stressed earlier in this chapter, it is often difficult to distinguish dramatic music, especially that which is atmospheric to a scene (such as the soft music to intensify Phylante's grief in *The Generous Conquerour*), from that which does not contribute to the plot in any active way but which is accommodated by the dramatic situation (such as the two songs to which Phylante must hearken). But incidental music, comprised of short instrumental pieces played before the play and between the acts--the only kind of music that one might safely assume to lie entirely outside the drama--is also capable of having an atmospheric effect on scenes in plays; in some cases, in fact, one can barely distinguish its function from that of the music which is clearly within the domain of the dramatic action.[21] The ambiguity between incidental and dramatic music is best seen in that introduced at the beginnings of acts or scenes to prepare an emotionally charged situation or the discovery of a spectacular scenic effect, or to bridge the emotional gap between two scenes of drastically differing moods.

Music for Discoveries

The melancholy song, which typically opens an act or scene, is mostly restricted to tragedy. But instrumental music would seem as capable of preparing a scene representing a Covent Garden coffee house as enhancing a prospect of the Elysian Fields. Yet it too was mainly limited to tragedy or to those plays with classical settings. Music, the playwrights felt, was necessary to help effect the considerable leap from the dim, candle-lit stage of the Theatre Royal into an ancient world under a brilliant Mediterranean sun; almost any scene in which one's imagination might have to be stretched in order to appreciate the full effect of the spectacle was prepared by music. The opening of the fourth act of Mary Manley's tragedy *The Royal Mischief* (1696) would be ambitious even for a dramatic opera:[22]

> The Curtain flys up, to the sound of Flutes and Hoboys, and discovers the River Phasis, several little gilded boats, with Musick [i.e., musicians] in them; a Walk of trees the Length of the House; Lights Fixed in Chrystal Candelsticks to the branches; Several Persons in the Walk, as in Attention [i.e., as listening to the music]. . . .

In contrast to this bright spectacle, the fifth act of Motteux's operatic *The Island Princess, or the Generous Portuguese* (1699) opens with a far gloomier scene; the music was probably needed to prepare the audience for seeing its heroine in prison, a rather incongruous episode framed by scenes of mirth and celebration: "The Curtain slowly rises to mournful Musick, and discovers a Prison, Quisara lying on the Floor, all in White, reading by the light of a Lamp. . . ." In both of these scenes music accompanies the ascent of the curtain, and the discoveries come not at the beginning of the play (where the curtain usually rose to fall again only after the epilogue when the stage was empty), but well into the play, before the fourth act in *The Royal Mischief* and at the beginning of the last act in *The Island Princess.* This study of Restoration plays has determined that the curtain is used far more frequently than has hitherto been observed[23] and that its ascent is characteristically accompanied by instrumental music, either a composition specifically designed for the purpose or, coincidentally, the overture or an act tune.

From the earliest years of the Restoration the ascent of the curtain was often associated with music. Or to be more precise, discoveries were accompanied by music; for the chief purpose of the curtain on the late 17th-century stage, as on the Elizabethan and Jacobean stages and on our own, is to conceal a special scene until such time that its discovery is in maximum contrast to what precedes it, whether that less magnificent scene was the bare thrust stage in front of the proscenium arch (where much of the action of Restoration drama was played) or dirty and narrow Drury Lane. The curtain was used to conceal something worth waiting for; to ensure that the often hastily constructed celestial realms did not appear to the spoiled courtiers considerably less grand than they were intended to be, the audience was usually prepared for the discovery by music calculated to enhance the scene to follow. Sir William Davenant, the anxious father of Restoration drama, makes extensive use of the curtain in his pre-1660 show *The first days Entertainment at Rutland House* (1657). At the beginning of this dramatic presentation, even before the prologue, is a rare stage direction for the preludial music which would later become obligatory for every stage work: "After a Flourish of Musick the Curtains are drawn and the Prologue enters." And each entry (or act) to follow is prepared by music: ". . . a Consort of instrumental Musick adapted to the Sullen disposition of Diogenes, being heard a while the Curtains are suddenly opened. . . ." "The Curtains are suddenly closed and the Company entertained by instrumental and vocal Musick. . . ." ". . . a consort of instrumental Musick, after the French composition[24] being heard a while the Curtains are suddenly opened. . ." and so forth until the epilogue. In his more legal dramatic offering *The Play-House to be Lett* (1673), performed in 1663 and incorporating his pre-Restoration works *The*

Cruelty of the Spaniards in Peru (1658) and *The History of Sr Francis Drake* (1658),[25] the opening curtain is accompanied by music: "The preparation of the Opening of the Scene is by a prelude and Corante. Afterwards the Curtain rises by degrees to an ascending Ayr, and a Harbour is discerned." Davenant's use of music at the opening curtain became a standard convention which has been with the play ever since as the overture.

From very early in the period almost every play (including farces and dramatic operas) had an overture, but not all curtain music is as carefully designed as Davenant's "ascending Ayr," a charmingly naive touch. Occasionally, overtures are downright unsympathetic to the first scene of a play. That is, the lively, fast section of a Lullian overture in a major key may precede the gloomy opening of a tragedy. And conversely, the optional, slow closing section may prepare a comedy, as happens, for instance, in Congreve's *The Old Batchelour* (1693). Here, the somber closing passage of Purcell's grand overture in A minor is a rather incongruous prelude to Ned Bellmour and Frank Vainlove's early-morning banter in the street. The overture (or curtain tune) and its smaller companions, the act tunes, are considered at length in Chapter Two.

Within the play two general categories of discoveries are accompanied by music: those revealing some horrid scene, such as a prison or torture chamber (as in *The Island Princess*, V.i) and those revealing splendid formal gatherings, usually involving the assembled cast;[26] the latter are typically banquet scenes, religious ceremonies, or most often representations of royalty sitting in state. Of the first category, the beginning of Dryden's *Oedipus* (1679) is perhaps the grisliest:

> Scene Thebes. The Curtain rises to a plaintive Tune, representing the present condition of Thebes; Dead Bodies appear at a distance in the Streets; Some faintly go over the Stage, others drop.

From Dryden's description music would seem of secondary importance to such a graphic scene. The opening of Congreve's *The Mourning Bride* (1697) is subtler, and the curtain tune is necessary to let the audience know at once the condition of the characters onstage: "The Curtain rising slowly to soft Music, discovers Almeria in mourning, Leonora waiting in mourning." Without music, the first scene of Dryden's dramatic opera *The State of Innocence, and the Fall of Man* (1677) would have been unthinkable. It was never staged, but one should not assume that Dryden's stage directions were the cause, as this first scene would have been well within the capabilities of Restoration stagecraft:

> The first Scene represents a Chaos, or a confus'd Mass of Matter;
> the Stage is almost wholly dark: A Symphony of Warlike Music is
> heard for some time; then from the Heavens, (which are opened) fall
> the rebellious Angels wheeling in the Air, and seemingly transfix'd
> with Thunderbolts . . . Tunes of Victory are play'd, and an Hymn
> sung . . . The Music ceasing, and the Heavens being closed, the
> Scene shifts, and on a sudden represents Hell . . . a Tune of
> Horrour and Lamentation is heard.

The music to accompany this scene, as it was never mounted, does not exist, nor does that for a great many other discoveries; this music was doubtless often improvised or of some other ephemeral nature. This, however, does not detract from the fact that playwrights considered music essential for such representations.

A more typical and usually less elaborate use of curtain with music is for ceremonials. Wilmot's *Valentinian* (1685) begins as "The Curtain flies up with the Musick of Trumpets and Kettle-Drums, and discovers the Emperor passing through to the Garden." In Granville's *The British Enchanters* (1706), the first act opens with the curtain rising "to a Flourish of all Sorts of loud Musick. The Scene is a Grove beautify'd with Fountains, Statues, &c. Urganda is discover'd as in the midst of some Ceremony of Enchantment. Thunder during the Musick."[27]

The setting of elaborate scenes during the course of a play, especially if many people and considerable scenery were involved, necessitated the lowering of the curtain. In Durfey's tragedy *Bussy D'Ambois, or the Husbands Revenge* (1691), Act III ends with several characters exiting as to a banquet. The stage direction "Curtain falls . . . The End of the Third Act" is most unusual. The purpose of the curtain-fall is obvious in that a banquet scene opens the next act. No music is called for in stage directions, as the third act tune would have been understood to provide the necessary music for the beginning of the banquet.[28]

Comedies, too, are replete with banquet scenes. Joseph Harris's *The City Bride, or, The Merry Cuckold* (1696) begins as "The Curtain draws up and discovers several sitting at a Banquet. An Entertainment of Instrumental Musick, compos'd by Signior Finger" (not extant); this probably began simultaneously with the ascent of the curtain. But the ringing up of the curtain in I.i of Southerne's comedy *The Wives Excuse* (1692) to reveal "the Company at the Musick-Meeting," does not open the scene, as a footman outside the concert (in an extended conversation with his lowly colleagues) declares, "A Pox on these Musick Meetings; there's no Fifth Act Here, a free cost, as we have at the Play-Houses, To Make Gentelmen of us, and keep us out of Harms way."[29] As the concert scene to follow suggests, most music in comedies is either blatantly para-dramatic or of integral importance to the play; music to accompany the discovery of special scenes is not common in comedies.

Marriage ceremonies in tragedies are often discovered in progress, music of course playing an important role.[30]   In two plays instrumental preludes function almost organically.   In Behn's tragi-comedy *The Forc'd Marriage, or the Jealous Bridegroom* (1671), a tableau is shown before the second act begins; the authoress is quite specific in her stage directions:

> The Curtain must be let down; and soft Musick must play: The Curtain being drawn up, discovers a Scene of a Temple . . . [during the wedding ceremony] all remaining without motion, whilst the Musick plays: this continues a while till the Curtain falls; and then the Musick plays aloud till the Act begins.

The first act of *King Edgar and Alfreda* (1677), by Ravenscroft, is very similar:

> The Curtain drawn up, an Altar is discovered.   Aldernald giving Alfreda to Ethelwold in Marriage, an Abbot joining their hands, with Monks attending him.   Ruthin Looking and smiling.   After a while the Scene closes. . . .

No music is indicated for this scene, but since it is totally without dialogue and is the first of the play, the overture or initial curtain tune probably accompanied the pantomime.

Music for Change of Scene

As the preceding discussion indicates, overtures and act tunes are frequently called upon to enhance and occasionally to participate in the drama.   But such pieces are termed "incidental" because they usually lie outside the play.   The music heard between the scenes of acts may, however, assume a more active role in reinforcing the drama, simply because it is closer to the action.

Although an act tune was performed immediately at the conclusion of each act except the last--regardless of the nature of the preceding scene, music was apparently played between the *scenes* only when what followed was to include a special discovery (as has been shown above) or when the two scenes differ so radically in emotional content that together they would appear incongruous without some breathing space, not of silence, but of music atmospheric to the following action.[31]   Davenant made use of such music early in the period, as most of the entries of the fourth and fifth acts in *The Play-House to be Lett* are preceded by music. But his stage directions specify that the music is to prepare what follows: some examples are in IV.ii, "A Symphony variously humoured prepared the change of the scene"; V.ii, "An Alman and Courante are play'd: after which a trumpet-ayre changes the scene"; V.iii, "A Symphony, consisting of four tunes, prepares the change of scene"; V.v, "A doleful Pavin is play'd to prepare the change of the Scene, which represents a dark prison at great distance. . . ." Later in the period, music is most often used to prepare scenes depicting dungeons or sacrifices. For example, in Granville's *The British Enchanters* (1706), III[ii], "The Scene changes to a Scene of Tombs and Dungeons . . . Plaintive Musick." The change to this dank scene from that of the idyllic forest preceding it would be too abrupt without musical preparation.

While music was needed to make a splendid discovery larger than life, it was also needed to make a less magnificent scene believable at all. In Scott's tragedy *The Unhappy Kindness: or, A Fruitless Revenge* (1697), a play nearly barren of scenic effects (probably because it was produced by the Theatre Royal company, at the time heavily committed financially to the more popular dramatic operas), the second scene of Act II, which shows "a Royal Throne on which the King places himself," is given "a Triumphal manner" by a song performed as Valerio enters. But this is merely preparatory to the discovery of the entire court seated for a masque (II[iii]). In *Imposture Defeated* (1698), a comedy by Powell, the second scene of Act I is prepared as "Artan (a spirit) waves his Hand, a Simphony of Musick, as it is playing the Scene Changes to a Beautifull Garden with Orange Trees on Each Side. . . ." This is *hors d'oeuvre* to even more splendid scenes later in the play.

In comedies, music is often incorporated into the final moments of a scene. The tune, which probably trailed off as the next scene began, was usually played by musicians leaving the stage. In Etherege's *The Comical Revenge: or, Love in a Tub* (1664), the masque of III.iii ends with the stage direction, "Exeunt Fidlers playing." In Payne's comedy *The Morning Ramble* (1673), II.i ends with Muchland, Townlove, Merry, "Fiddles, and Torches," on a midnight rampage:

> *Merry.* Strike up Boys, sound Alarm to the
>   sleepy Sentinels of the Fortification . . .
>   Sound a Charge, and Enter.
>   [Ex. Singing and Playing.][32]

Scenes of tragedies, too, often fade out as music is heard. For instance, a melancholy song bridges the gap between the first and second scenes of the bloody final act of William Phillips's tragedy *The Revengeful Queen* (1698). Rosamund says to her waiting lady that "These sad thoughts,

Musick and Love shall banish, / Retire with me to my Alcove, and try their Force. . . ." The song "Oh Love how mighty are thy Joys" follows, after which "the Scene draws and discovers Rosamund and Almachild sitting. . . ." In one play, Behn's *The Town-Fopp: or, Sir Timothy Tawdrey* (1677), III.i, music appears to be used simply to fill in time as several characters enter the stage: "Musick plays, till they are all seated."[33]

The intervals between scenes were also used to accommodate incidental songs. Three such are found in Southerne's comedy *The Disappointment* (1684): II.i-ii ("Scene changes to Erminia's Chamber. A SONG by an unknown hand"), "Poor, ill-instructed, wretched Woman-kind"; III.i-ii ("A SONG made by Colonel Sackville"), "Oh why did e'er my thoughts aspire" (D&M 2552 *m*R. King); V.ii-iii ("A SONG written by Sir George Ethridge"), "See how fair Corinna lies" (D&M 2867 *m*Pack). None of these songs is prepared by the dialogue, nor are they more than generally applicable to the dramatic situation. But they would be more obtrusive if they were integrally related, for then Southerne would have had to prepare their performance with dialogue perhaps inappropriate to the surrounding action. No matter how nonsensical or innocuous a lyric may be, it still carries some connotation, and playwrights nearly always preferred more neutral instrumental music to fill the intervals between acts and scenes.

Music for Love Scenes, Eulogies, and Hunts

The uses of atmospheric music outlined above are quite varied, although they fall into two categories: music to intensify melancholy situations and that to prepare unusual scenic effects. The remaining miscellaneous atmospheric uses of music discussed below are as diverse as the dramatic situations they accompany, but in general they are characterized by intense emotion. Love scenes are occasionally enhanced by an atmospheric lyric, and frequently the longing of a lover for the absent partner elicits a song.[34] For instance, in William Joyner's tragedy *The Roman Empress* (1671), I.i, Florus has fallen in love with a woman by looking at her picture. He has had a song written about her in which the author

> . . . has toucht the proper string of my affection,
> With commendation of his friend the Painter.
> Boy, lets see it, go now, and sing it.[35]

Scenes involving a confrontation of lovers are rarely accompanied by songs; the poets apparently felt a lyric was not as effective in intensifying the emotions as the words spoken by the lovers themselves. But instrumental music was used in such scenes, occasionally with great effect.

In W. Killigrew's tragi-comedy *Ormasdes* (1665), V.i, the extended love scene between the protagonist and Valeriana is accompanied by instrumental music which contributes significantly to the *tendresse* of the situation. Ormasdes asks Valeriana for her ring, but she replies that it was a gift from her mother and must be given only to her future husband. He suggests that they find some other way to test their love:

> *Valeriana.* I will consider on some way to try,
> But must submit unto this drowsinesse,
> For some minutes time, 'twill take me from you!
> Pray Sir, command the Musick now to play.
> [. . . Musick playes a while . . . Valeriana Counterfets to sleep,
> Ormasdes lyes on the ground by her Couch, and while he sleeps,
> she puts the Ring on his finger; then the Musick ends. . . .]

But Valeriana has second thoughts, because the ring carries a curse if given to one not destined to become her lord; she removes it while more music plays. But when Ormasdes awakens, he has dreamt about the ring being on his finger and realizes Valeriana loves him. The silence of their sleep (feigned or otherwise) is filled with atmospheric music. A lyric here would either provide unnecessary comment on a situation which requires no further elaboration or force onto the scene a connotation extraneous to the drama.

At the other extreme, music enhances scenes involving death. In V.ii of Otway's tragedy *Venice Preserv'd* (1682), the execution of Pierre is depicted. As the scene shuts on this hapless affair, soft music is played.[36] And in Crowne's *Darius King of Persia* (1688), V.iv, after the king has killed himself, the eulogy is delivered over soft music. Other much less common uses of atmospheric music include accompaniments for rather bizarre effects[37] and hunting scenes.[38]

Structural Lyrics

All of the uses of music outlined above in this chapter serve to enhance a dramatic effect already inherent in the various scenes, but in most cases the absence of this music would not create a hiatus in the structures of the plays. These scenes might not be as powerful without music, but its absence would not effect the plot nor change the overall meaning of the plays. But in several Restoration stage works one finds music which, if omitted, would weaken the fabric of the drama.

As Noyes observes, structural lyrics are unusual in plays of any period.[39] And in Restoration plays, heavier with music than those of any other era, songs which function organically are surprisingly rare. Perhaps the best example in a tragedy is found in Shipman's *Henry the Third of France* (1678), IV.ii. Gabriel is loved by the king and Grillon, colonel of the guards. While she is singing a song[40] to her confidante Armida to explain why she cannot return the king's love, her suitors enter and tell each other of the woman they love, not knowing that they both fancy Gabriel. Grillon expresses his worst fears: "'Twould be a plaguy Spite tho, when all's known, / If both these beauties, Sir, should prove but one." His fears are realized when Gabriel sings from within an arbor, and both men recognize the voice. (As will be shown in Chapter Three, Gabriel probably did not sing the song, and the voice they recognize was perhaps that of her attendant, Armida.) But in this example and others involving structural lyrics, it is not so much the music which is organic to the scene as the words of the song.[41] The king and Grillon could just as well have heard Gabriel reciting a poem or have spied her in the arbor, although the atmosphere would be lost without the song. One comedy includes a song which is more tightly bound to the action of a scene, although the lyric is not even printed in the play-book: I.i of Colley Cibber's *The Comical Lovers* [1707][42] is not unlike the situation in *Henry the Third*, except that here a man apparently mistakes the voice of an attendant for that of his prospective lover, and the consequences are not so fatal. Doralice asks her waiting lady, Beliza, to bring her lute and retire into an arbor so that she may hear a song. Palamede enters and listens to the song. As the women re-enter, Beliza, who probably sang the song,[43] seeing Palamede, says with a little embarrassment, "Madam, a Stranger." Doralice is quick to seize the opportunity and replies with feigned modesty, "I did not think to have had Witnesses of my bad singing." Palamede, however, does not consider it bad at all, and so the two begin a happy relationship founded on deception and misplaced flattery, the basic stuff of late Restoration comedies. This song (whatever it was, treating of love in French or sorrow in Italian, would make little difference) is of considerable importance to the action. Cibber deftly tells us in a brief musical scene exactly what kind of person Doralice is; there is no necessity for tedious dialogue. The song itself is only of atmospheric significance, but its use is crucial to the comic effect.

Music to Foreshadow Death [44]

Most Restoration tragedies are grim affairs. The incessant heroic rhymed couplets (of some early plays), the stiff, often one-dimensional royal or similarly exalted characters, and the explicitly depicted murder, torture, suicide, or other mayhem have made these plays inaccessible to most modern critics. With a few exceptions, they rank among the least revivable of all English dramas.[45] But the London audiences relished scenes of violence, and as the manner of death became stylized--daggers and poison, rants and eulogies--so too did its dramatic preparation. In the goriest of these tragedies music and dance characteristically foreshadow and intensify the bad end of some character, often the protagonist. This music (occasionally in the form of a full-blown ballet entry) is introduced well into the play, usually in Act IV or V, when it is clear to all, save perhaps the victim, that death is near. The music typically involves an allegorical acting out of the inevitable tragedy, shown in a court masque, for example, or in a dream.

Lee and Dryden's *The Duke of Guise* (1683) makes use of music to signal death with powerful dramatic effect. Malicorne, a conjuror and servant to the Duke of Guise, has made a pact with the devil (in the person of Melanax) to help his master secure a political victory over the King of France. The magician has been singularly indecisive in taking advantage of the hellish prognostications of Melanax, who tells Malicorne to kill the king in order to advance the Guise's cause. In the middle of Act V the flats are drawn to show Malicorne at a banquet celebrating the twelfth anniversary of his pact with Melanax, an arrangement which has brought him "Honours, Wealth, and Pleasure." But these private revels are interrupted by a fit of melancholy: "I want a Song To rouze me, my blood freezes: Musick there?" His request is ritualistically granted with a song and dance by a shepherd and shepherdess. The lyric, "Tell me Thirsis, tell your Anguish," is a light, amorous dialogue typical of the pastoral genre. But Captain Simon Pack's setting is as melancholy as Malicorne's spirits.[46] In the key of G minor and beginning with a stepwise descending bass line--two of the most potent emblems of death for the English baroque composer--the song is a harbinger of the horrific event to come. After the music a fierce knocking is heard at the door and Melanax enters. Malicorne believes that nine years remain in his contract, but a close study of the bond shows that he has been tricked: the figure "12" not "21" is there inscribed. The scene concludes as the dyslexic Malicorne is dragged down to hell. The Faustian derivation of this episode is clear, but perhaps it was more immediately inspired by a scene in Roger Boyle's unpublished play, "Zoroastres" [1675], V.ii.[47] Here several "Furys and Spirits arise and dance round ye Throne," shaking their torches at Zoroastres, singing "Awake! Awake! your fate draws near." After the dance the spirits tell the fated one that he is doomed, and "They all descend, pulling ye King down with them, ye heavens raining fire upon them and all ye while they are singing, several spirits fly across."

The dream sequence was a common device to introduce music and dance representing a murder. Boyle, at the beginning of Act III of his tragedy *Herod the Great* (1694), describes in unusual detail a dumb show (or ballet) that represents the king's ominous dream. As the scene opens,

> Herod appears asleep under a magnificent pavilion. Hircanus and Aristobulus's Ghosts enter, attended by several other Ghosts, in white, having great Stains of Blood all over their Garments. They dance antick Dances with black Javelins in their Hands. The dances ended they fall all into one Rank, and march up to Herod, brandishing the Points of the Weapons towards him. Herod wakes of a sudden, starts up, and draws his Sword, at which all the Ghosts vanish.

Only after this lengthy musical prologue to the act does the dialogue begin. Notice that this dance grows from the dramatic situation; its omission would deprive the audience of important information: Herod has been warned; he could mend his evil ways.

Another example of a portentous dream occurs in one of the few tragedies of Durfey, a playwright and lyricist known mostly for his doggerel verse and low wit. In V.ii of *Bussy D'Ambois* (1691) (a reworking of Chapman's play of the same name), a magician has been sent for to conjure for Bussy, but the latter falls asleep in the middle of the invocation, and after thunder and lightning, there appears "a Dance of Spirits, Representing the manner of d'Ambois's Murder. . . ." In John Crowne's *The History of Charles the Eighth of France* (1672), V[ii], a similar incantation has been prepared for the court. The duchess, Isabella, is aghast at a vision she sees and tries to investigate the strange forms before her. But she is touched with a wand, "at which she seems to fall into a slumber, and is placed on a chair by the magician: then the Masquers rise and dance; after the dance the Spirit descends, and the scene closes." What has disturbed Isabella is that she has learned through the masque that she will die.

The foreshadowing of death with music is consistent with Dryden's ideal that tragedy should raise the spirits and exalt characters, through a special way of speaking, vivid battle scenes, and, as his plays illustrate, through music. Tragic heroes are by definition exalted, and therefore their deaths are usually represented in extraordinary ways; and certainly the London audience never saw a thief hanged at Tyburn to the accompaniment of singing shepherds and shepherdesses.

Musical Allegories

Several of the musical foreshadowings mentioned above are presented as allegorical dances and songs, in some cases approaching the size of an independent masque. But unlike the Restoration masque, which, as will be shown below, is usually separate in plot and theme from its parent play, these musical allegories grow from the dramatic situation. Perhaps the best example of such a scene is found in Durfey's *Famous History and Fall of Massaniello* (two parts, 1700, 1699), one of the most remarkable plays of the period. A prose tragedy with persistent comic elements, it is concerned with the uprising of the common people of Naples against the corrupt government. The leader of the revolt is a poor fisherman, Massaniello, whose good-natured popularism turns violent as he begins to exercize his new-found authority. The object of numerous comic episodes is his fat, obscene wife, Blowzabella, whose temporary elevation to a high station and her vulgarizing of the trappings of nobility provide much biting satire. For example, in II.ii of the second part of the play, she tries to impress her aristocratic lady friends with a bawdy entertainment of "Clowns, Morris-dancers and Tumblers." Near the end of the play, shortly after Massaniello has been killed by the counter-revolutionaries, Blowzabella (ignorant of this climactic event) is entertained with a masque arranged by the same noblewomen who earlier had to suffer her sleazy musical show. She arrives in her garish finery and is presented a thinly-veiled, musical allegory of her ill-fated rise to glory. The masque begins with a dance by a fisherman and fishwife, who are afterwards dressed in fine clothes. Blowzabella has still missed the point of the show when a solemn song is performed by Rebellion, followed by a dance executed by Death and the Hangman. At the end of the masque these fearsome characters seize hold of the wretched woman, who resists. But a servant says, "'Tis part of the Entertainment, Madam, you must go with him," a line which should provide modern critics with an incentive to re-examine poor Durfey's much-abused dramatic works. The grim result of this extraordinary ballet is not realized until a few lines later, when the moralizing Viceroy of Naples opens the shutters to reveal Blowzabella's body "Hanging upon Gibbets."

In a more traditional tragedy, *Cambyses* (1671), IV.i, by Settle, the sleeping protagonist is presented with an elaborate allegory, the executants of which never touch the boards of the stage:

> The Scene representing a steep Rock, from the top of which descends a large Cloud, which opening, appear various shapes of Spirits seated in form of a Council, to whom a more glorious Spirit decends halfway, seated on a Throne; at which, the former Spirits rise and Dance: In the midst of the Dance arises a Woman with a Dagger in her hand; at which the Scene shuts. In the time of this Representation this Song is sung from within, as suppos'd, by Spirits. "Ye subtle Pow'rs that rule below."

The meaning of Cambyses's ominous vision of a celestial council of ministers is made clear in the final scene of the play (V.iii) with a blood-stained apotheosis. The spirits again appear in the clouds, this time above a wedding, one of the members of which is the villainous imposter of Smerdis; after another song ("Kings from the gods and from our elements"), "the Musick turns into an alarm, at which a bloody Cloud interposes between the audience and the Spirits and being immediately removed, the Ghosts of Cambyses and the true Smerdis appear in the seats of the former Spirits." This is one of the few examples in which a musical scene forms the climax of a spoken play.[48]

Musical allegories in Restoration plays are not always so gruesome as the scenes just described, but less macabre episodes, in which the desired effect is other than mere diversion of the audience, are rare. One example, which is only barely structural, occurs in *The Comical History of Don Quixote*, Part I (1694), by Durfey, now in his more comfortable element. The Don is about to set off on another adventure:

> Here Hostess and Maritorness raise up Don Quixote, and lead him
> to the farther Part of the Stage, and Arm him. Then a Dance is
> performed, representing Knights Errant Killing a Dragon.[49]

When one considers the nature of the other entertainments in this play and its sequels,[50] this dance is probably unintentionally representative of an activity usually associated with Don Quixote.

Music and Madness

In Restoration plays (and those of earlier periods), music is often associated with madness, either as exemplified by the "Ophelia complex" or the music sung or played to an insane person to ease his infirmity.[51] Since in these cases music is either a manifestation of a character's personality or appears to have an effect on his behavior, its use is nearly always of structural importance to the play. Except in comedies (in which a mad song is rarely integral to the action), songs in Restoration drama are not often sung by a mad person in the Ophelia fashion. An early exception is in V.i of Porter's *The Villain* (1663). Charlotte's lover Brisac (among others) has been killed; distracted, she is being held on a bed while singing snatches of song:

> *Charlotte.* Pray, Sirs, let me go, you use me too unkindly,
>   I never did any of you such wrong . . .
>   Ile never pray agen; but I will sing
>   My self into his [Brisac's] blest Society.

She sings "The Bells were rung, and the Mass was sung," and later, "Willy was fair, Willy was stout." But her singing is only a symptom, and Francibell hastens with the treatment: "May be some Musick may still her spirits, Sir: / Shall my Sister sing?" Charlotte's father consents and Marina sings "Lady preserve the Title of your head." But Charlotte is not so insensible that she is unable to be critical:

> Away, thou art out of tune and sence,
> Let it be my poor Boy's Voice;
> He once could please me with his melancholy Songs,
> Pray, let him sing.

A song ("Beyond the malice of abusive fate") is sung within by "the Boy." But her request is far from simply an excuse to sing another song, as Charlotte soon dies of a broken heart. The mad songs in Banks's late tragedy *Cyrus the Great* (1696), IV.i, are unusual. Lausaria (played by the great actress-singer, Mrs. Bracegirdle) has been driven insane with unrequired love; she enters "Distracted, drest like Cupid, with a Bow and Quiver, follow'd by her Women." After singing "O take him gently from the pile" (D&M 2527 mJ. Eccles sMrs. Bracegirdle) and loosing an arrow (without effect) at Cyrus, she exits and dies.[52]

As in the last act of *The Villain*, discussed above, music is more often seen as an antidote rather than as a manifestation of madness. In Vanburgh's comedy *The Pilgrim* (1700), III.iii, a mad scholar is uttering nonsense:

> No devouring Fish come nigh,
> Nor Monster in my empery
> Once shew his Head, or terrour bring,
> But let the weary Sailer sing,
> Amphitrite, with White Arms
> Strike my Lute, I'll sing Charms.

But before he can sing, his master remarks that "Now he must have Musick, his fit will grow worse else," and an unspecified tune is played. A less redeeming use of mad songs is occasionally found in the para-dramatic entertainments which clutter Durfey's comedies; he was perhaps attempting to satisfy the tastes of those courtiers who delighted in spending their afternoons peering over the wall at Bedlam.[53] But music is not used only to enhance the madness of a character. As it can serve equally well as cure or symptom, it can also be used to cause insanity or to prove that a character is sane. In Otway's *The History and Fall of Caius Marius* (1680), IV.ii, Marius senior expresses his misfortune in a paraphrase of a familiar line: "How am I fallen!" And then he hears soft music: "Musick? sure the Gods / Are mad, or have design'd to make me so." In Durfey's *Love for Money: or, the Boarding School* (1691), IV.iii, Jiltal (played by the actress-singer-dancer, Mrs. Butler) has been accused of being mad. She replies:

> Mad, indeed such injuries were enough to make me so; but Sir, I hope my Eyes will resolve that doubt; besides, if you doubt my sence, you shall hear me sing a Song of my own making.[54]

One must not discount the possibility that Durfey means the song to belie Jiltal's protestation of sanity (a hamming actress could certainly accomplish that), but here the song seems to serve quite a different purpose.

Music for Comic Effect

Unlike tragedies, comedies only occasionally use serious art music in such a manner that its omission would disrupt the dramatic structure. This is not to say that music of high quality is not used in the lighter stage forms; quite to the contrary. But in comedies music is rarely required to do any more than complement sophisticated fabrications involving either a quest for money (usually belonging to an innocent young heiress or crafty, licentious old widow) or sexual favors (those of anyone, man or woman, capable of giving them). The music in these affairs is mostly secondary, offered as a diverting respite from the action. When used for comic effect, it is simply a touchstone for witty dialogue or a background before which a comedian may exercise his non-vocal acting skills.

The after-dinner music provided by Major-General Blunt in Shadwell's comedy *The Volunteers: or the Stock Jobbers* (1693), III.i, is of little importance to the plot. But the play could hardly have survived without it, as it provided the audience with the almost obligatory concert of music which they expected from late 17th-century comedies (see Chapter Four). But Shadwell elevates the dramatic importance of this music so that it becomes essential for his dialogue; this he achieves, however, at the expense of the music, for both music and dialogue are heard at the same time:

> *Major-General Blunt.* . . . to help out your desert, you shall have a little Entertainment of Musick, when the Minstrels have Din'd. . . .
> [Enter Musick, they play and sing.]
> *Sir Nicholas.* Ah that's fine, that's Chromatick, I love Chromatick Musick mightily.
> *Sir Timothy.* Ah that Fuge! That Fuge's finely taken.
> *Sir Nich.* And bacely carried on.
> *Sir Tim.* All Italian Sir, all Italian. . . .

Certainly the pun is justification enough for this short passage, but the full comic potential would depend almost entirely on what music was played. These foolish knights are trying very hard to impress the gathering by demonstrating their knowledge of the latest musical vogue. But if their actions elsewhere in the play are any indication, Sir Nicholas's remarks about chromaticism were probably timed to coincide with the singing of an innocently diatonic song, and Sir Timothy probably made his contrapuntal observations during a section in recitative.

Often it appears that music was used simply to accompany the ridiculous antics of a foppish character. In Centlivre's *The Beau's Duel: or A Soldier for the Ladies* (1702), I.i, Sir William Mode calls for a group of musicians to play for him. He asks his servant, who is fashionably French, if they have arrived:

> *Reviere.* Yess Sire, here be de Fidle, de Hautbois, de Courtel, and de Base
> Vial, dey be all despose' for to receive your Command. . . .
> *Sir Will.* . . . Play some soft Air, a consort of Flutes wou'd have done well.

While the music is playing, Sir William "uses a great many odd postures" to increase his understanding of the music, but seeing the door open, he realizes that he is being observed from without; embarrassed, he stops the music. What the stage musicians played is obviously of little importance, provided that it pleased the paying audience. In Shadwell's thoroughly obscene comedy, *The Woman-Captain* (1680), III.ii, music must take over when the action supposedly occurring offstage becomes too risqué even for the licentious followers of Charles II. The preceding scenes have shown wanton violence, drunkenness, and the genteel night-time sports of breaking windows and blacking out street lamps; but when the action shifts to Sir Humphrey's closet, we must remain outside with a philosophical steward as soft music plays within:

> *Steward.* Heav'n how he melts his Time and Land away in Luxury
> and Sloath, and I by force must be an Instrument in his
> wickedness; now must I keep the Dore, while he, his Friends
> and Whores are lolling in their Baths. . . . [A Song is sung to
> 'em within.]

Whatever the audience imagined to be transpiring within Sir Humphrey's house, the scene involves only the steward; the music, which is supposed to conjure up a lewd image, is the background against which he displays his reaction to his master's behavior.[55]

Music played or sung "from within" is a common device to help create a humorous effect. A fine example is provided by Congreve's *The Way of the World* (1700), III.iii, an involved scene between Marwood and Millamant that culminates in an argument about their relative ages and beauty. When the discussion becomes a bit too heated, Millamant (played by the young Anne Bracegirdle; Marwood, by a slightly "decay'd beauty," Mrs. Barry) requests her maid to have a song sung in the next room; she assures her guest that there is not "any great matter in it--but 'tis agreeable to my humour." But the song, "Love's but the frailty of the mind," carries on the argument and is designed to embarrass Marwood with references to "inferior beauties" and sickly, wasting flames of love. As Stoddard Lincoln rightly observes,[56] the reaction to the song expressed on the faces of the actresses is of great importance in Millamant's victory over Marwood.

Perhaps the most notorious offstage music accompanying onstage foolery is in V.i of Dryden's Sr Martin Mar-all, or the Feign'd Innocence (1668), a scene which helped to make Sir Martin a stock character in Restoration comedy.[57] Millicent refuses to marry Sir Martin until he can give her "proof of his wit" (or better, his wits). His crafty servant, Warner, boasts that his master "sings, dances, plays upon the Lute." She requests a serenade. The talentless protagonist is placed in a window as Warner fetches his lute from a nearby barber shop. At the signal of a bell, Warner (or someone behind the scenes) plays a tune and sings a song ("Blind Love to this hour") while Sir Martin pretends to sing and play; he continues "fumbling, and gazing on his Mistress" even after the music has ceased. One cannot imagine that a theatre composer would have spent his best efforts on a song employed in this manner (it does not survive), yet without some music this scene would be lifeless.

Serenades

Besides the fifth-act "entertainments" that proliferate in comedies of the 1690s, the most extensive use of music in the lighter forms of the period is found in the serenade. In some tragedies (usually in the early acts) the serenade is comprised of tender songish entreaties of a prince or young warrior to his beloved. Usually serious in tone and introduced into a stable dramatic situation, it consists of set pieces of musical but rarely of dramatic importance.[58] The comic serenade, however, often features incompetent performances, feigned rebuffs, and the general confusion of foolish lovers blaming their amorous failures on the musicians, who grope together in the darkness under a fair lady's window.[59] Even if a serenading fool manages to have his musicians perform one song or air, his group often finds itself pitted against that of a rival.

Dryden, in An Evening's Love (1671), II.i, is the first Restoration playwright to create a scene involving rival serenades. The two Englishmen, Bellamy and Wildblood, pass through the streets of Madrid (at carnival time) in disguise with their musicians to serenade Jacinta. Wildblood orders "a song al'Angloise" ("After the pangs of a desperate Lover," D&M 17 *m*Marsh). But Jacinta is not impressed as she throws down her handkerchief with money in it: "Ill Musicians must be rewarded: there, Cavalier, 'tis to buy your silence. . . ." But then the Englishmen hear "Musick and Guittars tuning on the other side of the Stage," as the rival Spaniards, Don Lopez and Don Melchor, have arrived with their musicians. This scene ends in a fight as "the Musicians on both sides and Servants fall confusedly one over the other. . . ." This episode was frequently imitated, and the result is always pandemonium.[60]

Occasionally a playwright employs a serenade for a more subdued dramatic effect. In Motteux's tragedy *Beauty in Distress* (1698), IV.i, the hero, Don Vincento, disguised as a Moor and using the name Morat, and the villain, Ricardo, both love Placentia. They confront each other in the night near her house. They conceal their mutual jealousy and speak frankly about Placentia. Don Fabiano has arranged for "a Serenading Symphony" to strike up at this moment beneath her window, and the music helps to bring about a temporary alliance between protagonist and antagonist, who now realize Placentia has a third suitor.[61] This scene is not particularly humorous, but the lighter moments of many of the more serious dramatic forms include serenades. A particularly bawdy one occurs in Dryden's tragi-comedy *Troilus and Cressida, or, Truth Found too Late* (1679), III.ii. Pandarus has come to give the lovers named in the title a charivari:

> [Enter Pandarus; a Servant: Musick.]
> *Pand.* Softly, villain, softly; I would not for half Troy the Lovers
>   should be disturb'd under my roof; listen rogue, listen, do they
>   breathe?
> *Serv.* Yes, Sir, I hear by some certain signes, they are both awaken.
> *Pand.* That's as it should be: that's well aboth side:
>   [listens.]
>   Yes faith they are both alive: --there was a creake! there was a
>   creake: they are both alive . . . a ha boyes! --Is the musick
>   ready?
> *Serv.* Shall they strike up Sir!
> *Pand.* Art thou sure they do not know the parties?
> *Serv.* They play to the Man in the Moon for ought they know.
> *Pand.* To the Man in the Moon, ah Rogue! do they so indeed
>   Rogue! I understand, thee:[62] thou art a wag: thou art a wagg.
>   Come towze rouze! in the name of love, strike up boys!

This scene alone gives credence to Anne Ferry's generalization that "Dryden transposes the ideal of pastoral innocence into an image of prurient ignorance."[63]

Reading of Songs

Organic songs abound in Restoration comedy as the ballad-like catches or parts of songs that issue from drunken or half-witted characters. They are not often accompanied and are apt to be performed by comedians who were not skilled singers. Their subjects are low and bawdy, and their dramatic effect is so unsubtle as to require little exegesis. The independent art song, performed by a professional singer or skilled actor-singer, often introduced into comedies for the flimsiest of reasons, is occasionally given a more dramatic role when its text is read and then discussed, usually for the purpose of ridiculing its author.[64]   In Southerne's comedy *The Maid's Last Prayer* (1693), III.i, Granger has come into possession of a love song written by a talented young lady who "Sings, and Plays upon the Virginals so sweetly, and Dances Country Dances."   Asked what news there is of the virtuous girl, he replies, "Nothing extraordinary; she has play'd the Fool, and writ a Song, as most People do, that are in Love."   He then asks his friend Garnish to read it and tells him that "'tis all her own, I assure you."   The play-book does not make it clear if the song is performed, but the text is printed and begins "Prithee, my Dear, do not be so peevish."   The girl may have musical talent but is deficient as a poetess.   In other comedies the reading of a song, far from being a dramatic device to reveal the feeble poetic ability of a character, is done simply to rationalize its performance by providing it with some context in which to exist.   In C. Boyle's *As You Find It* (1703), I.ii, during a discussion of the more unusual manifestations of love, Eugenia says that she knows of a strange fellow who has expressed himself in verse: "A Gentleman of my Acquaintance, takes occasion to tell the Town, in a little Song, that he cannot love any Woman that's fond of him.   I believe I have it in my Pocket--Here's the Tune to it too."   She gives it to Orinda (played by Mrs. Bracegirdle), who reads it before singing, then remarks with certain false modesty that "I like the Words better than you will my Voice, I believe."[65]   This practice, rare in Restoration plays, probably developed as a result of the playwright's desire to incorporate into the action a song which would otherwise have been para-dramatic.   But the problems that faced the dramatist as regards the rationalization of these brief, often inconsequential musical diversions are in no way comparable with those inherent in having to accommodate the much larger musical excursions, the masque and entertainment, which are characteristic not only of the dramatic opera but of the comedy and tragedy as well.

II. MASQUES, ENTERTAINMENTS, AND DANCES

Court Masques and Masques in Plays

At the Restoration, the older London courtiers certainly had not lost interest in the former exercise of courtly entertainment, the masque, but with the beheading of the first Charles, the days of frequent lavish royal entertainments in which they could participate were gone. And what in Jacobean times had been a fairly common dramatic form, the play with masque, became even more common after 1660, as it was practically the only forum for that splendid kind of entertainment in which scenery, music, and dance are equal partners. In Porter's early Restoration comedy, *The Carnival* (1664), III.i, Lorenzo's nostalgia for bygone days at his foreign court probably reminded many of the English gentry in the audience of the good times a few decades earlier. Lorenzo is preparing to offer his guests a small private musical entertainment, but he recalls a far grander one: "Bartolo, bid them sing the Song was Sung when I acted the Sea-god with the Cornucopia. Ah, Bartolo, those were merry Days! thou didst Act Tantalus, I remember." He is even able to recall certain deficiencies of their dramatic presentation: "Troth It was a dainty Masque; for all The Company were kept in suspence till the last, and Did never comprehend what we meant. . . ." But this dramaturgical miscalculation was of no consequence, for whether their masque had a plot or even a unified theme mattered little, as long as all those dancing in it enjoyed themselves. The same is true with most of the representations of court masques grafted onto Restoration plays, performed now by the servants of the court rather than the courtiers themselves, and in which the late 17th-century English gentry could participate only vicariously. Just as the pastoral settings of the masques of the earlier Stuart court bore little resemblance to the intrigues of Whitehall Palace, the masques performed by the more ancient courtiers of the tragedies and tragi-comedies of the Restoration usually had little relation, symbolic or otherwise, with the sordid and bloody business of their plots. Charles I's courtly entertainments helped him to escape from an ominous political situation into a rich fantasy world, and the masques in plays often allow their similarly ill-fated protagonists to enjoy intermittent episodes of musical diversion amid the scenes of plotting and violence.

In most of the tragedies with "entertainments," the masque is usually placed in Act II or III and is occasioned by the return of a royal relative, a recent victory in battle, or a similar event. In the anonymous tragedy, *The Fatal Discovery; or, Love in Ruines* (1698), II.i, for example, a masque is presented by Beringaria for his son, recently returned from exile. The masque itself is of such little consequence to the plot that only the stage direction "Here follows the Masque" marks its existence. And even when stage directions for a masque are detailed, as in Rymer's *Edgar, or the English Monarch* (1678), IV, the masque usually bears little resemblance to the play, allegorical or otherwise, and the characters of the play within a play are emblematic rather than specifically symbolic of characters of the larger drama:

> A tempestuous Sea is represented, Neptune heaving the Billows with his Fork. Edgar with Alfrid entring [to observe, not to participate], the Tritons sound their Shells: A sudden Calm, Neptune lays his Trident at Edgar's Feet. The other Sea-gods, Proteus and Nersus, make likewise Obeisance to him. . . .

Later, after Proteus's address and a song of Sirens, "Three Celestiall Sirens approach, skymming on the surface of the water. The former Sirens dive hastily, and disappear . . . The 3 dance. . . ." The detailed stage directions suggest an elaborate representation of a masque in the Jacobean tradition. It has only a general theme and no story and would be entirely incidental if not for the fact that its characters acknowledge the presence of their king, Edgar.

Because the masque is often dramatically neutral--that is, simply a show of singing and dancing within a fanciful setting--the lighter dramatic types also incorporate it into their structures. A masque in honor of a wedding is presented in III.i of Dryden's tragi-comedy, *The Rival Ladies* (1664). Manuet, having just been told that the show is ready, indicates that he is a seasoned observer of such performances by letting the audience know what is the most significant aspect of the following presentation:

> desire 'em
> They would leave out the words, and fall to Dancing; The Poetry of
> the Foot takes most of late. . . .

His wish is granted in a swirl of descending Cupids, dancing swans and dragons, and a black flaming chariot.

Although such masques are but mere stage representations of the real thing, they were extravagant and costly. Even during the most prolific and successful years for the London theatre companies, only a few plays had masques, especially during seasons in which a dramatic opera or two was also offered.[66] Although a masque might require a greater expenditure of funds and rehearsal time than the rest of the play, the musical interlude is nearly always of secondary importance to the drama. This is not true of the dramatic opera, for the heart of these larger productions is the masque. Despite the profusion of songs, entry dances, and symphonies interspersed with spoken dialogue during the course of an act, the dramatic opera is most operatic during the masque, usually placed at the end of an act. Even though the all-sung section may have little to do with the surrounding drama, during the masque the play ceases and music reigns. Yet the Restoration playwright never released music drama from the confines of the spoken play. The more extended musical scenes have to be accommodated as the dreams or fantasies of "real" characters, as their royal entertainments, the celebrations of the more tangible battlefield victories, or (and this was perhaps the most successful solution) as the nonsensical, absurd antics of singing and dancing characters not really part of the play and for whom no excuse or explanation is offered at all. The next step, which was never quite taken during the Restoration, would have been to form these musical antics into drama or even melodrama, for which no apology (in the form of the guardian spoken play) would be necessary. But the play, the most enduring and firmly implanted of all English dramatic forms (indeed, one might argue that during the 16th and 17th centuries, it was the only indigenous dramatic form; certainly the dramatic opera is only a mutation of it), however much it might use music to enhance its spoken dialogue and scenic effects, would not yield to music. And the seemingly simple solution to the dilemma--opera, with its entirely different set of conventions, all of which were well known to the Restoration dramatist and composer--was only fully accepted as a continental importation. The play (which remains the most powerful stage form of the English) largely stifled British attempts at music drama for nearly two centuries. The Restoration masque, in which Purcell and a few others excelled briefly, is a miniature form, far too confined and dependent on its dramatic parent to have permitted the expansive musical expression provided first by Italian opera and then by the oratorio.

Organic Masques

Late 17th-century playwrights ordinarily make little attempt to integrate masques with their plays, other than to provide the musical interludes with some cursory dramatic justification (as in *Edgar, or the English Monarch*, IV). A few masques, however, function organically in their plays. They are closely related to the action and usually occur in the last two acts, where the drama tightens for the climax. (The less organic masque is usually presented in the early acts, before the graver episodes of the tragedy and the more frantic pace of action in the comedy.) The most skillful use of a masque to advance a plot is in Settle's *The Empress of Morocco* (1673), IV.iii. The queen mother and her villainous lover, Crimalhaz, present the court with a masque, unusual in that it is a familiar allegory. King Hamet is to play Orpheus and his young queen, Morena, takes the part of Eurydice. But the queen mother tells Morena that Crimalhaz, not Hamet, is under the mask of Orpheus, and the young queen, hoping to do away with the villain at the appropriate moment in the allegory, stabs her husband by mistake. It is a startling departure from the orderly presentation of a courtly entertainment. In no other play of the period does one find such an elaborate masque so closely related to its play,[67] for such scenes are usually ones of dramatic repose. Not all masques in Restoration tragedies are representations of the formal courtly type. In Payne's *The Fatal Jealousie*, published in the same year as *The Empress of Morocco*, 1673, gypsies dance and sing and tell Don Antonio's fortune in a kind of antimasque. And in V[ii] of Crowne's *The History of Charles the Eighth of France* (1672), a vision of a masque is conjured by a magician so that Isabella may foresee Charles's fate:

> There arises a Spirit and immediately the Scene is drawn and the supposed Shapes of Charles & Julia are presented, Royally habited, and seated on Chairs of State, at their feet several Masquers; and near the Chairs the Musick in white Robes and Laurels on their Heads [the characteristic costume of spirit musicians]. A Chorus of Voices and loud Musick heard.

From this vision Isabella learns that she is not destined to sit next to Charles as his queen.

In the more than 20 Restoration comedies that contain them, masques rarely function as organically as in the preceding examples from tragedies. The masque in the lighter form is mostly confined to those plays with foreign settings, as for example, Sir Robert Howard's comedy, *The Surprisal* (1665), set in Siena. And when such a musical episode finds its way into a Covent Garden comedy, its dramaturgical rational is often preposterous. For example, in Shadwell's *A True Widow* (1679), IV.ii, when the scene shifts to the theatre, and an actor announces that "We cannot go on with our Play, one of our young Women being frighted with the Swords, is fallen into a Fit, and carried home sick," Carlos saves the afternoon by telling his friends that he has prepared a masque-like entertainment. And Ravenscroft's three-act play, *The Anatomist, or, The Sham Doctor* (1697), represents no more than a playhouse within a playhouse in which the actors (as well as the audience) assemble to see Motteux's masque, "The Loves of Mars and Venus." Neither of these musical episodes is related to the spoken part of the play proper; they are both representative of most of the masques inserted into comedies. If a masque is related to its supportive play, it is usually only symbolic of the dramatic situation. For example, Colley Cibber's *Love's Last Shift* (1696), ends with a masque which consists of a debate among Love, Fame, Reason, Honor, and Marriage. All are eventually satisfied by Love in Marriage. This vaguely corresponds with the plot of the play in which a virtuous young wife is reunited with her wayward husband.

Entertainments

Closely related to the masque is the entertainment (also called banquet, show, antick dance, entry dance, and so forth), a loosely defined musical episode which at one extreme is as elaborate as the more formal masque and at the other extreme is a short, modest excursion from the spoken business of the play, often simply indicated by nothing more than the stage direction, "Here follows the Entertainment." Like the masque, the entertainment is almost always para-dramatic: in tragedies and tragi-comedies it is introduced when a masque would be inappropriate (for example, when the assembled persons to be entertained are not royalty, or when the plot will not bear a lengthy interruption); in comedies it occurs often with little preparation and is simply a concert-like musical offering to which the Restoration audience became more and more accustomed near the turn of the century. So common was the musical entertainment in comedies that its introduction became perfunctory. A typical rationale was to have music to accompany dinner; the cast usually sat down to their feast during or before the fourth act.[68] In Mountfort's *Greenwich-Park* (1691), IV.iv, Dorinda orders dinner to be brought in and asks Young Reveller to sit opposite her so "that with full Pleasure we may view each other." Reveller replies, "My Eye will have the greatest Banquet, Madam." She adds that "Your Ear too shall be entertain'd." As the servants bring in the food and drink, there is "An Entertainment of Music," its contents otherwise unspecified. To the audience, at least, the music was more important than a representation of people taking a meal, and the gastronomic show was often omitted, although the anticipation of a meal still occasions the introduction of music. For example, in Pinkethman's comedy *Love without Interest* (1699), II.i, Fickle has arranged to have the "Lord Mayors Musick" stop by to perform a sonata before dinner. Jonathan is anxious to have them perform, because "unless you'll give 'em Employment, they'll get so drunk, they'll be for playing on more Instruments than you imagin." But then he lets the real reason for his urgency slip out: "Then there's the Cook smoking like a Pasty, and swearing by his Chopping-block, unless You make haste, the Dinner won't be worth a Fig. . . ." He takes his place to hear the music, muttering, "Pox of this scraping afore Dinner, it serves only to set People's Teeth an edge, and spoil their Stomachs. . . ." Despite this humorous introduction, the music that follows is completely para-dramatic, although the sonata was doubtless of much interest to many of the musical dilettantes in the audience (see Chapter Four).

Occasionally a playwright makes little attempt to accommodate an entertainment with suitable dialogue. In Mrs. Manley's *The Lost Lover; or, The Jealous Husband* (1696), two musical entertainments are placed immediately at the opening of the scene: IV.i, "The Scene opens and discovers Lady Young Love . . . Song and entertainment of dancing"; V.ii, "Scene, Lady Young Loves House. Song and Musick."[69] In the latter, the music is performed before characters enter the stage. Whereas such musical interludes rarely pertain organically to the drama and therefore are not often described in detail (except for some dances, as will be shown below), often the play-book describes what music was played, much in the manner of a concert program.[70] Joseph Harris's comedy *The City-Bride, or, The Merry Cuckold* (1696) opens with a banquet which is simply a miniature concert: "The Curtain draws up and discovers several sitting at a Banquet. An Entertainment of Instrumental Musick, composed by Signior Finger: Then a Song, set by Mr. John Eccles, and Sung by Young La Roche . . . After this a dance and then the Scene shuts."[71] Although the scene has little relation to the rest of the play, its position at the beginning of an act does not disrupt the dramatic flow, since the play itself has not begun. In Thomas Dilke's *The City Lady; or, Folly Reclaim'd* (1697), a long entertainment is also placed at the beginning of a scene (III.ii), but in this case the action is halted in the midst of a thickening plot. Even the best comedies of the period were obliged to pause momentarily to satisfy the audience's "concupiscence of jigg and song." In Congreve's *The Way of the World* (1700), a play in which a song in III.iii is used for considerable dramatic effect, Lady Wishfort provides Sir Roland with an entertainment in IV.ii which does nothing to advance the plot: "Call in the Dancers--Sir Roland, we'll sit, if you please, and see the Entertainment." Shadwell, a playwright who never hesitated to exploit the fickle tastes of the courtiers (often to the detriment of his plays), inserts a fourth-act entertainment in his comedy *The Woman-Captain* (1680), IV.i, which probably involved no music at all, but which is related to the military subject of the play:

> *Mrs. Gripe.* Come on, I have provided some Entertainment instead
> of a Dance--you shall see my two new Souldiers Exerciz'd--
> fetch 'em in Serjeant.

Although most entertainments usually contained some music, late in the century they became the receptacles for almost any sort of theatrical activity, from tumbling to comic dialogues. Shadwell's drill exercise is an early example of the "music-hall turn" that many comedies were later to take. Although entertainments are seldom of such structural importance that they advance the plot (as seen in a few masques discussed above), occasionally they resemble the action of the play in the same way that

Mrs. Gripe's soldiers reinforce the military flavor of *The Woman-Captain*. For instance, in Dennis's comedy *Gibraltar: Or, The Spanish Adventure* (1705), V.i, "A Dialogue between an English Marriner, and a Spanish Shepherdess ('Come gentle Nymph')" is sung during a celebration at the end of the play.

The Restoration tragedy, which usually deals with the troubles of ancient or fictitious royalty, is more likely to present its formal music and dance in a masque than in an entertainment, although the latter is sometimes used if the plot of the tragedy has no convenient victory or royal homecoming to celebrate; the nebulous shape and contents of an entertainment could be molded to fit almost any dramatic situation. In Lee's tragedy *Mithridates* (1678), II[ii], a grim sacrifce provides the unlikely setting for an unspecified show:

> *Mithridates*. . . . Tryphon [a priest], begin, and let the Altar smoak
> With such rich Victims, to the well-pleas'd Gods,
> That they may smile from Heav'n, and give us joy.
> [Here follows the Entertainment.]

The gods are not pleased, however, as a graphic bad omen indicates: "An Image of Victory descends with two Crowns in her hands; but on a sudden the Engines break [i.e., brake?], and cast the Image forward on the Stage with such violence that they dash it in pieces. . . ."

In tragedies entertainments are dramatically static; the play-bound lords and ladies sit in attention and do not participate as they often do in the masque. Therefore, rarely do these shows further the plot, as happens, for example, in Settle's masque in *The Empress of Morocco* (1673). However, on occasion a skillful poet at least allows the action to continue during the entertainment, and in Crowne's *Ambitious Statesman, or the Loyal Favourite* (1679), IV[i], a song ("Long, long had great Amintor lain") performed during a musical show is dramatically functional:

> The Scene is drawn, the Dauphin and Louize are sat in State, and
> Entertain'd with Musick and Dancing. The Entertainment ended,
> Enter the Duke. . . .

But during the music, the duke has seen "the Dauphin Caressing Louize." She is married to the Dauphin but is in love with the duke, even though she believes the latter to be unfaithful. In the text of the song Celia is described as cruel to Amintor, though she secretly loves him.[72] Except for the song, the entertainment itself does not continue the plot but, importantly, neither does it hinder it.

Entry Dances

The entry dance is another kind of musical entertainment which is not usually organic to the plot and therefore is often as weakly prepared as the most para-dramatic masque or entertainment. These dances, however, are often representative of some aspect of the play. Both the Jacobean court masque and its stage imitation, as well as a few masques in Restoration plays, were comprised of several entries, roughly corresponding to the acts of a play. Because a full-length representation of a masque in a play would overbalance the spoken part, stage masques usually consist only of one or two entries (typically of the antimasque kind), plus, of course, all the trappings of an assembled court. As a simple song and dance were often necessary alternatives to the expensive masque, so also is the single entry dance of a masque (usually stripped of its more expensive play-within-a-play environment) a substitute for a grander show. Nevertheless, it provided the courtiers with the essence of a masque: an allegorical or pseudo-allegorical dance.

An entry dance can portray almost any activity or provide an emblematic representation of any character. Its definititon is so broad that even during the late 17th century there was some confusion about its meaning. In Crowne's comedy, *The Countrey Wit* (1675), IV.i, Sir Mannerly (with the help of his servant, Booby) is bragging to Lady Faddle about his dancing accomplishments. She asks him, "Canst thou Rise well?" Booby makes the quick reply, "In a morning, Madam." Lady Faddle misses the joke: "No, rise high in dancing, if you will rise high in Ladies favors here you must rise high in dancing. . . ." Sir Mannerly jumps ridiculously, and my lady approves: "Thy heels will be invited to show their parts to dance in every fine Entry, in the Masques and Plays." Sir Mannerly thinks she means an entry to a hall or a room, and she is forced to explain to the country bumpkin what an entry is: "to dance in an entry, that is to say, in an Entry, an Entry of any thing." But the worldly Lady Faddle is not able to define this thing, because as she stresses again, it could be literally anything. Finally, she is forced to give Sir Mannerly a specific example: ". . . in an Entry of Shepherds or Gods and Goddesses." This too fails to sink in, and in desperation she changes the subject to singing. Crowne's humor is directed at the practice of inserting any sort of dance into a play provided that its executants are fantastically attired and that the dance is a novel manifestation of the plot, theme, or setting of the play. An entry may be as integral to the play as that in I.i of Shadwell's operatic *Psyche* (1675), in which sylvans and dryads materialize naturally out of the pastoral scene to dance and present Psyche with fruits and flowers, or it may be as tangential as the entry of clowns in Shadwell's *A True Widow* (1679), IV.ii, which is generally compatible with the buffoonery displayed by

most of the characters in the play. Between these extremes, the entry
dance, in general, simply enhances the setting of a play. For example, a
play set in Spain often contains a dance accompanied by guitars and
castanets, as in Dryden's *The Indian Emperour* (1667), IV.iii:

> A pleasant Grotto discover'd: in it a Fountain spouting: round
> about it Vasquez, Pizarro, and other Spaniards lying carelessly
> unarm'd, and by them many Indian Women . . . two Spaniards arise
> and Dance a Saraband with Castanieta's. . . .

The dance with castanets became popular, and, inevitably, it is employed
in plays with or without Spanish settings.[73]

Antic Dances

Closely allied to the entry dance is the antic dance, also an
extract from the masque. Like the former, it defies simple definition and
may or may not be allegorically related to its dramatic surroundings, but
it characteristically involves dancers in bizarre or fantastic costume.
Stage directions are sometimes quite explicit in their descriptions of these
dances. In Ravenscroft's comedy *The Citizen Turn'd Gentleman* (1672),
Act III opens with an antic dance representing Cureal's fallacious medical
treatment given to Sir Simon Softhead:

> Enter two Chymists dress'd in antick habits with broad black caps on
> their heads, that flap down about their ears, no hair seen; Ruffs
> about their necks, strait bodyed doublets with long close sleeves;
> Spanish scant breeches, and pumps, followed by four Operators in
> antick dresses singing the symphony. . . .

Later in the act, Sir Simon describes what the charlatans actually did to
him:

> . . . then did these two buffle headed talkative fellows in broad-
> brimed hats speak nonsense for an hour, till my patience was
> wearied; then entered such a consort of Musick, as if they had plaid
> a flourish for the entry of Devils; but were followed by half a dozen
> Anticks singing, and dancing with Syringes and Glisters [i.e.,
> sparklers]   in   their hands, that they made me almost out of my
> wits. . . .

Less pertinent to the plot but just as explicit is a set of dances found in
Powell's *Imposture Defeated* (1698), I[ii], during a long frivolous
entertainment:

Here follows a Dance between a Lawyer and a Poor Clyent, a
Courtier and a Lame Soldier, a Userer and a Prodigal, a Physician
and a Fool.

Although no subsequent dialogue describes what occurred during these
dances, each was probably a vignette depicting the cruel treatment of the
lesser member of each pair by the higher placed.

The stage directions for antic dances are not usually as explicit as
those just mentioned, nor are the dances often of any structural
significance to the play. The display of an unusual costume was reason
enough to have a dance. In Behn's farce *The Emperor of the Moon*
(1687), for example, II.iii opens with a dance of antics dressed in "Gothic
Habits." And in Powell's *The Cornish Comedy* (1696), II.i, Captain Busy
calls in some of his friends to perform "A Posture Dance in imitation of
Soldiers Exercize." The dance is sympathetic to his military attitude but
is clearly a diversion for the audience rather than a constructive dramatic
device. The bizarre spectacle of most antic dances, their lack of serious
purpose, and their typical incongruity with the dramatic surroundings
precludes their being employed to advance the plot or to provide a
musical background during which the action of the play may continue.
The antic dance is the least organic to the drama of any of the musical
practices of the Restoration play.

Final Dances in Comedies [74]

The dramatic role of the final dance, the most persistent
Terpsichorean convention of the period, is difficult to assess. Most
comedies written between 1660 and about 1695 have as a standard
feature of their denouements a dance, usually involving the entire
dramatis personae. It is placed near the end of the last act and is
followed only by a few lines of dialogue and the final rhymed couplet,
the latter summarizing the moral of the story (when there is one) or
making one last joke about a foolish character. The final dance is
inserted into the last scene whether it is appropriate to the action or not;
since it frequently appears to interrupt the natural conclusion of an
otherwise well-constructed play, the dance may be seen to function
simply as a terminating device, something to slow down the rapid-fire wit
and to put a stop to the unraveling of a complicated or improbable plot
(hence its frequent omission from modern revivals).

The dance is nearly always occasioned by an anticipated
wedding. Any last minute difficulties between prospective bride and
bridegroom are quickly settled or pushed aside, the parson is sent for,
and someone orders the fiddlers, who have managed to work their way

into the scene on some pretext, to strike up. Importantly, final dances were cast dances (especially in the 1670s and 80s), even though other danced scenes may have included professionally executed masques and entertainments. Four couples usually performed a country dance, the so-called "Scotts' tune" or "Scotch measure" having enjoyed enormous popularity in the early 1690s.[75] Unlike the entry dances of the tragedies, country dances are not described in detail in stage directions, as they were common to nearly all comedies (and familiar to audiences as social dances) and seldom involved elaborate choreography or antic costumes. Yet Restoration audiences took great delight in them.

Congreve's *The Way of the World*, perhaps the best known English comedy of the period, includes a dance executed by the pairs of lovers. Near the end of the complicated plot, Sir Wilful suggests a dance, and Mirabell ritualistically asks, "What shall we do for Musick?" By coincidence, the fiddlers who played for Sir Rowland's entertainment in IV.ii are standing by. This is an incidental scene whose omission would not disrupt Congreve's plot. But *The Way of the World* needs the final dance. The denouement, like those of countless inferior plays, leaves the reader dizzied by plot complications. The audience requires a little time to reflect on the final romantic permutations of the intense partner-swapping. The dance, too, should summarize and objectify what Norman N. Holland calls "the pattern of building up and breaking down social structures that is the stuff of the play." He further believes it to be "an important part of the symbolism. For example, some seven speeches before it, the dim-witted Witwoud says, 'I'm in a Maze yet, like a Dog in a Dancing-School,' and, of course, that is just what Witwoud is when compared to the clever Mirabell and Fainall."[76] But perhaps Holland goes too far here. A sensitive director and choreographer could certainly give this final dance a symbolic meaning, but we have no idea of its impact on Restoration audiences, whether it was perfunctorily executed by tired and bored actors or if its choreography was meant to convey something more. To one brilliantly atypical final dance, however, we may safely ascribe a symbolic function.

The conclusion of Sir George Etherege's *The Man of Mode* (1676) is not altogether happy, and no anticipated wedding is celebrated. The dangling ends of the plot are not deftly tied off nor is acrimony assuaged with the announcement of a wedding, the usual panacea for any difficulties encountered in a Restoration comedy. Mrs. Loveit is discredited and humiliated (not the victim of a practical joke, but for what she is, a wretched ex-mistress), and the main pair of "lovers," Dorimant and Harriet (the latter offering love and money to the former, who is only mildly interested in either), decide not to fall in love and not to get married. Rather, Harriet and her mother, Lady Woodvil, are to retire to the country. The drama gradually slows to a halt. Granted, earlier in the play Young Bellair, risking disinheritance, has married his father's intended lover, Emilia, and Old Bellair forgives his son in the final scene; but the *fait accompli* does not receive a celebration and is of secondary importance to the subtle dissolution of the relationship between Dorimant and Harriet. The prospect of a sojourn in the country practically elicits a lament from Harriet; there is little humor in her final speech: ". . . pitty me, who am going to that sad place. Methinks I hear the hateful noise of Rooks already--Kaw, Kaw, Kaw--There's musick in the worst Cry in London! My Dill and Cowcumbers to pickle." This is no place for a dance of celebration, yet the fiddles are close at hand, and Old Bellair says, "Let 'em strike up then, the young Lady shall have a dance before she departs." A dance follows; it is perhaps best viewed as an ironic commentary on the lack of a happy ending. It also shows that despite the differences dividing the various characters participating in the dance (such as father and son Bellair's pursuance of the same woman and the cooling of the relationship between Harriet and the protagonist, as well as the general ridicule heaped upon Sir Fopling), the ten characters remaining onstage (five men--Dorimant, Medley, Old and Young Bellair, and Sir Fopling--and five women--Lady Townely, Emilia, Bellinda, Lady Woodvil, and Harriet) can still be harmonious if only in a dance. Mrs. Loveit, the odd one out, is disposed of earlier in the scene because she is the only person really hurt by Dorimant's immoral behavior; she is discredited by her own intransigence at refusing to accept what everyone else views as the follies of the human condition. Perhaps she is excluded because she would have no partner in the country dance, but her departure is also symbolic of an inability to accept the morals of the age. True, Etherege has bowed to the convention of the final dance, but without it, the ending of *The Man of Mode* would be unsettling, as the dance provides an order, a formality among its participants that the dialogue does not.

Final Entertainments

Most dramatists rarely elevate dances performed by actors as Etherege does in *The Man of Mode.* Audiences came to expect musical spectacle in almost all plays, and a final dance performed by ordinary actors, even though some were skilled hoofers, must have been anticlimactic especially if there had been a lavish fourth-act entertainment executed by fine professionals. Thus, in the last years of the century the final dance was regularly replaced by miscellaneous entertainments, although this occasionally happened in earlier plays. For example, in Thomas Shadwell's comedy *The Sullen Lovers: or, the Impertinents* (1668), V.i, Carolina announces that she has prepared a show that departs from the common practice: "in stead of a grand Dance according to the

laudable Custome of Weddings, I have found out a little Comical
Gentleman to entertain you with." The stage directions record that a
boy dressed as "Pugenello" enters, "traverses the Stage, takes his Chair,
and sits down, then Dances a Jigg." The diarist Samuel Pepys, a regular
theatre-goer in the 1660s, approved of this departure; his account reveals
how important a seemingly frivolous dance could be for a play's survival:

> [At the theatre] I had my place, and by and by the King comes and
> the Duke of York; and then the play begins, called *The Sullen lovers
> or The Impertinents*, having many good humours in it; but the play
> tedious and no design at all in it. But a little boy, for a farce, doth
> dance Polichinelli the best that ever anything was done in the world
> by all men's report--most pleased with that beyond anything in the
> world, and much beyond all the play.[77]

As the demand for music and dance in plays grew, dramatists
scoured their works for suitable places to insert music and dance. The
final dance, which is usually performed after the action of the play is
done, provided an optimum location for large para-dramatic musical
entertainments: it is dramatically neutral yet still within the drama; and
a wedding celebration is suitable for almost any kind of musical show.
Beginning about 1690 the final dance is increasingly replaced by
entertainments whose contents are often unspecified. The speaking cast
no longer participates. For example, in Baker's *The Humour of the Age*
(1701), V.i, the happy conclusion is quickly settled; Freeman calls for the
music, and the gathered company cools its collective heels: "An
Entertainment. They sit." But the wedding-dance origins are not
forgotten in these late plays. In another comedy by Baker, *Tunbridge-
Walks* (1703), V, Woodcock announces just before the end of the play
(the end of the spoken part, that is) that "some Neighbors of mine shall
divert you on this Occasion," as he has arranged for "an Entertainment
suitable to a Rural Marriage."

Paradoxically, the final entertainment had a role in ridding the
play of extraneous music. The replacement of a dance involving
characters celebrating their own wedding by an extended musical show
professionally performed by "some Neighbors" might appear to be just
one more musical excess. But a few playwrights realized that if most of
the music sprinkled throughout the acts (music often disrupting the flow
of the action and spoiling dramatic situations requiring no musical
elaboration) were concentrated at the end of the final scene, then the
drama would be left intact and practically unaffected by the music and
dance; in addition, the music-craving members of the audience would
not be dissatisfied with a denouement of dry, drawing-room dialogue

and could wallow in a lengthy musical show in which their favorite singers and dancers could perform unencumbered by the eventual necessity of continuing the play.[78]

Around the turn of the century, the demand for music and dance in plays increased, but the play simply could not assimilate the amount of music that audiences demanded. Earlier in the period, music had been used sparingly to intensify an emotion or to reinforce a scenic effect (such as a brief melancholy song to set a scene or a flourish of instrumental music at the ascent of the curtain). But even the earlier plays carried a musical burden in the form of masques, entry dances, and miniature concerts which often swell an act to over twice the length of time required for the delivery of the dialogue. As this burden increased late in the century, the final entertainment became a frequent receptacle for para-dramatic music. While songs and dances of no organic importance were largely removed from the acts of the play, so too was the music which had been used to enhance a love scene or to intensify a king's morose thoughts; and, unfortunately, the music which had been used to foreshadow death or to accompany a subtle battle of facial expressions, for example, was also mostly swept away by the reform. Spoken dialogue was reinstated as the principal medium of expression in the play, and music was forced to stand nearly outside the drama at the end of the play, as if to do penance for earlier excesses within.

The practices governing the performance of final entertainments and other musical shows on the Restoration stage are not as sophisticated as those pertaining to the music and dance used for dramatic effect. The play yields completely to the musical performers of the larger entertainments. No attempt is made to explain their appearance onstage. Since their music does not assist illusion nor intensify a dramatic situation, it is offered to the audience for what it is: music for its own sake. The performers require no elaborate rationale, since they are not actually a part of the play. The scenery for these episodes need not correspond to that of the rest of the play, nor do the instrumentalists need to be hidden or their instruments disguised (as would have happened, for instance, when they accompanied the mournful songs of ghosts or a celestial chorus). And because the speaking characters rarely participate in musical shows, actors need not be replaced with musical surrogates. Thus, the performance practices of the entertainment differ little from those of the concert room or dancing school. But the conventions governing the performance of music which is either organic to the drama or which is intended to be presented in the context of the play (a masque performed by play-bound courtiers, for instance) are complex and in some cases so stylized that an understanding of them is necessary for an understanding of the plays themselves. The most elaborate performance conventions involve the songs sung or supposedly sung by the main speaking characters and music performed within a grove.

III. MUSICAL SURROGATES AND MUSICAL GROVES

Songs from behind the Scenes

Throughout the period, the theatre companies had in their ranks actors and actresses who were capable singers. In the 1660s and 70s these players were not often the best actors of the troupes, as several of their late 17th-century descendants were, but they frequently acted important supporting roles demanding both musical and Thespian abilities. In early Restoration plays minor characters and occasionally major ones sing, though rarely a tragic protagonist. Concomitant with this practice is one in which a character's songs are sung for him either onstage by an attendant (that is, a professional musician) or offstage by an unspecified singer. Since the two conventions coexist (sometimes even in the same play), determining what character is to sing a particular song is often difficult, especially in plays produced early in the period. The play-books of early works only rarely list the most important actors, much less minor singers, in *dramatis personae.*[79] In early tragedies particularly, convention requires that songs, whether performed by the actor himself or by a surrogate, be sung from behind the scenes or from within a grove; the latter (as will be shown below) is the most common location for music and musicians on the Restoration stage. In W. Killigrew's tragedy *Selindra* (1666), II.i, the song that the protagonist supposedly sings to Phillocles is sung behind the scenes, probably because it was performed by someone other than the actress portraying Selindra. But in Dryden's *The Conquest of Granada by the Spaniards,* Part II (1672), IV.iii, a minor character, Esperanza, a slave, also sings from behind the scenes. Almanzor wants her to serenade the queen: "Now Stand; th' Apartment of the Queen is neer, / And from this place your voice will reach her ear." Esperanza probably does not sing the song, for she exits and re-enters after it.[80] The role was played by Mrs. [Anne] Reeve, a minor actress and therefore perhaps also a singer, although there is no record that she sang in any other play. Crowne's tragedy *Juliana, or the Princess of Poland* (1671), opens with a scene of a grove and gardens, within which Paulina and Joanna, minor characters, are concealed. Joanna sings the song, "Lo, behind a Scene of Seas" (D&M 2056 *m*Banister). She was played by Mrs. [Ann Gibbs] Shadwell, the dramatist's wife, who, because she sang in another play,[81] may have sung this song. But as is discussed more fully below, stage directions for grove scenes should not be trusted, because one of the main functions of the grove is to conceal something, not only small orchestras and choruses, but also the person who actually performs a song.

The convention of early tragedies that requires songs to be sung out of the audience's view applies to a few comedies as well, although in the earliest examples of the lighter form of drama, music sung or played onstage by main or secondary characters is common. In Durfey's *Madam Fickle: or the Witty False One* (1677), II.ii, Madam Fickle asks her attendant Silvia to "fetch thy Lute and sing." Silvia exits and while offstage, the song "Beneath a Shady Willow near" (D&M 359 *mnp*Turner) is sung. Silvia was played by Mrs. Napper [Nappier], an actress who in other plays was called upon to sing onstage;[82] her withdrawal from the stage to sing is puzzling. Other characters sing onstage in this play; for example, in V.i Jollyman (played by the comedian Cave Underhill) takes his part in the drinking song "And underneath the Greenwood Tree." Perhaps Mrs. Napper sang from behind the scenes to conceal her inability to play the lute (discussed more fully in Chapter Three). In another comedy by Durfey of the same year, *A Fond Husband: or, The Plotting Sisters* (1677), I.i opens with "A Dining-Room, a Table, Shuttle-Cock and Battle-Dor's [i.e., rackets]. Rashley and Emilla sitting. Betty [played by Mrs. Napper] sings."[83] But because Betty does not enter until later, after the song and some dialogue between Rashley and Emilla, she apparently sings from behind the scenes. The reason for this, again, is unclear. Apparently Durfey could not resist opening his play with a lyric, but the prospect of a maid standing by this adulterous couple (who perhaps have just finished a game of shuttlecock) singing an erotic little song would have stretched even the liberal musical conventions of Restoration comedy.

In later plays (both comic and tragic) songs are sung from behind the scenes, according, for example, to the convention of the atmospheric song; the performers are not usually specified. But late in the period the tendency is towards a display of music: singers and their accompanying musicians are nearly always seen onstage. Yet in a few late plays one finds an offstage performance of a song directly related to the dramatic situation. For example, in Higden's *The Wary Widdow* (1693), II.ii, Sir Noisy reads Clarinda a song he has written. The stage direction "The Musick sings the same Song" follows; but the musicians have not entered the stage. After Sir Noisy's song, Clarinda says, "Be pleased to command the Musick to sing the new Dialogue of Womens freedom thats much more agreeable to my humour." That he exits in order to speak to the musicians confirms that they are offstage. Their behind-the-scenes delivery of these two songs allows the audience to focus its full attention on Sir Noisy and Clarinda, who are probably to react with comical facial expression, similar to the scene between Millamant and Marwood in *The Way of the World* (1700), III.iii. This example is exceptional, however, as most songs in plays of the 1690s are sung onstage rather than off. Yet throughout the period the commonest location of singers and other musicians who are integral to or accommodated by the action of the play is neither on the bare forestage in clear view of the audience nor in the dark and jumbled confines of the backstage area, but rather in the pastoral world of "the musical groves and the cool, shady fountains."

Grove Scenes

There are three kinds of scenes in Restoration plays. The first is the purely functional one in which most of the business of the plot is carried on. It is not elaborate; indeed, such scenes are usually played on the forestage in front of the curtain or a painted pair of flats. The second kind has much more elaborate scenery (discovered by the ascent of the proscenium curtain or the drawing of the flats) and is specifically designed to provide either a static visual spectacle (such as the discovery of a supernatural world or a magnificent palace) or a dynamic dramatic effect involving stagecraft (such as a ship being tossed upon a stormy sea or a dragon, nostrils smoking, emerging from a magical cave). Like the first type, this also is designed principally to advance the action, but unlike the modest and often perfunctory scenes in which mere dry dialogue sets forth the argument of a plot, within the more elaborate scenes dramatic climaxes occur: armies are defeated, villains are con-sumed by hellish flames, gods and spirits descend to change a mortal's life, and martyred kings are deified. The third type of scene provides moments of dramatic repose, respites from the fustian rants of lofty characters and the frantic scurrying of dissembling lovers. In tragedies, such scenes usually include singing shepherds who, beneath the stars and laurel trees, present pastoral masques to weary kings and queens; and in the lighter dramatic forms, lovesick ladies retire to a cool arbor of weeping boughs and fragrant flowers to let a soothing song revive their spirits. During these scenes the dramatic flow of the play ceases (although a masque, for instance, might advance it allegorically), and characters reflect while music sounds. These interludes stand in marked contrast to the relentless bloody action of the tragedy and the continuous unraveling of plot and bombardment of wit in the comedy; dramatists consistently provide such scenes with a fanciful aura. The effect is not so much visual as aural. The "reality" of drawing room or dungeon gives way to the fantasy of the grove, from within whose leafy shade come the voices of singing Cupids, nymphs and shepherds, where flutes play to "the tunes of birds"; once within the almost magical confines of the musical grove, ordinary scullery maids discover that they can sing artful songs, and dull ladies of fashion are transformed into skillful lutenists.

Such scenes vary greatly in content from a single song to an extended masque. The grove itself may be as simple as a bench arched with a trellis of flowers, or as elaborate as "A Myrtle Grove in the Gardens of the Seraglio, adorn'd with Statues and Fountains."[84] Whatever form these various scenes take, music is allowed a free hand in them, unfettered by the dramatic constraints of more realistic scenes for which the dramatist must provide an elaborate rationale. For example, in comedy the serenade (often involving two groups of musicians, each consisting of several singers and instrumentalists) is the most common "realistic" vehicle for music; but how many late 17th-century London aristocrats wandered through the night with bevies of fiddlers to serenade a mistress, unless, of course, they were rakes bent upon humiliating some disreputable lady? The enchanted grove obviated the need for an improbable rationale; it was understood to be a setting where, in a lapse of reality, the subconscious thoughts of characters could be expressed in music.

Grove scenes are common in many early Restoration plays where they usually provide the background for rustic masques or some kind of pastoral entertainment; but the settings of these plays are often neither rustic nor pastoral. In Stapylton's *The Step-Mother* (1664), III[ii], the scene is "a Grove, in which is a Lawrell Tree, and three Poplar Trees"; a masque of Apollo is presented. In I[ii] of this tragi-comedy one finds another though less elaborate grove scene: "Filamor discover'd in an Arbor, with a Lute in his hand; on either side the Arbor, on two pedestals, Cupid stands. . . ." As Filamor's beloved Caesarina walks by the arbor, the Cupids come to life and sing. In this early play are evident two uses of the musical grove: a setting for an extended masque and a scene in which, via music, we are allowed to see into characters' minds. Other grove conventions combine its magical effects with more mundane matters of performance practice. In Etherege's *The Comical Revenge* (1664), II.ii, Aurelia is telling her problems to her waiting girl:

> Time to my bleeding heart brings no relief:
> Death there must heal the fatal wounds of grief:
> Leticia, come, with this shady Bower
> Wee'l joyn our mournful voices, and repeat
> The saddest Tales we ever learn'd of Love.

A stage direction confirms that they sing a duet ("Aurelia and Leticia walk into an Arbour, and sing this Song in Parts"),[85] but considering the early date of this play, the arbor probably concealed two professional singers (or at least one--to sing Aurelia's part), since main characters rarely sing in early plays. But even if these two actresses did sing the song, the arbor helped to solve another practical problem of performance: it brings singer and accompanist(s) into close proximity, for, as the following examples show, the grove (or arbor, garden, bower, and so forth) was literally alive with musicians from the first decade of the period. John Dover's tragedy *The Roman Generalls: or the Distressed Ladies* (1667) makes considerable use of such scenes; I[iv]:

> The Scene is a Grove. Enter the two former Ladies [who have been wandering in the grove]. They lye down, Flagilets play a Flourish within the Grove, to the Tune of Birds.

And in V.i, Oranges arranges a surprise for some ladies:

> [The Scene is the same Grove. Enter Oranges, Musick following of him; he having a paper in his hand, gives it to one of them.]
> *Oranges.* The Song--Goe place yourselves within the Grove . . . This is the Sign. When I do stamp begin, First play a strain or two and after sing.

But Oranges's musicians are not speaking characters in the play and were thus undoubtedly professionals; there was no need to hide their abilities, only to enhance the blurred reality of the grove.

Even when a main character's attendant appears to be her accompanist, the two often retire into seclusion for the song. For example, in Dryden's *Marriage A-la-Mode* (1673), I.i, Doralice asks her maid Beliza to "bring the lute into this Arbor, the Walks are empty: I would try the Song Princess Amalthea bad me learn." They retire from the clear view of the audience into viney shade perhaps because Doralice could not sing and Beliza was no lutenist; but the convention of the musical grove is persistent, and even late in the 17th century when many fine actor-singers were available, they too occasionally withdrew to sing. For instance, in the anonymous comedy *She Ventures and He Wins* (1696), II.ii, Juliana asks her maid Betty (played by the fine singer Mrs. Hodgson) to "sing the last new Song I gave you. . . ."[86] A stage direction states that "They go behind the Arbour."

The grove is also the setting for several atmospheric and (less frequently) organic musical effects of the kind discussed earlier in this chapter, but all of these are extensions of the general functions of the grove: to provide settings for pastoral masques; to give musical expression to a character's thoughts; to conceal the musical surrogates of speaking actors; and to provide an atmospheric and unobtrusive location for larger groups of musicians. In Gildon's tragedy *Phaeton* (1698), I.i, the protagonist and Althea sadly enter a grove so that they may "drown in Musick." Shepherds sing and dance for them. In two plays a grove is the setting for serenades: James Carlisle, in *The Fortune-Hunters: or,*

Two Fools well met (1689), III.i, and Cibber, in *The Rival Fools* [1709], III.i. Tate's *The Island-Princess* (1687), V.i, is unusual in that it is the setting for a grim affair: "A Grove . . . Solemn Musick.   Enter a Procession of Priests, as to the Sacrifice. . . ." Also uncharacteristic of the grove's usual hedonistic delights is V.i of Lee's *The Rival Queens* (1677):

> Statira is discovered sleeping in the Bower of Semiramis, The spirits of Queen Statira, her mother, and Darius appear standing on each side of her with daggers, threatening her.   They sing.

Only infrequently does a grove scene advance a plot.   In Cibber's *Comical Lovers* [1707], I.i, Palamede hears a maid singing to her lady in an arbor and mistakes her voice for that of the dishonest Doralice.   In Nicholas Brady's *The Rape: or, The Innocent Impostors* (1692), III.i, Eurione tells her attendant to "Fetch my Lute to yonder Arbor, there I'll sit awhile, and try if Musick can compose my mind." But the tranquility of the musical grove (as well as Eurione's chastity) is violated when the attendant returns to find "her Mistress gagged and bound."   And in Dryden's *The Indian Emperour* (1667), IV.iii, the musical entertainment presented to the Spaniards in a "pleasant Grotto" with "a Fountain spouting" is interrupted when "Guyman and his Indians enter, and e're the Spaniards can recover their Swords, seize them." Such disruptions of the dramatic repose of the grove are infrequent,[87] and unlike many other musical conventions which toward the end of the 17th century deteriorated into excuses for inserting para-dramatic music and dance, the grove remains throughout the period the commonest setting in which drama is intensified into music under stress of emotion. The grove was protected from excessive musical exploitation by the liberal and open-ended conventions governing its use of music. Almost any musical effect could occur within its fanciful world. The only significant change which the musical grove underwent during the entire period that could possibly be construed as a bending to current vogue is that, late in the 17th century, its shade became less dark and its floral boughs less dense, and thus the musicians within became more visible to the ogling audience. As the demand for music increased, so too did the demand for dancing, and dances, which are often inseparably joined to songs,[88] are pointless unless their executants can be seen by the paying as well as the paid audience.

Exploitation of Dramatic Music

Nearly all of the dramatic uses of music in Restoration plays discussed in this chapter were exploited as opportunities for introducing music, the main purpose of which was something other than the enhancement of a dramatic situation. One should keep in mind that a melancholy song might have been sung by a visiting Italian prima donna during a late 17th-century expeditionary London sojourn, or an unspecified piece played from within a grove may have been a movement from the latest Corelli sonata to come from Roger's Amsterdam press. In such instances music is no longer simply one of the auxiliary tools which (along with lighting, scenery, sound effects, pantomime, and so forth) a dramatist employs to enhance his principal medium of expression, spoken dialogue. To have the optimum effect, an ornament must not outshine what it is to embellish. Yet the most splendid ornament of late 17th-century English drama, music, was in such popular demand and so necessary for the success of a play that playwrights were compelled to include more of it in their works than was required for the most ambitious dramatic effects. As a result, drama often suffered and inevitably so did its attendant music. Perhaps the greatest damage to dramatic credibility resulted from the conviction held by some playwrights and theatre managers that if a previously successful play written by a great poet, acted by the best available actors and decorated by expensive scenery, is joined bodily to a musical entertainment composed by the greatest master of the age and sung and played by the finest English and foreign musicians, the resulting conglomerate will be more effective dramatically than either of its constituents would be if presented separately. The dramatic opera *King Arthur; or, The British Worthy* (1691), for example, is written by the greatest poet of the period, Dryden, and by the greatest composer, Purcell; the protagonist was originally played by the greatest actor, Betterton, and its music and dance performed by the best singers and dancers that the Theatre Royal company could muster. But whether this immense collaborative effort resulted in the best stage work of the period is doubtful. The most curious example of this practice and perhaps the one which best illustrates the ultimate frustration resulting from the imbalance of music and drama on the late Restoration stage is Gildon's *Measure for Measure, or, Beauty the Best Advocate* (1700); this is a careful reworking of Shakespeare's play which preserves much of the vigor of its model. But joined to each of the first three acts is one part of a three-part masque-like "entertainment," entitled "The Loves of Dido and Aeneas." The manager of the Lincoln's Inn Fields Theatre company (where this was first presented) and also the dean of British actors, Betterton, who had over the years watched the popularity of singers and dancers erode much of the prestige of his profession, spoke the prologue:[89]

... No more let Labour'd Scenes, with Pain, be Wrought,
What least is wanting in a Play, is Thought.
Let neither Dance, nor Musick be forgot,
Nor Scenes, no matter for the Sense, or Plot.
Such things we own in Shakespears days might do;
But then his Audience did not Judge like you. . .
[Going, Comes Back:]
Hold; I forgot the Business of the Day;
No more than this, We, for our Selves, need Say,
'Tis Purcels Musick, and 'tis Shakespears Play.

The entertainment is, of course, Purcell and Tate's *Dido and Aeneas* [1689],[90] at last wrenched from its innocent birthplace in Priest's Chelsea boarding school and placed firmly into the only possible medium for its public presentation--the playhouse, as a part of a larger work. For in the context of Restoration drama, Purcell's only opera is not an opera at all but an entertainment, a masque, a musical show to be placed awkwardly under the wing of a play. The conventions of the late 17th-century English stage allow music to enhance spoken drama to an extent unsurpassed by any other period of English dramatic literature, yet they make no provision for autonomous music drama. Regardless of the quality of the music performed in conjunction with spoken dialogue, music must always remain secondary to the play. That this, the greatest musical stage work of the era, is an anomalous foundling amongst its larger companions is strong evidence of the limitations of music in spoken drama, but the fact that its composer spent most of his creative life providing music for the best and worst of Restoration plays is equally strong evidence of the ultimate effectiveness of music to enhance spoken drama.

CHAPTER TWO

INCIDENTAL MUSIC

The play has rarely been performed without incidental music. In the modern theatre we may scarcely be aware of the *musique d'ameublement* selected by producer or director to set a mood, nor fortunate enough to have experienced Mendelssohn's enhancement of *A Midsummer Night's Dream* played by a pit orchestra rather than a phonograph. Yet during the Restoration most new plays were provided with orchestral music, often freshly composed by the greatest masters. Matthew Locke, Henry Purcell, John Eccles, and Jeremiah Clarke, as well as a train of lesser composers, wrote music for the best and worst plays of the period. Whereas not a single piece of instrumental music known to have been used in a play by Shakespeare or one of his contemporaries survives (although such music proliferated in Elizabethan drama), Restoration composers, beginning less than 50 years after the First Folio, have left a huge repertoire: music originally associated with more than 160 plays produced between 1663 and 1713 survives, incidental music for less than a third of the plays mounted during the period, yet a significant amount considering its ephemeral nature.[1]

Whether a dramatic opera, whose acts consisted almost entirely of music, or the rare tragedy shorn of internal musical entertainments by reform or (more likely) financial exigencies, the play was invariably preceded and relieved by music, almost always short instrumental pieces, known in the Restoration as "act music" and here given the not altogether satisfactory designation, "incidental music": at one extreme this music is perfectly incidental in that it often bears no relation to the drama and was performed to ease the genteel tedium of waiting in a good seat while the less desirable places (necessary imperfections of any proscenium-equipped theatre) were gradually occupied by latecomers. At the other extreme, the act music is integral to the play; an overture may prepare the mood of the opening scene, or the pieces between the acts may represent the action supposedly occurring during the intervals.

Despite a few playwrights' and composers' attempts to make act music organic to their plays, its commonest function was to provide contrast with and relief from spoken dialogue. Dryden, in his famous essay *Of Dramatick Poesie* (1668), speaks of act music as if it were a permanent fixture of the still young Restoration theatre and compares its function with comic interludes in heroic tragedy (p. 39):

> A Scene of mirth mix'd with Tragedy has the same effect upon us which our musick has betwixt the Acts, and that we find a relief to us from the best Plots and language of the Stage, if the discourses have been long.

During the second decade of the Restoration, however, music began to be inserted more frequently into the acts themselves--the songs, dances, instrumental music, and entertainments discussed in Chapter One above. That incidental music should relieve music-laden dialogue might seem paradoxical; the anonymous author of the prologue to a 1676 revival of Ben Jonson's *Volpone*,[2] writing shortly after the spate of "musical plays" in 1673-1675,[3] notices this anomaly:

> Musick, which was by Intervals design'd
> To ease the weary'd Actors voice and mind,
> You to the Play judiciously prefer,
> 'Tis now the bus'ness of the Theatre.

Act music continued to be used throughout the period in all kinds of plays, but because it usually lies outside the drama, and is therefore rarely mentioned in stage directions, drama historians have mostly overlooked this important accoutrement to the late 17th-century London playhouse.

The only detailed account by a contemporary dramatist of incidental pieces is the dedication to actor-playwright Richard Estcourt's comedy *The Fair Example: or The Modish Citizens* (1706). Estcourt addresses his dedication "To the Serene Christopher Rich, Esq; Chief Patentee, Governour and Manager of Her Majesty's Theatre Royal." Estcourt, one of Rich's principal actors at the time, turns praise to sarcasm as he pokes fun at Rich's supposed ignorance of dramaturgical matters:

> Dreadless Sir:
>
> . . . We will not trouble you, Sir, with Fable Manners, Fivyion, Sentiment, Subjects, Peripatic, Passion, Episode, Exode, Epopeeia, Character, Incidents, Surprises, Intrigues, Delicacy, and the Devil and all, which they tell us shou'd or shou'd not be in a Play, nor in their Poems of their Iambicks, Dithirambicks, Anapaesticks, and Trochee's, which last are one Foot long, and t'other short like the lame Miller in Oedipus. These have been all practised under your Patent, with the Great Seal of England undisturb'd these forty Years, and as familiar to you as the Play-House Tunes. The first is an Air, the second a Chacone, and the third an Overture, commonly called the Courtain Tune, the rest Act-Tunes.

While Estcourt's rudiments of drama and poetry border on the ridiculous,[4] the description of the "Play-House Tunes" is essentially correct, the humor arising from the necessity of describing them at all to a theatre manager.

Before the play began, two pairs of two pieces each were played, these pairs being called the "first music" and "second music," respectively. Estcourt implies that the "first" and "second" each consisted of a single piece, but the usual practice was to combine two contrasting instrumental types for each of the pairs: a slow piece followed by a fast one; a short piece (an air, for example) followed by a long one (a chaconne perhaps); or one in duple meter followed by one in triple meter. As Estcourt states the next music is the overture or curtain tune, usually played after the spoken prologue. The rest of the incidental pieces are the four act tunes, played immediately at the conclusion of each of the acts, except Act V, which was not usually followed by music. Therefore, most sets of act music for Restoration plays (including dramatic operas) consist of nine pieces: five preliminary pieces and four act tunes.

Each new play and revival given within a decade or so of a previous production was provided with new act music specifically written for it. Seldom are these short instrumental pieces used for more than one play. A brief instrumental piece, no matter how indistinguishable from any one of hundreds of other similar compositions, was considered to belong to a particular interval of a particular play. The practice of providing each play with its own incidental music was probably encouraged by the amalgamation of the two principal theatre companies, the King's Men at the Theatre Royal in Drury Lane and the Duke's Men at the theatre in Dorset Garden, in 1682, both of which were in financial trouble owing to poor attendance. With the surplus of theatre composers, managers probably commissioned new incidental music for each new production. Certainly extant act music ascribed to specific plays becomes more abundant at about this time. As likely an explanation, however, is that as part concert hall, the playhouse was required to provide the audience not only with a constant supply of new plays but also the latest instrumental music. Despite the unconcert-like behavior of some of the audience during the intervals and before the play began, the more musically sophisticated members awaited each new play both for its "humours" and its music. Many devotées came early especially to hear the orchestra play the latest airs, and late in the century when the scent of the new Italian music and Purcell's genius became strong in the music room, publishers issued sets of act music for the delectation of the dilettantes. Perhaps because incidental music was either ignored by those anxious to see the more spectacular musical offerings within the play or appreciated only by a sophisticated minority, act music rarely encroaches upon the drama. Even late in the century when para-dramatic music and dance grotesquely distend the acts of many plays, the act music for these works still consists of nine modest pieces. The limits that Dryden sets for incidental music in *Of Dramatick Poesie* were never exceeded, for act music is not only a "relief to us from the best Plots and language" of the heroic tragedy, but it also provides brief respites from the entertainments of music and dancing that proliferate in late plays.

I. PRELIMINARY MUSIC

Although the stage directions for the early and even pre-Restoration dramatic offerings of Sir William Davenant require that music be played immediately before the ascent of the curtain in the manner of an overture, the first indication that music was played in the London theatres before the play began (that is, the first and second music) is an account by a French visitor, Samuel de Sorbière, in his *Relation d'vn voyage en Angleterre* (Paris, 1664), p. 167: "La symphonie y fait atendre agreablement l'ouverture du theatre, & y va voluntiers de bonne heure pour l'escouter."[5] Except for the royal boxes, there were no reserved seats in the Restoration playhouse, and to obtain a good seat, one had to arrive at the theatre early, especially if a popular play were being offered. But if one left the theatre before the curtain went up, one's money would be refunded, for many courtiers attended the theatre not to see a play but to make their court, and often the latter could be accomplished before the play began.[6] In John Corey's *A Cure for Jealousie* (1701), I.i, Wildish and Loveday discuss this custom.

> *Wildish.* If I chanc'd to wander towards the Play-house, I was forc'd to watch the Musique and when the Curtain ascended I vanish'd.
> *Loveday.* Oh that's as Fashionable now, as sharping an act in the side Box.
> *Wildish.* It was not so much design as pure necessity-- I considered (I am a considering person) if I spent my half Crown at the Play, I might want it at the Tavern, and I always preferred Claret to Poetry.

Also taking advantage of the pay-if-you-stay procedure were the courtesans who flocked to the playhouses to risk half a crown and the boredom of a long play for the richer gains of their profession; as the second piece of the second music was played, there was often a frantic rush between gentlemen and prostitutes to complete the bargaining before the play began. The conversation between two rakes in the first scene of Settle's dramatic opera *The World in the Moon* (1697) is typical of many allusions to this practice found in the comedies of the period:

> *Frank Wildblood.* . . . Thou know'st I never take a turn to a Play, but either just pop in my Head before the Curtain rises, or before it drops again. . . .
>
> *Ned Stanmore.* But why are you so unkind to the Playhouses, especially at this Low-water time with them, to take a turn (as you call it) before the Curtain rises?
>
> *Frank.* Out of pure Charity, Ned. I gallop round the Pit, hear the last Musick, pick up a Mask, and carry her off before the Play; and so save the poor Whore her Half Crown. . . .

Frank's remarks also reveal a more practical use of the preliminary music: to let the audience know when the play was to begin. The "last Musick" (the second tune of the second music) is the forerunner of the final bell of our modern theatres.

The function of the first and second music differs from that of the remaining five compositions, even though in most cases a piece of preliminary music is stylistically indistinguishable from an act tune. Overtures and act tunes, because of their proximity to the drama, are capable of reinforcing or reflecting the mood and even the action of the scenes themselves.

When the second air of the second music was finished, the "prologue" walked onto the apron of the stage from one of the proscenium doors in front of the curtain to deliver his topical address to the audience. After the usual plea to the town not to be too hard on the play, the actor left the stage and the overture was played. So in addition to whatever dramatic function it may have had in preparing the opening scene, the overture served to set off the prologue from the drama to follow. The unusual prologue to Dryden's early tragi-comedy *Secret-Love, or the Maiden Queen* (1668) gives us a hint of this order of events. After what would appear to be the end of the preliminary address, a stage direction states that "The Prologue goes out, and stayes while a Tune is Play'd, after which he returnes again." He apologizes (in rhymed couplets, of course) that he has forgotten to speak the rest of his address. Later in the period the overture, let alone the first and second music, are almost never mentioned in stage directions. But the prologue to Farquhar's *The Inconstant* (1702) suggests that even in late Restoration plays the overture usually followed the prologue; the address ends with the lines ". . . up let the Musick strike: You're welcome all--Now fall to where you like."

Since the overture was often played before or during the ascent of the curtain, it is also called the "curtain tune." The two terms are used interchangeably in both musical sources and play-books.[7] But they are not necessarily synonymous. "Overture" usually refers to the musical type: the so-called Lullian overture, which begins with a slow section characterized by dotted rhythms, is followed by a fast section beginning fugally, and sometimes ends with a section similar in style to the first. "Curtain tune," on the other hand, usual¹y refers to a piece serving a definite function: music played at the drawing up of the curtain.[8] This may be almost any musical type, including a French overture.

Many Restoration plays probably had both an overture (played after the prologue) and a separate tune to ring up the curtain.[9] Evidence for this is provided by a manuscript note in the Royal College of Music copy of Purcell's *A Collection of Ayres for the Theatre* (1697). The act music for Dryden's comedy *Amphitryon* (1690) consists of eight pieces: a long overture and seven binary-form dances.[10] After the minuet on p. 30 (the second tune of the second music),[11] the following note is written in a contemporary hand: "this tune is also played after the Prologue."[12] If the minuet was played in the usual position of the overture, where was the overture played? Perhaps it too was heard after the prologue, but the longer composition probably did not accompany the ascent of the curtain. The stage directions for the first scene of Dryden's play indicate neither the ringing up of the curtain nor the playing of any music to accompany its ascent, but both events certainly occurred: "The Scene THEBES. Mercury and Phoebus descend in several [i.e., separate] Machines." In the production seen by the anonymous note-maker, the minuet likely served as the curtain tune, replacing the overture. This binary dance would be far more appropriate to accompany the *dei ex machinis* than Purcell's powerful overture, which abruptly changes tempo and meter near the end; and just as important, the less agitated minuet would provide an unobtrusive accompaniment to the witty dialogue between Mercury and Phoebus. Furthermore, this piece would be more easily expanded or truncated (by taking or omitting repeats) than the overture, if the machine effects needed more or less time to be accomplished.

Clearly the function of Purcell's minuet, like so much Restoration act music, depends upon its location, for nothing about the music itself indicates its role as curtain tune. With such preliminary music, the distinction between incidental and dramatic becomes most unclear. If the overture to *Amphitryon* immediately precedes the opening of the first scene, then it is (however inappropriately) the curtain tune and thus assumes a dramatic function. If, on the other hand, the overture is displaced by Purcell's minuet, it is incidental to the drama.

The overture to Motteux's dramatic opera *The Island Princess* (1699) appears to have been displaced in a similar manner. The reworking of Tate's 1687 alteration of Fletcher's play is unique in that it exists in a nearly complete form in Lbm Add. Ms. 15318, a manuscript that preserves almost all the dialogue, act music, songs, choruses, masques, and so forth, required for a production of this work.[13] Complete scores of late Restoration dramatic operas are by no means unknown (see, for example, Purcell's *Dioclesian*), but, extraordinarily, the *Island Princess* manuscript includes not only all of the incidental music for the work but the music for the dances as well, the latter among the most ephemeral of music in late 17th-century English plays.   If the various musical and spoken constituents of this work are recorded in order of performance, then Add. Ms. 15318 is an ideal source for testing the speculations regarding incidental music presented above. Beginning on fol. 1 (after the "title page") are the two pieces of the "1st Musick" followed by those of the "2^{d} Musicke" (all in four-part score). Next is the overture (fol. 2) followed (on fol. 3) by the *dramatis personae* and (on fol. 3') the "Prologue Spoken by Mr Powell," beginning, "Prologues some say, are useless, grave or Gay; / The first but Clog, the last ne're save a Play." Then the first scene begins (on fol. 4). Thus, the overture was apparently played before the prologue and no music intervened between Powell's address and the beginning of the play proper. However, the 1699 quarto, *The Island Princess, or The Generous Portuguese*, has the following stage direction immediately after the prologue, before I.i begins:

> Enter Mr. Leveridge, who Sings the following Words. "You've been with dull Prologues here banter'd so long, They signifie nothing, or less than a Song [etc.]."[14]

To call Leveridge's song the curtain tune would be to magnify its significance, but the sung prologue probably displaced the overture from its usual position. Separated from the play by a spoken as well as a sung prologue, it is, therefore, completely incidental and does not prepare the first scene. *The Island Princess* provides perhaps the best illustration of the danger of accepting too readily the interchangeability of the terms "overture" and "curtain tune."

This is not to say that some Restoration playwrights did not recognize the potential of specific pieces to enhance their dramas. One such poet, the dour critic and moral reformer John Dennis, intended the overture to his tragedy *Rinaldo and Armida* (1699) to be far from incidental:

> The Action of the Play begins with the Beginning of the Overture, which is a Trumpet-tune, supposed to be Play'd by the Good Spirits who have the Conduct and Care of Action, and the Guardianship of the Persons concern'd in it.[15]

Although the overture does not survive and Dennis's stage direction hardly reflects his dramaturgical ideals ("SCENE, A Delightful Wilderness on the top of a Mountain in the Canaries. Overture with Trumpets. . . ."),[16] the playwright apparently relied heavily on music to prepare the action of the opening scene of his tragedy.

II. ACT TUNES

In late 17th-century English play-books the beginnings and ends of acts are clearly marked; in performance, the division between acts was indicated by two conventions: the absence of all characters from the stage (often preceded by a final rhymed couplet delivered by the last actor to exit) and the playing of an instrumental piece (or other entertainment, usually unrelated to the action of the adjacent scenes). In the Restoration playhouse the curtain was only rarely lowered at the end of an act.[17] The number of intervals corresponded with the number of acts: four intermissions in an entertainment that seldom lasted over three and a half hours might seem excessive, but as the playhouse was partly a court theatre (especially before 1700), the audience considered itself as much a part of the show as the actors, and the courtiers took the opportunity between acts to display themselves.

A few surviving prompters' notes indicate that act tunes were played without pause at the end of each of the acts, but not usually the last.[18] Prompt notes are rare in printed versions of the plays, but a few missed editorial excision by 17th-century printers. From these it may be determined that one of the prompter's duties was to signal the theatre orchestra (a few lines before the end of an act) to prepare to play the act tune.[19] The musicians also listened for the customary terminal rhymed couplet for their cue. This signalling process is in fact the subject of the didactic introduction acted out before Sir Thomas St. Serfe's comedy *Tarugo's Wiles, or, The Coffee-House* (1668). After it has been explained that the author has not written his play in verse, a gentleman asks, "But how shall the Expectations of the Audience and the Musick be prepar'd at the ending of Acts"[?], to which a wag replies that a rattle will be used to "alarum the Minstrills to tune their Fiddles," as this noise-maker "will be better understood by a great many here then the best of Rhyme." Undoubtedly the final couplet of an act often caught the musicians unprepared to render the act tune.

Another allusion to the position of the act tune is in Cibber's *The Comical Lovers* [1707], III.i; Florimel is describing how some players portraying lovers ham up their exits at the end of an act. In the midst of her explanation, which includes a demonstration, she rather suspiciously breaks into rhymed couplets:

. . . So have I seen, in Tragick Scenes, a Lover,
With dying Eyes his panting Pains discover,
While the soft Nymph looks back to view him far,
And speaks her Anguish with her Handkercher:
Agen they turn still ogling as before,
Till each gets backward to the distant Door;
Then, when the last, last Look their Grief betrays,
The act is ended, and the Musick plays.
[Exeunt, mimicking this. The End of the Third Act.]

Florimel's parody is helped by the fact that after her last line, the third act tune began.

The unusually complete manuscript copy of *The Island Princess* provides further evidence that the act tune was played immediately after an act and as a conclusion rather than as an introduction to the next. The "1st Act Tune" (fol. 6') is written on staves added by hand to this page just below the closing couplet of the first act. Act II begins on the recto of the next folio (fol. 7), and this act ends with a dance (fol. 20', at the end of a long musical entertainment), which precedes the second act tune (fol. 21). A blank page (fol. 21') separates the dance and the act tune from the beginning of the third act. The happy dramatic circumstances at the end of the fourth act are reflected by the "4th act tune," a lively "Round[o]" (fol. 45). That this tune (like most act tunes) is dramatically sympathetic to the scene it follows rather than to that it precedes is confirmed by the beginning of the fifth act: "The Curtain rises to mournful Musick, And Discovers a Prison, Quisara Lying on ye Floor, all in white. . . ."

The *Island Princess* score includes no fifth-act tune, but many of the extant sets of act music for Restoration plays contain ten rather than the more usual nine incidental pieces; Locke's instrumental music for *The Tempest* (1675), for example, is comprised of 11 pieces: the first music has three tunes, beginning with an "Introduction," and the set ends with "The Conclusion, A Canon 4 in 2," that is, a double canon, which is apparently the fifth act tune.[20] Also, the prompt notes for *The Change of Crownes* and *The Sisters* (see n. 19 above) both have the direction "Act Ready" a few dozen lines before the end of the fifth act, thus indicating that these plays employed a fifth act tune. There is no correlation between plays (such as *The Island Princess*) that contain considerable music in their final acts and the absence of a fifth-act tune, nor does the presence of a final act tune depend on whether or not a play was followed by an afterpiece, as little is recorded about post-dramatic entertainments of the Restoration period.

Although much of the audience was apparently inattentive during the efforts of the orchestra between the acts,[21] playwrights often require act tunes to serve a dramatic or at least a quasi-dramatic function between scenes. Farquhar, in "A Discourse upon Comedy, In Reference to the English Stage,"[22] recognizes their value in filling a breach in the unities, as he suggests act music be used to connect the scenes of a hypothetical comedy which are separated by time and place: "Then in the second Act, with a Flourish of Fiddles, I change the Scene to Astrachan." And in his tragedy *Aureng-Zebe* (1676), Dryden joins the action of Acts II and III with the stage direction, "Betwix the Acts, a Warlike Tune is plaid, shooting off Guns, and shouts of Souldiers are heard as in an assault." Occasionally, a subtler dramatic role is required of an act tune. Godfrey Finger's for the fourth act of *The Husband His own Cuckold* (1696), by John Dryden, Jr., is apparently related to the play by a centuries-old musical pun: entitled "Cuckoe," the composition is built on the motive of a falling minor third.

Playwrights frequently construct the ends of acts so that the act tune appears to be an outgrowth of the dramatic action. For example, in Thomas Porter's *The Villain* (1663), at the end of Act III, Francibell and La'march are in search of a particular house. They finally locate it by the sounds of merriment within, and as the act ends Francibell says, "we might hear this House by the Musick," thus making a smooth connection between the action of the scene and the act tune. In III.i of Dennis's *Rinaldo and Armida* music played within the act is repeated as the act tune,[23] a rare occurrence in plays of the period. Urania is warned of Rinaldo's departure as "Here the Musick plays out. . . . Here the Alarm plays out again." At the end of this act is one of the few stage directions for act music in Restoration plays: "The foresaid Alarm is repeated for the Act Tune." As the poet explains, the music is repeated for dramatic reasons, not for the sake of economy: "In the Musick between this and the Fourth Act, the Instruments express the Alarm that the Infernal Regions take at Rinaldo's Departure." Dennis also imparts dramatic roles to the other act tunes in his tragedy, warning his audience that this is a departure from the normal practice: "The Musick between the Acts of this Play is part of the Action of the Play, and therefore for the better distinguishing the acts, the Reader [sic] is desir'd to take Notice, that when at any time the stage is quite Empty, then is the End of an Act."[24] But such organic uses of "incidental" music are not common in Restoration plays, and toward the end of the period little care was taken to make the music between the acts dramatically conducive to the action within.

The pieces published in John Walsh's *Harmonia Anglicana* (1701-c. 1706), by far the largest series devoted to early 18th-century incidental music (see Appendix II), are not given in their original act-music sequence. Each set is an orchestral suite, beginning with a French overture followed by various dances arranged roughly according to later continental practice: for example, courantes usually follow allemandes;

and sarabandes appear before gigues and hornpipes at the end of the suites. Except for the general correlations between pieces in minor and tragedies and ones in major and comedies, these suites do not often reflect their dramatic origins. Interestingly, slow pieces in the minor mode are found only in sets of act music for tragedies,[25] although such pieces, some of which were perhaps fourth-act tunes played in the midst of murder and grief and thus the final music heard in the play, never conclude a set. *Harmonia Anglicana* has apparently been purged of all programmatic curtain tunes or music for special dramatic effects, such as ghosts' risings and gods' descents. This reflects an attempt by Walsh or his contributors to present a "satisfying" concert suite, rather than the sequence demanded by the playhouse.[26]

III. ACT SONGS

As noted earlier, sets of act music usually consist of eight short pieces and a longer overture (or curtain tune). However, over 20 sets of act music ascribed to specific plays have fewer than the standard nine pieces, in most cases lacking only one or two tunes. In a few instances the preliminary music is missing a piece; that is, either the first or second music is comprised of one long piece rather than the more usual two short pieces. For example, the act music for John Lacy's comedy *The Old Troop: or, Monsieur Raggou* (1672) consists of eight tunes. The first music is a ground (or chaconne), the second music being two shorter pieces.[27] But for many of the other sets of act music with fewer than nine compositions, the missing piece appears to be an act tune: in many of these cases a song or an inter-act entertainment likely replaced the instrumental tune.

Before 1700 songs rarely replaced act tunes. In Lee's tragedy *Theodosius* (1680), for instance, the inter-act songs were considered remarkable enough to be printed with the play-book.[28] Among them is Henry Purcell's first offering for the London stage, "Ah Cruel bloody fate." None of these songs (except for Purcell's) is more than vaguely related to the scenes they follow; at most they provide atmospheric punctuation of the dramatic action immediately preceding them, as do most act tunes.[29] One may add to Lee's tragedy only a handful of other plays in which lyrics printed in the play-books were sung between acts.[30] But the practice of replacing act tunes with songs may have been more widespread than these few examples suggest. Several late 17th-century plays have songs not printed in their quartos (but ascribed to them in other sources) that appear to replace incidental tunes. For instance, the act music to Cibber's *Love's Last Shift* (1696)[31] is lacking those for the third and fourth acts. Two songs, not printed in the play-book, are ascribed to this play in their musical source, *Thesaurus Musicus* (1696).[32]

Cibber's *She wou'd and She wou'd not* (1703) and Thomas Baker's *The Humour of the Age* (1701) also fall into this category.[33] The exact position between the acts of the songs ascribed to these plays must be conjectured, for none of their lyrics bears more than tangentially on the dramatic action. Like most act tunes, they are simply atmospheric.

The act songs for Katherine Philips's *Pompey* (1663) are remarkable in several respects. Not only are they the earliest extant pieces for a Restoration play, but they effectively link the acts of this tragedy in a way unique to the drama of the period. More is known about the preparation of the music for this translation of Corneille's tragedy than for any other 17th-century play. Not only does the authoress's account survive, but a rude printer has written a preface to the 1663 play-book which is stripped of all panegyric. He apologizes for his lack of eloquence, stating bluntly that Mrs. Philips did nothing but translate Corneille's play and pen the songs between the acts, "which were added only to lengthen the Play, and make it fitter for the Stage." Mrs. Philips's own falsely modest account is recorded in a series of letters to her friend and mentor Sir Charles Cotterell.[34] She was so encouraged by his approval of the translation itself, that she decided "to lengthen the Play by adding Songs in the Intervals of each Act, which they flatter me here [in Ireland] are not amiss. . . ."[35] But in her next letter (14 January 1663), written after the first song had been set to music by one "Philaster," she hints that the music should do more than simply fill the intervals between acts; and her stage directions at the end of the first act state that Ptolomy and Photin "should be discovered, sitting and hearkning to the Song" ("Since Affairs of the State are already decreed").[36] The lyric, which Mrs. Philips remarks is set to "brisk" music, speaks of the difficult affairs of kings, who must balance lofty decisions of state with soft diversions. Considering that Ptolomy has just ordered Pompey's murder and has ascended a tower to watch the vile deed performed below him, Mrs. Philips's song is somewhat inappropriate. It was followed by "an Antick dance of Gypsies" (that is, Egyptians), which was perhaps meant to depict Pompey's death.

The song at the end of Act II, "See how Victorious Caesar's Pride Does Neptune's Bosom sweep,"[37] serves a similarly reflective function. In the second act the plot has thickened considerably with the emergence of Cleopatra's ambition and Caesar's arrival in Egypt and subsequent consternation upon learning of Pompey's death. The song extols Caesar's greatness and comments on the intricacies of the political situation.

The song between Acts III and IV is Mrs. Philips's most ambitious, being integral to the plot. In the last scene of the third act, Caesar has made conciliatory gestures to Cornelia, Pompey's distraught widow. At the end of the scene she falls asleep on a couch; then

Pompey's ghost appears and sings "From lasting and unclouded Day," a long lyric designed to comfort Cornelia. The stage direction requires a "Recitative Air," but Mrs. Philips was not happy with this term, and before the play was published in London she asked Cotterell to change it (this was not done): "After the third Act I have us'd an Expression which I take to be improper: *Recitative Air.* I desire it may be made *Recitative Musick.*"[38]

She had perhaps learned from the composer of the song, John Banister,[39] that to use "recitative" to qualify "air" is contradictory: in the 17th century "air" usually referred to a short instrumental piece or song in a definite meter, while "recitative" generally meant what it does now-- vocal music, often unmetered, in which the rhythm is closely tied to speech declamation. In a later letter Mrs. Philips is able to remark confidently that the fifth song (by Philaster) is "between Recitative and Air."[40] By this informed observation we see that she was not ignorant of musical matters.

"From lasting and unclouded Day" is in three discrete sections. The first, which was probably the cause of Mrs. Philips's terminological indecision, is an arioso (that is, "between Recitative and Air"), being the formal enunciation of Pompey's ghost to Cornelia. He sings that he has shed pure blood while falling a martyr to Rome. The words are vividly set to music. Beginning in G minor, the key most favored by 17th-century English composers to symbolize death, the music rises a full octave at the phrase "from a Spring without decay." Then a deceptive cadence in Bb major on the word "beams" sends a shaft of light into Cornelia's gloom. The second part of the song is more akin to Italian recitative, being rhythmically freer and more dramatic than the first part. Here Pompey vows revenge on Caesar and Egypt, as the music returns to G minor at the words "Roman & Egyptian blood." Both voice and bass parts descend graphically at the line "he [Caesar] shall fall by treason too." The third section is a gentle, triple-meter aria of comfort addressed to Cornelia, a welcome lyrical interlude. The song is followed by "a Military Dance, as the Continuance of her Dream," after which Cornelia awakens and speaks a line that Mrs. Philips added to her translation: "What have I seen? and whether [sic] is it gone!" Far from simply "lengthening the play," this interpolated musical scene carries the action forward by welding Acts III and IV together. And, frankly, this dream sequence is the only moment in the first three acts of this stilted tragedy that could be safely called dramatic.

Act IV rushes past in a series of plots and counterplots that pave the way for Cleopatra to ascend the throne. At this turning point, she "sits hearkening to" "Proud Monuments of Royal Dust!"[41] The act song asks if Egypt will be a province of Rome or a kingdom and muses on the transience of political power.

After the final act, Mrs. Philips's song "Ascend a Throne Great Queen" (a coronation anthem that also laments the death of Pompey) is expanded into a grand masque presented to Caesar and Cleopatra.[42] Since she makes no mention of the masque in her letters, Mrs. Philips likely had no hand in creating it or the dramatic trappings to accompany her act songs. Restoration playwrights generally had little control over what form their works would ultimately take on the stage, and doubtless Lord Orrery's hundred pounds advance "towards the Expence of buying Roman and Egyptian Habits"[43] helped the theatre decide to transform her incidental songs into sumptuous dramatic transitions between the acts of *Pompey*.

No other Restoration play uses songs to link its acts to this extent, and only Dennis's *Rinaldo and Armida* attempts the continuous drama of *Pompey*, but with instrumental music. Perhaps because the words of any song, however foolish or trifling, carry some dramatic connotation, act tunes were preferred for the intervals until about 1700 when foreign singers made ever more frequent entr'acte appearances. Mrs. Philips's imaginative songs showed the newly restored theatre one of the ways that music, which was to assume an increasingly important role in the plays of the next 40 years, could be incorporated into spoken drama in an integral way. That this direction was not followed by other playwrights well illustrates what Dryden meant when he wrote that the music between the acts should give relief "from the best Plots and language of the Stage."

To distinguish what is dramatic, para-dramatic, or even adramatic on the Restoration stage is difficult. The physical nature of the playhouse itself produced an intimate and informal atmosphere rarely encountered in the modern theatre. The audience often conversed with the prologues, and wits bent on bringing down a play interjected remarks during the play itself, often eliciting improvised replies from the actors. Plays of the 1690s in particular must have presented a motley assortment of music and spoken dialogue. Entertainments within the acts, during which the speaking characters sat back and observed as did the audience, were barely distinguishable from the shows performed between the acts.[44] Similarly, there must have been little difference between a song or instrumental piece played to a tired king to soothe his play-bound weariness and the so-called incidental music which allowed the audience to relieve their tired backs and cramped legs. The function of any music in these late plays depends upon its position in the whole of the afternoon's entertainment at the playhouse: a tune played to a character might serve equally well as an act tune played to fill the silences in courtly chatter. Therefore, any music, within or between the acts, became in a sense incidental to the drama when its auditors singly or collectively chose to shift their attention from what was occurring on the stage in order to converse with those sitting nearby or to peel an orange. One finds as many opportunities within the plays themselves as during the intervals for music to give relief "from the best Plots and language" and "To ease the weary'd Actors voice and mind." Perhaps for this reason Restoration writers do not use the word "incidental" to describe the music played between the acts of plays.

CHAPTER THREE

THE MUSICIANS

The position of the musician in the Restoration theatre is curious. Throughout most of the period the dramatist and actor were the masters of the playhouse, the most outstanding being Vanbrugh and Betterton. As patentees, they determined which plays would be mounted, which would be favored with scenic and musical enhancement, which would fall victims of a diminished treasury, which would be strengthened by their Thespian superiority, and which would be condemned to play to an empty house because of a late spring or an early summer mounting. Since the main staple of the late 17th-century English stage was the play, spoken dialogue--either wit expressed in the sophisticated vernacular or passions in often stilted poetry--was cultivated by playwrights and encouraged by actors and theatre managers. Yet from the first years after the Restoration, dramatists realized that even the best plays required music, both because the audience expected it and because playwrights and managers considered music capable of reinforcing dramatic illusion. The musician, like the painter and architect, was the ally of the actor.

For the first 20 years of the period this was a comfortable alliance, largely because the musician never threatened the actor's position of eminence. The Thespian could draw at will on music to save a limping play from failure but rarely credited music financially or artistically in amount commensurate with its role in the success of a play. The audience's "concupiscence of jig and song," the dramatists thought, was a function of current vogue, something that could be easily satisfied by lowly, anonymous musicians. Spoken drama was a British tradition, an art form that required a great actor as its almost heroic advocate. But the importance of music on the London stage began to grow rapidly from about 1680. Henry Purcell applied his dramatic skills to the existing theatrical establishment to help create stage works in which music was a vital ingredient rather than a mere ornament. Theatre musicians accordingly gained considerable stature. But this era also saw the gradual drifting apart of the musical and spoken parts of stage works. Main characters were less often required (or able) to sing art songs, and the best music was reserved for the masque or formal entertainment in which nonspeaking, professional singers dominated. No longer could the modest musical abilities of the actor-singer meet the demands of the composer, and more important, the spoken play could not accommodate the professional musician dramatically. The theatre companies were still managed mostly by actors, and plays--no matter how heavily laden with music--were the main form of entertainment. Even Betterton and Mrs. Barry were often required to act in shabby scenes--the mere interstices of musical shows. Paradoxically, the actor, now under-paid and rebellious, was still the most venerated, if no longer the most popular, personality of the stage. The musician commanded applause, the actor respect.

I. THE ACTOR AS MUSICIAN

Actor-Singers

A Restoration actor who lacked all musical ability was a rarity. Most of them were at some time called upon to sing and dance; though seldom was a player as acclaimed for his musical accomplishments as was a professional singer, some practical musical experience was a prerequisite for all but a few actors. On the other hand, theatre musicians were expected to be able to bear what are often important though minor speaking parts, acting a small role in one play and dancing or playing the fiddle in the next. The staged introduction to Part II of Vanbrugh's *Aesop* (1697) illustrates this point. The protagonist meets a group of actors:

> *Aesop.* Well, good People, who are all you?
> *Omnes.* Sir, we are Players--
> *Aesop.* Players? What Players?
> *Player.* Why, Sir, we are Stage-Players;
> That's our Calling:
> Tho' we play upon other things too; some of us play Upon the Fiddle; some play upon the Flute; We play upon one another, we play upon the Town, And we play upon the Patentees.

Perhaps Vanbrugh's puns are a little strained, but the fact that theatre musicians were also considered members of the acting troupe is similarly suggested by William Cavendish's *The Humorous Lovers* (1677), III[ii]. Sir Anthony is at the theatre to see a rehearsal of a musical entertainment; he converses with "Two Women Players":

> *Sir Anthony.* You are perfect in your parts[?]
> *1. Player.* Yes.
> *Sir Anth.* You sing the Songs[?]
> *2. Player.* Yes, Sir.
> *Sir Anth.* You have an Angelical Voice, and deserve good ones.

These players, like those in *Aesop*, have only minor speaking parts, and their musical skills were probably more highly developed than their acting abilities. Throughout the period, however, a few actors specialized in roles requiring them to sing art songs as well as to portray important speaking characters. The most famous of these was Anne Bracegirdle, whose career (like those of many of her singing colleagues) was surprisingly short-lived (she first sang in a play in the early 1690s and retired from the stage in 1707). Yet she was hardly the first major actress to be entrusted to sing her own songs.[1]

By 1690 *dramatis personae* usually include the names of all but very minor characters, and stage directions often state explicitly who is to sing a song. Also the song-books and songs printed on separate sheets which began to be issued at about this time frequently mention the name of the player who sang it. For example, the stage direction in V.ii of Durfey's *Don Quixote*, Part II (1694), which states that Marcella (played by Mrs. Bracegirdle) sings "I burn, my Brain Consumes" is corroborated by its musical source, *The Songs to the New Play of Don Quixote* (1694) (see D&M 1497 *m*J. Eccles *s*Bracegirdle).[2]

The plays published before the last decade of the 17th century, however, do not always give complete cast lists, and the stage directions are often ambiguous as to who is to sing a song. The earlier musical sources, too, only infrequently provide the names of singers. This is not to say that musical practices in plays produced in the first 20 years of the period differed drastically from those of the plays of the musically rich final years of the century. That a few players were also required to sing their own songs in early plays is indicated by the frequency with which certain actors are mentioned as singers. Elizabeth Knepp, for instance, appears to have been called upon often to sing in plays produced between 1668 and 1675.[3] Mr. Harris[4] also seems to have sung in early Restoration plays; he is probably the same actor that Pepys mentions as having danced in Shadwell's tragi-comedy *The Royal Shepherdess* (1669).[5] Moll Davies, celebrated for her dancing in plays of the first decade of the period,[6] may have also acted the small role of Gatty in Etherege's *She wou'd if she cou'd* (1668), which required her to sing two songs.[7] Most of the songs performed by these early actor-singers are not musically sophisticated, and those sung by Mrs. Knepp, in particular, are generally humorous in nature.

The more demanding art songs of the early Restoration were usually sung by professional singers (that is, minor characters such as maids and waiting ladies, who, since they do little else in a play, presumably specialized in singing). Many actor-singers of the last decade of the century, however, seem to have been capable of high levels of performance. John Boman, Thomas Dogget, and Letitia Cross sang "in character" in the plays proper and performed singing parts in masques and dramatic operas as well.[8] These players, however, are exceptional, as the actor-singers did not usually encroach upon the domain of the professional singers--the masque. Musical competence rather than virtuosity was required. Boman and Cross were not celebrated actors,

but, surprisingly, many important actors did sing in plays.   Mrs.
Bracegirdle, Elizabeth Barry, Estcourt, Mrs. Verbruggen, Mountfort, and
Wilks--all important players--also performed songs on the late 17th-
century London stage.   Wilks and Mountfort, besides Mrs. Bracegirdle,
are the only actors of high stature to be named in song-books,[9] and
Mountfort was a theatre composer as well as a singer; he set Durfey's
song "Great Jove once made love like a bull" (D&M 1201) in *The
Marriage-Hater Match'd* (1692) and apparently furnished some of the
instrumental music for his own play *Greenwich Park* (1691) (see
Appendix I).   Cibber speaks highly of Mountfort, both as an actor and as
a singer:[10]

> If it could be remembered how much he had the Advantage of me,
> in Voice and Person, I could not, here, be suspected of an affected
> Modesty, or of over-valuing his Excellence: For he sung a clear
> Countertenour, and had a melodious, warbling Throat, which could
> not but set off the last Scene of *Sir Courtly*[11] with an uncommon
> Happiness; which I, alas! could only struggle thro', with the faint
> Excuses, and real Confidence of a fine Singer, under the
> Imperfection of a feign'd, and screaming Trebble, which at best
> could only shew you what I would have done, had Nature been
> more favourable to me.[12]

Cibber's envious remarks reveal how important a singing part could be in
a Restoration play.   The role of Sir Courtly Nice was probably written
for Mountfort during the heyday of the singing actor, and when
Crowne's play was revived with Cibber in the title role, probably first in
1703,[13] the apparent unavailability of a singing actor necessitated
compromising the original requirements of the role.   Surprisingly, in his
account of the most famous of the hybrid actresses, Mrs. Bracegirdle,
Cibber makes only a brief reference to her musical abilities.   He is most
impressed with her nonsinging roles but states that in her acting of the
other kind of characters, "where Singing was a necessary Part of them,
her Voice and Action gave a Pleasure, which good Sense, in those Days,
was not asham'd to give Praise to."[14]   The reason for Cibber's coolness
towards the roles requiring singing is not, as will be shown in Chapter
Five, completely the result of envy.
        Although the song-books published between about 1690 and
1710 usually confirm that the actors mentioned in *dramatis personae* and
stage directions did actually sing the songs demanded of them, one finds
a few discrepancies between play-books and song-books which indicate
that occasionally an actor had his song performed by someone else.   For
example, in Dryden's *Amphitryon* (1690), III.i, in which Jupiter (played
by Betterton), disguised as Amphitryon, is trying to seduce Alcmena, a
stage direction states: "Jupiter signs to the Musicians.   Song and

Dance." Apparently he is to sing the song "Celia, that I once was blest" (D&M 515 mH. Purcell), but the song-book records John Boman as the singer. The *dramatis personae* lists Boman as playing Phoebus (who does not appear in III.i); did he also play a musician in this scene? That Betterton, the dean of Restoration actors, does not sing here is not surprising, for he is practically the only member of his profession who is not recorded to have sung on the stage. The stage direction for this song is ambiguous; it could simply mean that Jupiter calls to the musicians to perform. But in Durfey's *The Bath, or, The Western Lass* (1701), the stage direction for a song in V.iii is explicit. Crab (played by Cibber) and Gillian (played by Mrs. Verbruggen) decide to sing a dialogue:

> *Crab.* . . . I gave thee a Song this Morning . . . you know; come, we'll sing
> it together. . . .
> *Gillian.* Odslid, with all my heart--

The stage direction for this song follows: "Second DIALOGUE between Crab and Gillian." But in *Wit and Mirth: or Pills to Purge Melancholy*, IV (1706), the song, "Where Oxen do low" (D&M 3846 mD. Purcell) is stated to have been sung by the professional singers Mrs. Harris and Mr. Pierson. Cibber, by his own admission, was reluctant to sing, and Mrs. Verbruggen did so infrequently, and then only bawdy songs.[15] Since nearly five years intervened between the first production of the play and the publication of the music, perhaps the mention of Mrs. Harris and Mr. Pierson indicates a revival, but none is recorded in *The London Stage*, II:1, as having been mounted later than December, 1702. Other instances of disagreement between song-books and play-books are rare,[16] and most actors, regardless of the quality of their voices, sang the songs required by their roles.

Professional Singers

In the plays published shortly after 1700, roles for actor-singers are less common, and by 1706 or 1707 independent songs sung by important speaking characters are infrequent. (Cibber's difficulty in managing a part originally designed for this special kind of player is also testimony of the rapid disappearance of the former tradition.) Music was not eliminated from the plays produced during these years, but (as suggested in Chapter One) it became compartmentalized. The whole of the dramatic music is often contained in a masque or final entertainment, during which the speaking characters sit and listen: hence the ascent of the professional singer, an artist who rarely spoke but expressed himself completely in song. Mrs. Ayliff, John Freeman, Mrs. Hodgson, Mrs.

Hudson, Mr. Pate, John Reading, and a few others became extremely popular as the nymphs and shepherds and the spirits and devils of the late Restoration masque.[17]   Unlike their anonymous predecessors who sang in the dramatic operas of Locke and Shadwell, these singers are frequently and conspicuously mentioned in the play-books. But despite their popularity, high salaries, and the large proportion of an afternoon's entertainment devoted to their singing, the more traditional actors considered these performers only a necessary evil and occasionally reminded them of their low dramatic station; prologues used them as whipping boys to berate the audience's decaying tastes. Motteux, in his comedy *Love's a Jest* (1696), alludes to this theatrical class distinction. During Act II, two singers performed a ribald para-dramatic entertainment: "Enter Mr. Redding [Reading] in a Smith's Habit, a Bottle in his Hand. He sings, seemingly drunk."   While singing he "Drinks; then throws away his Bottle, and takes up a Quart Pot. Enter Mr. [John] Lee drest as the Smith's Wife and big-bellied."   The two characters complete their song[18] and Sir Topewel rewards them: "here Friends, there's a couple of Shillings for you to drink," and he casts two coins at their feet.   But Christina is shocked at his niggardly condescension: "Fye, Sir Topewel, you affront 'em, and us too; they never sing under a couple of Guineas."   Perhaps not coincidentally, Christina was played by Mrs. Bracegirdle, who might well take the insult personally.

II. THE INSTRUMENTALIST ONSTAGE

The actor-singer and, to a lesser extent, the professional singer were the elite members of the theatre's musical establishment. They were highly paid, popular, and, in a few cases, respected actors. Also attached to the London playhouses were a few dozen musicians--singers and instrumentalists--who were responsible for the performance of much of the music and also for the many minor roles--citizens, rabble, masquers, bravos, soldiers, drawers, serving wenches, link boys, and attendants--that provide the kings and rakes of the plays with an animate environment in which to spin their plots. Their duties ranged from rendering the music of larger musical scenes, such as masques and final entertainments, to performing independent songs, dances, instrumental pieces, flourishes, and so forth. Regardless of the type of music they sang or played, either onstage or off, these musicians--choristers, fiddlers, lutenists, and wind players--were called "the Musick."

In the 17th century the term "musick" had a much broader connotation than it does now. It may mean any aspect of the practice of the musical art but refers most often to performers: for example, in Cibber's *She wou'd and She wou'd not* (1703), V.i, a servant announces that "the Play-house Musick are come." The term is used to designate singers as well as instrumentalists, as in Crowne's *The History of Charles the Eighth of France* (1672), V.ii: ". . . and near the chairs the Musick in white Robes and Laurels on their heads. A chorus of voices and loud Musick heard."[19] Besides its modern general meaning, it often refers specifically to an instrumental piece or a short prelude before a song: Dryden, *Troilus and Cressida* (1679), III.ii, "Musick, and then Song: during which Pandarus listens"; Settle, *The Heir of Morocco, with the Death of Gayland* (1682), III.i, "The King discovered in his Night-Gown, sitting, Meroin by him. A Song and Musick." In some cases the meaning may be determined only by the context: Gildon, *The Roman Bride's Revenge* (1697), IV.i, "Enter from the other side the Emperor, Attendants, Lights, Music . . . Music and Song." "Musick" may refer to the written or printed notation, and it may also mean a musical instrument: Behn, *The Young King* (1683), I.i:

> *Pimante.* Besides, he is very ill-bred for a King, he knows nothing of the World, cannot dress himself, nor sing, nor dance, or play on any Musick. . . .

And in V.iv of the same play is the following stage direction: "They seat themselves. Enter Amin. Ura[nia], masked, shepherds, shepherdesses, followed with Pipes, or wind-Musick. . . ."

The Fiddler

The mainstay of the stage musicians was the fiddler. In comedies he accompanied the songs of lovesick ladies and played for final dances; during drunken rampages or abortive serenades, rakes often "drove the Fidlers before them like a flock of geese."[20] In tragedies they played from within a grove or were called into royal chambers to soothe a troubled king. Even during masques and entertainments, the musical accompaniment was often provided by richly dressed stage musicians rather than the orchestra hidden from view in the pit or music room. And in a few comedies fiddlers have small speaking roles, usually nothing more than wretched foils for genteel abuse and ridicule. The position of the instrumentalist, particularly the violinist, greatly improved during the second half of the 17th century: the descendants of the poor, ale-house fiddlers who entertained the revelers celebrating King Charles's restoration became the fashionable drawing-room exponents of the Corelli sonata; but on the stage of the London playhouses, even after the turn of the century, the acting fiddler of the comedy remains the abused and knocked-about half-musician, half-acrobat of the 1660s. In addition to his traditional roles of impertinent buffoon and provider of dance music and accompaniments to songs, the fiddler was charged with a variety of musical duties on the stage.[21]

Like "musick," "fiddler" also had a wider meaning during the Restoration than it does at present, as it could refer to any stage musician, singer or instrumentalist. In Behn's *The Amorous Prince* (1671), II.iii, the drunken Lorenzo asks his fiddler to provide the music for a serenade:

> *Lorenzo.* Away with the Song, I'll take it on your word that 'tis fit
>   for my purpose.
> *Fidler.* I'll warrant you my Lord.

It is not clear how many musicians have entered the stage, but the fiddler probably sings the song ("In vain I have labour'd the Victor to prove"). In Dryden's *An Evening's Love* (1671), II.i, a stage direction ("Enter Musicians with disguises; and some in their hands") and the ensuing action suggest the presence of several musicians. Wildblood explains to them the necessity of the disguises, and Bellamy asks Maskall to "help on with 'em, while they tune their Instruments." Wildblood commands the fiddles to strike up: "we'll entertain 'em [the ladies] with a song al'Angloise, pray be ready with your Chorus." Obviously, the "fiddles" were capable of more than playing their instruments. In Durfey's *The Fool Turn'd Critick* (1678), II.ii, a fiddler gives his audience a choice of music:

> *1st Fiddler.* Will it please you Gentlemen to hear a new Lesson,[22]
>   or a Song A-la-Mode.

Smallwit's choice of the latter prevails over Sir Formall's request for a battle song, and the fiddlers sing "The Age is refin'd" (D&M 19). A singing fiddler in V.i of Porter's comedy *A Witty Combat* (1663) boasts that he can sing "A hundred and fifty [songs], two hundred if need be . . . ." And in Shadwell's *The Miser* (1672), III.iii, Timothy puts a group of fiddlers to what would seem a strange use after they have announced themselves in the typical manner ("Flourish of Musicianers"). He is careful how he addresses them:

> *Timothy.* . . . wee'l have a Song faik now; Violinmen, (I dare not call 'em
>   Fiddlers, for fear they should be angry) sing us a catch. . . .

A stage direction confirms that his request is granted: "They Sing. A Catch in four Parts."[23] Fiddlers sing in a few other plays,[24] but as these examples show, their introduction into a scene is almost always for comic effect. In a few comedies a fiddler is given a fairly important speaking part in addition to his musical responsibilities.

In Shadwell's *The Woman-Captain* (1680), III.i, three villains commandeer a group of fiddlers on their way to a place of employment:

> [Enter three or four Fidlers.]
> *Blunderbus.* Who's here? stand.
> *Heildebrand.* Stand Rogues; ha! they'r Fidlers.
> *Fidler.* We are going to Play under a window for a Wedding.
> *Sir Christopher.* We'll stop your Journey, Rascal; strike up, and play to us while we break windows.
> *Fidl.* Good Gentelmen! we shall lose our Wedding; there are other Companies out that will be there before us.
> *Sir Chr.* We will cut and hack you first, and then your Fiddles.
> *Fidl* Hold, hold Gentlemen! we will Play--
> [They play scurvily.]
> *Sir Chr.* Now let's break Windows to this Musick. 'Tis good for nothing else.

In *Epsom-Wells* (1673), III.i, by the same author, a musician is even allowed to get the upper hand. While enjoying a holiday away from the hectic life of London, Peg is anxious that her friends, Mrs. Jiltall and Mr. Clodpate, hear a song apropos to their pleasant condition:

> [Enter Peg and Fidler.]
> *Peg.* Here's the honest fellow that sings the Song. . . .
> [Fidler sings.] "Oh how I abhor the Tumult and smoak of the Town"[25]
> *Mrs. Jiltall.* Excellent, there's a Crown; pray come and sing this to me twice a day as long as I stay in Epsom.
> *Fidler.* I will, Madam.
> *Clodpate.* 'Tis incomparable, let me embrace thee, there's ten shillings for thee; and if thou wilt live with me in Sussex, thou shalt never see London again.
> *Fidl.* Pardon me, Sir, I was born and bred in London, and would not live out on't for five hundred pound a year.
> *Mrs. Jilt.* Out on you, you scurvy Fellow.
> *Clod.* [aside] A pox on him for a Rascal. Thou art a very honest Fellow, give me my ten shillings agen, and I'l make it a Guinney.

But Clodpate tricks the poor fiddler out of his money, and grumbles, "An insolent London Rogue to sing against his Conscience. . . ."

Dance Music and Fiddlers

Although the stage musician occasionally has a few lines to speak in some comedies, a more important duty was to accompany singers, for in Restoration plays, most songs (not a part of larger entertainments) performed onstage were also accompanied onstage. The musicians are usually worked into the action on some pretense and stand aside until the song is sung. After playing, they depart immediately unless their skills are required later in the scene. As will be shown below, the singer was in most cases accompanied by a guitarist or lutenist. Nearly all of the extant songs originally associated with Restoration plays consist of a voice part and bass line on which the instrumentalist builds his accompaniment. But the stage directions for some of the scenes in which these songs appear clearly indicate that several musicians in addition to singer and accompanist are onstage while the songs are sung. Since many of the independent songs are followed and, less often, preceded by dances, the musicians were present to play the dances and probably not to supplement the accompaniment of the continuo.[26] These dances occupied the fiddlers[27] more than any other music of the late 17th-century London stage, yet, except for a few meagre fragments, the music is almost completely lost.

Stage musicians were members of the cast and not only did they have to memorize their few spoken lines but also the music they played while onstage. Undoubtedly much of their dance music was semi-improvised or taken from the well known repertoire of popular tunes, such as the old standards printed and reprinted in the numerous issues of *The Dancing Master* and similar publications. Any professional musician would probably have had many of these tunes in his fingers, and the livelihood of a stage fiddler (who probably also played at balls and in the alehouses)[28] would certainly have depended on his ability to play popular dances. But there is evidence to show that much of the dance music used in a Restoration play, like the songs, masques, and act tunes, was written or arranged anew for each production; for if audiences demanded the latest songs and airs, they surely would not have been satisfied with out-of-fashion dance music.

One must resist the temptation to rely too heavily on the lavish and remarkably complete scores of dramatic operas, such as the manuscript copy of Motteux's *The Island Princess* (1669) (Lbm Add. 15318) or Purcell's *The Vocal and Instrumental Musick of the Prophetess, or The History of Dioclesian* (1691), as guides to Restoration performance practice, for these scores were compiled because the stage works for which they provide the music were extraordinary productions; therefore, they may not reflect the musical practices of ordinary plays. But as regards dance music, they provide clues as to what music might have been used in less elaborate plays. In *Dido and Aeneas* (the existing scores for which are by no means complete, especially with respect to dance music),[29] for example, several of the songs and choruses are followed by dances. In the case of the "Sailors' Dance" in Act III, Purcell provides separate music for the dance which is stylistically akin to the sailor's song, "Come away, fellow sailors." But the final piece in the masque, the "Cupids Dance," has the same music as the preceding chorus, "With drooping wings." In many plays of the period, dances performed after the songs were probably instrumental arrangements of the songs themselves.

The play-books reveal very little about this practice; as shown elsewhere in this study, they provide only scant records of the instrumental music in a play. A few provocative stage directions have survived, however. For instance, in IV.ii of Otway's comedy *The Atheist* (1684), after the song, "Welcome Mortal to this place" (D&M 3578 *m*Pack) is the note: "Enter four Black Women, that dance to the same Measure of the Song. . . ." This is ambiguous. Do the women dance to the song itself or only to the same metric units (the rhythm or phrase structure) of "Welcome Mortal," as it is played by instrumentalists? Dancers occasionally sing the tune to which they dance, as, for example, in I.i of *The Grove* (1700), by Oldmixon: "The Front Scene opens and discovers a Circle of Seven Pillars adorn'd with Garlands of Flowers, The Shepherds and Shepherdesses dancing within it, to the Tune of the Chorus, which they sing as they Dance."[30]

Song-Tunes

More substantial evidence that dances were derived from vocal music is provided by the so-called song-tunes, instrumental arrangements of popular songs. Numerous flute and violin tutors, such as *Apollo's Banquet* (various editions) and *The Compleat Flute-Master* (1695), almost always include some song-tunes, and after 1700, the publications of vocal music by John Walsh and others often include the melodies of songs transposed for recorder (see Appendix I). These arrangements of popular songs should not be taken alone as evidence of the derivation of dance music from the songs in plays, because any popular tune, vocal or instrumental, was often arranged countless times for whatever instruments happened to be in vogue. But, curiously, a few four-part arrangements of songs from plays are found in manuscript collections of instrumental act music. Some of these were possibly used as dance music in plays. One striking example is an arrangement of Purcell's song, "No, no, poor suff'ring Heart" (D&M 2347 *m*H. Purcell *s*Mrs. Butler) for Dryden's tragedy *Cleomenes The Spartan Heroe* (1692), II.ii, found in Lbm Add. 24889 (fol. 21'), a manuscript that was perhaps used by theatre musicians,[31] since (as the title-page states) it contains "Playhouse Tunes." In this scene a brief entertainment is presented to Ptolomy and Cassandra:

> The SCENE opens and discovers Cassandra's Apartment. Musicians
> and Dancers--Ptolomy leads in Cassandra, Sosybius follows--They Sit.
> Towards the end of the Song and Dance; Enter Cleomenes and
> Cleanthes on one side of the Stage. . . .

The stage direction is important because it specifies how much music is
performed during the entertainment (a song and dance) and that there
were musicians onstage. The instrumental version of Purcell's song was
perhaps the dance.

Continuo Instruments

If the four-part arrangement of "No, no, poor suff'ring Heart"
provided the music for the dancers, then at least four musicians must
have been present. Seldom do stage directions specify the exact number
of fiddlers onstage, but occasionally this may be determined by other
means. For example, in III.iii of Shadwell's *The Miser* (1672), fiddlers
sing "A Catch in four Parts." And in *The Woman-Captain* (1680), III.i,
"three or four Fidlers" are on their way to play for a wedding. All of
these musicians were probably not violinists, and undoubtedly some in
the party were burdened with the rather cumbersome instruments
necessary for the execution of the basso continuo. As will be shown
below, either a bass viol or violoncello was often carried on and off the
Restoration stage, and the usual partner of these instruments, in both the
accompaniment of songs and the playing of instrumental pieces, was the
lute, theorbo, or guitar, and rarely the harpsichord. Stage directions
frequently mention the various plucked stringed instruments as providing
the accompaniment to songs. In general, those of the lute family are
used mostly in early plays or plays with classical settings and are played
by unspecified professionals or, if a speaking character is supposed to
accompany himself or another character, the lute is played behind the
scenes. The guitar, on the other hand, was the favorite instrument of the
actor-singer and is used in plays produced throughout the period.

For the Restoration dramatist, the lute was the musical
instrument of antiquity. It accompanied songs performed for legendary
or mythological kings, and rarely was it ever heard in a topical comedy,
except those written in the early years of the period.[32] In Roger Boyle's
tragedy *The Black Prince* (1669), for instance, I.ii opens with a grotto
scene. Alizia's servant, Sevina, is playing upon the lute. Sevina was
acted by Mrs. Napp (that is, Knepp), one of the few singing actresses
recorded as having played the lute. But even in this case, the grotto may
have concealed the fact that she did not play; an arbor probably served a
similar purpose in Ravenscroft's *King Edgar and Alfreda* (1677), I[iii]:
"The King and Queen sleeping in an Arbor hand in hand. Matalda

sitting on the other hand of the King awake, Alicia playing a soft Ayr on the Lute, and singing to't." Although the lute is a common instrument in tragedies, only rarely did the audience actually see it being played.[33] More often it served simply as a stage property. For example, in Stapylton's *The Step-Mother* (1664), I[ii], "Filamor [is] discover'd in an Arbor, with a Lute in his hand; on either side the Arbor, on two pedestals, Cupid stands, and the Flamen kneels; as Caesarina walks by they sing." Filamor does not play, but rather the lute is probably meant to suggest his musical frame of mind. The theorbo is much less frequently mentioned in stage directions, and, as with its smaller relative, references to it are confined to early and mid-Restoration plays. In Francis Fane's comedy *Love in the Dark* (1675), I.i, "Parhelia sings a Song to the Theorbo" ("Let us turn usurers of time"). The only other mention in a play of this instrument as a playhouse fixture is the famous note in Shadwell's version of *The Tempest* (1674), I.i ("The Front of the Stage is open'd, and the Band of 24 Violins, with the Harpsicals and Theorbo's which accompany the Voices, are plac'd between the Pit and the Stage"), but undoubtedly it was frequently used as a continuo instrument throughout the period.[34] The plays, however, tacitly reflect the gradual demise of the lute in the second half of the 17th century in England, as actors and the fashionable dilettantes that they portrayed rejected Thomas Mace's favorite instrument for the guitar.

Even in plays produced during the first decade or so after the Restoration, the guitar is more frequently played onstage by speaking characters than the lute. The actor probably found the guitar more suitable to provide an accompaniment to his songs, not because the lute is more difficult to play, but rather because it was in fashion and the lute was not. Most of the guitar's appearances in plays are designed to enhance settings which are supposed to represent the country of its origin. It was frequently played onstage for more or less serious purposes, as in III.i of Dryden's *An Evening's Love* (1671),[35] but comedians often used it to accompany their humorous songs. One cannot imagine that in Dryden's *The Assignation: or, Love in a Nunnery* (1673), I.i, Joe Haines (who played Benito) need have had much skill on the instrument:

> Scene ROME. A great Glass Plac'd. Enter Benito with a Guittar in his Hand. Benito bowing to the Glass . . . He playes on the Guittar, and Dances and Sings to the Glass.

His clowning is interrupted by his master, Aurelian, who remarks that Benito should not lower himself by playing "the younger brother of the Cittern." In Durfey's *The Banditti* (1686), IV.ii, the effect of Frisco's

similarly humorous song (". . . Frisco [played by Mr. Jevon] Acts a
Spanish Song affectedly to his Guittar. . .") probably did not depend on
Jevon's musical ability.

Because of its portability, the guitar, and before it the lute, were
ideal stage instruments; they were probably common in the small bands
that tumbled on and off the stage during serenades or stole quietly in
and out of the musical groves. The harpsichord, while a fixture of the
music room or orchestra pit, was necessarily used much less frequently
on the stage. A keyboard instrument is mentioned only four times in
stage directions; on three occasions it is said to be onstage. In these
cases the dramatists appear to be exploiting the special musical abilities
of actress-singers, but in *Womans Wit: or, The Lady in Fashion* (1697),
III.i, Cibber satirizes the precocious young ladies of quality who, after
being urged to display their skills at the keyboard, play a little too long.
In this scene he drew upon the talents of his wife, Catherine Cibber,
daughter of the King's trumpeter, Mathias Shore. Emilia says, "here's
the Harpsichord to divert us," and she pushes a reluctant Olivia (played
by Mrs. Cibber) towards the instrument. She smiles and begins to play.
But the music grows tedious for Emilia who begins to talk. Finally she
asks Olivia to sing. She obliges with "Tell me Belinda, prithee do"
(D&M 3155 *m*Leveridge?); she apparently accompanied herself on the
harpsichord. In the anonymous tragi-comedy *The Triumph of Virtue*
published in the same year (1697), a spinet is used in a much different
situation, but again the musical talents of a young actress rather than a
desire to create a dramatic effect probably occasioned its use. The
second act opens with "A Bed-Chamber, and a Spinette set forth.
Isidore [played by Mrs. Cross] plays upon the Spinette, and sings." In
Steele's comedy *The Lying Lover* (1704), II.i, Penelope reads and
comments to her friend Lettice about a song entitled "To Celia's Spinet,"
which begins "Thou soft Machines." A stage direction states that "Here
the Song is perform'd to a Spinet," but it is not clear who sings it,
although perhaps Mrs. Lucas, who plays Lettice, rendered it.[36]

One of the reasons that the harpsichord was not frequently used
onstage in Restoration plays is because of its lack of portability. For this
reason one may ask what bass instrument typically formed the other half
of the continuo unit, for even though the bass viol and violoncello
certainly do not present their players with the transportation problems of
the clavicinist, these are rather unwieldy objects, especially if one
imagines a gambist threading his way through a proscenium door or a
maze of scenery with a viol in one hand and that other nonmusical
though nevertheless equally essential device in the other, a chair. But
why should we suppose that 17th-century stage managers were any less
ingenious in solving minor technical problems than their modern
counterparts? If several musicians could descend harmoniously in a

machine, surely some lowly gambist's favorite straight-backed chair could have been unobtrusively accommodated within a prospect of the Elysian Fields. A few stage directions indicate the presence of bass viols on the stage. In Behn's comedy *The Feign'd Curtizans, or A Nights Intrigue* (1679), near the end of Act III, Fillamoor and Galliard come stumbling through a door with "all the Musick." Galliard asks the musicians to "tune your pipes," and after they play some unspecified music, a song is performed. Then a fight breaks out, "the Musick confusedly among them." Galliard loses his sword and "in the hurry gets a Base Viol." Although a playable instrument was probably not used here, this scene does suggest that such instruments were included in the typical stage band. In Centlivre's *The Beau's Duel* (1702), I.i, the French servant Reviere says that "de Fidle, de Hautbois, de Courtel, and de Base Vial" have arrived to play for his master. And in the music meeting represented in IV.ii of Southerne's *The Maid's Last Prayer* (1693), a bass viol figures prominently as Sir Symphony's instrument: "He takes a Base-Viol, and while he is Tuning, one of the Bullies unwinds the Pegs over his head: Then he lays down the Bow, which the Bully draws through the Candle; when Sir Symphony tries to play, he can't make it sound." Pictorial evidence for the viol as a stage instrument is an engraving included in the 1707 edition of Abraham Cowley's *Cutter of Coleman-Street* (première, December 1661).[37] The "fiddlers" in V.vi are depicted: two violinists and a gambist, all three standing, with the latter resting his viol on a small stool.

III. THE PLAYHOUSE ORCHESTRA

While the stage musicians provided much of the music required by the action of the play, the act tunes and that instrumental music associated with larger musical scenes (such as entertainments and masques in which many singers and dancers were involved) were played by the theatre orchestra. This group of musicians varied in size from a handful of fiddlers to a large orchestra of over 30 members. The amount of music within the acts varied considerably from work to work, and a few plays require no music whatsoever in their stage directions; yet musicians were always present in the playhouse to provide the preliminary music and the act tunes. In 1667 the theatre-wise traveller Samuel Chappuzeau remarked that the London playhouses usually had 12 players in the orchestra, whereas in Paris six was the normal number.[38] And in the same year, Pepys reports that Killigrew planned to have nine or ten fiddlers in his new theatre (12 February 1667). The various Lord Chamberlain records, which include warrants for the costumes of theatre orchestra players, not surprisingly mention 20 or more musicians as comprising the "play-house Musick," but these documents usually pertain to special productions and lavish court entertainments for which personnel were borrowed from court musical establishments.[39]   For example, the 1674 production of Locke and Shadwell's version of *The Tempest* was an especially elaborate one in which "the Band of 24 Violins" (that is, the strings of the Royal Musick) is mentioned as having provided part of the music. As the size of the orchestra varied according to the musical requirements of the drama itself (and the budget allotted to a particular production), so the position of the offstage musicians varied from the music room to the pit, and to the stage itself: the musician and dramatist placed the orchestra where it would be most advantageous for a particular stage work mounted in a given theatre.

The Music Room

Modern scholars have largely overlooked the flexibility allowed the 17th-century dramatist with regard to the physical arrangements in the playhouses. Theatre managers made maximum use of improvements and new facilities, and when these became out-moded or could not accommodate innovations in stagecraft or musical performance practice, they improvised and worked around the limitations until funds could be raised to build a new one or to remodel the existing structure. This is particularly true of the music room. There probably never was a separate chamber in a 17th-century London playhouse reserved solely for the musicians, but in the early years of the period, a small group of players probably performed in a room raised above the level of the stage. After a few seasons, managers found the tiny music room inadequate to accommodate the fiddling personnel of what was becoming increasingly a musical theatre. Whenever necessary, the orchestra was placed on the stage itself, or the first few rows of benches were removed from the pit to provide a temporary location for the musicians.

Despite the insistence of many modern drama historians that all Restoration theatres had music lofts placed above the stage in the center of the proscenium arch,[40] conclusive evidence for the existence of this suspiciously Elizabethan structure is sorely lacking. Besides Pepys's ambiguous references to "the musique-room" and the few clues provided by play-books, the only evidence that the early Restoration playhouses had proscenium rooms are the well known engravings of five scenes from Settle's *The Empress of Morocco* (1673), printed with the play-book. Two of these, depicting the "Moorish Dance" of II.ii and the masque of Orpheus in IV.iii, are reproduced as Plates I and II, respectively. Both of these scenes (as well as the three others not included here) are set into the same ornamental border; many scholars have taken this border to represent the Duke's Theatre, Dorset Garden, in 1673, the year when Settle's play was produced at that playhouse. Each engraving clearly shows a protruding structure overhanging the stage. The interior of the room is hidden by what appear to be screens, and the curved balustrades on either side of the room are decorated with musical emblems: at stage-left is a wind instrument and a drum and at stage-right some sort of stringed instrument and perhaps a cornetto. This would appear to be the same sort of structure that Pepys mentions on 7 November 1667. He was anxious to see Dryden and Davenant's new adaptation of *The Tempest* being presented at Lincoln's Inn Fields; he arrived late and was "forced to sit in the side balcone over against the musique-room."[41] But the statement is ambiguous and certainly does not pinpoint the location of the music room at the center of the proscenium arch. While the various engravings of *The Empress of Morocco* obviously depict scenes described in stage directions and implied by the action of the play, the proscenium arch and music room which surround these scenes form no more than a picture frame. The value of any engraving of this period in establishing the actual dimensions of a structure is questionable. More reliable pictorial evidence is provided by a cross-sectional plan of a theatre designed by Christopher Wren, probably the new Theatre Royal of 1674, the only extant architectural section of a Restoration playhouse.[42]

Anyone hoping to find neo-Elizabethan devices in Wren's drawing (reproduced as Plate III) will be disappointed, for this diagram depicts a structure not dissimilar to many west-end London theatres of today. The only significant differences between this and most modern theatres are the thrust stage, which extends half the total length of the stage beyond the proscenium into the auditorium, and the two doors leading onto this "extension" of the stage. The plan (probably drawn about the same time as *The Empress of Morocco* engravings were published) shows no music loft at the top of the proscenium. Yet if this drawing actually represents a Theatre Royal and is therefore perhaps similar in construction to other Restoration theatres, how can we reconcile the apparent lack of music room with the numerous references throughout the period in Pepys's *Diary*, ballads,[43] and plays, to some sort of elevated room reserved for the theatre orchestra? Perhaps Wren's drawing does show the music room: the two side boxes situated over the stage, above the proscenium doors. When Pepys states that he was "forced to sit in the side balcone over against[44] the musique-room," he was probably referring to side boxes similar to those above the stage in Wren's playhouse. Apparently, he sat in the upper box nearest the proscenium arch across from the corresponding one on the other side of the house,[45] two of the worst locations for observing the scenic effects of even the pre-operatic 1667 version of *The Tempest*. Barring the possibility of the overhanging music room in the center of the arch (as depicted only in *The Empress of Morocco* engravings), the side box nearest the curtain is the most likely location for the music room in the late 17th-century London theatre. The few play-books containing stage directions that mention a music room also suggest that musicians occasionally occupied these undesirable (from the audience's point of view) boxes; and considering the musical requirements of many Restoration plays, the absurdity of a music room hanging over the front of the stage becomes even more apparent.

In IV.ii of *The Chances* (1682), a comedy by the Duke of Buckingham, George Villiers, Don John hearkens as "Musick plays above." He is presumably standing on the thrust stage and glances up at the balcony, exclaiming, "What's here, Musick and Women? would I had one of 'em." A stage direction states that "One of 'em looks out at the Window." The window was probably fixed in one of the side boxes nearest the stage, as these were frequently used for balcony scenes. In R. Boyle's unacted *Tragedy of King Saul* (1703), II.ii, both side boxes were to be employed by actors: "The Palace. After several shouts a sound of Trumpets; Merab with other ladies appear in one window . . . others over against[46] them in another window. . . ." And in the unusual prologue to Durfey's *The Virtuous Wife* (1680), an antiphonal address is delivered by two famous comedians: "Lee [Antony Leigh] peeps out of a little window over the Stage . . . Nokes peeps out of a little Window the other side of the Stage." Since the prologue was almost always delivered before the curtain went up, Leigh and Nokes probably spoke from the side balconies. Occasionally stage directions mention the music room when it is not involved in the action of a scene, as in *The Humorous Lovers* (1677), III[ii], by Cavendish ("A SONG in the Musick Room"). But usually it is alluded to only if it is employed as a part of a dramatic situation. For example, in Dryden's comedy *The Kind Keeper; or, Mr Limberham* (1680), I.i, Woodall is concerned about the predicament of a young lady when he hears "Musick at the Balcony over head," and a song is sung from above ("'Gainst Keepers we petition"). Clearly the music room had many uses in Restoration plays, and its fairly frequent employment for balcony scenes illustrates how awkward it would be to coordinate music performed in a proscenium music room with dialogue, singing, or dancing on the part of the stage behind the proscenium arch. If any 17th-century London theatre had such a room, it must have been of little use and soon abandoned.

The Orchestra Pit

The side boxes could probably have accommodated a harpsichord, a few singers, and perhaps even the dozen fiddlers mentioned by Chappuzeau, but when plays requiring elaborate musical effects were mounted and the size of the orchestra swelled to 30 or more players, the musicians quitted the music room for more commodious quarters. The stage directions for the opening scene of the 1674 version of *The Tempest* are well known. For this production the area in front of the stage was altered to make room for the 24 violins of the King, harpsichords, and theorbos. The note "The Front of the Stage is open'd" suggests that some members of this sizable orchestra sat under the front of the thrust stage. In fact, a stage direction in II.iii of the play, overlooked by most writers on the subject of the Restoration theatre orchestra, states: "Another flourish of Voyces under the Stage . . . a Masque Sung under the Stage." This proto-Wagnerian pit was not new to the London playhouses in 1674; Pepys mentions a similar structure in the second of the new theatres built after the Restoration. On 8 May 1663 he attended the Theatre Royal, Drury Lane, "the second day of its being opened," to see a revival of Beaumont and Fletcher's old comedy, *The Humorous Lieutenant*:

> The house is made with extraordinary good contrivance; and yet hath some faults, as the narrowness of the passages in and out of the pit, and the distance from the stage to the boxes, which I am confident cannot hear. But for all other things it is well. Only, above all, the Musique being below, and most of it sounding under the very stage, there is no hearing of the bases at all, nor very well of the trebles, which sure must be mended.

One should not assume from this report that a permanent pit had been constructed for the musicians, for there was probably no fixed location for the orchestra. But an under-stage room was not completely abandoned by the instrumentalists, and on at least two other occasions music was heard from beneath the boards. In Dennis's *Rinaldo and Armida* (1699), III.i, Urania, frightened by subterranean growls, exclaims, "already, Hells grizly Tyrant takes the dire Alarm." A stage direction records what must have been a rather hellish sound: "The Serpent and Basses softly under the Stage." Urania quickly perceives that "Th' Infernal Trumpet throu' the Abiss profound, / Horribly Rumbles with its dreary Sound." In Ravenscroft's *The Careless Lovers* (1673), two prompt notes ("Musick ready below" in IV.i and "Flourish below" in V.ii) suggest that perhaps the prompter needed to warn musicians under the stage to prepare to play; but "below" might refer to the spacial characteristics of the printed page rather than to the physical arrangements of the theatre in which this play was first performed (that is, the Duke's, in Dorset Garden). One occasionally finds the musicians sitting on the stage rather than in the pit in front of it. Congreve, in an account of the performance of John Eccles's setting of *The Judgement of Paris* (1701)[47] (a masque written by Congreve and set to music by Eccles and three other composers as a competition for the "musick prize"),[48] reports that this lavish Dorset Garden production necessitated removing the musicians from their usual position:

> The number of performers, besides the verse-singers, was 85. The front of the stage was all built into a concave with deal boards; all which was faced with tin, to increase and throw forwards the sound. It was all hung with sconces of wax-candles, besides the common branches of lights usual in the playhouses. The boxes and pit were all thrown into one; so that all sat in common; and the whole was crammed with beauties and beaux, not one scrub being admitted. The place where formerly the music used to play, between the pit and the stage, was turned into White's chocolate-house: the whole family being transplanted thither with chocolate, cool'd drinks, ratafia, Pontacq, etc., which every body that would called for, the whole expence being defrayed by the subscribers.

Since Congreve writes that the musicians were removed from their usual position between the stage and the pit, one must assume that they were placed somewhere on the stage and that the acoustical reflector was erected upstage, the orchestra being in front of it. In Ravenscroft's *The Anatomist* (1697) the musicians, whose chief duty was to provide the music for Motteux's masque, *The Loves of Mars and Venus*, were also probably in clear view of the audience, perhaps even onstage. Beatrice tells Angelica that the latter's lover, who is despised by Angelica's parents, has come down from university before the holidays to try to see her. So desperate is the young man to deliver a message to Angelica that, risking discovery, he has come to her parent's musical entertainment:

> *Angelica.* How can that be? He is known both by my Father and Mother.
> *Beatrice.* No matter for that, he is in disguise, and sits amongst the Instrumental Musick as one of them. . . .

This conversation, spoken "before the Curtain," suggests that the orchestra for the masque, which begins later in the scene at the ascent of the curtain, is on the stage behind the curtain, for the rest of what Angelica says in this scene does not indicate that she anxiously looks into the pit to attempt to see her truant lover but that she (and the audience) must wait for the masque to begin to discover who among the orchestra is the bogus musician.

Both *The Anatomist* and *The Judgement of Paris* were special productions in which music is the main attraction, and therefore the placement of the orchestra was probably unusual. Congreve's remark, that "the place where formerly the music used to play, between the pit and the stage," suggests that the orchestra pit was a common feature of the Restoration playhouse--common, that is, for plays and other stage works that required large musical forces. No pictorial evidence from the late 17th century shows unequivocally that such a special place was reserved for the orchestra, but the frontispiece to Grabu and Perrin's *Ariane, ou le Mariage de Bacchus* (1674), which purports to depict the first scene of this French opera, produced 30 March 1674 at the newly opened Theatre Royal in Drury Lane,[49] hints at the presence of an orchestra pit. The theatre represented in this engraving (see Plate IV) is perhaps the same as that diagramed in Wren's cross-section discussed above.[50] The vertical dotted line in the drawing (see Plate III) near the front edge of the stage probably indicates that it was curved.[51] This curvature is seen in the *Ariane* frontispiece. That the front of the stage (or perhaps a partition between the front of the stage and the first row of benches) is decorated with various musical emblems might suggest the presence of musicians behind. Considering the placement of the band for the operatic version of *The Tempest*, the orchestra for this French opera might have been similarly situated.

The only music heard in many comedies and tragedies were the act tunes, and these were probably indifferently played on occasion by a handful of bored fiddlers tucked away in some inconspicuous location, such as a cramped side box, left vacant because of the small crowds that attended the theatre when a poor, simple play rather than a spectacular musical show was the bill of fare. The Restoration theatre had to serve as both opera house and playhouse. The musical requirements of any two productions varied considerably, and the musicians were constantly shifted from one location to another, depending on how important a musical and dramatic role they were to play.[52] Towards the end of the 17th century when the audience's demand for music and dance strained the balance between music and drama, the instrumentalists often played directly under the audience's noses; the actor-singers and their accompanists strutted on the thrust stage, and the music room, the modest hideaway of the musicians of an earlier age, became the lover's balcony, only occasionally occupied by a serenading band.

Plate I

The "Moorish Dance" in II.ii of Settle's *The Empress of Morocco* (1673)

Plate II

The masque in IV.ii of Settle's *The Empress of Morocco* (1673)

Plate III

Christopher Wren's plan for a Restoration playhouse. All Souls College,
Oxford, Wren Drawing II.81

By permission of the Warden and Fellows of All Souls College, Oxford

Plate IV

The frontispiece to Louis Grabu and Pierre Perrin's *Ariane, ou le Mariage de Bacchus* (1673)

CHAPTER FOUR

THE ABUSE OF MUSIC IN RESTORATION DRAMA

> I grant the Abuse of a Thing is no Argument against the use of it.
> However Young people particularly, should not entertain themselves
> with a Lewd Picture; especially when 'tis drawn by a Masterly Hand.
>
> Jeremy Collier, *A Short View of
> the Immorality and Profaneness
> of the English Stage* (1698), p. 5

In 1700 the London theatrical world was in crisis. The quality of
plays had slowly deteriorated during the 40 years of restored Stuart rule,
and some critics, particularly the unwittingly witty clergyman quoted
above, saw an alarming decline in the last decade of the 17th century.
The two theatre companies were locked in bitter competition for the
small audience, and poets and actors complained loudly of the music-hall
entertainments--from ventriloquists to tumblers--that the managers
increasingly relied on to fill the playhouses. Music and dance, as much
as anything else, were at the center of the crisis.

Vanbrugh, one of the better playwrights of the time, must have
been loath to report to Lord Manchester on 25 December 1699 that

> Miss Evans the dancer at the New Playhouse is dead. . . . She's
> much lamented by the Towne as well as the House, who can't well
> bare her loss; Matters running very low with 'em this Winter, if
> Congreve's Play don't help 'em they are undone.[1]

The new play was *The Way of the World* (1700), not much of a success
for the struggling Lincoln's Inn Fields Theatre.[2] Congreve's disgust for
his audience was so intense that he never wrote another. That the loss of
a little-known dancer could bring to its knees a company fortunate
enough to première Congreve's masterpiece is strong testimony of the
importance of music and dance to this fragile theatrical system. Twenty
years earlier, Tate was more explicit:

> Our loudest Critiques are generally Pleas'd or Displeas'd with What
> is least Material in a Play, or perhaps not so much as a Part of it;
> for sometimes Five good Acts have not been able to make amends
> for One ill Dance.[3]

Tate's remarks are somewhat blunted by the fact that late in life he
turned to writing the kind of plays (and libretti) into which a maximum
amount of music and dance could be poured.

    Both Restoration poets and critics (often the same) were aware that the enormous emphasis on music in the plays of the time was a significant departure from the Elizabethan and Jacobean traditions: the plays of their predecessors certainly used music, but never had it so inundated drama. A manuscript prologue for a late 17th-century production of Ben Jonson's *Volpone* [1676], the revival of which probably made the anonymous writer of this introductory address acutely aware of differences between the plays of his generation and those of the previous age, states:

> Did Ben now live, how would he fret, and rage,
> To see the Musick-room envye the stage?
> To see the French Haut-boyes charm the listening Pitt
> More than the Raptures of his God-like wit!"[4]

The idea that music (which its strongest critics would on occasion admit was valuable at least for diversion) was mainly a threat to a poet's wit is frequently expressed by Restoration observers.

    Although musicians and dancers (especially foreign ones) were severely criticized, the dramatic potential of music was always respected, even though the critics were never quite willing to admit that music's power was legitimate. Thomas Rymer, that persistent champion of the plays of an earlier age, freely acknowledges the considerable effect that dramatic frills may have on an audience; he also insists that a distinction must be made "between what pleases naturally in it self, and what pleases upon the account of Machines, Actors, Dances and circumstances which are meerly accidental to the Tragedy."[5] Even the most effective critic of the excesses of the Restoration play, Jeremy Collier, admits that "Show, Music, Action, and Rhetoric are moving Entertainments; and, rightly employ'd, would be very significant." So moving does Collier consider them that when in the enemies' hands, that is, when commanded by "a very dangerous Management," they are "Like Cannon seized . . . pointed the wrong way. . . ."[6]

    Colley Cibber, an important actor and playwright despite formidable criticism from literary luminaries of his time, is most objective and subtle in his assessment of music in plays--a remarkable fact when one considers that he was significantly responsible for ridding the play of its more ludicrous and wasteful musical practices. At one point in his *Apology* he compares the control and modulation of the stage voice of his mentor and idol, Thomas Betterton, with "the sweeter Notes of Vocal Musick" and remarks that as a fine actor may waste his skills on a bad play, so "the finest Musick, purchas'd at such vast Expence, is so often thrown away upon the most miserable Poetry. . . ." But he sees a further danger in music, one that he knew all too well could charm an audience away from plot and player: ". . . when the Movement of the Air, and Tone of the Voice, are exquisitely harmonious, tho' we regard not one *Word* of what we hear, yet the Power of the Melody is so busy in the Heart, that we naturally annex Ideas to it of our own Creation, and, in some sort, become our selves the Poet to the Composer. . . ."[7] Cibber has hit upon perhaps the most devastating criticism of the way in which the late 17th-century London theatre companies abused the powers of music: they introduced music not to make the skin creep as a tragic end approached nor to let the audience see clearly a lover's madness; they employed song and dance--yes, even Purcell's and Priest's best efforts-- simply to please and divert.

Early Complaints Against Musical Excess

The attacks by Collier and others on "extraneous" music in Restoration plays are well known to students of the drama. Because these critics principally condemn practices evident in the works of their contemporaries, the misconception has arisen that the abuse of music is limited to those turn-of-the-century works which were grotesquely distended by whatever type of musical entertainment the audience desired. But para-dramatic music and dance had since the earliest years of the period been vigorously attacked. The writers most critical of the early dominance of music and dance are the poets themselves, caught between what was on occasion an idealistic desire to make their plays dramatically sound and at the same time the necessity of making their works palatable to the music-demanding audience. Playwrights commonly went on record (in prologue and preface) as deploring excessive music inserted into their plays. Typical of such disclaimers is the prologue to Shadwell's *The Royal Shepherdess* (1669), which reeks of satirical disdain:

> We've stuff'd in Dances, and we have Songs too
> As senceless, as were ever sung to you.
> If all these things will not support our Play,
> Then Gallants you may damn it, yes you may;
> But if You do, you'l suffer such a Curse--
> Our Poet swears he'll write one Ten times worse.

But if a poet makes bold to joust with the gallants of the pit (albeit through his mouthpiece, the prologue) in the more serious preface or dedication, usually addressed to those people of quality who leaped at the chance to sponsor a notorious play (hoping that some of the notoriety might rub off on them), he is often compelled to rationalize his music on firmer historical grounds. Shadwell's tone in his message "To the Reader" in the same play is discernibly subdued:

I have endeavour'd to carry on those few Humors, which were but
begun by him;[8] and (to satisfie the Concupiscence as Mr. Johnson
call's it, of Jigge and Song)[9] I designed as fit occasions for them as I
could, there being in the former Play but one short Song which is
the last but one.

French Vogues

If poets frequently use historical precedence to thwart criticism,
they rarely blame their theatrical predecessors for the practice of stuffing
music into plays. From the restoration of the stage until well into the
next century, the blame was placed on insidious foreign incursions, early
in the period, almost exclusively those which Charles had brought from
France. In the prologue to *The Morning Ramble, or, the Town Humours*
(1673), Henry Nevil Payne expresses disbelief at how easily he wrote this
successful comedy, after laboring so painfully on his first dramatic
offering, a tragedy. He then adds the barb:

> . . . but truly there might be
> As good a Play spoke Ex tempore.
> For Whip and Spur, 'tis A-la-mode de France;
> A thing made up of Fiddle, Song, and Dance.
> All three your dear Delights, no matter then
> Whether of sence there be one line in ten. . . .

Five years later, the author of the prologue to *Tunbridge-Wells: or, A
Day's Courtship* (1678) is more specific about where the trouble with
English drama lies and is quick to exonerate his scribbling predecessors,
but with little regard for historical accuracy:

> Th'Old English Stage, confin'd to Plot and Sense,
> Did hold abroad but small intelligence [i.e., was little known],
> But since th'invasion of the forreign Scene,
> Jack pudding Farce, and thundering Machine,
> Dainties to your grave Ancestours unknown.
> (Who never disliked wit because their own)
> There's not a Player but is turned a scout,
> And every Scribler sends his Envoys out
> To fetch from Paris, Venice, or from Rome,
> Fantastick fopperies to please at home.[10]

Etherege, writing at about the same time, launches a more effective
attack by making his critics laugh rather than rail. He is resigned to
accommodating French vogues in his plays:

> But I'm afraid that while to France we go,
> To bring you home fine Dresses, Dance, and Show,
> The Stage like you will but more Foppish grow.

Of Foreign Wares why shou'd we fetch the scum,
When we can be so richly served at Home?[11]

Music vs. Wit

For the critics to ridicule what they considered to be the source of musical excess in plays was no challenge; everyone at court and theatre unabashedly strove to be *à la mode de France*. But they were genuinely concerned about the effect that French vogues were having on English drama. Although entries and masques were already making light entertainment of some tragedies and songs and dances were delightfully though interminably postponing dreadful deeds, music for the early Restoration critic was chiefly the enemy of wit. Elkanah Settle, whose dramatic muse would scarcely have held the stage at all if not for music's assistance, considers what a play would need for success if it suddenly found itself without its musical clothes:

Plays without Scene, Machin, or Dance, to hit,
Must make up the defect of shew, with Wit.
As sometimes course Girle takes in homely Gown
Whose Beauty, though 'tis little, is her own,
Before a gaudy Flutterer of the Town.
So 'tis with Plays; and though a Gaudy sight,
Song, Dance, and Shew, more briskly, move delight;
And there th'advantage get o're plain drest sense;
Yet Wit and Object have this difference. . . .[12]

In fact, the fear that music might consume wit is practically the only thing that could dissuade a poet from the usual practice of including as much song and dance as his play could bear. In *The Woman turn'd Bully* (1675), the anonymous author recognizes the onslaught against wit and promises that his play will have "hardly a Song or Dance, / Scene, nor Machine, its Credit to advance. . . ." But this must have been delivered for its shock value, for considerable amounts of music did manage to creep into this play, doubtless to the relief of the audience.

The idea that comic dances could replace wit in plays is often sarcastically expressed. The prologue to Rawlins's *Tunbridge-Wells* (1678) remarks

. . . that each act may rise to your desire,
Devils and Witches must each Scene inspire,
Wit rowls in Waves, and showers down in Fire.
With what strange Ease a Play may now be Writ,
When the best half's composed by painting it?
And that in th'Ayr, or Dance lyes all the Wit?

Tone in Restoration plays is often difficult for modern readers to discern, but one may assume that the following passage is not entirely tinged with satire. In John Caryll's *Sir Salomon: or, The Cautious Coxcomb* (1671), near the end of Act III, a dance has just been "rehearsed" for Timothy's benefit; he makes a general comment ⌐n music and wit:

> Bravely performed! This will do: And let me tell you, There is more wit in this dance than in a dozen of your best modern plays: They with the gingle of Rhime and playing with words, go just like the chimes of St. Bart'elmy: and please the ladies eares, but effect not the understanding at all.

If the reader is surprised that Timothy finds more wit in his dance than in a play and then uses a musical allusion to condemn "the gingle of Rhime and playing with words," he has not suffered through a play in heroic rhymed couplets by a lesser poet of the period.

John Dryden is not a lesser poet, and therefore 17th-century writers do not criticize the jingle of rhyme in his heroic tragedies. (This has not been the case with more recent criticism, however.) Joseph Arrowsmith is surely having fun at Dryden's expense in his comedy *The Reformation* (1673), IV.i. Tutor is foolishly describing in detail how he writes a heroic play. Musical nuances he considers most important: "What grace a drum and trumpet give a play. . . ." And to ensure absolutely that a play will succeed, "Last of all raise a dancing singing ghost."[13] Arrowsmith's satire is an early example of a Restoration critic broadening his attack to condemn even the most dramatic musical practices, perhaps after these practices had degenerated into clichés. Dryden's defense of including music in heroic plays, particularly in battle scenes, is vigorous and well founded on the practices of his predecessors:

> . . . To those who object [to] my frequent use of Drums and Trumpets; and my representations of Battels, I answer, I introduc'd them not on the English Stage, Shakespear us'd them frequently: and tho' Jonson shows no Battel in his Catiline, yet you hear from behind the Scenes the sounding of Trumpets, and the shouts of fighting Armies. But, I add farther; that these war-like Instruments, and, even the representations of fighting on the Stage, are no more than necessary to produce the effects of an Heroick Play. . . .[14]

But in practice, Dryden, like other successful fellow playwrights, wrote plays, particularly comedies, that included music which was less than necessary for any dramatic effect but "no more than necessary" for popular success.

Rationalizing Musical Excess

Music introduced into plays purely because the latest vogue demanded it is sometimes difficult to detect; the more skillful poets and directors did their best to employ any music dramatically, designing their plays so that if, for example, a currently popular dancer were to appear, his performance would not overbalance the rest of the play. Instead of performing in an entry specifically prepared for him, a dancer might appear instead as the main character in a masque, perhaps in place of the actor-protagonist. Unfortunately, skillful poets and directors were not plentiful in the Restoration, and as a result, para-dramatic music and its executants were often clumsily accommodated by the plays.

Dramatic verisimilitude rarely seems to have been important to the audience in their pursuit of fine music and dance, no matter how shabbily these delights were prepared by the dramatic situation. Malagene and Saunter are not being entirely facetious in the following conversation with Lady Squeamish and Caper in I.i of Otway's comedy *Friendship in Fashion* (1678). Caper has just asked Lady Squeamish if she will attend the new play in the afternoon:

> *Lady Squeamish.* No, I saw it the first day, and don't like it. . . .
> *Saunter.* Does your Ladiship know who writ it?
> *L. Sq.* Yes, the Poet came and read it to me at my Lodgings: He
>   is but a young man, and I suppose he has not been a Writer
>   long: besides, he has had little or no conversation with the
>   Court, which has been the reason he has committed a great
>   many Indecorums in the conduct of it.
> *Saunt.* I did not like it neither for my part, there was never a Song
>   in it, ha?
> *Caper.* No, nor so much as a Dance.
> *Malagene.* Oh, it's impossible it should take if there were neither
>   Song nor Dance in it.

The play in question is a tragedy. David Crauford, realizing that his comedy *Love at First Sight* [1704] may lack humor, has his prologue put the audience at ease by announcing that he has taken precautions:

> Tho' Subsidies of Wit he [Crauford] can't advance
> He'as larded his supply, with Song and Dance,
> Two things of late that with a gust go down,
> And catch the whole surprize of all the Town. . . .

The most difficult task that Crauford and his fellow second-rate dramatists faced was to fashion a pathetic patchwork to hold together unrelated musical episodes. One finds countless attempts in late plays to rationalize independent songs (those not a part of a larger entry or masque) that are neither organic to the plot nor atmospheric to the dramatic situation. These diverting, entertaining songs, instead of merely being requested of an attendant or some lesser character (the usual practice in earlier plays) are said to have been composed for some special occasion, usually by the character requesting them, or to illustrate a point someone is trying to make, or for any number of reasons which considering their incidental nature would seem better left unsaid.

In Will Pinkethman's comedy *Love without Interest: or, The Man too hard for the Master* (1699), V.i, Trulove, after announcing that he is leaving for supper, says:

> Mean time, if you please, I'll entertain you with a Song I lately compos'd, which is both instructive and suitable to this present occasion.

Two musicians enter and sing the song,[15] which is only remotely related to the "present occasion." In Mary Pix's *The Beau Defeated: Or, The Lucky Younger Brother* [1700], II.ii, Sir John Roverhead declares that he has written "a Stanza, to shew how awkwardly an old Woman makes advances," a point which in light of the rest of the play certainly requires no musical elaboration here.[16] In *The Mock-Marriage* (1696), II.ii, by Thomas Scott, the action is delayed as Lady Barter says, "let us first have Mr. Willmot's judgment of the Song I was so pleas'd with last night." But Willmot, expressing a feeling probably held by many a cynic in the pit, attempts to excuse himself from yet another song: "Madam, I know 'tis excellent." But my lady is quick to counter, "What, before you have heard it?" Once promised, rarely is a song not delivered, and Lady Barter obliges.[17]

On occasion a more skillful poet is able to avoid the awkward introduction of music which characterizes the preceding examples, even though the song he must accommodate is just as incidental. In his farce *Cuckolds-Haven: or, an Alderman No Conjurer* (1685), I.iii, Tate provides his audience with spectacle to accompany song, as Girtred commands a page to perform "the French Song, it will help off this fatigue of Dressing." The two events, Girtred's dressing and the French song, neither of which by itself would be of much interest, were probably made to complement each other humorously, if nothing else.

A song is often introduced for no other reason than to allow the gathered courtiers to hear the latest tune from the court which was the envy of all Europe. The following dialogue is from Rawlins's *Tom Essence: or, The Modish Wife* (1677), IV.i, and even though the words of the song are not related to the situation, the tune to which they are sung certainly tells us much of their author:

[Betty Feels in her Pocket, pulls out a Song.]

Betty. My Master Sir, has sent me to know how Madam Theo. does this morning, and presents her with the effects of his Love, in a Song which he writ last Night before he went to Bed.

Old Monylove. Hum, pretty Childish silly stuff;--can you sing it Little one?

Betty. Yes Sir, my Master made it to one of the new Tunes he heard in an Opera at Paris.[18]

Even the great playwrights of the period had to satisfy the audience's voguish whims, and although they usually accommodate their songs more skillfully than do the less successful poets, some of their songish scenes are forced. Even Congreve is not immune, as one may see from *Love for Love* (1695), III.iii:

> *Scandal.* Come I'll recommend a Song to you upon the hint of my two proverbs and I see one in the next room who will sing it.
>
> .   .   .   .
>
> Pray sing the first song in the last new play.[19]

Although the lyric (sung by an attendant) is not found in any other play-book, Congreve's message is clear: songs from the native drama could become as stylish as those of the Paris *opéra*.

Genteel Assistance

We can too quickly condemn a playwright for bowing to current vogue: often the pressure was internal. The gentry did not perform in the Restoration play, as they had done in the Jacobean masque; nevertheless, they insisted on participating. If a nobleman lacked the perseverance to write a complete play, he could make a conspicuous contribution by writing the words for a song. This vain and insidious practice was known from the first years of the period[20] but became prevalent late in the century. From about 1685 play-books regularly include some dramatically inappropriate song before which the author's noble name often appears in large typeface.[21] Sadly indicative of the poor quality of some plays is the fact that playwrights did not openly object to this practice; they probably felt their foppish patrons were meddling with an aspect of the play in which they could do the least harm. Nevertheless, Thomas Baker cannot resist a jibe at the would-be poets of an exclusive club in his comedy *Hampstead-Heath* (1706), I.i; Lampoon, who was played by the master mimic of foppery, Cibber, lets his foolish pride get the better of him:

> A Kick! I'm one o'the Kit-cat Club, and a sort of Poet, that is, I pay Poets that write for me, and there's ne'er a Wit among us, but

> will stand a Kick at any time rather than lose a Jest; and to give
> you Proof of my Courage, I'll present you with a Song that's a
> general Satyr upon all the Rakes, Fops, and Coxcombs in the
> Kingdom.[22]

Para-dramatic songs, of course, are not the only form of musical entertainment that shake the dramatic credibility of Restoration plays, though perhaps they are the most notorious. That dances, for instance, have been added to a play at the last minute is apparent from the more feeble attempts to justify their inclusion in certain plays. In *The She-Gallants* (1696), III.i, by George Granville (later the Lord Lansdowne), one finds a variation of the stock serenade beneath a mistress's window. Angelica announces to her mistress, Lucinda, that some dancers are below to perform a dance composed by a friend. Philabel remarks that

> 'Tis fit, Madam that some new Ways should be invented to engage
> the Ladies; 'tis dull to tread always in the same path. And nothing
> is found so prevailing as these mute accomplishments. Writing and
> saying fine things have given place to Caper, the Flute and the
> Voice.

Despite the mollifying pun, one is struck by the curious necessity of explaining and justifying why the author has chosen not "to tread always in the same path."

Three-Act Play with Masque

Several plays of the period have didactic dialogues in which the author attempts to rationalize what he obviously realizes is a less than integral use of music. One of the most delightful (as well as genuinely instructive) is the prelude to Edward Ravenscroft's *The Italian Husband* (1698), an unusual tragedy in several respects. Critic, Poet, and Peregrine are discussing why the play has only three acts, a form unheard of in England:

> *Poet.* I'll tell you: A Play is not call'd a Farce from any number
>   of Acts, but from the lowness of the Subject and Characters;
>   which are not true characters in Nature, nor just representations
>   of humane actions (as Comedy is or should be) but from the
>   oddness and extravagancy of the Characters and Subject:
>   Which, tho not natural, yet not always against Nature; and tho
>   not true, yet diverting, and foolishly delightful. A Farce is like
>   a Dutch piece of Painting, or a Grotesque Figure, extravagant
>   and   pleasant.
> *Peregrine.* In my judgment it is so.
> *Critic.* Well, we'll pass over that point. But why do you make a
>   Tragedy but three Acts?

Peregrine. O, that's customary in other Countries.

Poet. I have observ'd that many Plays of late are all talk and no business; others have some business, but so much talk, that the business is almost lost in the multiplicity of words, and the Plays lag and grow tedious. Therefore, to avoid this, I have now laid the business so close, that every Scene may seem necessary to carry on the design and story of the Play, and with as few words as I cou'd suppose sufficient; therefore I confine my self to three Acts, which gives me also opportunity to introduce some Musical Entertainments, and those seeming natural to the Play; which few Poets have yet observ'd.

At last the real reason why he has written only three acts emerges from his lecture: an entry of a masque (*Ixion,* by William Taverner) is to follow each of the three acts of the tragedy, which on closer examination is revealed to be simply a paltry skeleton on which to hang music. Just before the curtain rises, however, Critic has a last sceptical word: "I confess [the playwrights] bring in their Musick by head and shoulders, and [it] may serve in one Play as well as another. . . ."

If one excludes the dramatic opera, the late Restoration three-act play (not the farce) is the result of a 50-year trend in which music gained more and more on drama, and though music never managed to exist without the play, the parasite came very close to consuming its host. But this special kind of play--truncated in such a way as to prevent the spoken part from intruding on the musical part--was perhaps the most satisfactory (though short-lived) solution to the problem of excessive music in the five-act play. The three-act play with masque makes little pretense of being serious drama (as even the most ludicrous of the dramatic operas usually do) but attempts to provide simply a dramaturgical context (something English audiences and playwrights could not do without until Italian opera showed them the way) for an extended musical entertainment, which often has no plot, no theme, and usually no continuity whatsoever.[23] The full-length plays of the period, which tried to provide both dramatic and para-dramatic music, were in a more precarious position. On the whole these five-act productions did far more to bring about reform than did the three-act hybrid form. The authors of the traditional type sensed the dilemma and made the necessary apologies.

In the comedy *Imposture Defeated: or, A Trick to Cheat the Devil* (1698), written the same year as Ravenscroft's *The Italian Husband,* actor-playwright George Powell tells the reader that

this triffle of a Comedy, was only a slight piece of Scribble, purely design'd for the Introduction of a little Musick,[24] being no more than a short weeks work, to serve the wants of a thin Playhouse, and Long Vacation. . . .

This full-length play is as heavy with music as any three-act play with masque; Powell himself bravely spoke the prologue:

> To this poor Treat, these Honour'd Guests t'invite,
> I come my own Embassador to Night,
> To tell the truth, your Bill of fare is small,
> It is a little Humble Comedy, that's all:
> For standard Sense, mine is too course Allay,
> Alas, that Talent does not lie my way:
> But though this Play in Wit be not so strong,
> 'Thas that will do as well, it trouls along,
> With a whole train of Fiddles, Dance and Song. . . .

Theatre managers found that the bolder members of their troupes could produce plays (in which wit was apparently no longer necessary) as effectively as the more established playwrights.[25]   Nevertheless, some legitimate playwrights thrived on providing dramaturgical skeletons for music for the late 17th-century London playhouses. Thomas Durfey was surely the most contented of them.

Durfey and Shadwell Make the Best of a Bad Situation

Durfey never complains about having to provide settings for music and dance in his plays, only that bad performances might spoil his work:

> The Songish part which I used to succeed so well in, by the indifferent performance the first day, and the hurrying it on so soon, being streightned in time through ill managment--(tho extreamly well set to Musick, and I'm sure the just Critick will say not ill Writ) yet being imperfectly performed, was consequently not pleasing; and the Dances too, for want of some good Performers, also [were] disliked. . . .[26]

While Durfey rarely admits the failure of a play for any reason other than deficiency in the performance of the music, neither does he claim success for any reason other than musical.   Indeed, in the dedication to his comedy *The Richmond Heiress: or, A Woman Once in the Right* (1693), he speaks of the music and dancing as if they were his own:

> The entertainment of Songs and Dances in it, as they gave more diversion than is usually seen in Comedy's, so they were perform'd with general Applause, and I think my Enemies have cause to say with greater than is ordinary; and though this had its Inconvenience by lengthening the whole Piece a little beyond the common time of Action, which at this time o'th'Year [April] I am sensible is a very great Fault . . .

Even a critic could pay him a compliment on his songs; except in the context of the Restoration, the following might be interpreted as anything but complimentary:

> But if you cou'd meet with generous [i.e., many?] Enemies, they would forgive those Errors their quick sight might discover, for the Beauties and delightful Entertainment of the Lyric part, the Songs I mean, in which I think there is none will (I am sure none ought to) dispute your Title to the Preheminence.[27]

Durfey was well aware of his limitations as a dramatist, but he knew that he could provide what his audience desired. After all, even if the success of a play was owing largely to the music which it carried, the playwright was still entitled to his "third and sixth days."[28]

As stressed earlier in this chapter, the abuse of music is not limited to late Restoration plays. Granted, the problem is acute in some of these monstrosities of music and drama, but an over-reliance on music to help ensure a play's success is a characteristic of stage works written during the entire era. Shadwell, whose long career spans practically the whole period, derived much of his success from plays and entertainments in which music is often dubiously employed.

Like Durfey, Shadwell is never reticent to acknowledge a musician's help in making a play successful.[29] He even goes so far as to condemn those authors who are reluctant to credit their musical allies. In the preface to *The Sullen Lovers: Or, the Impertinents* (1668), he thwarts criticism by freely admitting that singers and dancers may very well help a play, but he adds parenthetically with sophomoric wisdom that to accommodate them dramatically is not an easy task. Foppish critics, he writes,

> will huff, and look big upon the success of an ill Play stuff'd full of Songs and Dances, (which have that constraint upon 'em too, that they seldome seem to come in willingly;) when in such Playes the Composer and the Danceing-Master are the best Poets, and yet the unmerciful Scribler would rob them of all the Honour. . . .

In the prologue he expresses the anxiety that the audience will not like his play, for "He has no cautionary song, nor Dance, / That might the Treaty of his Peace advance. . . ." In his subsequent plays Shadwell is not so sparing with music.

In his comedies published between 1685 and 1690, such as *Bury-Fair* (1689) and *The Amorous Bigotte: with the Second Part of Tegue O Divelly* (1690), music often has a dramatic, even a dynamic role. Fiddles "play scurvily" as rambling, drunken knights smash windows; lyrics are introduced to exhibit the coarseness or foolishness of some boorish character. Except for an occasional serious song, often in a ludicrous context, or an entry dance, usually disintegrating into pandemonium, music is used for comic purposes, we could almost say for sound effects, rather than as a diverting interlude, a brief respite from the bawdy, fast-moving action. "A Lewd Picture," Collier might mutter, but drawn partly by the masterly hands of Henry Purcell[30] and Will Mountfort.[31] The "show" of these plays is strictly comedy, and music certainly serves rather than relieves the heavy-handed wit; but unlike the plays of most of his contemporaries in which song and dance vie with spoken dialogue for prominence, Shadwell's works place music in the lowest subservient position. No one can accuse him of not providing the songs and dances in his plays with viable dramatic situations, but this he achieves at the complete expense of the music.

Blank Songs

In Shadwell's late plays one notices a tendency to omit the text of a song from the play-book.[32] "Musick A Song" and "A Song here" are typical stage directions in these works and in dozens of those by his contemporaries. Nor is this practice confined to songs: "A consort of Instrumental Musick" and "Here follows an Entertainment of Musick and Dancing" are common stage directions for otherwise unspecified music. Even though these musical episodes are often accommodated by the dramatic situation, the fact that the poet had no particular music in mind suggests that it mattered little what was heard. One recalls Critic's disgruntled remark in the prelude to Ravenscroft's *The Italian Husband* (1698) that playwrights are rather indiscriminate in their choice of music and that it "may serve in one Play as well as another." To understand how such a situation endured so long without reform, one must appreciate that the late 17th-century London playhouse was as much a concert hall as it was an establishment for the presentation of spoken drama.

Playhouse and Concert Hall

By the turn of the century, public concerts had become very popular in London. John Banister, who composed music for plays of the 1660s and 70s, also held some of the first concert meetings. During the last decade of the century the gatherings at York Buildings offered enlightened entertainment.[33] But before the concert (or, more specifically, those gatherings which could be relied upon to provide the best music played and sung by the best performers) became a regular occurrence, Londoners went mainly to the playhouse to hear professionally performed music. The greatest composers of the period

were principally theatre composers, even if also members of the elite
Royal Musick, because the playhouses provided the most lucrative
market for their wares.   Similarly, the best performers, both
instrumentalists and singers, were more or less permanently attached to
the theatres. The audience expected the music to be as fresh and as
ever-changing as the plays in which it appeared. This the playhouse
accomplished for many years; the unavoidable result was that the plays
could not creatively accommodate the large quantities of new music
constantly demanded by the audience: hence the necessity of including
music para-dramatically rather than organically. But when the concert
attained sufficient sophistication and popularity to alleviate some of the
musical burden hitherto borne by the playhouse, music had become so
fixed a tradition of the stage that competition between the theatres and
the concert rooms rather than cooperation ensued.

Many plays produced in the last decade of the old century and
the first years of the new one reflect this competition; allusions to
concert meetings are frequent, and occasionally one encounters elaborate
scenes simulating a concert-room atmosphere. The best known is I[ii] of
Southerne's comedy *The Wives Excuse: or, Cuckolds make themselves*
(1692), which takes place at a music meeting. A short concert (of both
vocal and instrumental music) is presented to the gathered audiences, one
on the stage and the other in the pit and boxes. In Southerne's next
comedy, *The Maids Last Prayer: or, Any, rather than Fail* (1693), IV.ii,
there is also a scene depicting a music meeting, with the noble host, Sir
Symphony, ridiculously participating on "a Base-Viol." Mercifully, his
bow has been drawn through a candle by a bully. If this scene in any
way reflects real life, then the concert, like the play, doubtless suffered
from genteel assistance.

Motteux mentions similar aristocratic participation in an allusion
to one of the more fashionable music rooms. Christina, in *Love's a Jest*
(1696), I.i, describes what kind of a person may safely be considered a
beau, and to illustrate her description, she lists the mandatory places
where a beau must be seen in order to impress a lady of quality:

> . . . how fine 'tis to see one of you follow some foolish Celia like
> her Shadow, and even to St. Jame's or St. Ann's, for a single look
> cross a Pew; pelt her with Billets Doux commonly stol'n,
> Nonsensical, or Romantic, write dull Madrigals on her, and get 'em
> sung to duller Tunes at your weekly interviews in York-buildings. . . .[34]

In Cibber's *Love's Last Shift*, II.i, Young Worthy is desperately trying to
convince Narcissa of his love; he says it should be apparent to all,
because "the last song I made of you has been sung at the Musick-
meeting and you may imagine Madam, I took no little care to let the

Ladies and Beaux know who 'twas made on." The concert had apparently become as fashionable a place for vain participation as the theatre and, inevitably, similarly abused.

The allusion to public concerts was soon recognized as another way to rationalize extraneous music in plays, a doubly effective device to prepare the introduction of music totally unrelated to any dramatic situation and to provide the audience with what they might otherwise be missing by electing to spend the afternoon in Drury Lane rather than at York Buildings. This technique is expertly employed in Baker's *Tunbridge-Walks*, II.i, with a reference to the well known music meetings of Thomas Britton, the coal dealer and book collector who transformed his modest dwelling in Clerkenwell into a fashionably bizarre music room, faithfully attended each week for over 40 years by the best musicians and most splendid gentry.[35] In this scene the assembled women of quality are presented with a song, and a further bit of realism is added when coffee is served, as the humble Mrs. Britton is said to have done for her guests:

> *Mr. Maiden.* Ladies, I have brought a fine Singer, came down [from London] last night to Entertain you with a Composure; one that's mightily admir'd at the Small-Coal Musick Meeting.

This is surely one of the least objectionable techniques (even if it falls short of being dramatically constructive) of introducing music which has little connection with the dramatic situation; it is frequently employed, if not always with such an elaborate rationale, at least in such a way that it is clear from the play that the music to be heard is new and popular and therefore will please both its play-bound auditors and those observing from a somewhat greater distance. This practice is surely responsible for the tendency apparent late in the period to omit song-texts in the play-books and not to specify what music in general is to be used in certain situations. Indeed, the songs and instrumental pieces were probably changed from time to time; as one did not expect to hear the same music each day at a concert, similarly, if one attended the same play on successive nights, one probably expected to hear different music. The mobility of music in plays is alluded to in Durfey's remarkable dedication to *The Banditti.* He reports that the première got off to a bad start, and then subsequent scenes "were all promiscuously decry'd both good and bad, the Songs and Musick hoop'd and whistl'd at, tho' they have been Sung in several other Plays with generall Applause, which I think sufficiently discovers the ungenerous Malice, and poor partiallity that was us'd. . . ."[36] The extraordinary belief that if a song works well in one context therefore it should work equally well in another, indicates either Durfey's monumental naiveté or, more likely, a dramatic aesthetic

largely unrecognized in Restoration plays.   But is this not the very
foundation of the modern variety show and the poorer though not
necessarily less successful musical comedies?   In other words, the quality
of many of the songs used in late Restoration plays, like that of their
modern counterparts, is so trifling as to have little effect on a dramatic
situation which is equally as mundane.

Sonatas in Plays

The competition between the playhouse and the concert hall,
though lively and at times intense, never really threatened to weaken
music's hold on the play.   If reform gradually dissuaded playwrights and
theatre managers from filling the acts of their plays with quite so much
music as before, the entr'acte and afterpiece provided infinitely
expandable media through which the audience could glut itself with
music, leaving the play whole, if rather disjointed.   It is a mistake,
however, to assume from the surfeit of advertisements (beginning around
1700) for music presented with dramatic offerings, that all of this
extraneous music was incidental to the plays.[37]   At about this time
London (as well as much of the rest of western Europe) was in the grips
of an insatiable vogue for Italian instrumental music, principally the
works of Corelli.   At concerts and during the intervals of plays little else
was heard.[38]   It is not generally known, however, that this kind of music
is found within the acts of plays as well.

An advertisement in *The Daily Courant* 10 November 1703 for a
performance of *Aesop* (a revival of Vanbrugh's comedy of 1697) at the
Theatre Royal in Drury Lane announces that Visconti will perform
"some new Sonata's for the Violin lately brought from Rome, Compos'd
by the Great Arcangelo Corelli."[39]   The stage directions for *Aesop* do not
specifically call for a Corelli sonata to be played during any scene, and
Visconti probably performed between acts.   Nevertheless, this Italian
violinist might have been included in the play itself, ostensibly as a
member of the cast.

In Cibber's *Love's Last Shift*, III.ii, Flareit is expecting a group
of musicians, including "the hautboys," to drop in to play for him.   They
arrive and Sir Novelty says "Here Gentlemen, place yourself on this spot
and pray oblige me with a Trumpet Sonata."   A stage direction indicates
that "The Musick prepare to play and all sorts of people gather about
it."[40]   In Pinkethman's *Love without Interest* (1699), II.i, the action is
temporarily halted by "An Entertainment of Musick," which could easily
have accommodated the performance of a visiting musician, as "A
Sonato" is required.   Finally, in Durfey's *The Old Mode & the New, or,
Country Miss with her Furbeloe* [1703], II.ii, dinner is graced with
"Musick playing, a Sonnata; then a Song sung."

This was the state of many late Restoration plays: playwrights and theatre managers were unwilling to rid their works of excessive para-dramatic music, even though the emergence of the public concert afforded them an excellent opportunity to lighten the musical burden which had transformed some of their works into mockeries of dramatic representation. The tastes of the audience, whetted by the clear-sounding harmonies and driving rhythms of the new Italian music, must in part be blamed. The London courtiers had first experienced previous innovations in musical style--from the grandness of the Lullian overture to the expressive depths of a Purcellian song--in the pit, boxes, and gallery of the playhouse. One might expect, then, that if the musical practices of the stage were to be reformed, reform would not be imposed from without, from the concert halls and fashionable drawing rooms where the new Italian music first surfaced in London, but from within the playhouses themselves, where on ever increasing occasions the players removed themselves to allow an elite group of singers to hold the stage with recitative and arias in Italian, without the aid of a shoddily prepared dramatic framework of spoken English dialogue.

Italian opera and its various constituents, introduced piecemeal into British drama long before a complete opera was staged in London, allowed playwrights and managers to restore dramatic credibility to their plays by providing the audience with a fresh and more attractive setting in which to enjoy theatre music. The reform of the play facilitated by the foreign opera was sweeping, and even dramatic music, composed by the greatest masters of the era and creatively employed by the greatest poets and players, largely disappeared from the play. But that is the story of the final chapter of this study. Londoners did not stop going to plays, nor did playwrights cease to use music dramatically in the 18th century; neither tradition has been broken since 1660. But playgoers no longer attended the theatre to hear the finest art music used to enhance spoken drama.

CHAPTER FIVE

ITALIANATE OPERA AND THE REFORM OF THE PLAY

In the last decade of the 17th century the balance between music and drama on the London stage was disrupted. The play had not been so seriously threatened since the playhouses were closed and the theatre companies dissolved during the Puritan rule. From the beginning of the Restoration period, the spoken play had been the receptacle into which songs, dances, and masques were poured. By 1700, playwrights rarely took pains to incorporate these musical elements organically into their plays, and the longer musical scenes in particular could easily be detached from the dramas without doing any damage to their plots. The results were an entertainment which existed on two levels--spoken dialogue and episodes of music and dancing--and a theatrical organization deeply divided into actors and musicians. The infusion of Italian opera into this structure, at first seen by the actors as catastrophic to their interests, paradoxically restored them to their former prominence and saved British drama from further destruction. With the onslaught of the foreign opera, the play no longer had to supply both spoken and music drama. Thespians returned to providing relatively unadorned plays, while the audience's desire for stage music was sufficiently supplied by the new opera. The main victims of this change in theatrical structure were the English dramatic opera and the native composers who contributed the masques for these lavish productions.

The threat to English plays by the foreign musician was greatest during the years around 1700, before Italian opera appeared in London. Playwrights were frustrated in their attempts to produce dramas in the uninterrupted tradition of Dryden and (so they believed) Shakespeare, and simultaneously to provide a forum for the expensive Italian singers and French dancers. These performers ensured packed houses, but the theatrical establishment was geared to produce plays, not operas and ballets. As a result, the best poets, such as Congreve, were pushed aside by inferior scribblers who, probably not too reluctantly, agreed to compromise their muse in favor of notoriety and purse. A few years before, Henry Purcell, perhaps the greatest operatic composer between Monteverdi and Mozart, had been confined to writing masques for dramatic operas and brief songs for ordinary plays. The amount of music heard in the playhouses increased significantly after his death, but instead of using it to enhance spoken dialogue, playwrights and theatre managers found it more efficient to confine music to intervals and afterpieces. The actors, whose names were still proudly displayed in a place of honor at the beginning of play-books, suffered. They portrayed characters who, after introducing shepherds and masquers into their play-bound milieu, shrank to the insignificance of the occupants of the pit and gallery. A letter written around 1706 by a Drury Lane actor to a friend in Nottingham understates the situation:

> Our stage is in a very indifferent condition. There has been a very fierce combat between the Haymarket and Drury Lane, and the two sisters, Music and Poetry, quarrel like two fishwives at Billingsgate. . . . Though Farquhar meets with success, and has the entire happiness of pleasing the upper gallery, Betterton and Wilks, Ben Jonson and the best of them, must give place to a bawling Italian woman, whose voice to me is less pleasing than merry-andrew's playing on the gridiron. 'The Mourning Bride,' 'Plain Dealer,' 'Volpone,' or 'Tamerlane,' will hardly fetch us a tolerable audience, unless we stuff the bills with long entertainments of dances, songs, scaramouched entries, and what not.[1]

The English actor-singers, such as Leveridge, Pate, and Bracegirdle, could sing incantations and mad songs in plays, and native as well as French dancers might advance plots in allegorical ballets; but foreign singers were singularly useless to the early 18th-century English theatre, except, of course, as entr'acte attractions. Their Italian arias may have been effective weapons in the battle for audiences; dramaturgically, however, the imported music was in the same category as tumblers and rope dancers.

I. THE ITALIAN INFILTRATION [2]

Considering the traditional resistance of the English audience to autonomous music drama, the seemingly easy victory of Italian opera in London in the first decade of the 18th century might appear difficult to explain. The first opera "after the Italian Manner" was performed in early 1705, but the London audience was well acquainted with all elements of the foreign opera, except secco recitative in Italian, by the early 1690s. Several castratti and prima donnas had already made expeditionary forays into the northern country. For example, Giovanni Francesco Grossi (known as Siface) was in England during the reign of James II.[3] Whether or not this famous singer performed on the stage is not known, but "Italian songs" are called for in plays from this period and even earlier.[4] In the 1690s the Italian invasion quickened and the visiting artists performed at public concerts. In early 1693 an "Italian Lady" is recorded as singing at the concerts in York Buildings; a contemporary account reveals that her passage to England was paid by another Italian immigrant, Giovanni Battista Draghi, who made certain that the young prima donna was heard by the future queen, Princess

Anne of Denmark, during whose reign Italian opera later flourished in London.[5] We have no record that "the Italian Lady" sang on the stage, but a few years later other imported singers certainly did, either before the curtain went up or between the acts of good English plays.[6] As shown in Chapter Four, Italian instrumental music, too, was extremely popular in London beginning in the late 1680s, and this new style, more than anything else, prepared the way for all things Italian in the first half of the next century. As if under a secret master plan, the foreign singers were soon joined by opera-wise instrumentalists and impresarios, many of whom could, when necessary, throw together an Italian pasticcio. In 1703, one season before such a pasticcio had its début in London, one of the foreign singers, Margarita de l'Epine, trying very hard to be Italian although her nationality has never been determined, sang at the playhouse an aria from Giovanni Bononcini's *Camilla*, which two years later would be the first enduring Italian opera performed on the London stage.[7] With these "critical masses" of foreign performers and quasi-composers, as well as an audience accustomed to hearing fragments of Italian music drama on their native stage, it is remarkable that an Italian opera was not mounted earlier than January 1705. The distinction of producing the first such opera in London (or perhaps the dubious achievement when one considers its quality) fell to Christopher Rich, the manager and chief shareholder of the Theatre Royal.

There were two playhouses in London at this time: the Theatre Royal in Drury Lane, which had formerly been Henry Purcell's house, and the recently completed Queen's Theatre in the Haymarket, the new home for the troupe of veteran actors who had seceded from Rich and the Theatre Royal in 1695.[8] The Drury Lane company carried a staff of fine singers and dancers and was equipped to perform lavish dramatic operas in the Purcellian tradition. Their manager, Rich, was widely recognized as an opportunistic businessman, who paid high salaries to the imported musicians while starving his actors, and who was willing to bring to the stage any fad, whether musical or not, to ensure packed houses. This theatre was an ideal greenhouse in which to grow an Italian opera in hostile climes. The Haymarket playhouse, on the other hand, had been designed and built by the gallant architect and playwright, Vanbrugh, and was managed by him and the greatest dramatist of the era, Congreve. They had hoped to make their new theatre and its troupe of distinguished actors vehicles for their own new plays, works which would return spoken drama to its former prominence.[9] But the enterprising Vanbrugh, whose diverse talents kept him in close contact with some of the most influential aristocrats of the era, would soon compromise his devotion to his native drama and follow the vogue for Italian opera started by the rival theatre.[10]

On 16 January 1705, less than four months before Vanbrugh's new theatre opened, Rich's Drury Lane company presented Thomas Clayton's *Arsinoe, Queen of Cypress*, an Italianate pasticcio with clumsily translated English verse affixed to the notes of diverse (and as yet unidentified) Italian arias.[11] This opera, with its pathetically diminutive plot and antiquated arias--performed, ironically, by an all-English cast-- became very popular. Between January 1705 and March 1707, *Arsinoe* was performed 35 times. It is damned by the anonymous author of "The Critical Discourse on Opera's and Musick in England," who calls it "the Hospital of the old Decrepid *Italian* Opera's."[12] But the editor of *The Muses Mercury* for February 1707 (written in March, however) holds *Arsinoe* in a rather higher regard, as he compares it to Clayton's next attempt at an opera, *Rosamond* (performed in March 1707): "The Harmony of the Numbers, and the Beauty of the Sentiments are universally admired. It has been disputed, whether the Musick [of *Rosamond*] is as good as that of *Arsinoe*; but, without entering into Comparisons, it must be confess'd, that the Airs of *Rosamond* are fine, the Passions well touch'd. . . ."[13] Regardless of its quality, and it must be admitted to be very poor by any standards, *Arsinoe* is significant because its story is borne completely by music; it is the first work without spoken dialogue to achieve such success on the London stage. But the English audience's acceptance of the operatic convention was not so immediate as the success of this one opera would indicate.

Most of the extant newspaper advertisements and playbills for performances of *Arsinoe* show that it was mounted with fragments of other works, usually acts of plays. For example, on 7 June 1705 it is advertised as being performed with the fifth act of Centlivre's comedy *Love's Contrivance* (1703) and on 28 February 1706 with the fourth act of Congreve's *The Old Batchelour* (1693). As one authority has pointed out, *Arsinoe* is quite short in comparison with other Italianate operas of the period (containing only 37 brief arias compared to the 56 in *Camilla*) and, therefore, probably needed such supplementary attractions to fill out an evening's entertainment;[14] but I would propose that *Arsinoe*'s fellow travelers were not simply padding but the keys to its acceptance on the Drury Lane stage.

One might assume that the acts of the various plays performed with *Arsinoe* were afterpieces to the featured opera, but as one advertisement states, an act of a comedy was "to be perform'd before the Opera begins."[15] A brief examination of one comedy associated with *Arsinoe* will show why the two types were performed together. The fifth act of Centlivre's *Love's Contrivance* is as dramatically inert as any in a Restoration comedy. The central "turn" of the rather simple plot has already occurred in Act IV. The high point of the last act, a humorous scene involving a sham philosopher, has no bearing on the main plot.

All that actually happens here is that a cantankerous old father acquiesces to his beautiful daughter's original inclinations to marry and, more important for *Arsinoe*, preparations are made for a musical entertainment to celebrate this happy event. At the end of the play-book, after the command to "let the Diversion begin," is a stage direction for a song to be sung by Leveridge, the premier bass of the Drury Lane company. But for a few performances of this act of Centlivre's play, Leveridge did more than sing a simple song, as he rendered the role of Feraspe, captain of Queen Arsinoe's guards. Thus the function of this act of *Love's Contrivance*, like the fourth act of Congreve's *The Old Batchelour*,[16] was to provide *Arsinoe*, which in Rome or Vienna would have been considered an autonomous music drama, with a rational context in which to exist. Much as the masques of the dramatic operas had been surrounded by loosely related but not usually integral spoken dialogue, England's first Italian opera was introduced by actors, who, once the music began, sat wordless at the side of the stage and watched the masque as did the audience proper.

Vanbrugh and Congreve, the managers of the nearly completed Haymarket theatre, observed Clayton's pathetic opera drawing full houses at Drury Lane, and the two playwrights debated whether or not to follow Rich's lead and to open their house with an Italianate opera. Two months before the opening, Congreve wrote in a 3 February 1705 letter to his friend Keally in Dublin that ". . . I know not when the house [i.e., the Haymarket theatre] will open, nor what we shall begin withal; but I believe with no opera. There is nothing settld yet."[17] The continuing success of *Arsinoe* made their decision easier, and on 9 April 1705 the barely completed[18] Queen's Theatre in the Haymarket opened with an Italian pastoral opera, Jakob Greber's *The Love's of Ergasto*. The diminutive opera, probably the first London stage work to be sung completely in Italian, was a costly failure. Roger Fiske believes that *Ergasto* was sung in English by native as well as foreign singers,[19] but the libretto is printed both in Italian (on the verso of an opening) and in English (on the recto), in the manner of the later bilingual pasticci; and John Downes, the indefatigable prompter, states that it was ". . . Perform'd by a new set of Singers, Arriv'd from Italy; (the worst that e're came from thence) . . . and they being lik'd but indifferently by the Gentry; they in a little time marcht back to their own Country."[20] Vanbrugh and Congreve may have imported one or two Italian singers during the frantic preparations for the opening of their theatre,[21] but more likely they assembled most of their shabby cast from among the foreigners at the rival Drury Lane theatre. For instance, the "Baroness," who frequently performed at Rich's theatre, probably sang in *The Loves of Ergasto*. If Greber's pastoral was sung completely in Italian, this evidently proved to be a premature move against an audience that would prefer to suffer several years of bilingual concatenations before hearing another opera sung in Italian throughout. Also, the Haymarket's opera, which is much more masque-like than *Arsinoe*, was not provided with a dramaturgical rationale; this undoubtedly contributed to its failure.

The Haymarket company struggled for survival for the rest of the 1704-05 season and for much of the next, while Drury Lane continued to milk *Arsinoe* for large audiences. But on 21 February 1706 the Haymarket finally mounted a successful musical production, not an Italian one, but an English dramatic opera, George Granville's *The British Enchanters*.[22]   It had been five years since either theatre had presented a new semi-opera,[23] although the Drury Lane company frequently mounted revivals of Purcell's famous works even after the initial success of *Arsinoe*. *The British Enchanters* is in the *King Arthur* mold, with heroic spoken dialogue punctuated by grand masques and incantation scenes. Granville used old-fashioned rhymed couplets throughout his drama (thus reverting to Dryden's early Restoration practice), but it "pleas'd the Town as well as any *English* Modern Opera."[24]   Its long run of 12 performances between February and May probably prompted the Drury Lane company to revive *King Arthur* on 2 March 1706.[25] The considerable success of *The British Enchanters* in the midst of the foreign onslaught has been overlooked by students of the Italian opera. But the run of this dramatic opera, like the careers of its composers, John Eccles and William Corbett,[26] would soon be curtailed, not simply by an audience clamoring after the new Italian music, but also by politically motivated changes in the organization of two playhouses.

A month after *The British Enchanters* opened successfully at the Haymarket, Drury Lane mounted its second Italianate opera, Bononcini's *Camilla*. This opera is the catalyst which triggered a permanent change in the position of music on the London stage. Performed entirely in English, mostly by a native cast, and with freshly composed English recitatives, *Camilla* was the first full-length, heroic Italian opera mounted in London; it was enormously successful. In *Camilla* the audience found an ideal concoction: the kind of music they most desired, their favorite English singers sharing the stage with a few exotic newcomers, and, perhaps the most important ingredient of all in a theatre in which Congreve and Otway had once woven their stories, a developed, fast-moving, and believable plot, whose absurdities are ameliorated by Bononcini's arias. Unlike *Arsinoe*, *Camilla* is a substantial drama and, therefore, did not need to be prepared by actors playing loose scenes of old comedies, although it was introduced and bade farewell each night by well-known actors who spoke the prologue and epilogue.[27]   The actors and playwrights felt more threatened by music than ever, and they bitterly attacked the tastes of the audience and their own managers,[28] particularly Christopher Rich, who was responsible for bringing *Camilla* to the stage.[29]   His fellow shareholders in the Drury Lane company complained of his shady financial dealings and apparent disregard for the difficult condition in which his actors now found themselves.   In 1706, after *Camilla*'s successful first season, they reported that Rich boasted "Last year that he Lost by his Players what he got by the opera," and that by cooking the books of his "double company" of actors and opera singers, he could conceal the huge profits and thereby avoid paying dividends to the other shareholders.[30]   The situation was exacerbated by the singers, who demanded higher salaries while the actors received lower ones.[31]   The first of the three great revolutions of the critical decade was about to happen.

II. THEATRICAL REVOLUTIONS

The history of the next five years of the London theatres is a confused tangle of official orders and counterorders, plots and counterplots. Yet it is essential to know the seemingly prosaic details of the theatrical management in order to understand the ultimate victory of the Italian opera over the English form and the revitalization of spoken drama on the London stage. The most frequently cited account of this period is Cibber's *Apology*. This self-serving chronicle, upon which parts of the following diagrams are based, reflects the bias of the beleaguered actors; although his outlines of the three major revolutions are essentially correct, Cibber's explanations of the motivations behind them are naive.

Diagram 1 shows the management of the London playhouses during the 1704-1706 seasons, before the first revolution in the late summer of 1706. At the top of the hierarchy is the Lord Chamberlain, Henry Grey, the Earl of Kent. Endowed with dictatorial powers over the theatres and answerable only to the Queen and her ministers,[32] Kent, a dilatory Chamberlain easily influenced by the rich and powerful, apparently had only a vague understanding of the crises facing his playhouses. Cibber stood in awe of his supposedly Solomon-like orders, but punctuating most of the laureate's facile explanations of the theatrical revolutions discussed below are cautionary remarks indicating that the actors and the lower echelons of management really knew very little of what transpired among the wealthy and powerful to bring about the changes. William Collier, a shareholder in the Drury Lane company, had a more cynical opinion of the orders emanating from the Lord Chamberlain's office; he described them as so confusing and contradictory that one had to violate them in order to learn their meanings.[33] Responsible for the day-to-day running of the theatres and for carrying out the policies of the Earl of Kent was Sir Thomas Coke, the Vice Chamberlain. Vanbrugh described Coke as a "great Lover of Musique and Promoter of Operas" and confided that the Lord

Chamberlain left such matters entirely to his assistant.[34]   Fortunately, many of Coke's official papers survive, and these documents form the backbone of the following discussion.[35]

As Diagram 1 shows, both the Drury Lane and Haymarket theatres were in fact double companies, each with a separate troupe for plays and operas, although in practice, of course, the opera singers sang between the acts of plays, while the actors aided the operas with prologues and epilogues and, occasionally, fragments of plays.   The Drury Lane company was owned by a group of shareholders, chief among them Rich, the manager, and Sir Thomas Skipwith, who at this time exerted little of his influence. After the great success of *Camilla* in March 1706, the musical director of this company was probably Nicola Haym, a Roman 'cellist and composer who had adapted Bononcini's opera for the London stage.

To speak of this important musician as a "musical director" in the modern sense may be misleading, because opera in London was still being produced under the auspices of *play*houses, not opera companies. But during the 1705-06 season Haym appears to have been in control of the Drury Lane singers and instrumentalists, performers of ever-increasing value. Not surprisingly, then, Haym reported directly to the opera-loving Vice Chamberlain at this time and not to the manager of the theatre, Rich. For example, in a 21 April 1706 letter to Coke, he explains that Margarita de l'Epine cannot sing for the Vice Chamberlain because "she is obliged to Learn ye part of Camilla by heart for Tuesday next." He suggests that instead of the soprano he send Johann Pepusch and some "violins."[36] One must not assume that the source of Haym's considerable power was simply a self-professed musical superiority,[37] for he also maintained good English and Italian connections. As the master of the private musical establishment of the powerful Duke of Bedford, Haym obtained many scores and libretti of Italian operas (including those for *Camilla*) for his patron, who played an important role in the Italian victory in London.[38] Bedford and other aristocratic opera lovers, such as the Earl of Halifax,[39] probably exerted their influence on the malleable Chamberlain as well as on the manager of the Drury Lane theatre. There is proof of such influences for later seasons. Haym also helped Vanbrugh and Congreve with their abortive pastoral opera, because he negotiated the loan of his prize pupil, the Baroness, for *The Loves of Ergasto*.[40]

Revolution I

Diagram 1 reflects an unstable condition. For the two companies to continue to produce both operas and plays was financially impossible. Congreve had dropped out of the Haymarket partnership by December

1705; he is not forthcoming with details in a 15 December 1705 letter to Keally in Dublin: ". . . so I have nothing to add but only that I have quitted the affair of the Hay-market. You may imagine I got nothing by it. . . ."[41] Vanbrugh, too, was ready to abandon the project. Rumors of an impending change in the organization of the London playhouses were abroad. Cibber reports that "It was, now, the Town-talk, that nothing but a Union of the two Companies could recover the Stage, to its former Reputation. . . ."[42] This gossip was undoubtedly fanned by Vanbrugh's 19 July 1705 proposal submitted to the Lord Chamberlain requesting a union of the two theatre companies. In a long reply, Rich pleaded with Kent's secretary, Sir John Stanley, to forestall the union, since it would be prejudicial to him and his shareholders.[43] The Drury Lane actors were also aware of the reorganization plan even before Vanbrugh proposed it. They thought that it would cause them great hardship, and in a broadside petition printed in June 1705, they begged the Lord Chamberlain to stop the plans for uniting the two companies. These players (see Diagram 1) were younger and less experienced than Betterton's distinguished company at the Haymarket and therefore probably feared that when the two troupes were joined, there would be fewer parts for the inexperienced actors.[44] Nearly a year later, the Lord Chamberlain had still not acted on Vanbrugh's proposal, and Congreve, writing on 30 April 1706, doubts that the Haymarket could survive another season, adding that he has "heard there is to be a Union of the two houses. . . ."[45] He may have learned of these efforts from his former colleague Vanbrugh, who during this month was politicking among his aristocratic acquaintances for "an agreement betweene the two playhouses. . . ."[46] His efforts finally paid off, because at the end of the long summer vacation in 1706, before the theatres reopened for the season in September, the Lord Chamberlain ordered (or at least condoned) a sweeping reorganization of the theatres. As Diagram 2 shows, most of Rich's principal actors were transferred to the Haymarket, and "for the Future all Operas & other Musicall Entertainm[ts]" could be performed only at Drury Lane. Furthermore, the Lord Chamberlain restricted the Haymarket to plays without musical episodes and dancing and transferred all musicians and dancers in the Haymarket company to Drury Lane, leaving only a small band of instrumentalists to perform the overtures and act tunes for plays.[47]

There are conflicting reports of what precipitated this reorganization. At about this time, Vanbrugh leased the Haymarket theatre to Owen Swiney. Cibber reports that the lease gave Swiney complete control, the new manager being required to pay Vanbrugh only £5 per day of acting.[48] But as is shown below, Vanbrugh remained much involved with the management of his theatre. Cibber was puzzled

MANAGEMENT OF THE LONDON THEATRES
FROM 1704 TO 1710
DIAGRAM 1

1704-1706 Seasons

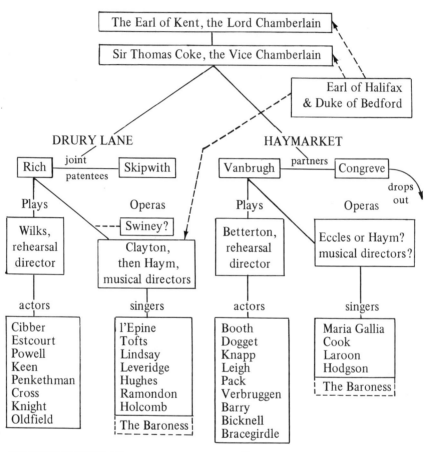

"ITALIAN" OPERAS

Arsinoe (Clayton)
Camilla (G. Bononcini and Haym)

DRAMATIC OPERAS (all revivals)

Island Princess
Bonduca
King Arthur
Tempest
Indian Queen

"ITALIAN" OPERAS

Loves of Ergasto (Greber)
Temple of Love (Saggione)

DRAMATIC OPERAS (premières)

British Enchanters
Wonders in the Sun

REVOLUTION I
DIAGRAM 2
1706-1707 Season

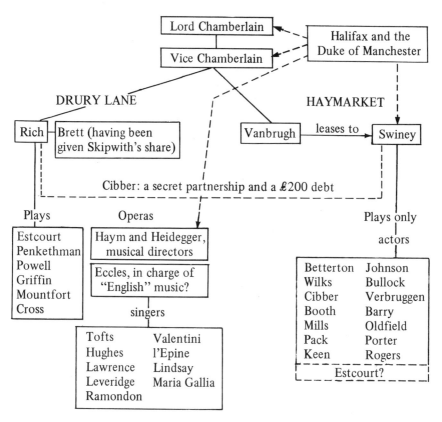

Lord Chamberlain

Vice Chamberlain

Halifax and the
Duke of Manchester

DRURY LANE

HAYMARKET

Rich — Brett (having been
given Skipwith's share)

Vanbrugh   leases to   Swiney

Cibber: a secret partnership and a £200 debt

Plays

Estcourt
Penkethman
Powell
Griffin
Mountfort
Cross

Operas

Haym and Heidegger,
musical directors

Eccles, in charge of
"English" music?

singers

Tofts   Valentini
Hughes   l'Epine
Lawrence   Lindsay
Leveridge   Maria Gallia
Ramondon

Plays only

actors

Betterton   Johnson
Wilks   Bullock
Cibber   Verbruggen
Booth   Barry
Mills   Oldfield
Pack   Porter
Keen   Rogers
        Estcourt?

"ITALIAN" OPERAS

Rosamond (Clayton)
Thomyris (Heidegger)

DRAMATIC OPERAS (all revivals)

Island Princess
Tempest
Timon of Athens
Macbeth

Prepared but not performed:

Semele (Eccles and Congreve)
Orpheus (?)
Orlando Furioso (D. Purcell)

NO MUSICAL PRODUCTIONS

by this action, because Swiney had been closely associated with Rich at Drury Lane: Swiney probably oversaw the production of *Camilla*, for example.[49] Why would Vanbrugh enter into an agreement with an agent of his arch-enemy Rich? Cibber saw only one explanation: that the entire transfer was a collusion between Swiney and Rich, the protégé apparently owing his master £200.[50] But why would the greedy Rich allow his best actors to be sent to the rival theatre, even if he were allowed to keep the most profitable segment of his company, the opera? Cibber reports that Rich did in fact resist the union at first, because the manager feared that his many creditors and investors would be able to see his large profits more clearly after the company was divided.[51] Cibber's account is corroborated by a document written in support of the other investors in the Drury Lane company, who believed that ". . . if he [Rich] has the Opera Single & entire ye Profit must be so Certain and ye accounts will be in so . . . Plain a Compass that 'twill be impossible for him to deceive the People any Longer. . . ."[52] But when Rich saw the possibility of controlling both theatres through his protégé Swiney, he happily conformed to the Lord Chamberlain's plan, or at least this is what Cibber would have us believe.[53] Congreve thought otherwise. The playwright, who had resigned his partnership in the Haymarket but who still had well-informed sources, reports in a letter of 10 September 1706 that Rich was furious at the Lord Chamberlain's order, which Congreve clearly saw as a move to improve the condition of the actors oppressed by the evil Rich:

> The play-houses have undergone another revolution; and Swinney, with Wilks, Mrs. Olfield, Pinkethman, Bullock, and Dicky, are come over to the Hay-market. Vanbrugh resigns his authority to Swinny, which occasioned the revolt. Mr Rich complains and rails like Volpone when counterplotted by Mosca. My Lord Chamberlain approves and ratifies the desertion; and the design is, to have plays only at the Hay-market, and operas only at Covent Garden [i.e., Drury Lane]. I think the design right to restore acting, but the houses are misapplied, which time may change.[54]

The effects of the 1706 reorganization, which at first appeared to please almost no one, were gradually felt. For the first time in years the actors were now being paid regularly by Swiney at the Haymarket.[55] Rich, who had jealously guarded his right to produce both plays and operas, gave more performances of Italianate operas than ever before. And using the skeleton crew of actors left by the transfer (listed at the far left in Diagram 2), he also produced at least four revivals of old musical plays. But this sweeping change which Congreve saw as "right to restore acting" victimized England's last major dramatic opera and nipped in the bud the finest, all-sung English opera of the period.

In compliance with the Lord Chamberlain's order, the Haymarket theatre retained a modest musical establishment, and new act music was even commissioned for Farquhar's successful comedy *The Beaux Stratagem*, which opened on 8 March 1707.[56] But no elaborate musical episodes were possible in the plays mounted at the Haymarket during the 1706-07 season. Granville's *The British Enchanters* had been the new theatre's only successful musical production, but the 1706 revolution now prevented it from being performed, because it requires considerable musical forces. This did not, however, deter Swiney from announcing a performance of the work on 9 December 1706.[57] Granville saw the advertisements and wrote an outraged letter to the Vice Chamberlain: ". . . the Players in the Hay Market have put forth Bills for acting the British Enchanters tomorrow without Singing and Dancing . . . which I can deem no other than a design to murder the Child of my Brain. . . ."[58] Granville asked his friend at court to suppress the performance. The dramatic opera was never again performed with its musical scenes, although later in the season, Granville was apparently persuaded to let it be staged "with all the Original Scenes, Machines, and Decorations."[59]

A greater tragedy for English music drama resulted from the 1706 Lord Chamberlain order, however. With a monopoly on opera, Rich planned several new productions for the 1706-07 season. Among these were English semi-operas as well as Italianate pasticci. Daniel Purcell was working on an "Orlando Furioso," adapted from Quinault, and the sober critic and playwright John Dennis had concocted a masque of "Orpheus and Euridice" that was set to music by an anonymous composer.[60] Nothing came of these essays in native music drama; they were presumably pushed aside by *Thomyris,* one of several Italianate operas being adapted for the London stage at the time.[61] Yet another opera was composed for this watershed season: Eccles and Congreve's *Semele,* the only English opera of worth to survive from the critical decade.[62] Considering its fine quality and lack of Italian traits, it could perhaps have signaled a new direction for an English baroque opera tradition. Since Congreve was a close friend of Vanbrugh and a former partner in the Haymarket venture, scholars have assumed that *Semele* must have been designed for Vanbrugh's Haymarket theatre.[63] But *The Muses Mercury,* a monthly periodical devoted to the arts, reports in January 1707 that Eccles's opera was ready for rehearsal at Drury Lane;[64] and a document in the Vice Chamberlain's papers confirms that Congreve and Eccles had come to an oral agreement with their old arch-rival, Rich, to have their opera produced at Drury Lane, which, of course, had the opera monopoly.[65] Witnessing this dubious agreement was the influential Earl of Halifax, the Lord Treasurer. Halifax was a generous patron of the arts, native as well as foreign, and during this season he was engaged in an unsuccessful project to bring the creator of *Camilla*, Giovanni Bononcini, from Vienna to London.[66] While he and his influential friends courted the continental opera composer, Congreve's *Semele* sank into oblivion. It was never performed and probably never even rehearsed. Instead, *Thomyris* began its long run in April 1707. It is not known what role Rich played in selecting operas for his Drury Lane theatre nor the extent of the pressure put on him by the Lord Chamberlain and the patrons, but the balance had finally swung decisively in the Italian direction: English music drama, both the old Purcellian semi-opera and a new, all-sung type which Eccles showed himself capable of mastering, was dead.

But Rich's operatic empire had begun to crumble. His relationship with Swiney, the new manager of the Haymarket, ruptured. The former protégé had apparently paid off his debt to Rich and showed no desire to continue any private agreements.[67] The collusion suspected by Cibber had apparently occurred between Vanbrugh and Swiney, not Rich and Swiney. The Earl of Halifax, who had earlier taken a keen interest in Rich's operatic productions, now turned against the old manager and helped the Haymarket company stage a successful series of revivals of famous plays.[68] Halifax's rekindled interest in Shakespeare may be an advance warning of the next theatrical revolution, one which depended upon a solvent Haymarket theatre and a bankrupt Rich. More serious difficulties, however, came from within Rich's own organization, as he began to have major disagreements with his singers, dancers, and orchestral musicians. Katherine Tofts, in particular, England's first great operatic soprano, felt that Rich had cheated her out of salary,[69] and she and other singers petitioned the Lord Chamberlain for allegedly unpaid fees.[70] The crisis flared into the public view when on 15 November 1707 of this stormy season a performance of *Camilla* had to be canceled, because Mrs. Tofts and Margarita de l'Epine refused to sing; they now considered their contracts with Rich to be void.[71] But the critical turn of events which finally stripped Rich of his monopoly to perform operas took place among powerful aristocrats, who thought the interests of Italian opera in London better served by Vanbrugh and Swiney at the Haymarket.

Revolution II

As early as September 1707 rumors of a plot to return opera to the Haymarket had been circulating. The anonymous editor of *The Muses Mercury* may have known something of the behind-the-scenes plans. He is usually meticulous in his reports of rumored opera productions, often correcting minor misstatements in subsequent issues.

He also respected the confidentiality of his obviously well-placed informants. In the September 1707 issue (p. 218) he reports that several operas are being prepared but that the one "in the greatest Forwardness" is Scarlatti's *La Didone Delirante*.[72]   "We have Reason to know something of this Opera, but that Reason hinders us from Saying any more of it." Perhaps he had been told of a plan to rehearse operas surreptitiously at the Haymarket. On 1 December of the same season, the Lord Chamberlain gave Rich's best Drury Lane instrumentalists permission to rehearse an opera secretly at the Haymarket.[73] The theatre, supposedly reserved exclusively for plays, even announced a performance of *Thomyris* for a week later, but this apparently never happened.[74] Rich's monopoly on opera had been thoroughly undermined, and he promptly dismissed the defecting musicians and stopped his singers' salaries.[75] The production of opera at Drury Lane lurched to a halt.[76]

In the middle of the second revolution of the critical decade, the Lord Chamberlain issued a sweeping order which again reorganized the London theatres, as shown by Diagram 3. The order, issued on 31 December 1707--the same day that Kent had received word of the stalemate between Rich and his musicians--requires that all singers, dancers, and instrumentalists be transferred to the Haymarket, where (beginning on 10 January 1708) only operas could be performed, and that all actors should report back to Drury Lane.[77] This order, which left only musicians at the Haymarket, created London's first theatre devoted exclusively to opera.

By virtually all accounts of this period, the complete separation of musicians and actors was satisfactory to both parties, although the actors, again under the thumb of the despised Rich, did not immediately see its benefits. Cibber, who considered the action the turning point in the recovery of his profession into a golden age, reports that Swiney was given sole control of the Haymarket opera.[78] But the Vice Chamberlain documents clearly show Vanbrugh to be in charge during the first few difficult months of 1708.[79] In fact, in a 24 February letter Vanbrugh takes credit for the change in management, stating that he exerted his influence in the highest places. He writes to the Earl of Manchester, at the time Ambassador Extraordinary to Venice: ". . . I got the Duke of Marlborough to put an end to the play-house factions, by engaging the Queen to exert her authority, by the means of which, the actors are all put under the Patent of Covent Garden house, and the operas are established at the Haymarket. . . ." He adds a word of encouragement for Manchester, whose unofficial duties in Italy included scouting singers and opera composers for possible service in London: "[the separation of dramatic forces is] to the general liking of the whole town, and both [operas and plays] go on in a very successful manner, without disturbing

REVOLUTION II
DIAGRAM 3
After 10 January 1708

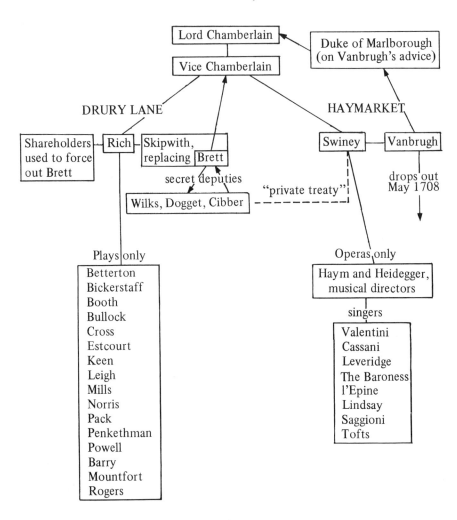

NO MUSICAL PRODUCTIONS

"ITALIAN" OPERAS

Love's Triumph (Valentini)
Pyrrhus & Demetrius (Haym)
Clotilda (Heidegger)

Prepared but not performed:

Didone Delirante (Scarlatti?)

one another."[80] Vanbrugh must have felt it politic to paint a rosy picture for the ambassador, because despite Marlborough's influence, the Queen's compliance, and the Vice Chamberlain's love and encouragement of Italian opera, the Haymarket theatre was in a financially precarious position for the early months of 1708. Vanbrugh's chief difficulties were the salary demands of the singers and a fear that the devious Rich was counterplotting. A letter from Vanbrugh to Coke graphically illustrates both of these worries; it almost certainly dates from 20 January 1708, little more than a week after the Lord Chamberlain's order took effect:[81]

> Tuesday Night
>
> I endeavour'd twice today to wait on you--I hope you can spare an hour to morrow, that some Conclusion may be made with these singers and musick; for without your aid, nothing can be done with 'em. There was but £150. last time and £120. to night. 'Tis impossible to go thorough with it, if the Performers are not reduc'd to Reason. I have appointed severall of 'em to attend you to morrow--I'll likewise wait on you about ten a Clock and shew you what I have drawn up, wch I think is all can possibly be offer'd em. There will be an other misfortune, a great one if not nip'd in the Bud. I mean musick meetings. There's one given out to morrow at York Buildings, and the Bills larger & much more remarkable than usuall. I'm told, (and believe) Rich is in the Bottom on't. But I hope you'll move my Ld Cham^{b}: for an Order to stop their Performances. Which will be a great means to make our musitians both accept reasonable sallarys and be carefull in their Business.

Apparently heeding the playwright's advice, the Lord Chamberlain canceled the York Buildings concert.[82] Mr. Rich, stripped of his right to perform operas and fighting his last battle for managerial control of the Drury Lane theatre, could still be a thorn in Vanbrugh's side.

Cibber's account of the momentous reorganization of December 1707 differs considerably from Vanbrugh's, and since it involves people at the lower echelons of authority, it is probably ingenuous. As Diagram 2 shows, Skipwith, one of the main shareholders in the Drury Lane company, gave his shares outright to Henry Brett, a close friend of Cibber's, in the early autumn of 1707.[83] The reasons for the transfer are not altogether clear; apparently Skipwith had lost interest in the financially troubled company and had grown weary of battling with the chief patentee. According to Cibber, Brett took an active role in the running of the theatre upon receipt of Skipwith's shares. He angered Rich by insisting that the actors be paid regular salaries, and, more important, "he made use of the Intimacy he had with the Vice-Chamberlain to assist his Scheme of this intended Union . . .,"[84] that is, the December 1707 revolution, for which Vanbrugh also takes credit. But Brett's stint as a shareholder in the Drury Lane company was short-lived. When the financial condition of that theatre began to improve after the reorganization, Skipwith decided to reclaim his shares. Rich was probably behind this maneuver (shov·n in Diagram 3), because he enlisted the aid of several minor shareholders to help force Brett out of the company.[85]   But before his ouster, Brett appointed three influential actors, John Wilks, Thomas Dogget, and Cibber,[86] as his secret deputies with managerial responsibilities, a move designed to split Rich's company and to bring eventual stability to the London theatres. Sometime during the 1707-08 season, Swiney, the titular manager of the Haymarket theatre, took the three actors into a secret partnership,[87] thus laying the groundwork for the third revolution of the critical decade.

At the end of the 1707-08 season, with the Italian opera firmly in the hands of Swiney at the Haymarket, Vanbrugh finally dropped out as an active participant in the managerial struggles. On 11 May 1708 he writes: "I have parted with my whole concern to Mr Swiney; only reserving my Rent; So that he is entire Possessor of the Opera And Most People think, will manage it better than any body."[88]   But Vanbrugh retained an interest in his theatre for several years, as he continued to give Swiney advice, and as late as November 1713 he provided the Vice Chamberlain with an account of the location and value of the Haymarket stock (scenery, costumes, and so forth).[89]

The December 1707 reorganization, like the first in 1706, was detrimental to English music drama.   G[iles] J[acob], a perceptive chronicler of the early 18th-century London stage, bluntly expresses what other champions of the English dramatic opera must have believed to be the reason for the Lord Chamberlain's new order: "for the better Encouragement of the *Italian* Operas, at that time the prevailing Passion of the Town."[90] Drury Lane, formerly the home of Henry Purcell's stage works, no longer had the musical forces to present even a simple play with incidental songs,[91] while the Haymarket, now reserved exclusively for Italian opera, had no actors and only two or three English singers with whom to mount a dramatic opera. This form, which had begun with Shadwell's 1674 version of *The Tempest*, ended in 1706 with Granville's *The British Enchanters*.[92]   One native prima donna, Mrs. Tofts, was evidently unaware of just how restrictive the new order would be: among her four demands in a contract submitted c. December-January 1707-08 is that she "not be debar'd singing at a Play wch is comeing out upon condition it does not interfere wth an Opera."[93] Someone has marked this item with a cross, perhaps to remind Mrs. Tofts that plays could no longer be produced at her new theatre, the Haymarket. The Italian bilingual pasticcio now reigned as the only type of music drama on the London stage. Purcell's dramatic works enjoyed a resurgence of popularity two seasons later, but no new dramatic operas were offered during this period.

Revolution III

The next major change in the London theatrical organizations was a natural result of the various designs set in motion by the December 1707 order. Rich quarreled with his actors over how much they should be paid for their benefit plays, and he even ignored the Lord Chamberlain's order which decided in favor of the actors,[94] a disobedience which led to his downfall. Again Kent condoned private agreements prejudicial to Rich before actually issuing an official order, as he allowed Swiney and the three actor-managers to enlist players for an eventual secession from the Drury Lane company.[95] Rich was in a very low condition when in the early part of the 1708-09 season he tried to placate his actors by appointing some of them as deputy managers, a desperate move probably designed to counteract Brett's assignment of his authority to Wilks, Dogget, and Cibber. This futile act is alluded to in "A Long Vacation Prologue Writ by Mr. [Thomas] B[a]k[e]r; and spoke by Mr. Es[tcour]t, at the *Theatre-Royal* in *Drury Lane*," apparently during September 1708.[96] In a passage pertaining to theatre managers, a printed marginal note states that "Mr. R[ic]h *appointed 8 Managers*," and listed are Powell, Keene, Johnson, Bullock, Norris, Leigh, Bickerstaff, and Mrs. Powell. Perhaps this act prompted Cibber to remark that Rich "was as sly a Tyrant, as ever was at the Head of a Theatre; for he gave the Actors more Liberty, and fewer Days Pay, than any of his Predecessors. . . ."[97] The impudent prologue also reveals that the actors hoped Richard Norton of Southwick, for whom some of them had performed during the summer vacation, would "Buy out these sordid *Pattent-Masters* [i.e., Rich, Skipwith, et al.], And make a *Free Gift* of it to the *Actors*. . . ."

On 6 June 1709 the Lord Chamberlain finally removed Rich as manager of the Drury Lane theatre,[98] and early next season, two new companies were established,[99] as shown in Diagram 4: Drury Lane could act plays and was once again allowed to interlard them with musical entertainments other than operas. Several experienced actors were transferred to the Haymarket, but the theatre retained its operatic establishment; Swiney could present plays, musical entertainments, and, of course, Italian operas. During the chaotic autumn of 1709, there was a struggle for control of the Drury Lane playhouse, and William Collier and Aaron Hill emerged as the new managers. Collier, who had been one of the shareholders in the company for several years, cleverly subverted Rich's attempt to run the company in "exile."[100] Hill, too, learned his new trade the hard way: in the early summer of 1710, after Collier had removed some actors as sharing managers, the rebellious players broke into the theatre on 5 June, assaulted Hill with swords drawn, and invited the deposed Rich to retake command of the theatre. Fortunately for Collier and Hill, the Lord Chamberlain interceded and stopped the rebellion.[101] Rich apparently still controlled a majority of the shares in the company, and during the 1710-11 season, he temporarily regained his position as manager by ousting Collier in a financial maneuver.[102] But Rich finally abandoned Drury Lane and began to build a new theatre in Lincoln's Inn Fields, which opened shortly after his death in 1714. His power never depended much upon aristocratic connections, but rather upon wise investments.

The Haymarket company was mostly free of the managerial disputes plaguing Drury Lane during the 1709-10 season. Wilks, Dogget, and Cibber and their partner Swiney spent the summer of 1709 having Vanbrugh's theatre remodeled. It had been notoriously poor for spoken drama, and Cibber even believed the playhouse's operatic acoustics to be an important factor in the December 1707 decision to make it the opera house.[103] Plays fared well under the trio's management, but the actors were not good opera impresarios. Cibber admits as much (in *An Apology*, p. 226), and his confession in confirmed by an undated letter from Nicolini Grimaldi, the first great operatic castratto to sing in London.[104] He complains that not only has Swiney disregarded his contract, but that the manager's associates, "tous trois Comediens," have done far worse: "leur interest, et leur but est de detruire les Operas, et de faire insulte à ceux qui s'opposent à leur dessein. . . ." The Lord Chamberlain apparently recognized the English actors and Italian singers at the Haymarket as strange bedfellows, because on 6 November 1710 he transferred Swiney and all actors back to Drury Lane, appointing Collier and Hill to manage opera at the Haymarket.[105] A measure of stability was thus achieved in the London theatres for several years. This is certainly not the last major change in the management of the early 18th-century London stage, but it is the last one which significantly affected the balance of music and drama.

After the separation of Thespian and musical forces was ended at the beginning of the 1709-10 season, plays with musical episodes, a type which had been officially vanquished by the Lord Chamberlain and his opera-loving peers, surprisingly re-emerged on the London stage. For example, on 28 November 1709 the Haymarket *opera* house presented *Macbeth*, "With all the Vocal and Instrumental Musick and Dances proper to the Play"; and a month later, the Drury Lane house announced a performance of *Timon of Athens*, "With all the Original Sonatas, and other Pieces of Musick set by the late Mr. Henry Purcell."[106] This season also saw a return to the former custom of opera singers

REVOLUTION III
DIAGRAM 4

After 6 June 1709

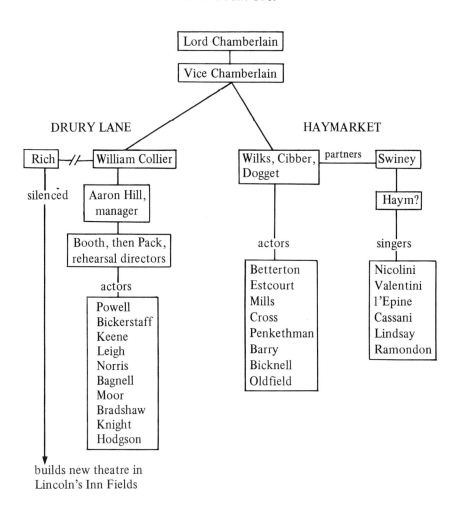

PLAYS WITH MUSIC (revivals)

Timon of Athens
Tempest

ITALIAN OPERAS

Almahide (Heidegger)
Hydaspes (Nicolini)

PLAY WITH MUSIC

Macbeth

performing between the acts of plays, a practice which galled Nicolini, who considered it a "Means to Vilifie and Prejudice the Opera."[107]   The imported music drama, now emerging from the bilingual pasticcio disguise in which it first appeared in London, certainly remained the most popular musical type on the London stage, but a segment of the ever-more-middle-class audience still preferred to hear music drama within the context of a spoken play.

The revolutions discussed above, though variously motivated and producing diverse effects, had two common goals: to accommodate Italian opera in a theatrical system which had long resisted the all-sung form and which had not the resources nor the audience to sustain both plays and operas; and to assure that the introduction of continental music drama did not weaken what was then and is now the most important stage genre of the English: the spoken play.   The casualties of this collision and subsequent reconciliation of music and drama on the London stage were the Restoration play with music and John Eccles and his out-of-fashion colleagues.   Even Henry Purcell, had he lived into the critical decade, would, I believe, have succumbed to the foreign foes and playhouse politics.

The native music which remained on the stage after 1709 paled next to the Italian operas of Handel and Bononcini.   The greatest musicians of the era were at the disposal of the opera companies, while the playhouses were forced to use only actors in their musical entertainments.[108]   The diminished condition of English music drama is well expressed in a famous essay by Joseph Addison in *The Spectator* of 1711,[109] the first important opera criticism in the English language:

> There is nothing that has more startled our *English* Audience, than the *Italian Recitativo* at its first Entrance upon the Stage.   People were wonderfully surprized to hear Generals singing the Word of Command, and Ladies delivering Messages in Musick. . . . But however this *Italian* Method of acting in *Recitativo* might appear at first hearing, I cannot but think it much more just than that which prevailed in our *English* Opera before this Innovation: The Transition from an Air to Recitative Musick being more natural, than the passing from a Song to plain and ordinary Speaking, which was the common Method in *Purcell's* Operas.

This passage is remarkable in that it shows a formidable English critic embracing the operatic convention: people could actually converse in recitative without the benefit of a dramaturgical context.   The Restoration convention of "passing from a Song to plain and ordinary Speaking," in other words, the practice of having musical episodes dependent upon the context provided by a spoken play and its actors, now seemed old-fashioned to Addison.   It may be puzzling that the critic speaks of Purcell's dramatic operas in the past tense and with a detachment far greater than the nine or ten years that had elapsed since the Drury Lane theatre specialized in such musical shows, for Addison was probably familiar with "the Frost Scene" in *King Arthur*, "the Conjuror's Scene" in *The Indian Queen*, and the masque in *Dioclesian*, all of which were heard in London about the time he wrote this passage.[110] But Purcell's miniature dramas now only infrequently appeared with their original plays. The masques in these works were carved up and intermingled with music of indifferent quality to make diverting afterpieces and entr'actes. In the years following the first decade of the 18th century, English art music rarely enhanced the scenes of English plays, and the London stage entered an era of music hall.

Postscript

The process by which the English play was relieved of most of its music is complicated. Italian opera at first disrupted the existing dramatic conventions but later permitted the play to shed the musical excesses which had turned it into a variety show. The reform of the play was not, then, so much a restructuring of the dramatic conventions governing music on the stage as it was a reorganization of the theatrical establishment itself. The reform created a clear separation between spoken drama and music drama. Although the play could still occasionally draw on music to intensify illusion and to relieve "the best Plots and language," it no longer had to accommodate musical scenes which never quite achieved musico-dramatic autonomy.

Throughout the Restoration, the play was alternately enhanced and weakened by music. Settle's *The Empress of Morocco* (1673), in which a masque strikingly advances the plot, is perhaps the best example of the full realization of music's dramatic potential in a spoken play, though taken separately, Settle's tragedy and Locke's masque are hardly significant achievements. Durfey's *Don Quixote* trilogy (1694-1696), in which strings of musical entertainments strangle the meagre amounts of plot, is probably the best example of weakening by music, although several of those entertainments include some of Purcell's finest songs. Paradoxically, the best music dramas of the era are entertainments that bear little relationship to their parent plays. These musical miniatures were a restrictive form, a dead end for the composer and a hindrance to the playwright. But as one of the tools of the dramatist, music was capable of intensifying almost any dramatic situation. Stage effects representing supernatural occurrences demanded musical accompaniment, and the psychological state of a character in a more realistic setting is often vented musically. A hero who expresses himself with English words could be diverted by an Italian song, perhaps even moved, but it could not effect an organic change in him.   A protagonist could command a masque to be performed in which his allegorical counterpart might "rant by Note, and through the Gamut rage; / In Song and Airs express [his] martial Fire, / Combate in Trills, and in a Feuge expire";[111] but after the musical diversion, when the tragic hero must himself succumb, he rants with words and expires with unmusical groans. The conventions of late 17th-century English drama placed severe limitations on musical expression, but at the same time allowed the maximum use of music to enhance the spoken play.

APPENDIX I

A CATALOGUE OF INSTRUMENTAL MUSIC
IN RESTORATION PLAYS
1665-1713

The following catalogue lists plays produced in London theatres from 1665-1713 for which there is extant instrumental music. It is designed to give not only the sources for the music but also to indicate the total musical requirements of the plays listed.

The information is presented in the following order: plays are listed alphabetically by title, and each title is preceded by an indication of its dramatic genre (see the List of Abbreviations). Cross references are provided for plays with double titles or variant titles found in the musical sources. The complete name of the playwright (when known), an abbreviation of the name of the theatre where the play was first produced, and the year of publication of the play-book follow. Next, the most complete source of the act music is listed. Standard RISM sigla are used for manuscripts, and short titles for prints. The keys to the sigla and the full titles of the publications are found below in the List of Sources. The ascriptions to play and composer are reproduced within quotation marks exactly as they appear in the main source, and the state of completeness of the instrumental parts is indicated ("a1" means treble part only, "a3" means two trebles and a bass, "a4" indicates two trebles, tenor--that is, viola--and bass, and "keyb." means a setting for keyboard). Where part-books are concerned, the page or folio reference is to the first treble part-book only. Each of the act tunes is then listed by title (if known) in the order of pieces in the main source. After each piece appear any concordances, the information presented in the same form as that for the primary source. Next, the songs for the play are listed by act and scene, and when the music for the song is extant, its D&M number is given, or the reader is referred to the printed source catalogued in *The British Union-Catalogue of Early Music*, ed. Edith Schnapper (London, 1957). Dances required by the stage directions of the play are then listed (by act and scene), and indications of any miscellaneous or unspecified music follow.

Dramatic operas for which there is surviving act music are included in this catalogue, but the complete requirements for music in these works are not given; rather, the most complete musical sources (when known) are listed. For those plays and dramatic operas whose instrumental music is by Henry Purcell, the reader is referred to the catalogue number given to these works in Franklin B. Zimmerman, *Henry Purcell 1659-1695: An analytical catalogue of his music* (London,

1963).   Note that the only concordances provided for the individual pieces of Purcell are those not listed by Zimmerman.   All references to performance dates are taken from Emmett L. Avery, *The London Stage 1660-1800* (Carbondale, Illinois. 1960).

The reader is cautioned that this catalogue is not complete. Although I have made every effort to record all sources of Restoration act music, manuscripts, particularly in libraries in the United States, continue to turn up.   For instance, the so-called Filmer collection at Yale University has not been thoroughly examined, although the act pieces of the two most important sets of part-books have been included below. And as this catalogue goes to press, I await microfilms of manuscripts in various other institutions.   The reader may rest assured, however, that, barring the discovery of a source of the magnitude of the Magdalene College, Cambridge, part-books, the following catalogue is as complete as eight years' work and modest research funds will permit.

List of Abbreviations

BUCEM	=	*The British Union-Catalogue of Early Music,* ed. Edith Schnapper (London, 1957)
C	=	comedy
DG	=	Dorset Garden Theatre
DL	=	Theatre Royal, Drury Lane
D&M	=	Cyrus L. Day and Eleanore Boswell Murrie, *English Song-Books 1651-1702 A Bibliography* (London, 1940)
DO	=	dramatic opera
F	=	farce
Hist.	=	history
LIF	=	Lincoln's Inn Fields Theatre
M	=	masque
O	=	opera
P	=	play
Past.	=	pastoral

QT   =   Queens Theatre in the Haymarket

Smith, *Walsh I*   =   William C. Smith, *A Bibliography of the Musical Works Published by John Walsh during the Years 1695-1720* (London, 1948)

T   =   tragedy

TC   =   tragi-comedy

TR   =   Theatre Royal, Vere-street

Z   =   Franklin B. Zimmerman, *Henry Purcell 1659-1695: An analytical catalogue of his music* (London, 1963)

List of Sources

I. Manuscripts Note: standard RISM sigla are used

EIRE, DUBLIN, TRINITY COLLEGE LIBRARY

Dtc MS 413

GREAT BRITAIN, CARDIFF PUBLIC LIBRARY

CDp MS 1.39 (A-H)

GREAT BRITAIN, CAMBRIDGE, FITZWILLIAM MUSEUM

Cfm 52.B.7
Cfm 640-642

GREAT BRITAIN, CAMBRIDGE, KING'S COLLEGE LIBRARY

Ckc MS 122

GREAT BRITAIN, CAMBRIDGE, MAGDALENE COLLEGE LIBRARY

Cmc pt-bks (a set of five part-books without press-mark)

GREAT BRITAIN, LEEDS PUBLIC LIBRARIES

LEp MS Q784.21 L969 (a set of four part-books)

GREAT BRITAIN, LONDON, THE BRITISH LIBRARY

Lbm Add. 15318
Lbm Add. 17853

Lbm Add. 22098
Lbm Add. 22099
Lbm Add. 24889
Lbm Add. 29283, 29284, 29285 (a set of three part-books)
Lbm Add. 29371
Lbm Add. 29378
Lbm Add. 29398
Lbm Add. 30839
Lbm Add. 31576
Lbm Add. 34204
Lbm Add. 35043
Lbm Add. 38189
Lbm Add. 39565, 39566, 39567, and Add. 30839 (a set of four part-books)
Lbm R.M.20.c.5

GREAT BRITAIN, LONDON, ROYAL COLLEGE OF MUSIC

Lcm MS 862
Lcm MS 988
Lcm MS 1144
Lcm MS 1172

GREAT BRITAIN, MANCHESTER PUBLIC LIBRARY

Mp MS 130 Hd 4, Vol. 189

GREAT BRITAIN, OXFORD, BODLEIAN LIBRARY

Ob MS Mus. Sch. c.61
Ob MS Mus. Sch. c.72
Ob MS Mus. Sch. c.73
Ob MS Mus. Sch. c.95
Ob MS e.397

GREAT BRITAIN, OXFORD, CHRIST CHURCH LIBRARY

Och Mus. MS 3
Och Mus. MS 352
Och Mus. MS 620
Och Mus. MS 944
Och Mus. MS 1183

GREAT BRITAIN, YORK MINSTER LIBRARY

Y MS M.24(s) 17-18

UNITED STATES, NEW YORK PUBLIC LIBRARY

NYp MS Drexel 3849

UNITED STATES, UNIVERSITY OF CALIFORNIA AT LOS ANGELES LIBRARY

LA Finney pt-bks (a set of four part-books owned by the late Theodore Finney and now on deposit at this library)

UNITED STATES, WASHINGTON, D.C., LIBRARY OF CONGRESS

Wc M1515.All Case

UNITED STATES, NEW HAVEN, YALE UNIVERSITY MUSIC LIBRARY

NH Filmer MS 6
NH Filmer MS 9

II. Printed sources   Note: Only the italicized portion of the following titles is used in the catalogue. For compositions that appear in several editions of the same publication (such as *The Dancing Master*), the reference is to the earliest edition in which the piece is found. For publications for which only one copy is known, the locations of these unique copies are given. If the location of a copy is not given, the reader may assume that it is found in Lbm.

40 Airs Anglois à dessus & une basse . . . choisis & mis en ordre par George Bingham, II, Amsterdam: E. Roger [c. 1710].   Only copy in US LA.

40 Airs Anglois . . . & trois Sonates, Livre second . . . Roger [c. 1701]. Only copy in B Bc.

40 Airs Anglois pour la Flûte . . . de Monsieur Finger . . . et . . . Monsieur George Bingham . . . III [c. 1705]. Only copy in B Bc.

40 Airs Anglois . . . composez par M. George Bingham . . . IV [c. 1705]. Only copy in B Bc.

50 Airs Anglois . . . Amsterdam: E. Roger [c. 1700-1710]. Only copy in B Bc.

Apollo's Banquet; containing Instructions and variety of new Tunes, Ayres and Jiggs, for the Treble-Violin . . . The 2d edition, with additions. London: W. Godbid for John Playford, 1678.

Apollo's Banquet . . . The sixth edition, with new additions. London: E. Jones for H. Playford, 1690.

Apollo's Banquet: containing Variety of the Newest Tunes, Ayres, Jiggs, and Minuets, for the Treble-Violin, Now in Use at Publick Theatres, and at Dancing-Schools . . . The second book.   London: E. Jones for Henry Playford, 1691.

Apollo's Banquet. The first book of Apollo's Banquet . . . The 7th Edition Corrected [London]: E. Jones, for Henry Playford, 1693.

Apollo's Banquet. Newly Reviv'd: Containing New and Easie Instructions for the Treble-Violin, With Variety of the Best and Choicest Ayres, Tunes, Jiggs, Minuets, Sarabands, Chacones, and Cybells, that have been Perform'd at both Theatres, and other Public Places . . . London: W. Pearson, for H. Playford, 1701. Only copy in Durham, Cathedral Library.

[Apollo's Banquet, c. 1705], an issue of this publication without title-page is found in the Royal College of Music Library, London.

Bray, Thomas, *Country Dances*. . . London: William Pearson, 1699. Only copy in Lcs.

A Brief Introduction to the Skill of Musick . . . London: John Playford, 1664, 1666, 1670, 1671.

A Choice Collection of Ayres for the Harpsichord or Spinett With . . . Directions for young beginners . . . London: J. Young, 1700.

A Collection of Lessons and Aires for the Harpsichord or Spinnett. Compos'd by M^r. J: Eccles M^r. D: Purcell . . . London: I. Walsh and I. Hare [1702]

A Collection of New Ayres: composed for Two Flutes, with Sonata's. By some of the Ingenious Masters of this Age. The First Collection. London: J. Heptinstall for J. Hudgebutt, 1695.

The Compleat Flute=Master or the whole Art of playing on ye Rechorder . . . London: Walsh, 1695. Only copy in Lbm K.5. b. 32 (a recent acquisition).

Compleat Instructor to the Flute. The Second Book. London: J. Young, 1700. Only copy in US NH.

Courtly Masquing Ayres: Containing Almanes, Ayres, Corants, Sarabands, Morisco's, Jiggs &c. of two parts, Treble and Basse, for Viols or Violins . . . London: W. Godbid for John Playford, 1662.

The Dancing Master. London: J. Playford et al., 1670, 1675, 1679, 1686, 1690, 1695, 1696, 1698, 1701, 1705, 1709, 1713, 1716, and 1718.

The Division Flute. The First Part of The Division Flute Containing A Collection of Divisions upon Several Excellent Grounds for the Flute being Very Improving and Delightfull to all Lovers of that Instrument . . . London: I. Walsh and I. Hare, 1706.

The Division Flute. The Second Part of the Division Flute. Containing the Newest Divisions upon the Choicest Grounds . . . London: I. Walsh and I. Hare [1708].

The Division Violin. The First Part of the Division Violin Containing A Collection of Divisions upon Several Excellent Grounds for the Violin The Sixth Edition Corected and enlarged with Aditions of the newest Divisions upon Grounds and Chacons by the most Eminent Masters.   London: I. Walsh and I. Hare [1705].

The Division Violin. The Second Part of the Division Violin Containing the newest Divisions upon Grounds for the Violin as also seueral solos by Arcangello Corelli and others the Fourth Edition Corected and enlarged with Additions of the newest Chacons Allmands Preludes and Choice Cibells Composed by the best Masters . . . London: I. Walsh and I. Hare [1705].

The Division-Violin. The second part of the Division-Violin: containing the newest divisions to a ground, and Scotch tunes of two parts for the treble-violin . . . London: H. Playford, 1693.

Eccles, John.   *A Collection of Songs* for One, Two, and Three Voices, together with such Symphonies for Violins or Flutes as were by the Author design'd for any of them . . . London: I. Walsh [1704].

Flute Master. The Fifth Book of the New Flute Master Containing The most Perfect Rules and Easiest Directions for Learners on the Flute yet Extant, together wth an Extraordinary Collection of Aires both Italian and English Perticularly the most celibrated Arietts in the New Opera of Arsinoe Queen of Cyprus, and severall other Excellent Tunes never before Printed.   London: I. Walsh and I. Hare, 1706.

Harmonia Anglicana Or the Musick of the English Stage, Containing Six Sets of Ayers and Tunes in 4 Parts, made for the Operas Tragedys and Comedyes of the Theatre Royal . . . London: I. Walsh and I. Hare [1701-1706].

> Note: Apparently nine collections of this series were issued, but title-pages for only the first two survive. For a complete listing of this publication, see Appendix II.

Harpsichord Master. The Second Book of the Harpsichord Master Containing A choice Collection of Lessons for the Harpsichord or Spinnett as Almands, Sarabrands, Ayres, Minuetts, and Jiggs . . . London: I Walsh, 1700.   Only copy in Lcm I.F.9 (3).

Harpsichord Master. The Third Book of the Harpsichord Master . . . London: I. Walsh, 1702.   Only copy in Lcm I.F.9 (4).

A Hundred and Twenty Country Dances for the Flute . . . London: L. Pippard, 1711.

An Introduction to the Skill of Musick . . . London: J. Playford, 1674.

Ladys Banquet. The Second Book of the Ladys Banquet Being A Choice Collection of the Newest . . . Lessons for the Harpsichord . . . London: I. Walsh, 1706.

Lock[e], Matthew. *The English Opera: or the Vocal Musick in Psyche* . . . to which is Adjoyned the Instrumental Musick in the Tempest.   London: T. Ratcliff, and N. Thompson, 1675.

Melothesia,: or, certain general rules for playing upon a continued-bass . . . The first part. London: J. Carr, 1673.

Musick's Delight on the Cithren, Restored and Refined to a more Easie and Pleasant Manner of Playing than formerly . . . London: W[illiam] G[odbid], 1666.

Musicks Hand-maide. Presenting New and Pleasant Lessons for the Virginals or Harpsycon. London: John Playford, 1663.

Musicks Hand-maid: New Lessons and Instructions for the Virginals or Harpsichord. London: J. Playford, 1678.

Musicks Recreation on The Viol, Lyra-way. Being a new Collection of Lessons Lyra-way. To which is added a Preface, Containing some Brief Rules and Instructions for young Practitioners. London: W. Godbid, for John Playford, 1669.

The Pleasant Companion: or, New lessons and Instructions for the Flagelet. By Thomas Greeting . . . London: John Playford, 1672. Only copy in Cambridge, University Library.

The Pleasant Companion . . . London: John Playford, 1675. Copy in Ob.

The Pleasant Companion . . . London: John Playford, 1680. Copy in Lcm.

The Pleasant Companion . . . London: John Playford, 1682. Copy in Lbm.

Purcell, Henry. *A Collection of Ayres, Compos'd for the Theatre,* and upon Other Occasions . . . London: 1697.

Select Lessons for the Violin, as Preludes Almands Sarabands Corants Minuets and Iiggs . . . London: I. Walsh, 1702. Only copy in Durham, Cathedral Library.

The Self-Instructor on the Violin, the 1st, Second, & Third Books . . . London: I. Walsh, 1700.

Songs In The New Opera Call'd the World in the Moon . . . London: I: Walsh and I: Hare, 1697.

Theater Musick Being A Collection of the newest Ayers for the Violin, with the French Dances perform'd at Both Theaters, as also the new Dances at ye late Ball at Kensington on ye Kings Birth day and those in the new Opera of Rinaldo & Armida, with a Through Bass to each Dance, Compos'd by Mr: Iohn Eccles. London: I: Walsh [1698]. Only copy in Durham, Cathedral Library.

Theatre Musick. The Second Book of Theatre Musick . . . London: I: Walsh, 1699. Only copy in Durham, Cathedral Library.

Theater Musick. The Third Book of Theater Musick . . . London: I Walsh. 1700. Only copy in Durham, Cathedral Library.

The Theatre of Musick: or, A Choice Collection of the newest and best Songs sung at the Court, and Public Theatres . . . Also Symphonies and Retornels in 3 parts to several of them for the Violins and Flutes . . . London: J. Playford, for Henry Playford and R[ichard] C[arr], 1685-1687.

Thesaurus musicus: being, a collection of the newest songs performed at their majesties theatres; and at the Consorts in Villier-street in York-buildings, and in Charles-street . . . To which is annexed a collection of aires, composed for two flutes, by several masters. 5 books.   London: J. Heptinstall for John Hudgebut, 1693, 1694, 1695, and 1696.

Twenty Four New Country Dances for the Year 1718.   With New Tunes and Figures to each Dance . . . London: I. Walsh and I. Hare, 1718.

Vade Mecum for the Lovers of musick, shewing the excellency of the recorder . . . London: J. Hudgebutt, 1679.

Vinculum Societatis, or the Tie of good Company.   3 Vols. London: F. Clark, T. Moore, and J. Heptinstall, for John Carr and R. C., 1687-1691.

Walsh, John [Act Music of the Queens Theatre, 1705-1710].

Note: For a complete listing of this publication, see Appendix II.

The Catalogue

T   *Abdelazer, or the Moor's Revenge,* Aphra Behn, DG (1677)

Act music (for a revival, c. 1693):   Henry Purcell, *A Collection of Ayres for the Theatre* (1697), pp. [40]-41.   See Z 570.

1 Overture

2 Rondeau   = *Self-Instructor,* I (1700) [No. 18], "Horn-pipe," a1; Lcm
                        [*Apollo's Banquet,* c. 1705] [No. 106], "Round O by Mr.
                        H. Purcell," a1

3 Aire   = *Compleat Flute=Master* (1695) [fol. 18], "Ayre M.^{r}
                        Purcell," a1; Lcm [*Apollo's Banquet,* c. 1705], No. 64,
                        "Ayre," a1

4 Aire   = LA Finney pt-bks., p. 105, "5," a4

5 Minuett   = LA Finney pt-bks., p. 106, "6," a4

6 Aire   = LA Finney pt-bks., p. 77, "8," a4

7 Jigg   = *Self-Instructor,* I (1700) [No. 28], "Jigg," a1; *50 Airs
                        Anglois,* p. 29, "Air Presto, Mr H. Purcell," a3

    8 Hornpipe

    9 Aire   = LA Finney pt-bks., p. 76, "6," a4; *Self-Instructor*, I (1700) [No. 27], "Aire," a1

Songs: I.i [Abdelazer sullenly leaning his head on his hands; After a little while, still Musick plays. Song.] "Love in Phantastick triumph sat"

          II.ii [SONG] "Make haste, Amintas, come away" (D&M 2158 *m*Forcer)

          not printed in play-book: "Lucinda is bewitching fair" (D&M 2141 *m*H. Purcell *s*"the boy")

Dance: II.ii [A Dance of Shepherds and Shepherdesses.]

T *Abra-Mule: Or, Love and Empire*, Joseph Trapp, LIF (1704)

Act music: Walsh. *Harmonia Anglicana* [VI, 1704], "M.ʳ [John] Lentons Musick in the Play call'd Abra Mule," copies in Lgc G.Mus. 153 (second treble), Lcm XXIX.A.11 (a4), Lcm XXIX.A.12 (second treble, tenor, bass)

    1 Overture

    2 Minuett   = Lbm Add. 24889, fol. 22, a4

    3 Aire

    4 Aire

    5 Slow Aire

    6 Slow Aire

    7 Minuett

    8 Slow Saraband

    9 Iigg

Song: IV.i [SCENE, A pleasant Grotto . . . Enter Eunuchs with Six Women of the Seraglio: The Kisler places them with Abra. Then enter Mahomet, and seats himself. A Symphony of soft Musick, after which the Song.] "Happy Monarch, who with Beauty"

The Accomplish'd Fools (see *The Tender Husband*)

The Agreeable Disappointment (see *Love Betray'd*)

T *The Albion Queens: or the Death of Mary Queen of Scotland*, John Banks, DL [1704]

Act music: Walsh, *Harmonia Anglicana* [collection a, 1704], "M^r [John] Barretts
               Musick in the PLAY call'd Mary Queen of Scotts," copies in Lbm
               b.29.a (first treble), Lbm d.24 (first treble and bass), Lgc G.Mus. 153
               (second treble), Lcm XXIX.A.11 (a4), Lcm XXIX.A.12 (second treble,
               tenor, bass)

[1] Overture

2   = Cmc pt-bks., fol. 66', "Slow," a4

3 Iigg

4 Saraband   = *Harpsichord Master*, III (1702), p. 9, "Minuet by Mr.
                          Barrett," keyb.

5 Aire

6 Iigg

7 Round O   = Cmc pt-bks., fol. 58', "Slow," a4; *Flute Master*, V (1706),
                          p. 23, "Round O by Mr Barrett," a1

8 Gavott   = Cmc pt-bks., fol. 58', a4; *Ladys Banquet*, II (1706), p. 9,
                          "Gavott," keyb.

9 Iigg

C *The Alchymist*, Ben Jonson (1612)

Act music (for a revival 14 January 1710, QT): Walsh [Act Music of the Queens
               Theatre, 1710], "First Treble Musick in the Play call'd the Alchimist
               by a Italian Master [i.e., G. F. Handel]," copy in the Gerald Coke
               Collection, a4

[1] Overture   = Lbm R.M. 20.c.5, "Rodrigo" [c. 1707] [fol. 1]. "Overture
                          di G. F. Handel," a4

2 Prelude   = [see below]

3 Minuet   = Lbm R.M. 20.c.5, fol. 8', "4 Menuet," a4

4 Saraband   = Lbm R.M. 20.c.5, fol. 5, "2 Saraband," a4

5 Boree   = Lbm R.M. 20.c.5, fol. 5', "5 Bourre," a4

6 Aire   = Lbm R.M. 20.c.5, fol. 7, a4

7 Minuet   =   Lbm R.M. 20.c.5, fol. 7', "Menuet," a4

8 Aire   =   Lbm R.M. 20.c.5, fol. 4, "3 Matelot," a4

9 Jigg   =   Lbm R.M. 20.c.5, fol. 3, "Gigue," a4

Note: Two other copies (lacking the tenor part) are found in Mp MS 130 Hd 4, Vol. 189, and in *Handel's Works* [ed. Samuel Arnold, c. 1790], Vol. 17, No. 64, "The Music in the Alchymist, Composed by G. F. Handel." For a manuscript copy almost identical to the Walsh print, see Lbm Add. 31576, fols. 118-122, "Handel's Music in the Alchymist," a4.

Alexander the Great (see *The Rival Queens*)

C *All for the Better: Or, The Infallible Cure* [Francis Manning], DL (1703)

Act music: Walsh, *Harmonia Anglicana* [IV, 1702], "Mr Ier:[emiah] Clarke's Aires in the Comedy call'd all for the Better," copies in Lbm b.29.a (first treble), Lbm d.24 (first treble and bass), Lgc G.Mus. 153 (second treble)

[1] Overture   =   Cmc pt-bks., fol. 91', a4; Och 3, fol. 41', "J. Clarke Overture in All for ye better," a4

2 Gavott   =   Och 3, fol. 42', "Gavott," a4; *Harpsichord Master*, III (1702), p. 7, "Gavott by Mr. Clark," keyb.

3 Hornpipe Round O   =   Och 3, fol. 42', "Hornpipe Round O," a4; *Harpsichord Master*, III (1702) [p.8], "Hornpipe by Mr Clark," keyb.

4 Aire   =   Cmc pt-bks., fol. 66, a4; Och 3, fol. 42', "Aire," a4

5 Round O Slow   =   Cmc pt-bks., fol. 8, a4; Och 3, fol. 43', "Round O Slow," a4; Och 620, p. 21, "By Mr Clark," a2

6 Aire   =   Och 3, fol. 43, "Aire," a4; *Harpsichord Master*, III (1702) [p. 6], "A Farewell (Slow) by Mr Clark," keyb.

7 Farwell Slow   =   Och 3, fol. 43', "Farwell Slow," a4: *Harpsichord Master*, III (1702) [p. 6], "A Farewell (Slow) by Mr Clark," keyb.

8 Aire   =   Och 3, fol. 44, "J. Clarke Aire," a4

9 Minuet Round O   =   Och 3, fol. 44, "Minuet Round O," a4

Songs: I.i [SONG. Set by Mr. Daniel Purcell.] "Come, let us be jolly"

              II.i [A Song and soft Musick here. SONG Set by Mr. D. Purcell.] "Awake, fair Nymph, awake, and dream No more"

              IV.ii [A short Consort of Musick. SONG by a Friend.] "Oft have I heard our Poets"

              V.iv [Musick Plays . . . DIALOGUE by a Friend. Set by Mr. Barret. Enter a Cupid and Girl.] "Tell me, Precious, my you prove so Coy"

? All in Confusion

Dance: *Apollo's Banquet* (1691), No. 65, "Dance in the Play All in Confusion," a1 = *Apollo's Banquet* (1701), No. 103, "Tune by Mr. Montford," a1

Comment: This is possibly an alternative second title for Joseph Harris's tragicomedy *The Mistakes, or, The False Report* (1691). See Price, "Eight 'Lost' Restoration Plays 'Found' in Musical Sources," *Music & Letters*, LVIII (1977), 299.

T   *The Ambitious Step-mother*, Nicholas Rowe, LIF (1701)

Act music: Walsh, *Harmonia Anglicana*, I [1701], "Mr Lenton's Ayres in the Tragedy of the Ambitious Stepmother," copies in Lbm d.24 (first treble and bass), Dc C.37 (a4), Lgc. G. Mus. 153 (second treble), Lcm XXIX.A.11 (a4)

1 Overture

2 Aire

3 Hornpipe   =   Cmc pt-bks., fol. 92', a4

4 Slow aire

5 Gavott

6 Hornpipe   =   Cmc pt-bks., fol. 92', a4

7 Jigg   =   Cmc pt-bks., fol. 93, "Slow," a4

8 Scotch Aire   =   *Select Lessons* (1702), fol. 6, "Scotch Aire by Mr Lenton," a1

    9 Slow Aire   =   Cmc pt-bks., fol. 12, "Slow," a4

Songs: III.i [A Garden belonging to Mirza's Palace. Cleone is discover'd lying on a bank of Flowers, attending. SONG, by B. Stote, Esq.] "Upon a shady Bank repos'd"

             III.ii [The Scene opening shews the Altar of the Sun, Magas and several other Priests attending. Solemn Musick is heard . . . HYMN to the Sun, by W. Shippen, Esq;] "Hail Light, that doubly glads our sphere"

The Amorous Jilt (see *The Younger Brother*)

C *Amphitryon: or, The Two Socias*, John Dryden, DL (1690)

    Act music: Henry Purcell, *A Collection of Ayres for the Theatre* (1697), pp. 28-30. See Z 572.

    1 Overture

    2 Saraband

    3 Hornpipe

    4 Scotch Tune

    5 Aire   =   LA Finney pt-bks., p. 81, a4

    6 Minuett   =   LA Finney pt-bks., p. 80 a4

    7 Minuett   =   LA Finney pt-bks., p. 81, a4; Lbm Add. 22098, fol. 14', a1; *Dancing Master* (1703), p. 252, "Enfield Common," a1

Songs and Dances: see Z 572.

C *The Anatomist: or, the Sham Doctor*, Edward Ravenscroft, LIF (1697)

    ? Dance: *Dancing Master*, II (1698), p. 26, "The Sham Doctor," a1

Comment: This perhaps was danced in the masque *The Loves of Mars and Venus* (1697) by P. A. Motteux, performed with *The Anatomist.* The vocal music of the masque is found in *Single Songs, and Dialogues, in The Musical Play of Mars & Venus. Perform'd with the Anatomist, or the Sham Doctor. Set to Musick by Mr. Finger, and Mr. John Eccles* (1697). See D&M 332, 593, 1031, 1463, 2090, 2105, 2121, 2247, 2266, 2858, 3072, 3223, 3301, 3348, 3419, 3431, and 3446.

T *Antony and Cleopatra*, Charles Sedley, DG (1677)

Act music (for a revival in 1696? See *The London Stage*, I, 450): Lcm 1172, fol. 15, "[Jeremiah] Clarke Overture in Antony & Cleopatra," a4

? Miscellaneous music: Lcm 1172, fol. 20', "Clarke, Lady Warton's Farewell in [Antony?] & Cleopatra," a4

Armida and Rinaldo (see *Rinaldo and Armida*)

C *The Artful Husband*, William Taverner, LIF [1717]

See Smith, *Walsh I*, No. 507, an advertisement in *The Post Man* 30 March-2 April 1717: "A Set of Tunes in 4 Parts for Violins and Hoboys, in the Comedy call'd The Artful Husband, compos'd by Mr. [William] Turner." This music is not extant.

C *As You Find it*, Charles Boyle, LIF (1703)

Act music: Walsh, *Harmonia Anglicana* [VI, 1703], "M^r [William] Corbetts Musick in the Comedy call'd As you find it," copies in Lbm d.24 (first treble and bass), Lgc G. Mus. 153 (second treble), Lcm XXIX.A.11 (a4), Lcm XXIX.A.12 (second treble, tenor, bass)

1 Overture

2 Aire

3 Hornpipe

4 Aire

5 Aire

6 Scotch Aire

7 Aire Slow

8 Minuett

Songs: I.ii [SONG, Set by Mr. John Eccles.] "Sabina's Haughty as she's Fair"

II.iii [Enter Musicians . . . SONG in the Second Act. Sett by Mr. John Eccles. Sung by Mrs. Hodgson.] "He that has whom he lov'd" (in Eccles, *A Collection of Songs* [1704], p. 84, also arranged "For the Flute," a2; and a broadsheet published by T. Cross, in Ckc)

P *The Banditti, or, A Ladies Distress*, Thomas Durfey, DL (1686)

? Dance: *Apollo's Banquet*, III (1690), No. 11, "The Banditti; a Round O," al

Note: This "Round O" is the tune to "The Joys of court or city" (D&M 1888) in III.i of this play.

C   *The Bassett-Table*, Susannah Centlivre, DL (1706)

See Smith, *Walsh I*, No. 194, an advertisement in *The Post Man* 22-24 January 1706: "Mr. D.[aniel] Purcell's Musick in 4 parts, in the Comedy called The Bassett-Table." This music is not extant.

Beauty the Best Advocate (see *Measure for Measure*)

C   *The Beaux Stratagem*, George Farquhar, QT (1707)

Act music: Walsh [Act Music of the Queens Theatre, 1707], "M^r [Jean-Claude] Gilliers Musick in the Play call'd the Stratagem," copy in Lbm g.15 (a4)

1   Overture

2   Trumpet tune

3   Allemand

4   Aire

5   Saraband

6   Gavot

7   Aire

8   Iigg

9   Iigg

Dance: V.iv. *Archer*. Madam, there's a Country Dance to the Trifle that I sing to Day; your Hand, and we'll lead it up.   [Here a Dance.]

Dancing Master (1718), p. 169, "The Beaus Stratagem," a1. This dance may have been associated with this play.   See also BUCEM, II, 855.

T   *Boadicea, Queen of Britain*, Charles Hopkins, LIF (1697)

Act music: US NH Filmer MS 9 [pp. 50-52], "M^r. Forcer in ye Queen of Brittain," a3

1
2
3
4
5
6
7
8
9

The Boarding School (see *Love for Money*)

T *Bonduca: or, The British Heroine,* George Powell, DL (1696)

    Act music: Henry Purcell, *A Collection of Ayres for the Theatre* (1697), pp. 42-45. See Z 574.

    1 Overture   = LA Finney pt-bks., p. 83, "Overture," a4

    2 Song Tune   = LA Finney pt-bks., p. 52, a4; Lcm [*Apollo's Banquet,* c. 1705], No. 55, "Ayre," al

    3 Song Tune   = LA Finney pt-bks., p. 51, a4; Lcm [*Apollo's Banquet,* c. 1705], No. 54, "March by H. Purcell," al

    4 Aire   = LA Finney pt-bks., p. 50, a4

    5 Hornpipe   = CDp 1.39(j), fol. 49, "Purcell," keyb.

    6 Aire   = LA Finney pt-bks., p. 50, a4

    7 Hornpipe   = LA Finney pt-bks, p. 51, a4

    8 Aire

    9 Minuet   = LA Finney pt-bks., p. 77, a4

    Songs, etc.: see Z 574.

DO *The British Enchanters: or, No Magick like Love* [George Granville], QT (1706)

    Act music: Walsh, *Harmonia Anglicana* [collection c, 1706], "M.^{r} [William] Corbetts Musick in the OPERA call'd the British Inchanters or no Magick like Love," copy in Lbm d.24 (first treble and bass)

    1 Overture

    2 Prelude

3 Minuet

4 Aire

5 March

6 Aire

7 March

8 Boree

9 Minuett

The British Heroine (see *Bonduca*)

The British Worthy (see *King Arthur*)

T *Bussy D'Ambois, or the Husbands Revenge,* Thomas Durfey, DL (1691)

? Act music: Lcm 1144, fols. 48-49, "Mr [Henry] Purcells in The Husbands Revenge," a2

Comment: This set of act music appears in *A Collection of Ayres for the Theatre* (1697) ascribed to *The Old Batchelour,* Congreve (1693). Three of these act tunes appear in 1691 publications (*Apollo's Banquet,* Nos. 55, 56, and 57 and *Vinculum Societatis,* III [pp. 31 and 33]. See s.v. *The Old Batchelour,* below. Perhaps this music was used for both plays, but the ascriptions in Lcm 1144 are in many other instances faulty.   See also Z 607.

The Canting Astrologer (see *The Cheats*)

Capua (see *The Fate of Capua*)

C *The Cheats* [or The Canting Astrologer?], John Wilson (1664)

Act music (for revival, 1684 or 1693?): Och 944, pp. 1-9 "[Thomas] Tolletts [act music] in The Cheats or The Canting Astrologer," a4

Comment: The play-books for various editions of this play do not give the second title "The Canting Astrologer," but considering the subject of the play, it is appropriate.

[1] Overture

[2] Bore

[3] Hornpipe

[4] Scotch tune

[5] Aire

[6] Entre   =   Cmc pt-bks., fol. 128', a4

[7] Jigg

[8] Chacone

Song: II.iv [Bilboe Sings.] "Come give me the Wench that is mellow"

Dance: V.v. *Jolly.* Servavit Apollo!--Strike up, strike--One noise best drownes
               another . . . [They dance.   Tyro pipes.]

Miscellaneous music: V.i. [The Lute Playes]

Cinthia and Endymion (see *A New Opera, call'd Cinthia and Endimion*)

C   *The City-Heiress: or, Sir Timothy Treat-all*, Aphra Behn, DG (1682)

Act music: Lbm Add. 29283-5, fols. 65'-68, "Egles [Solomon Eccles] tunes in S^r
               Timothy Treatall," a3

      1   =   US NH Filmer MS 6 [fol. 34'], p. 52, a3

      2   =   US NH Filmer MS 6 [fol. 34'], p. 52, a3

      3   =   US NH Filmer MS 6 [fol. 35], p. 53, a3

      4   =   US NH Filmer MS 6 [fol. 35], p. 53, a3

      5   =   US NH Filmer MS 6 [fol. 33'], p. 50, "Overture," a3

      6   =   US NH Filmer MS 6 [fol. 34], p. 51, a3

      7   =   US NH Filmer MS 6 [fol. 34], p. 51, a3

      8

      9

      10

      11

Songs: III.i [Enter Musick playing, Sir Anthony Merriwell dancing with a
               Lady in his hand . . . Sir Anth. singing.] "Philander was a jolly swain"

(III.i) [Song sung by Charlot] "Ah Jenny Jen your eyes do kill" (D&M 61)

(III.i) [Here is an Italian Song in 2 parts]

IV.i [Song sung by Betty] "In Phillis all vile jilts are met" (D&M 1762 *m*Draghi)

Dances: (see III.i, above)

III.i [They all sit. Charlot and Fopington dance]

Miscellaneous music: V.iv [Musicians play]

C   *The City Lady: or, Folly Reclaim'd,* Thomas Dilke, LIF (1697)

Act music: Ob c.72, pp. 24-26, "Mr [Godfrey] Finger['s act music in] The City Lady," a3

[1] Overture	=	LA Finney pt-bks., p. 114, "Mr Finger 1 Overture," a4; Lbm Add. 35043, fol. 79, "Finger Overture in the City Lady," a1; US NH Filmer MS 9 [p. 54], "Overture," a3
2	=	LA Finney pt-bks., p. 115, "3," a4; Lbm Add. 35043, fol. 79, a1; *Self-Instructor,* II (1700) [No. 31], "Minuet Mr. Finger," a1; US NH Filmer MS 9 [p. 55], a3
3	=	LA Finney pt-bks., p. 115, a4: Lbm Add. 35043, fol. 79', a1; *Select Lessons* (1702), fol. 14, "The Stratham A Country Dance," a1; US NH Filmer MS 9 [p. 55], a3
4	=	LA Finney pt-bks., p. 116, a4; Lbm Add. 35043, fol. 79', a1; *Self-Instructor,* II (1700) [No. 30], "Minuet Mr. Finger," a1; US NH Filmer MS 9 [p. 55], a3
5	=	LA Finney pt-bks., p. 116, a4; Lbm Add. 34204, fol. 4, "A Scotch tune by Mr Finger," a1; Lbm Add. 35043, fol. 79', a1; *Self-Instructor,* II (1700) [No. 33], "Scotch tune Mr. Finger," a1; US NH Filmer MS 9 [p. 55], a3
6	=	LA Finney pt-bks., p. 116, a4; Lbm Add. 35043, fol. 79', a1; *Self-Instructor,* II (1700) [No. 24], "Aire Mr. Finger," a1; US NH Filmer MS 9 [p. 53], "Mr Finger in ye Citty Lady," a3
7	=	LA Finney pt-bks., p. 117, a4; Lbm Add. 35043, fol. 80, a1; US NH Filmer MS 9 [p. 53], a3

8   = LA Finney pt-bks., p. 117, a4; Lbm Add. 35043, fol. 80, a1; *Self-Instructor*, II (1700) [No. 25], "Aire Mr Finger," a1; US NH Filmer MS 9 [p. 53], a3

9   = LA Finney pt-bks., p. 117, a4; Lbm Add. 35043, fol. 80, a1; US NH Filmer MS 9 [p. 53], a3

Songs: II.i [Lucinda sings Song.] "Love is an empty airy Name" (in Lbm Add. 22099, fol. 69', by [John] Eccles; *A Song in the City-Lady* . . . sung by Mrs Hudson, copies in Lgc and Mpl)

     (II.i) [Formosa sings.] "All beauty were a foolish toy"

     III.ii [Scene opens, and the Company goes in to a Banquet, flourish of Trumpets as they lead up: During the Banquet an Entertainment of Music, Singing and Dancing. Ode Triumphant.] "Give to the Warrior loud & lasting praise"

     IV.ii [Cicely Sings] "There lately was a maiden Fair" (D&M 3218)

     V [Pedantry makes a Song on the laundress at Oxford] "Fine laundry Nell"

Dances: (see III.ii above)

     V [Final dance]

Note: In NYp MS Drexel 3849, p. 117, is a piece (a3) entitled "Formosa." There is a character of that name in this play; possibly the music is related to the play.

The City Wives Confederacy (see *The Confederacy*)

T *Cleomenes The Spartan Heroe*, John Dryden, DL (1692)

Song: II.ii [The SCENE opens and discovers Cassandra's Apartment. Musicians and Dancers . . . Song and Dance . . . SONG] "No no, poor suff'ring Heart" (D&M 2347 *m*H. Purcell *s*Mrs. Butler)

Note: In Lbm Add. 24889, fol. 21', is an a4 arrangement of this song.

Cleopatra (see *Antony and Cleopatra*)

C *The Comical History of Don Quixote*, three parts, Thomas Durfey, DG (1694, 1694, 1696)

? Dances: Lcm 1172, fol. 35', "Minuet in Don Quixet," a1

     Dancing Master (1695), p. 162, "Sancho-Pancho," a1

See also Z 578.

C *The Comical Revenge; or, Love in a Tub*, George Etherege, LIF (1664)

> ? Dance (for a revival 13 November 1671?): *Pleasant Companion* (1672), No. 8, "Love in a Tubb: a Dance M:[atthew] L:[ocke]," al

A Comical Transformation (see *The Devil of a Wife*)

C *The Confederacy*, John Vanbrugh, QT (1705)

> See Smith, *Walsh I*, No. 189, an advertisement in *The Post Man*, 20-22 December 1705: "The Musick in 4 parts perform'd in the Comedy called the Confederacy. Composed by Mr J.[ohn] Eccles, Master of her Majesty's Musick." This music is not extant.

C *The Constant Couple or a Trip to the Jubilee*, George Farquhar, DL (1700)

> Miscellaneous instrumental music: *Compleat Instructor to the Flute*, II (1700), pp. 1, 4, 5, 6, 11, 12, seven pieces in "ye Iubilee," al

[1] A Round O	= *Theater Musick*, III (1700), sig. b, "Round O in ye Jubile," al; Cmc pt-bks., fol. 78', a4; Ob e.397, p. 38, "Rondo in ye Jubille," keyb.
[2] an Aire	= *Theater Musick*, III (1700), sig. c, "Aire," al; Cmc pt-bks., fol. 79, a4
[3] The Country Dance	= *Theater Musick*, III (1700), sig. p, "Country Dance in the Jubile," al; *Dancing Master* (1701), p. 289, "The Trip to the Jubilee, as 'tis Danc'd at the Play-House," al
[4] "Thus Damon Knockt," Song tune in the Iubilee	= see below
[5] a bore	
[6] A Iigg	= *Theater Musick*, III (1700), sig. c, "Jigg," al
[7]	= *Theater Musick*, III (1700), sig. a, "Slow = Aire in ye trip to ye Jubile," al; Cmc pt-bks., fol. 78', a4

Comment: The "Slow-aire," No. [7] above, "Aire," and "Round O" are probably act tunes, and the dance was probably performed in the entertainment in V.iii.

Songs: IV.ii [Wildair sings] "Thus Damon Knocked at Celia's Door" (D&M 3351 *m*D. Purcell *s*Pate and Freeman); also see BUCEM, II, 855

V.iii [Here singing and dancing]

Comment: On the title-page of *The Compleat Instructor to the Flute*, II (1700), is the statement that the book contains "ye rest of ye Musick in the Iubilee," suggesting that more music for Farquhar's play was printed in an earlier Young collection, now apparently lost.

The Converted Twins (see Saint Cecily*)*

C   *The Country-Wake*, Thomas Dogget, LIF (1696)

? Dances: Lbm Add. 38189, fol. 31 "[dances] in the Country Wake," a1

[1] Hornpipe . . . very slow: 4 times

[2] play this [dance] till you see they have done

[3 Dance] In the 4th Act

Comment: Lbm Add. 38189 is apparently a dance-book used by theatre musicians. The marginalia are unusually complete. The note "very Slow: 4 times" is indicative of how a brief tune could serve as the music for an extended dance.

Songs: not printed in the play-book "Come Hodge come Robin come John" (D&M 653 *m*J. Eccles *s*Wiltshire and Mrs. Hudson)

              "Of all simple things we do" (D&M 2571)

Dances: IV.ii [Enter Hob with the Potts of Ale, stares on the Dancers . . . Dance.]

Comment: The music for this dance is probably that headed "In the 4th Act" in Lbm Add. 38189, listed above.

              V.ii (Hob is supposedly ill and his mother tells Mary to kiss him. His wedding is then arranged and there is a dance. Perhaps kissing was a feature of the dance.)

Dancing Master, II (1696), p. 16, "Hobb's Wedding: A Kissing-Dance in the Country Wake," a1

C   *Courtship A-la-mode*, David Crauford, DL (1700)

Act music: Walsh, *Harmonia Anglicana*, I [1700], "Mr Wm Croft Ayres in the Comedy of Courtship Alamode," copies in Dc C.37 (a4), Lgc G. Mus. 153 (second treble), Lcm XXIX.A.11 (a4), Lcm XXIX.A.12 (second treble, tenor, bass)

[1] Overture   =   Och 620, p. 54, "Overture Mr Crafts," a4

2 Aire   = Och 620, p. 61, "Aire (2), Mr. Crafts," a4; *Harpsichord Master*, III (1702) [fol. 11], "Aire by Mr Crofts," keyb.

3 Aire   = Och 620, p. 62, "Aria (3) Mr Crafts," a4

4 Round O   = Och 620, p. 63, "Round O Mr. Crafts," a4

5 Round O Minuet   = Och 620, p. 64, "Round O Minuet Mr. Crafts," a4; *Apollo's Banquet* (1701), No. 27, "Slow Minuet," a1; *Harpsichord Master*, III (1702), fol. 10, "Song tune by Mr Crofts," keyb.; *Compleat Instructor to the Flute*, II (1700), p. 17, "A Round o by Mr Wm Croft," a1

6 Aire   = Och 620, p. 65, "Aire Mr. Crafts," a4

7 Hornpipe   = Och 620, p. 67, "Horn Pipe Mr Crafts," a4; Lbm Add. 22099, fol. 12', "Hornpipe," keyb.; *Harpsichord Master*, II (1700) [No. 25], "Aire Mr. Crofts," keyb.

8 Round O Scotch Tune = Och 620, p. 68, "Round O Scotch Tune . . . Mr Crafts," a4; *Apollo's Banquet* (1701), No. 28, "Scotch Tune," a1; *Harpsichord Master*, III (1702) [fol. 12], "Scotch Tune by Mr Crofts," keyb.; *Select Lessons* (1702), fol. 11, "The Northern Ladd A Country Dance," a1; *Compleat Instructor to the Flute*, II (1700), p. 16, "Mr Croft A Round O," a1

Songs: V.ii [Here Dick sings a Comical Song.]

            (V.ii) [Here a Song, then a Figure Dance]

Dances: V.ii. *Willie.* Play up thaun Fidlers, aun be haung't tea ye, aut let me hea au verray bonny Spring.   [Here a Dance by Willie.]

O *The Cruelty of the Spaniards in Peru,* William Davenant, Cockpit (1658)

? Dance: *Brief Introduction* (1664), p. 109, "Saraband," a1 = *Dancing Master*, II (1665), No. 51, "A Sarab.[and] for to Dance with [ca]stanets," a1

Comment: This may be part of the music used in the fourth entry: ". . . a Saraband is play'd whilst two Spaniards enter . . . they solemnly uncloak and unarm themselves to the Tune and afterwards dance with Castanietos."

Cuckolds make themselves (see *The Wives Excuse*)

The Curious Impertinent (see *The Married Beau*)

Cynthia and Endymion (see *A New Opera, call'd Cinthia and Endimion)*

The Death of Alexander the Great (see *The Rival Queens)*

C *The Devil of a Wife, or, A Comical Transformation,* Thomas Jevon, DG (1686)

    ? Act music: NYp MS Drexel 3849, p. 74, "Mr Banisters Divell," a3

        [1] Divell

        [2] The Ground

        [3] Almaine

        [4] Corant

        [5]

        [6] Hornepipe Finis

Dioclesian (see *The Prophetess*)

P *The Disappointment: or, The Mother in Fashion,* Thomas Southerne, DL (1684)

    Act music: Lbm Add. 29283, fols. 74'-77 "[Lewis] Grabus for ye Play call'd Ye Dissappointment, or ye Mother in fashion. 1684," a3

        1

        2

        3

        4 Round O

        5

        7 [NB]

        6

        8

        9

10

11

Songs: I.i [Albertus Dressing. A SONG written by the Honourable Colonel Sackvile.] "I Never saw a face till now" (D&M 1574 *m*Pack)

II.ii [Scene changes to Erminia's Chamber. A SONG by an unknown hand.] "Poor, ill-instructed, wretched Womankind!"

III.i [A SONG made by Colonel Sackvile.] "Oh why did e'er my thoughts aspire" (D&M 2552 *m*R. King)

V.ii [A SONG written by Sir George Ethridge.] "See how fair Corinna lies" (D&M 2867 *m*Pack)

The instrumental ritornelli to three of the four songs survive in *Theatre of Musick*, I (1685), 1, a3:

"I never saw a face 'til now," Capt. Pack

"See how fair Corrina," Capt. Pack

"Oh! why did e're my Thoughts aspire," Robert King

Comment: To find instrumental ritornelli to solo songs in plays of this period is rare, although in performance, many songs surely had them. These instrumental pieces thus make the original music of this play unusually complete, the only apparent lacuna being the song in II.ii.

? Dance: *The Dancing Master* (1715), p. 184, "Disappointment," a1

T *Distress'd Innocence: or, The Princess of Persia,* Elkanah Settle, DL (1691)

Act music: Henry Purcell, *A Collection of Ayres for the Theatre* (1697), pp. 34-36. See Z 577.

1 Overture

[2] Aire

3 Slow Aire

4 Aire

5 Hornpipe

6 Rondeau   = LA Finney pt-bks., p. 78, "9 Round O," a4

7 Aire   = LA Finney pt-bks., p. 105, a4

8 Minuet

Song (not printed in the play-book): "Why Oh! why should the World Mistake," in
      J. Eccles, *A Collection of Songs* [1704], p. 7, "A SONG in The
      Princess of Persia," a2

Divell (see *The Devil of a Wife*)

Don Quixote (see *The Comical History of Don Quixote*)

C *The Double Dealer,* William Congreve, DL (1694)

Act music: Henry Purcell, *A Collection of Ayres for the Theatre* (1697), pp. 30-33.
              See Z 592.

1 Overture

2 Hornpipe

3 Minuett

4 Air

5 Hornpipe

6 Minuett   = LA Finney pt-bks., p. 82, a4

7 Minuett

8 Aire

9 Aire

Songs: II.i [Song.] "Cynthia frowns whene'er I woo her" (D&M 782 *m*H.
            Purcell *s*Mrs. Ayliff)

            III.iii [Song, sung by Lord Froth] "Ancient Phillis has young Graces"
            (D&M 166 *m*Boman)

The Double Discovery (see *The Spanish Fryar*)

T *The Double Distress,* Mary Pix, LIF (1701)

Act music: Cfm 640-642, fol. 1, "M^r [John] Eccles['s music] in ye Double
              Distress," a1

1st tune   = Cmc pt-bks., fol. 21, "Slow," a4

2   = Cmc pt-bks., fol. 82, a4

3   = *Select Lessons* (1702), fol. 1, "March," a1

4 Scotch tune

5   = Cmc pt-bks., fol. 81', "Slow," a4; *Select Lessons* (1702), fol. 2, "Slow Aire by Mr Eccles," a1

6

7 Round O "Strike up with Lute and harps"

8 Slow

9 M^r. Williames Farwell

Miscellaneous music: I.i [Scene Persepolis. Drums and Trumpets . . .]

        III.ii [Hymn to Apollo. Solemn Musick, Antick Dances . . .]

        IV.ii [SCENE, the Palace. Overtures of Victory.]

T *The Double Marriage,* Philip Massinger and John Fletcher

 Act music (for a revival, 6 February 1688): Henry Purcell, Lcm 1144, fols. 38-39, a2. See Z 593. Note: This set of act tunes is also found in US NH Filmer MS 9 [pp. 26-28], a3, ascribed to "Mr. Grabue," thus lending credence to Zimmerman's suspicion that *The Double Marriage* music is not by Purcell. See Z, pp. 268-269.

Dr. Faustus (see *The Life and Death of Doctor Faustus*)

T *The Duke of Guise,* John Dryden and Nathaniel Lee, DL (1682)

 ? Act music: Ob c.95, pp. 22-23 "[five tunes in] The Duke of Guise," a1

  [1] Overture

  [2] Bore Angleterre = *Apollo's Banquet,* II (1678), No. 34, "Bore Angleterre," a1; *Apollo's Banquet,* II (1690), No. 11, "Bore Angleter," a1

  [3]   = *Apollo's Banquet,* II (1678), No. 23, "La Monmouth," a1

[4]   = *Apollo's Banquet*, II (1678), No. 25, "A French
                                   Bore,"   a1

[5]

Comment: The concordances with *Apollo's Banquet* (1678) suggest that three of
these tunes were not originally associated with this play.

Songs: III.i [Marmoutiere Sits. Song and Dance . . . Spirit within Sings.]
             "Malicorn, Malicorn, ho!" (D&M 2164)

             V.i [A SONG.] "Tell me Thirsis, tell your Anguish" (D&M 3172 *m*Pack)

Dances: (see III.i)

             V.i [Dance]

Edward the Third (see *King Edward the Third*)

F *The Emperor of the Moon*, Aphra Behn, DG (1687)

Dances: *Vinculum Societatis*, II (1688), p. 27, "A Dance in the Emperor of the
             Moon," a1 = US NH Filmer MS 9 [p.20] [Grabue], a3

             Vinculum Societatis, II (1688), p. 28, "Mr. Motley's Magot," a1 =
             Musick's Hand-maid, II (1689) [No. 46], "Motleys Maggot," keyb.;
             Apollo's Banquet, III (1690), No. 52, "The Emperour of the Moon,"
             a1; *Dancing Master* (1690), p. 217, "The Emperor of the Moon," a1;
             120 Country Dances (1711), p. 16, "Emperor of the Moon," a1

             Lcm [*Apollo's Banquet*, c. 1705], No. 130, "Slow [. . . the Card Dance
             in the Emprer of ye moon]," a1

Comment: It is not possible to determine where this dance (ascribed to this play
only by the marginal note in Lcm [*Apollo's Banquet*]) or the other two dances listed
above are to be performed in this farce. This work requires considerable music and
dance, and besides the three tunes mentioned above, only two songs from it were
printed: III [A SONG] "All joy to Mortals" (D&M 118) and D. Purcell, "A curse
upon the faithless maid," see BUCEM, II, 855.

Enchanted Island (see *The Tempest*)

C *Epicoene; or, The Silent Woman*, Ben Jonson [1609]

Miscellaneous music (for a revival in December, 1700?): Lbm Add. 38189, fol. 34',
             "Silent Woman 3[d] act play til they speak to leave of," a1

Comment: Apparently this piece was played in III.ii, "Enter Clerimont, followed by
a number of musicians."

C *Epsom-Wells*, Thomas Shadwell, DG (1673)

? Miscellaneous music: *Pleasant Companion* (1680), No. 51, "Epsom Wells Mr. John Banister," al

Apollo's Banquet (1678), No. 86, "Epsom Wells," al = *Pleasant Companion* (1682), No. 31, "A Tune by Mr. John Banister," al

Lbm Add. 24889. fol. 24'. "Epsom Wells," a4 = *Thesaurus musicus* (1694), pp. 38-39, "Hornpipe Paisible," a2; Lbm Add. 39565, fol. 77', "Paisible 9^e aire Escosoisse," a3; *Dancing Master*, II (1696), p. 12, "Epsom Wells," al; *Compleat Flute=Master* (1695) [fol. 16], "Waa is me what mun I do" (D&M 4008); *Self-Instructor*, I (1700) [No. 23], "Waa is me what mun I do," al; *120 Country Dances* (1711), p. 17, "Epsom Wells," al

An Equipage of Lovers (see *The Fine Lady's Airs*)

M *Europe's Revels for the Peace*, P. A. Motteux, LIF (1697)

Five entry dances: Bray, *Country Dances* (1699), p. 31, John Eccles, "An Entry of Nations," a2

Bray, *Country Dances* (1699), p. 31, "Second [Entry] a Dutch-Man and his Wife," a2

Bray, *Country Dances* (1699), p. 33, "Third [Entry] a French-Man and his Wife," a2

Bray, *Country Dances* (1699), p. 33, "Fourth [Entry] an English-Man and his wife," a2

Bray, *Country Dances* (1699), p. 35, "An Entry of Clowns," a2

? Dance: *Dancing Master*, II (1698), p. 25, "Europes Revels," al

For John Eccles's vocal music in the masque, see Lbm Add. 29378, fols. 96-138.

T *The Fair Penitent*, Nicholas Rowe, LIF (1703)

Act music: Walsh, *Harmonia Anglicana* [V, 1703], "M^r [John] Lentons Musick in the Tragedy call'd the fair Penitent," copies in Lgc G.Mus. 153 (second treble), Lcm XXIX.A.11 (a4)

1 Overture

2 Aire two in one

3 Aire Slow

4 Aire Slow

5 Aire

6 Round O Slow

7 Hornpipe

Songs: II.i [Here an Entertainment of Musick and Dancing. SONG. By Mr.
              CONGREVE.]   "Ah stay! ah turn!"   (D&M 3058 *m*J. Eccles *s*Mrs.
              Hudson, and in Lbm Add. 22099, fol. 49'; see also BUCEM, I, 307)

              V.i [SCENE is a Room hung with Black . . . After Musick and a
              Song, Calista comes forward. SONG] "Hear, you Midnight Phantoms"
              (in Lbm Add. 31455, fol. 18, by [John] Eccles, entitled "The passing
              Bell"; imperfect in Lbm Add. 31405, fol. 151', "The Passing Bell")

C *The Fair Quaker of Deal, or, The Humours of the Navy,* Charles Shadwell, DL (1710)

   See Smith, *Walsh I,* No. 347, an advertisement in *The Tatler* 28-30 March 1710:
   "Mr. [John] Barret's Musick, in 4 Parts, for Violins and Hautboys, performed in the
   last new Comedy called, The Fair Quaker of Deal."   This music is not extant.

DO *The Fairy-Queen,* DG (1692)

   Act music: Henry Purcell, *A Collection of Ayres for the Theatre* (1697), pp. 9-17.
                See Z 629.

      1 Overture

      2 Hornpipe   = LA Finney pt-bks., p. 82, a4

      3 Aire   = LA Finney pt-bks., p. 81, a4

      4 Aire

      5 Rondeau

      6 Preludio   = LA Finney pt-bks., p. 75, a4

      7 Hornpipe

      8 Overture

      9 Song Tune

10 Jigg

11 Dance for Furies   = LA Finney pt-bks., p. 104, a4.

12 Aire 4 in 2

13 Song tune

14 Aire   = LA Finney pt-bks., p. 84, a4

15 Aire   = LA Finney pt-bks., p. 85, a4

16 Song Tune

17 Chacone

18 Aire   = LA Finney pt-bks., p. 87, a4

P *The Faithful Bride of Granada* [William Taverner], DL (1704)

    Act music: Walsh, *Harmonia Anglicana* [IV, 1702], "Mr D.[aniel] Purcells Second
               Treble in the Faithful Bride of Granada," copies in Lgc G.Mus. 153
               (second treble) and Lcm XXIX.A.12 (second treble, tenor, bass)

    1 Overture

    2 Aire

    3 Aire

    4 Minuett

    5 Round O

    6 Iigg

    7 Aire

    Note: The first treble part of this set is found in US Wc M1515.A.11 Case, pp.
232-245.

    Miscellaneous music: III.i [SCENE A Mosque. The Tomb of Ozman . . .
                     Solemn Musick, Drums, Trumpet . . .]

The Fall of Mortimer Earl of March (see *King Edward the Third*)

C *The False Friend,* John Vanbrugh, DL (1702)

Act music: Walsh, *Harmonia Anglicana* [III, 1702], "Aires in the Play call'd the
               False Friend Composed by a Person of Quality [William Lord
               Byron?]," copies in Lbm b.29.a (first treble), Lbm d.24 (first treble and
               bass), Lgc G.Mus 153 (second treble), Lcm XXIX.A.11 (a4)

[1] Overture

2 Aire

3 Iigg   = Cmc pt-bks., fol. 125, a4

4 Minuett   = Cmc pt-bks., fol. 124, a4; D. Purcell, *A Collection of
                  Lessons* [1702], p. 9, "Minuet," keyb.

5 Allmand   = Cmc pt-bks., fol. 124, a4

6 Gavott   = Cmc pt-bks., fol. 124', a4; D. Purcell, *A Collection of
                  Lessons* [1702], p. 8, "Aire," keyb.

7 Minuet   = Cmc pt-bks., fol. 125, a4

8 Slow Aire   = Cmc pt-bks., fol. 124, "Slow," a4; Lbm Add. 22099, fol.
                  7', "A Slow Aire [by] a person of quality," keyb.; D.
                  Purcell, *A Collection of Lessons* [1702], p. 9, "Slow Aire,"
                  keyb.

9 Sibell   = D. Purcell, *A Collection of Lessons* [1702], p. 10,
                  "Cibell," keyb.; Lcm [*Apollo's Banquet*], p. 40, "Cibell by
                  my Lord Byron," a1; *Division Flute*, II [1708], p. 16,
                  "Cibell by my Ld Byron," a1; *Division Violin*, II (1693),
                  p. 48, "Cibell by my L^{d} B," a1

The False Report (see *The Mistakes*)

Falstaff (see *K. Henry IV*)

C   *Farewel Folly: or, The Younger the Wiser . . . With A Musical Interlude, call'd The
    Mountebank: or, The Humours of the Fair* [P. A. Motteux], DL (1707)

? Act music: Lcm 1172, fols. 31'-32 "[four tunes in] Farewell," a4

   [1]

   [2] = *Theatre Musick*, II (1699) [No. 24], "Bore Mr Finger," a1

   [3]

   [4]

T   *The Fate of Capua,* Thomas Southerne, LIF (1700)

> Act music: US NH Filmer MS 9 [pp. 69-71], "M^r [John] Lenton In ye Fate of Capua," a3
>
> 1
>
> 2
>
> 3
>
> 4
>
> 5   Overture
>
> 6
>
> 7
>
> 8   =   Cmc pt-bks, fol. 119', a4
>
> 9   =   Cmc pt-bks, fol. 46', a4

See Smith, *Walsh I,* No. 438, an advertisement in *The Post Boy* 23-26 March 1713, for act music apparently used in a revival: "The Musick perform'd in the Tragedy of Capua in Parts for Violins, Trumpets and Hautboys: composed by Mr. John Eccles of Her Majesty's Musick."   This music is not extant.

The Fate of Troy (see *The Virgin Prophetess*)

Faustus (see *The Life and Death of Doctor Faustus*)

The Feign'd Innocence (see *Sr Martin Mar-all*)

C   *The Female Advocates: Or, The Frantick Stock-Jobber* [William Taverner], DL (1713)

> ? Act music: Lbm Add. 17853, fols. 39 and 52', two tunes in "ye Female Advocates," keyb.
>
> [1] 3^d: Act tune In ye Female Advocates
>
> [2] Jig in ye Female Advocates [fragment]

Female Warrior (see *Friendship Improv'd*)

C   *The Fine Lady's Airs: Or, an Equipage of Lovers,* Thomas Baker, DL [1709]

Act music: Walsh [Act Music of the Queens Theatre, 1709], "M^r [John] Barretts
              Musick in the Comedy calld the Ladys fine Aires for Violins and
              Hoboys," copy in Lbm g.15 (a4)

1 Overture   = Cfm 52.B.7, p. 113 "Overture," keyb.

2 Prelude

3 Hornpipe

4 Jigg

5 Aire

6 Jigg Round O

7 Aire Round O

8 Minuet

Song: IV.ii. *Shrimp.* By this Light, here's Betty the Orange Woman from the
              Play-house . . . [She Sings. SONG.] "How happy are we" (D&M
              1413 *m*Barrett *s*Pack)

Dance: V.ii [A DANCE]

Folly Reclaim'd (see *The City Lady*)

C *A Fond Husband: or, The Plotting Sisters,* Thomas Durfey, DG (1677)

    Miscellaneous music: *Apollo's Banquet* (1678), No. 105, "A Scotch Tune in the
                            Fond Husband," al = *Apollo's Banquet* (1687), No. 55,
                            "Scotch tune," al; *Pleasant Companion* (1682), No. 69, "A
                            new Tune to a Northern Song," al (this is the tune to
                            D&M 1752, "In January last")

? The Fool in Fashion (see also *Love's Last Shift*)

    Act music: Lcm 1144, fol. 15 "[seven pieces in the] 2^d part of Fool in Fashion,
                  by [John] Barret," a2

    1   = Cmc pt-bks., fol. 7, a4

    2

    3

    4   = Cmc pt-bks., fol. 7', a4

[5] Overture

6

7   =   Cmc pt-bks., fol. 7, a4

Comment: This is perhaps the act music for the first production of Vanbrugh's *The Relapse* (1697), called the "sequel" to *Love's Last Shift; or, The Fool in Fashion.* See Hume, *The Development of English Drama in the late Seventeenth Century*, pp. 411-412, and below, s.v. *The Relapse.*

The Fop's Fortune (see *Love Makes a Man*)

Formosa (see *The City Lady*)

The Frantick Stock-Jobber (see *The Female Advocates*)

T *Friendship Improv'd, or The Female Warrior*, Charles Hopkins, LIF (1700)

Act music: US NH Filmer MS 9 [pp. 72-74], "M:^{r} Solomon Eccles in the Female Warrior," a3

1   =   Cmc pt-bks, fol. 109, a4

2   =   Cmc pt-bks, fol. 58, a4

3   =   *Apollo's Banquet* (1701), No. 31, "Hornpipe," a1; [*Apollo's Banquet* c. 1705], No. 31, "Hornpipe," a1

4 Overture   =   Cmc pt-bks, fol. 127', "Ouverture," a4

5   =   Cmc pt-bks, fol. 86', a4; *Compleat Instructor to the Flute*, II (1700), p. 2, "by Mr Eccles in Henry ye fourth," a1

6   =   Cmc pt-bks, fol. 108, a4; *Compleat Instructor to the Flute*, II (1700), p. 2, "by Mr Eccles," a1

7   =   Cmc pt-bks, fol. 109, "Slow," a4; *Apollo's Banquet* (1701), No. 36, "A Tune of Mr. Eccles," a1; [*Apollo's Banquet*, c. 1705], No. 36, "A Tune of Mr. Eccles," a1; *Self-Instructor*, III (1700) [fol. 15], "Scotch Aire by Mr. Eccles," a1

8   =   Cmc pt-bks, fol. 87, "Slow," a4; *Apollo's Banquet* (1701), No. 32, "Slow Jigg," a1; [*Apollo's Banquet*, c. 1705], No. 32, "Slow Jigg," a1; *Self-Instructor*, III (1700) [fol. 15], "Iigg," a1; *Compleat Instructor to the Flute*, II (1700), p. 3, a1

C   *The Funeral: Or, Grief A-la-mode*, Richard Steele, DL (1702)

Act music: Walsh, *Harmonia Anglicana*, III [1701], "Mr Wm Croft's Ayres in the
               Comedy call'd the Funeral, or Grief Allamode," copies in Lbm b.29.a
               (first treble), Lbm d.24 (first treble and bass), Lgc G.Mus. 153 (second
               treble), Lcm XXIX.A.11 (a4), Lcm XXIX.A.12 (second treble, tenor,
               bass)

   [1] Overture

    2 Scotch Aire

    3 Slow Aire   =   Cmc pt-bks., fol. 38, "Slow," a4

    4 Iigg   =   Cmc pt-bks., fol. 38, a4

    5 Slow Aire

    6 Aire   =   Cmc pt-bks., fol. 38, a4

    7 Aire

   [8] CHACCONNE

Songs: II.ii [Song] "Let not Love on me bestow" (D&M 1982 *m*D. Purcell
               ʃMrs. Harris; see also BUCEM, II, 855)

               IV.i [Boy Sings.] "Ye Minutes bring the Happy Hour" (D. Purcell, *A
               song in the comedy call'd the Funeral*, sung by Mrs. Campion [London,
               c. 1702], copy in Lbm)

               V.i [Here a Dance and the following Songs. Set by Mr. Daniel
               Purcell. Sung by Jemmie Bowin.] "On Yonder Bed supinely laid"
               (D. Purcell, *A song* [London, c. 1702], copy in Lbm)

               (V.i) [Sung by Mr. Pate.] "Arise great Dead"

C   *The Gamester*, Susannah Centlivre, LIF (1705)

Act music: Walsh [Act Music of the Queens Theatre, 1705], "M^r [John] Lentons
               Musick in the Comedy call'd ye Gamester," copy in Lbm g.15 (a4)

    1 Overture   =   Lcm [*Apollo's Banquet*, c. 1705], p. 57, "Overture," a1

    2 Gavott   =   Lcm [*Apollo's Banquet*, c. 1705], p. 57, "Gavot," a1

    3 Minuet   =   Lcm [*Apollo's Banquet*, c. 1705] [p. 58], "A Minuet," a1

    4 Bass minuet   =   Lcm [*Apollo's Banquet*, c. 1705] [p. 58], "A Minuet," a1

5 Aire slow

6 Iigg   =   *Ladys Banquet,* II (1706), p. 10, "Jigg," keyb.

7 Hornpipe

8 Scotch aire

9 Iigg

Songs: II.i [A Song, Sung to the Widow.] "In vain you sable Weeds put on"

              (II.i) [A Song, Sung to the Gamester, when he has won Money.] "Fair Caelia, she is Nice and Coy"

              Dance: V.ii [A Country Dance.]

T *The Generous Conquerour: or, The Timely Discovery,* Bevil Higgons, DL (1702)

Act music: Walsh, *Harmonia Anglica,* III [1702], "M.^{r} [John] Barretts Ayres in the Tragedy call'd the Generous Conquerour or the timely Discovery," copies in Lbm b.29.a (first treble), Lbm d.24 (first treble and bass), Lgc G.Mus. 153 (second treble), Lcm XXIX.A.12 (second treble, tenor, and bass)

    [1] Overture   =   Cmc pt-bks., fol. 51', "Ouverture," a4

    2 Allemand   =   Cmc pt-bks., fol. 52, a4; LA Finney pt-bks., p. 96, a4; *Harpsichord Master,* II (1700) [No. 14], "Almand Mr Barrett," keyb.

    3 Corrant   =   Cmc pt-bks, fol. 52, a4; LA Finney pt-bks, p. 96, a4

    4 Aire

    5 Iigg

    6 Aire   =   Cmc pt-bks., fol. 52', a4; *Harpsichord Master,* II (1700) [No. 21], "Aire Mr Barrett," keyb.; *Theater Musick,* III (1700), sig. o, "Aire Mr Barrett," a1

    7 Saraband   =   Cmc pt-bks., fol. 52', "Slow," a4; LA Finney pt-bks., p. 97, a4; *Harpsichord Master,* II (1700) [No. 16], "Saraband Mr. Barrett," keyb.; *Theater Musick,* III (1700), sig. n, "Saraband Mr. Barrett," a1

8 Aire   = Cmc pt-bks., fol. 53, a4; *Harpsichord Master*, II (1700)
                  [No. 20], "Aire Mr. Barrett," keyb.; *Theater Musick*, III
                  (1700), sig. n, "Aire," a1

9 Slow Aire

Song: II.ii [SONG] "How long, my Flavia"

Miscellaneous music: III.ii [Martial Loud Musick Plays, the King Listens . . . Soft
                        Musick Plays, the King listens.]

                  V.i [Consorts of Musick, Shouts and Acclamations at distance.]

C   *The Generous Enemies or the Ridiculous Lovers,* John Corye, TR (1672)

? Act music (for a revival?): Lcm [*Apollo's Banquet,* c. 1705], two marginal notes
                        ascribe two tunes to "Rediculos Lover 1697 by [Thomas] Tollet," a1

No. 49 [Mr Tollet in
Rediculos Lover 1697]   = *Apollo's Banquet* (1701), No. 49, "Ayre," a1;
                        Self-Instructor, I (1700) [No. 22], "Scotch
                        Tune," a1; Ob c.72, p. 11, "Tollett 2d tune,"
                        a3

No. 50 Mr Tollett
Hornpipe [in
Ridiculous Lovers]   = *Apollo's Banquet* (1701), No. 50, "Mr. Tollett
                        Hornpipe," a1; *Self-Instructor* (1700) [No. 21],
                        "Hornpipe," a1; Ob c.72, p. 11, "Tollett 3^d
                        tune hornpipe," a3

The Generous Portuguese (see *The Island Princess*)

The Gentleman Quack (see *Justice Busy*)

Good Luck at last (see *The Virtuous Wife*)

? The Gordian Knott unty'd [William Walsh?] [1690?]

Act music: Henry Purcell, *A Collection of Ayres for the Theatre* (1697), pp. 36-
              [39].   See Z 597.

1 Overture   = LA Finney pt-bks., p. 74, "1. Overture," a4

2 Aire   = LA Finney pt-bks., p. 76, a4; Lcm [*Apollo's
                       Banquet,* c. 1705], No. 91, "Ayre by Mr.
                       Purcell," a1

3 Rondeau Minuett   = LA Finney pt-bks., p. 76, "Round O," a4

4   Aire

5   Jigg   =   LA Finney pt-bks., p. 107, a4

6   Chacone

7   Aire

8   Minuet

T   *The Governour of Cyprus*, John Oldmixon, LIF (1703)

     Act music: "A New Set of Tunes in four Parts, In the Governour of Cyprus
                  Acted at the New Theatre, and Composed by Thomas Deane of
                  Worcester. London Printed by Tho. Cross for the Author, & Sold at
                  the Musick Shops. Tho: Cross Sculp." Bound in with Lcm
                  XXIX.A.11   (a4)

     1   Overture

     2   A Ground

     3   A Scotch Aire

     4   A Minuet

     5   A Saraband

     6   A Scotch Tune

     7   A Hornpipe

     8   A Jigg

     Songs: I.i [Scene a Garden, Lucinda lying on a Bank of Flowers, a Grove
              near it; after the Song is over, Zarma, and She come forward.
              SONG.]   "When Sylvia runs to Woods and Groves"

              (I.i) "Since tis to Sin"

C   *Greenwich-Park*, William Mountfort, DL (1691)

     ? Act music: *Apollo's Banquet* (1691), five tunes "of Mr. Montfort's in the Play of
                  Greenwich Park," a1

     [Nos.] 60

       61

62

63

64 = US NH Filmer MS 9 [p. 59], "The 1st Lesson in Grinwich Park," a3

? Dance: *Dancing Master*, II (1698), p. 33, "Greenwich Park," a1 = *120 Country Dances* (1711), p. 30, "Greenwich Park," a1; Lbm Add. 22099, fol. 6', "Come sweet lass Mr. Clark," keyb.

Note: In US NH Filmer MS 9 [p. 59], is another tune following that mentioned above as a concordance to *Apollo's Banquet*, No. 64. Since it is numbered "2," perhaps it also was heard in this play.

Grief A-la-mode (see *The Funeral*)

DO *The Grove, or, Love's Paradice*, John Oldmixon, DL (1700)

Act music: Lcm 1144, fols. 33-33', five tunes by "Dan[iel] Purcell in Loves Paradice," a2

1

2 = *Theater Musick*, III (1700), sig. g, "Aire in ye Opera call'd ye Grove," a1

3 Round O = Cmc pt-bks., fol. 61', a4; *Theater Musick*, III (1700), sig. g, "Minuet," a1

4 = Cmc pt-bks., fol. 106', a4; *Theater Musick*, III (1700), sig. h, "A March in ye Grove," a1

5

In addition to these five pieces, in *Theater Musick*, III (1700), there are two more ascribed to this dramatic opera on sig. w, a1.

[6] Aire Cibell = Cmc pt-bks., fol. 105, a4; Lbm 39565, fol. 60, a4

[7] A Dance in ye Opera Call'd ye Grove

Daniel Purcell's full score to this opera is in Lcm 988. See also D&M 502, 586, 1237, 1240, 1808, 1947, 2883, 3514, 3851, and 4030, as well as BUCEM, II, 855.

C *Hampstead-Heath* [Thomas Baker], DL (1706)

See Smith, *Walsh I*, No. 191, an advertisement in *The Post Man* 20-22 December 1705: "The Musick in 4 parts perform'd in the Comedy called Hamstead Heath. Composed by Mr J.[ohn] Barret[t]."   This music is not extant.

Hist. *Henry the Second, King of England; with the Death of Rosamond,* John Bancroft, DL (1693)

? Act music: US NH Filmer MS 9 [pp. 31-33], "M:^{r} [Thomas] Tollet in King henry ye 2d" [from second treble part-book], a3

    8[=1]

    9[=2]   = Cfm MS c.431, "Tolit," a3

    10[=3] Ground

    11[=4] Ouverture

    12[=5]

    13[=6]   = Cfm MS c.431, "Tolit," a3; Cmc pt-bks, fol. 46, a4

    14[=7]   = Cmc pt-bks, fol. 13, "Slow," a4

    15[=8]   = Cmc pt-bks, fol. 44', "very slow," a4

Henry ye fourth (see *K. Henry the Fourth: With the Humours of Sir John Falstaff*)

? Henry IV

    Act music: Walsh, *Harmonia Anglicana* [VI, 1703], "M^r [William] Corbet's Musick in the Comedy call'd Hen.^{r} the 4th Play'd all the time of the Bublick [sic] Act in Oxford," copies in Lbm d.24 (first treble and bass), Lgc G. Mus. 153 (second treble), Lcm XXIX.A.11 (a4), Lcm XXIX.A.12 (second treble, tenor, bass)

    1 Overture

    2 Prelude

    3 Gavott

    4 Aire

    5 Minuett

    6 Slow Round O

7 Rigadoon

8 Aire

9 Aire

T *Heroick Love*, George Granville, LIF (1698)

Act music: US NH Filmer MS 9 [pp. 63-65], "M:^{r} [John] Lenton in Heroick
Love," a2 and a3

   1 Slow

   2

   [3]   = Cmc pt-bks, fol. 21, a4

   [4] Overture   = Cmc pt-bks, fol. 81', "Ouverture," a4

   [5] Round o   = Cmc pt-bks, fol. 64, a5

   [6] Round o   = Cmc pt-bks, fol 63', a4

   [7]   = Cmc pt-bks, fol. 63', "Slow," a5

   [8]   = Cmc pt-bks, fol. 130', "Slow," a4

The History of Dioclesian (see *The Prophetess)*

O *The History of Sr Francis Drake*, William Davenant, Cockpit (1659)

  ? Dances: *Courtly Masquing Ayres* (1662), No. 279, "Symerons Dance [Matthew]
Locke," a2 = *Musicks Hand-maid* (1663), No. 38, "The Simerons
Dance by Mr Lock," keyb.; *Musicks Recreation on the Viol* (1669),
No. 12, "The Simerons Dance," a1

                Dancing Master, II (1665), No. 33, "The Simerons Dance," a1 =
Apollo's Banquet (1678), No. 31, "The Simerons Jigg," a1

Comment: These dances might be some of the music used in the sixth entry, "The
Grand Dance begins, consisting of two Land-souldiers, two Sea-men, two Symerons,
and a Peruvian. . . ."

T *The History of Timon of Athens, The Man-Hater*, Thomas Shadwell, DG (1678)

Act music (for a revival c. 1694?): Lcm 1144, fols. 54-55, "M^r [Henry] Purcell in
Timon of Athens," a2

Note: As may be determined from the concordances listed below, this act music (except for the overture) was probably composed by James Paisible, not Henry Purcell. See also Z 632 and *Timon of Athens*, ed. Jack Westrup, in *The Works of Henry Purcell*, II (1974), xii.

[1 Overture]

2   = *Compleat Flute=Master* (1695) [fol. 17], "March M. Peasable," a1

3

4   = *Compleat Flute=Master* (1695) [fol. 17], "Borre Mr Peasable," a1

5   = *Compleat Flute=Master* (1695) [fol. 18], "A minuet Mr Peasable," a1

6

7

8

9

See Z 632 for listings of other music associated with this play.

C   *The Humorous Lieutenant*, John Fletcher

Act music (for a revival, July 1697?): Lcm 1172, fols. 23-25', "Mr. Gorten's [music] in The Humorous Lieutenant," a4

Overture

[first music?]   = Lbm Add. 29283, fol. 84', "Mr. Gorton," a3

1st Act [tune]   = Lbm Add. 29283, fol. 85, a3

3^{d} Act [tune]

4th Act [tune]

[first music?]

2^{d} Act [tune]   = Lbm Add. 29283, fol. 85, a3

[second music?]

[second music?]

The Humors of Sir John Falstaff (see *K. Henry IV*)

C *The Humour of the Age*, Thomas Baker, DL (1701)

> Act music: Walsh, *Harmonia Anglicana*, II [1701], "M.^{r} [Godfrey] Fingers Ayres in the Comedy call'd the Humors of the Age," copies in Dc C.37 (a4), Lgc. G. Mus. 153 (second treble), Lcm XXIX.A.11 (a4)

> 1 Overture

> 2 Aire   = *Select Lessons* (1702), fol. 7, "Rigadoon," a1

> 3 Round O Sebell   = *Select Lessons* (1702), fol. 7, "Sebell Round O," a1; *40 Airs Anglois*, III, p. 14, "Sybell," a2

> 4 Trumpet aire   = *Select Lessons* (1702), fol. 8, "A Trumpet Aire by Mr Finger," a1; *40 Airs Anglois*, III, p. 8, "Jigg," a2

> 5 Minuett   = *Select Lessons* (1702), fol. 8, "Trumpett Minuett," a1

> 6 Aire

> 7 Aire

> 8 Iigg

Songs: III.iv [A SONG.]

> not printed in play-book: "Beneath a gloomy shade" (D&M 356 *m*D, Purcell *s*Bowen)

> "Fixed on the fair Miranda's eyes" (D&M 1012 *m*D. Purcell *s*Bowen)

> "'Tis done the pointed arrow's in" (D&M 3377 *m*D. Purcell *s*Mrs. Shaw)

Miscellaneous music: V.i [An Entertainment. They sit.]

The Humours of the Navy (see *The Fair Quaker of Deal*)

C *The Husband His own Cuckold*, John Dryden, Jr., LIF (1696)

> Act music: Lbm Add. 35043, fols. 80'-81', "M^r [Godfrey] Fingers First Trebles in the Play Call'd The Husband his own Cuckold," a1

[1] Overture = LA Finney pt-bks., p. 54, "Mr Finger 1 Overture," a4; Lcm 1144, fol. 27, "Finger overture," a2; Ob c.72, p. 1, "Mr. Finger's Musick Overture," a3

2 = LA Finney pt-bks. [n. 55], a4; Lcm 1144, fol. 27', a2; *Apollo's Banquet* (1701), No. 42, "A Tune by Mr. Finger," a1; *40 Airs Anglois,* II [c. 1701], p. 19, "Air Mr. Finger," a2; Ob c.72, p. 1, a3

3 = Cmc pt-bks., fol. 81, a4; LA Finney pt-bks. [p. 55], a4; Lcm 1144, fol. 28, a2; Ob c.72, p. 2, a3; *40 Airs Anglois,* II [c. 1701], p. 19, "Air Mr Finger," a2

4 = LA Finney pt-bks., p. 56, a4; Lcm 1144, fol. 28, a2; Ob c.72, p. 2, a3; *40 Airs Anglois,* II [c. 1701], p. 20, "Air Mr G. Finger," a2

5 = LA Finney pt-bks., p. 56, a4; Lcm 1144, fol. 28', a2; Ob c.72, p. 2, a3

6 = LA Finney pt-bks., p. 57, a4; Lcm 1144, fol. 29, a2

7 = LA Finney pt-bks., p. 57, a4; Lcm 1144, fol. 29, a2; Ob c. 72, p. 2, a3

8 = LA Finney pt-bks., p. 58, a4; Lcm 1144, fol 28', "Finger Cuckoe Air," a2; Ob c.72, p. 3, a3

9 = LA Finney pt-bks., p. 58, a4; Lcm 1144, fol. 28', a2; Ob c.72, p. 3, a3

Songs: I.i [SONG] "Help, help, ye Pow'rs Divine" (John Eccles, *A song in the Husband his own Cuckold* . . . Sung by Mrs. Aliff [London, c. 1696], copies in Lbm and Lgc)

V. "Why so coy and so strange" (in Ob c.95, p. 138, "John Eccles, a dialogue sung by Mr. Doggett & Mrs. Bracegirdle in The Husband his own Cuckold"; see also BUCEM, I, 308)

Dance: IV.ii [Johny Thump dances John Stoakes his Jigg.]

Miscellaneous music: V [Soft Musick.]

The Husband's Cure (see *The Wife's Relief*)

The Husbands Revenge (see *Bussy D'Ambois*)

C *The Inconstant: or, The Way to Win Him,* George Farquhar, DL (1702)

Act music: Walsh, *Harmonia Anglicana*, III [1702], "Aires in the Comedy call'd the Inconstant or ye way to Win him Compos'd by Mr D.[aniel] Purcell," copies in Lgc G.Mus. 153 (second treble), Lcm XXIX.A.11 (a4), Lcm XXIX.A.12 (second treble, tenor, bass)

1 Overture

2 Aire   = D. Purcell, *A Collection of Lessons* [1702], p. 7, "Aire," keyb.; *Theatre Musick,* II (1699) [No. 3], "Aire," a1; Lbm Add. 15318, fol. 20', "Dance" in *Island Princess,* a4

3 Minuett   = D. Purcell, *A Collection of Lessons* [1702], p. 7, "Minuet," keyb.

4 March   = Cmc pt-bks., fol. 133, a4; D. Purcell, *A Collection of Lessons* [1702], p. 6, "March," keyb.

5 Hornpipe   = Cmc pt-bks., fol. 110, a4; D. Purcell, *A Collection of Lessons* [1702], p. 6, "Hornpipe," keyb.

6 Aire   = D. Purcell, *A Collection of Lessons* [1702], p. 5, "Allemand," keyb.

7 Gavott   = D. Purcell, *A Collection of Lessons* [1702], p. 5, "Gavott," keyb.

8 Aire

9 Minuett

Songs: V.ii [SONG]

            a song at end of play (location not specified) [SONG. By Mr. O--r. Set by Mr. Daniel Purcell] "Since Caelia 'tis not in our Power" (D. Purcell, *A song in ye comedy call'd ye Inconstant . . .* Sung by Mr. Hughes [London, 1702], copies in Lbm and Eu)

T *The Indian Queen,* John Dryden and Robert Howard, TR (1665)

? Act music: NYp MS Drexel 3849, pp. 71-72, "J.[ohn] Banister, The Indian Queene," five pieces, a3

     [1] Prelude   = Lbm Add. 24889, fol. 21, "Prelude second pt. of Indian Queen," a4

     [2] The Indian Queen = Lbm Add. 24889, fol. 21, "Indian Queen 1st pt.," a4; Ob c.95, p. 32, "Indian Queen (2)," a1

[3]   = Lbm Add. 24889, fol 21, "Dance," a4

[4]

[5]

In Ob c.95, p. 32, is another piece entitled "The Indian Queen."

See Z 630 for Henry Purcell's music for an operatic revival of this play, c. 1695, and p. 333 for mention of a dance ascribed to this play in *Apollo's Banquet* (c. 1669).

The Infallible Cure (see *All for the Better*)

C *Injur'd Love, or, The Lady's Satisfaction*, DL [1711]

See Smith, *Walsh I*, No. 386, an advertisement in *The Daily Courant* 15 May 1711: "A new Sett of Tunes in three Parts for Violins and Hoboys with a through Base composed by Mr. N.[athaniel] Kynaston for the Play, call'd, The Injured Lover." This music is not extant.

C *The Innocent Mistress*, Mary Pix, LIF (1697)

Act music: US NH Filmer MS 9 [pp. 56-58], "Mr Forcer in ye Innocent M.^{ss}," a3

1

[2]

[3] Overture

4

5

6

7

8

T *Iphigenia*, John Dennis, LIF (1700)

?Act music: *Compleat Instructor to the Flute*, II (1700), pp. 14-15, three pieces ascribed to "Ephegenia," a1

[1] Minuet

[2] a bore

[3] A Slow Aire

> Theater Musick, III (1700), sig. i, "Slow Aire In Iphigenia," a1; *40 Airs Anglois*, II [c. 1701], p. 10, "Allegro Symphony Mr Finger," a2; *40 Airs Anglois*, III, p. 2, "Adagio," a2; Cmc pt bks., fol. 108', a4; LEp MS Q784.21 L969, p. 31, a4; see also BUCEM, II, 856.

DO   *The Island Princess, or the Generous Portuguese*, P. A. Motteux, DL (1699)

See Lbm Add. 15318 for a complete score of this dramatic opera, including the act music (a4), which was composed by Jeremiah Clarke.   Lcm 1172, fols. 32'-34' contains all the act music (a4), except the "2^d Act tune." This piece is in a major key, and all of the music in Lcm 1172 is in minor.   In fact, every piece in Lcm 1172 is in the key of G minor; this curious system of collecting the music for this manuscript appears to explain why many of the sets of act music it contains are lacking one or more tunes.

1st Musick [1]	= Lcm 1172, fol. 34, "1st musick," a4; *Songs In The New Opera Call'd the World in the Moon* (1697) [No. 5], "Is'e no more to Shady Coverts [for the flute]," a2 (this is an instrumental arrangement of D&M 1653)
[2]	= Cmc pt-bks., fol. 6', a4; Lcm 1172, fol. 34', "1st musick," a4; *Theatre Musick*, II (1699) [No. 19], "Iigg Mr Clark," a1
2^d Musicke [1]	= Lcm 1172, fol. 34', "2^d musick," a4; *Theatre Musick*, II (1699) [No. 15], "Aire Mr Clark," a1
[2]	= Lcm 1172, fol. 35, "2^d musick," a4
Overture	= Lcm 1172, fol. 32', "J. C.[larke] overture in Island Princess," a4
1st Act Tune	= Lcm 1172, fol. 34, "1st act tune," a4; *Theatre Musick*, II (1699) [No. 18], "Aire," a1; *Apollo's Banquet* (1701), No. 92, "Ayre by Mr. Clarke," a1
2^d Act tune	= Ob e.397, p. 32, "Trumpet tune by Mr Purcell," keyb.; *Theatre Musick*, II (1699) [No. 1], "Trumpet Aire Mr. Clark," a1

3^{d} Act tune   = Lcm 1172, fol. 35', "3^{d} Act tune," a4; *Theatre*
                                      Musick, II (1699) [No. 21], "Aire Mr Clark,"
                                      a1; *40 Airs Anglois,* II [c. 1701], p. 9, "Air," a2

4th Act Tune Round [0]   = Lcm 1172, fol. 33, "J. Cl[arke] Round 0 4th
                                      Act tune in Island Princess," a4; *Theatre*
                                      Musick, II (1699) [No. 16], "Minuet M.^{r}
                                      Clark," a1

For other sources of the music in the Island Princess, see *Theatre Musick,* II (1699),
for the following tunes, all found in Lbm Add. 15318, except the last:

(5) Summer Dance by
     Blacks in ye Island
     Princess   = *Apollo's Banquet* (1701), No. 95, "Ayre," a1

(6) Autum Dance by a
     French Clown & a
     Country Woman in
     Wooden Shoes   = Ob e.397, p. 30, "Wooden Shooes," keyb.;
                                Apollo's Banquet (1701), No. 96, "The Wooden
                                Shew Dance," a1; *120 Country Dances* (1711),
                                p. 27, "Wooden Shooes," a1

(7) Sebell Mr Clark in
     ye Island Princess   = *Theater Musick,* III (1700), sig. u, "Cibell M^{r}
                                Clark," a2; *Division Violin,* II (1693), p. 49,
                                "Cibell by Mr Clark," a1; *Division Flute,* II
                                [1708], fol. 8, "Clark a Cibell," a1; Lcm
                                [*Apollo's Banquet,* c. 1705], p. 41, "Cibell by
                                Mr. Jer. Clark," a1

(8) The Grand Dance in
     Ye Island Princess

(9) An Entre Danc't by
     Mr Prist in ye Island
     Princess   = *Self-Instructor,* III (1700), fol. 17, "Entre," a1

(10) Spring Dance two girls
     with Nose gay's   = Lcm 1172, fol. 33', "Cla[rke] Spring Dance in
                                Island Princess," a4

(11) Winter Dance by a
     Duch Woman & a
     Old Miser in ye
     Island Princess   = *Division Violin,* II (1693), p. 42, "Chacone by
                                Mr Morgan," a1; Lcm [*Apollo's Banquet,* c.

1705], p. 37, "Chacone by Mr. Morgan," al;
Division Flute, II [1708], fol. 8, "Chacone by
Mr Morgan," al

(29) The Prologue in
ye Island Princess

For songs see D&M 131, 1385, 1991, 2128, 2230, 2509, 4118. See also Ob c.95, p.
72, "Tis Sultry weather pretty Maid," and Ob c.95, p. 129, "Let soft desire your
heart engage" (D&M 1991). And see BUCEM, II, 856.

The Italian Conspiracy (see *The Patriot*)

T *The Italian Husband,* Edward Ravenscroft, LIF (1698)

Act music: Ob c.72, pp. 32-34, seven pieces by "John Eccles in The Italian
Husband," a2

1   = Cmc pt-bks., fol. 2, a4; US NH Filmer MS 9 [p. 60],
"Mr John Eccles in the Ittalian Husband," a3

2   = Cmc pt-bks., fol. 2', "Slow," a4; US NH Filmer MS 9
[p. 60], "Slow," a3

3   = Cmc pt-bks., fol. 4', "very slow," a4; US NH Filmer MS
9 [p. 60], "Very Slow," a3

4   = Cmc pt-bks., fol. 6, a4; *Self-Instructor,* III (1700) [fol.
21], "Iigg," al; *Apollo's Banquet* (1701), No. 142, "The
Zear," al; *Ladys Banquet,* II (1706), p. 7, "Baloons Jigg,"
keyb.; US NH Filmer MS 9 [p. 60], a3; Ob e.397, p. 6,
"Sr John Guise," keyb.; *Compleat Instructor to the Flute,*
II (1700), p. [18], "A new French dance call'd ye Zar of
Moscow by Mr Eccles," al

5 Overture   = US NH Filmer MS 9 [p. 61], "Overture," a3

6   = US NH Filmer MS 9 [p. 62], a3

7   = US NH Filmer MS 9 [p. 62], a3

Note: This tragedy has only three acts; hence, only two act tunes are needed.

Songs: I.i [An Anniversary Song on the Dukes Wedding.] "Joy to the
youthful happy pair"

II.i [A SONG to the Dutchess.] "Nymphs that now are in your prime"

Miscellaneous music: I.i (An Entertainment)

                             III[ii] "IXION, A Masque," by William Taverner

The Jealous Husband (see *The Lost Lover*)

C   *The Jovial Crew*, Richard Brome (1652)

    Miscellaneous music (for a revival, c. 1682?):   *Apollo's Banquet* (1678), No. 64, "The Jovial Crew," a1

The Jubilee (see *Sir Harry Wildair* and *The Constant Couple*)

?   Julius Caesar

    Miscellaneous music: *Apollo's Banquet* (1687), No. 48, "Julius Caesar," a1

C   Justice Busy; or, The Gentleman Quack, John Crowne, LIF?

    ?   Dance: *Dancing-Master* (1718), p. 164, "Justice Busie," a1 = Cmc pt-bks., fol. 54,   a4

    Song: "No every morning my beauties renew" (D&M 2320, *m*J. Eccles *s*Mrs. Bracegirdle)

See Nicoll, *A History of English Drama 1660-1900*, I (Cambridge, 1967), 400. This song and a remark in Downes, *Roscius Anglicanus*, p. 45, mark the existence of this play. Also see Eccles, *A Collection of Songs* [1704], p. 55, "A SONG for 3 Voices in the Comedy call'd Justice Buisy ('Wine does Wonders every day')" and Ob c.95, p. 135, a song ("I'll hurry") by John Eccles in "Justice Busy or The Gentleman Quack." See B. J. McMullin, "The Songs from John Crowne's *Justice Buisy, or the Gentleman-Quack*," *Review of English Studies*, N.S., XXVIII (1977), 168-175.

TC   *K. Henry IV with the Humours of Sir John Falstaff*, Thomas Betterton, LIF (1700)

    ?Act music: Walsh, *Harmonia Anglicana*, III [1701], "Mr Peasable's [James Paisible] Ayre's in the Comedy call'd the Humors of Sr Iohn Falsstaf," copies in Lbm b.29.a (first treble), Lgc G.Mus. 153 (second treble), Lcm XXIX.A.11   (a4)

        1 Overture   = Cmc pt-bks., fol. 54', "Ouverture," a4

        2 Aire

        3 Trumpet aire   = Cmc pt-bks., fol. 56. a4

        4 Trumpet aire   = Cmc pt-bks., fol. 55, a4

        5 Iigg   = Cmc pt-bks., fol. 56, a4

6 March   = Cmc pt-bks., fol. 138, a4

7 Passagalia

In *The Compleat Instructor to the Flute,* II (1700), pp. 2-3, are two pieces ascribed to "Mr Eccles in Henry ye fourth." The first is also found in US NH Filmer MS 9 [p. 74], in a set headed "Mr Solomon Eccles in the Female Warrior," a3, and in Cmc pt-bks., fol. 86', a4.

C *Kensington-Gardens; Or, The Pretenders,* John Leigh, LIF (1720)

See Smith, *Walsh I,* No. 574, an advertisement in *The Post Boy* 28-30 January 1720: "A new Sett of Tunes, in three Parts, for Violins and Hoboys; perform'd in the Comedy call'd Kensington-Gardens." This music is not extant.

The Kind Impostor (see *She wou'd and She wou'd not*)

DO *King Arthur; or, The British Worthy,* John Dryden, DG (1691)

Act music: Henry Purcell, *A Collection of Ayres for the Theatre* (1697), pp. 4-9. See Z 628.

1 Overture

2 Aire   = LA Finney pt-bks., p. 80, a4

3 Aire

4 Song Tune

5 Hornpipe

6 Aire   = LA Finney pt-bks., p. 104, a4

7 Song Tune

8 Aire

9 Song Tune

10 Song Tune

11 Trumpet Tune   = LA Finney pt-bks., p. 85, a4

12 Trumpet Tune

P *King Edward the Third, with the Fall of Mortimer Earl of March,* John Bancroft, DL (1691)

? Act music (for a revival?):   Walsh, *Harmonia Anglicana* [IV, 1702], "Mr Peasables [James Paisible] Aires in the Play call'd Edward the Third," copies in Lgc G.Mus. 153 (second treble), Lcm XXIX.A.11 (a4)

1	Overture	=	Cmc pt-bks., fol. 67'. "Ouverture," a4; Lbm Add. 39565, fol. 60', "Paisible ouverture," a4
2	Minuett	=	Lbm Add. 22099, fol. 11', "Min:," a3; Lbm Add. 39565, fol. 61, a4
3	Aire	=	Cmc pt-bks., fol. 70, a4; Lbm Add. 39565, fol. 61', a4; *Self-Instructor*, III (1700), fol. 7, a1
4	Minuett	=	Cmc pt-bks., fol. 69, a4; Lbm Add. 39565, fol. 61', a4; *Self-Instructor*, III (1700), fol. 6, "Mr. Peasables," a1
5	Round O	=	Cmc pt-bks., fol. 114, a4; Lbm Add. 39565, fol. 8', "Paisible Rondeau," a4
6	Prelude	=	Cmc pt-bks., fol. 70, a4; Lbm Add. 39565, fol. 61, a4
7	Bore	=	Cmc pt-bks., fol. 69, a4; Lbm Add. 39565, fol. 61, a4; *40 Airs Anglois*, II [c. 1701], No. 23, "Air Mr. Peasable," a2
8	Minuet	=	Cmc pt-bks., fol. 95, a4; Lbm Add. 39565, fol 61'. a4; *Self-Instructor*, III (1700), fol. 7, "Peasables," a1; *40 Airs Anglois*, II [c. 1701], No. 24, "Air Mr Peasable," a2

The Kingdom of the Birds (see *Wonders in the Sun*)

A Ladies Distress (see *The Banditti*)

The Ladies Friendship (see *The Lying Lover*)

The Lady in Fashion (see *Womans Wit*)

The Ladys fine aires (see *The Fine Lady's airs*)

C   *The Lady's last Stake, or, The Wife's Resentment*, Colley Cibber, QT [1708]

See Smith, *Walsh I*, No. 277a, an advertisement in Smith No. 282a: "Musick in the Ladys last Stake."   This music is not extant.

Lady's Satisfaction (see *Injur'd Love*)

T   *Liberty Asserted*, John Dennis, LIF (1704)

Act music: Walsh, *Harmonia Anglicana* [VI, 1704], "M^r [John] Lentons Musick in the Play call'd Liberty Asserted," copies in Lbm d.24 (first treble and bass), Lgc G. Mus. 153 (second treble), Lcm XXIX.A.11 (a4)

1 Overture

2 Trumpet tune

3 Iigg

4 Rigadon

5 Slow Aire

6 Scotch Malancholly aire

7 Hornpipe

8 Aire

9 Iigg

F   *The Life and Death of Doctor Faustus,* William Mountfort, DG (1697), first produced in December, 1685

? Dance: *Apollo's Banquet,* III (1690), No. 54, "New Posture Dance in Dr. Faustus," a1

Comment: If associated with this farce at all, this tune is most likely for the dance in Act III: "Faustus Limbs come together, A Dance, and song."

C   *The Lost Lover; or, the Jealous Husband,* Mary de la Riviere Manley, DL (1696)

Act music: Lbm Add. 35043, fols. 47'-48 [William Lord Byron's act music in The Lost Lover], a1

1st Musick   [1]

[2]

2^d Musick   [1] = Lcm 1172, fol. 22', "2^d Musick, Lord Byron in the Lost Lover," a4

[2] = Lcm 1172, fol. 22', a4

Overture

1st Act Tune

2^d Act Tune   = Lcm 1172, fol. 22', "1st Act Tune," a4

[third act tune]

4th Act Tune

Songs: I.i [SONG] "Ah Dangerous Swain tell me no more"

IV.i [The Scene opens and discovers Lady Young Love . . . Song and Entertainment of Dancing.]

V. ii [Lady Young Loves House. Song and Musick.] "To love and all its sweets adieu" (see BUCEM, II, 856)

C *Love and a Bottle*, George Farquhar, DL (1699)

? Dances: Lbm Add. 29371, fol. 104', "Love and a Bottle," a2

120 Country Dances (1711), p. 1, "Love in a Bottle," a1

? Songs (not printed in play-book): Ob c.95, p. 119, "by [Richard] Leveridge in Love in a Bottle ('Early in ye Dawning of a Winter Morn')," a2

Ob c.95, p. 122, "by [Richard] Leveridge in Love in a Bottle ('When cupid from')," a2

Love and Empire (see *Abra-Mule*)

C *Love and Honour* [William Davenant, LIF, 1661]

? Dance: *Pleasant Companion* (1672), No. 15, "Love & Honour a Dance M.[atthew] L.[ocke]," a1

C *Love at a Loss; or, Most Votes carry it,* Catharine Trotter, DL (1701)

Act music: Walsh, *Harmonia Anglicana,* I [1701], "M^r [Godfrey] Fingers Ayres in the Comedy of Love's at a Loss," copies in Lbm b.29.a (first treble), Dc C.37 (a4), Lgc G.Mus. 153 (second treble), Lcm XXIX.A.11 (a4), Lcm XXIX.A.12 (second treble, tenor, bass)

[1] Overture

2 Iigg

3 Scotch Tune   = *Apollo's Banquet* (1701), No. 25, "Slow," a1

4 Hornpipe

5 Aire

6 Aire

7 Round O

8 Bore   = *40 Airs Anglois*, III, p. 7, "Allegro," a2

Dance: V.iii (a final dance)

C *Love Betray'd; or, The Agreable Disappointment* [William Burnaby], LIF (1703)

Act music: Walsh, *Harmonia Anglicana* [V, 1703], "M^r [William] Corbett's Musick in the Comedy call'd the agreeable Disappointment," copies in Lgc G.Mus. 153 (second treble), Lcm XXIX.A.11 (a4), Lcm XXIX.A.12 (second treble, tenor, bass)

1 Overture

2 Allmand

3 Sarraband

4 Minuett

5 Corrant

6 Slow Aire

7 March

8 Slow Aire

9 Round O

Songs: II.i [SCENE opens, and discovers Moreno on a Couch, and Caesario kneeling by . . . Caesario sings.] "If I hear Orinda swear" (D&M 1681 *m*J. Eccles *s*Bracegridle), also in Eccles, *A Collection of Songs* [1704], p. 145, and arranged there "For the Flute," a2; and in J. Eccles, *A song in the comedy call'd Love betraid* [London, c. 1720], copy in Mc)

III.i [Emilia Sings.] "Cloe met love for his Psiche in Fears" (D&M 545 *m*J. Eccles *s*Mrs. Prince)

Miscellaneous music: V.i [A Masque]

C *Love for Love*, William Congreve, LIF (1695)

Act music: Ob c.72, pp. 8-10, "Love for Love [Godfrey] Finger," a3

[1] Overture   = LA Finney pt-bks., p. 38, "Mr Fingers Overture," a4; Ckc 122, fol. 5, "Overture," a2; Lcm 1144, fol. 24, "Love for love," a2; *40 Airs Anglois,* III, p. 1, "Ouverture," a2; US NH Filmer MS 9 [p. 37], "overture Mr Fingers musick in love for Love," a3

2   = LA Finney pt-bks., p. 39, a4; Ckc 122, fol. 5, a2; Lcm 1144, fol. 24', a2; *Compleat Flute = Master* (1695) [fol. 28], "Slow Ayre Mr Finger," a1; *Self-Instructor,* I (1700), "Ayre Mr Finger," a1; US NH Filmer MS 9 [p. 38], a3

3   = LA Finney pt-bks., p. 40, a4; Ckc 122, fol. 5', a2; Lbm Add. 39565, fol. 51, a4; Lcm 1144, fol 24', a2; *Compleat Flute = Master* (1695) [fol.24], "Ayre Mr Finger," a1; US NH Filmer MS 9 [p. 38], a3

4   = LA Finney pt-bks., p. 40, a4; Ckc 122, fol. 5', a2; Lcm 1144, fol. 24', a2; *Compleat Flute = Master* (1695) [fol. 24], "Scotch tune Mr Finger," a1; *Self-Instructor,* I (1700), "Scotch Tune Mr. Finger," a1; *Apollo's Banquet* (1701), No. 107, "Scotch Tune," a1; US NH Filmer MS 9 [p. 38], a3

5   = LA Finney pt-bks., p. 40, a4; Ckc 122, fol. 5', "Gigue," a2; Lcm 1144, fol. 24', a2; *Compleat Flute = Master* (1695) [fol. 28], "Iigg Mr Finger," a1; US NH Filmer MS 9 [p. 39], a3

6   = LA Finney pt-bks., p. 41, a4; Ckc 122, fol. 5', a2; Lbm Add. 39565, fol. 50', a4; Lcm 1144, fol. 25, a2; US NH Filmer MS 9 [p. 39], a3

7   = Finney pt-bks., p. 41, a4; Ckc 122, fol. 6, a2; Lbm Add. 39565, fol. 50', a4; Lcm 1144, fol. 25, a2; US NH Filmer MS 9 [p. 39], a3

8   = LA Finney pt-bks., p. 42, a4; Ckc 122, fol. 6, a2; Lbm Add. 39565, fol. 50, a4; Lcm 1144, fol. 25, a2; *Compleat Flute = Master* (1695) [fol. 20], "Slow Mr Finger," a1; US NH Filmer MS 9 [p. 40], a3

9   = LA Finney pt-bks., p. 42, a4; Ckc 122, fol. 6, a2; Lbm Add. 24889, fol. 21, "Countrey Dance called 'The Maids happy meeting'," a1; Lbm Add. 39565, fol. 51, a4; Lbm

Add. 35043, fol. 80, "Finger Hornpipe," a1; Lcm 1144, fol. 25, a2; *Compleat Flute=Master* (1695) [fol. 20], "M.ʳ Finger," a1; US NH Filmer MS 9 [p. 40], a3

Songs: III.iii. "A Nymph and a swain to Apollo once prayed" (D&M 2443 mJ. Eccles sPate, and J. Eccles, *A song in the comedy call'd Love for Love*, London, c. 1696, copy in Gu)

III.iv. "A Soldier and a sailor a tinker and a tailor" (D&M 3019 mJ. Eccles sDoggett)

IV.iii. "I tell thee, Charmion, could I time retrieve" (D&M 1603 mFinger sPate and Reading, and BUCEM, I, 336)

Dances: III.iv. *Ben.* If some of our crew that came to see me are not gone, you shall see that we sailors can dance sometimes as well as other folks. [Whistles] I warrant that brings 'em an they be within hearing. [Enter Sailors] Oh, here they be!-- and fiddles along with 'em. Come, my lads, lets have a Round and I'll make one. [They dance]

The Dancing Master, II (1696), p. 20 "[a tune] Danc'd in the Play Love for Love," a1 (this is probably the music for the sailors' dance)

V.ii [A Dance]

C *Love for Money: or, the Boarding School*, Thomas Durfey, DL (1691)

? Act music: *Apollo's Banquet* (1691), "Mr. [Thomas] Tollett's [tunes] in the Play of Love for Money" a1

44 A Minuet

45 A Minuet

46 A New Tune

47 A Tune

48 A New Theatre Tune = Cmc pt-bks., fol. 91, "Slow," a4

49 A New Tune

50 A Tune

Songs: I.i [A Song here mimicking the French. SONG] "As soon as day began to peep"

II.ii [Here Coopee Re-enters, and Sings this Song to the Minuet that he is dancing with Jenny.] "Make your Honour Miss" (D&M 2163)

IV.iii [SONG] "Royal and Fair, great Willy's dear Blessing" (D&M 2835)

Dances: (see II.ii, above)

III.ii [Here the Romps perform a Ridiculous dance with Guittars out of Tune.]

(III.ii) [Here Jiltal dances.]

Apollo's Banquet (1691), No. 1, "A Dance in the Play of the Boarding-School," a1 = H. Purcell, *A Collection of Ayres for the Theatre* (1697), p. 30, "Hornpipe in Amphitryon," a4; *Dancing Master* (1703), p. 252, "Enfield Common," a1; Lbm Add. 22099, fol. 14', a1; LA Finney pt-bks., p. 81, a4

Apollo's Banquet (1691), No. 2, "A Tune in the Boarding-School," a1

Love in a Bottle (see *Love and a Bottle*)

Love in a Tubb (see *The Comical Revenge*)

C *Love makes a Man; or, The Fop's Fortune*, Colley Cibber, DL (1701)

Act music: Walsh, *Harmonia Anglicana*, II [1701], "M.ʳ [Godfrey] Fingers Ayres in the Comedye of Loue makes a man or ye Fops Fortune," copies in Lbm b.29.a (first treble), Lbm d.24 (first treble and bass), Dc C.37 (a4), Lgc G.Mus. 153 (second treble), Lcm XXIX.A.11 (a4), Lcm XXIX.A.12 (second treble, tenor, bass)

[1] Overture   = Cmc pt-bks., fol. 36', "Ouverture," a4

2 Iigg   = Cmc pt-bks., fol. 135, a4

3 Slow Aire   = Cmc pt-bks., fol. 134', a4; *Select Lessons* (1702), fol. 4, "Slow Aire by Mr. Finger," a1

4 Corrant   = Cmc pt-bks., fol. 134', a4; *Select Lessons* (1702), fol. 4, "Corrant," a1; *40 Airs Anglois*, III, p. 7, "Allegro," a2

5 Round O   = Cmc pt-bks., fol. 135, a4; *Select Lessons* (1702), fol. 5, "Round O," a1; *40 Airs Anglois*, III, p. 11, "Round O," a2

6 Prelude   = Cmc pt-bks., fol. 37', a4; *Select Lessons* (1702), sig. i. "Prelude by Mr. Finger," a1

7 Minuet   = Cmc pt-bks., fol. 37', a4; *Select Lessons* (1702), sig. i, "Minuet," a1

8 Slow Aire   = Cmc pt-bks., fol. 24', a4

9 Iigg   = Cmc pt-bks., fol. 24', a4

Song: IV.ii [A SONG here . . .]

Dance: V.iii (a final dance)

Miscellaneous music: IV.ii [A flourish . . . Musick here.]

                         V.iii [Enter Hautboys playing . . .]

C *The Lover's Luck*, Thomas Dilke, LIF (1696)

Act music: Lbm Add. 24889, fols. 10-11, the act music in "Lovers Luck T[homas] T[ollett]," a4

   1   = Lbm Add. 35043, fol. 102, "Tollett (2) in Lovers Luck," a1

   2   = Lbm Add. 35043, fol. 102', a1

   3   = Lbm Add. 35043, fol. 102', a1

   4   = Lbm Add. 35043, fol. 102', a1

   [5] Overture = Lbm Add. 35043, fol. 102, "1 Overture in ye Lovers Luck," a1

   [6]   = Lbm Add. 35043, fol. 103, a1

   [7]   = Lbm Add. 35043, fol. 103, a1

   [8]   = Lbm Add. 35043, fol. 103, a1

   [9]   = Lbm Add. 35043, fol. 103, a1

Songs: II.i [A SONG] "Rich mines of hot Love are rooted here" (D&M 2810 *s*Boman)

               III.iv [A SONG. Set by Mr. John Eccles.] "Full of the God I feel my raging soul" (D&M 1106 *m*J. Eccles and BUCEM, I, 308)

               IV.i [A SONG] "Let us Revel and Roar" (D&M 2020 *m*J. Eccles *s*Reading and Curco, and BUCEM, I, 308)

               V.ii [An Entertainment of Singing and Dancing by Sheppards and Satyrs . . . A Song, in Dialogue, Sung by Mr. Reading and Mrs.

Hodgson. Set by Mr. John Eccles] "Come, Thyrsis, come; let us our Voices try"

C *Love's Last Shift; or, The Fool in Fashion,* Colley Cibber, DL (1696)

Act music: Lcm 1172, fols. 6-6', four "Lessons in Loves last shift [by James] Paisible," a4

    1st Lesson   = LA Finney pt-bks., p. 33, a4; Lbm Add. 35043, fol. 60, al; Lbm Add. 39565, fol 45', "Paisible," a4

    2^{d} Lesson   = LA Finney pt-bks., p. 34, a4; LEp MS Q784.21 L969, p. 1, a4; Lbm Add. 35043, fol. 60, al; Lbm Add. 39565, fol. 74', "Paisible 6^{e} aire," a3

    3^{d} Lesson Bore   = LA Finney pt-bks., p. 34, a4; LEp MS Q784.21 L969, p. 1, a4; Lbm Add. 35043, fol. 60, al; Lbm Add. 39565, fol. 45', "Paisible," a4; *Thesaurus Musicus* (1696), p. 34, "Paisible," a2

    4th Lesson   = LA Finney pt-bks., p. 35, a4; Lbm Add. 35043, fol. 60, al; Lbm Add. 39565, fol. 45', "Paisible," a4; *Thesaurus Musicus* (1696), p. 34, "Minuet Paisible," a2

Songs: IV.i [A Song here.]

not printed in play-book: "Go home unhappy wretch and mourn" (D&M 1141 *m*Frank *s*Mrs. Cross and "the boy")

"What ungrateful devil moves you" (D&M 3668 *m*D. Purcell, also in Ob c.95, p. 122, and see BUCEM, II, 857)

"Jockey was as brisk" (D&M 1874), also in Ob c.95, p. 124, "Mr. Clerke"

Miscellaneous music: V [A Masque]

Lbm Add. 38189, fol. 31' [a tune], "Play this [?] times over, & the Last play the Repeit in The Love's last shift," al

24 New Country Dances (1718), p. 18, "Loves last Shift," al

Loves of the Deities (see *A New Opera, call'd Cinthia and Endimion*)

Love's Paradice (see *The Grove*)

C Loves Stratagem ?

Act music: Walsh, *Harmonia Anglicana,* I [1701], "M.^{r} [James] Peasable [Paisible] Ayres in the Comedy of Loves Stratagem the Tunes for alsorts of

Instruments," copies in Lbm b.29.a (first treble), Dc C.37 (a4), Lgc G.Mus. 153 (second treble), Lcm XXIX.A.11 (a4)

[1] Overture   = Cmc pt-bks., fol. 139', "Ouverture," a4; Lbm Add. 39565, fol. 29', "Paisible Overture," a4

2 Prelude   = Lbm Add. 39565, fol. 29', "Paisible," a4

3 Aire

4 Bore   = Lbm Add. 39565, fol. 30, a4

5 Minuet   = Lbm Add. 39565, fol. 30, a4

6 Saraband   = Lbm Add. 39565, fol. 29', a4

7 March   = Lbm Add. 39565, fol. 30, a4

8 Entry   = Lbm Add. 39565, fol. 30', "Paisible 1^e Air," a4

9 Paspy   = Lbm Add. 39565, fol. 30', "Paisible 2eme air," a4

Comment: This play does not survive. See Price, "Eight 'Lost' Restoration Plays," pp. 300-301.

C *The Lying Lover: or, The Ladies Friendship,* Richard Steele, DL (1704)

Act music: Walsh, *Harmonia Anglicana* [VI, 1703], "Mr Wm Croft's Musick in the Comedy call'd the Lying Lover," copies in Lbm d.24 (first treble and bass), Lgc G. Mus. 153 (second treble), Lcm XXIX.A.11 (a4), Lcm XXIX.A.12 (second treble, tenor, bass)

[1] Overture   = Och 620, p. 69, "Overture Mr Croft," a4

2 Hornpipe   = Cmc pt-bks., fol. 50', a4; Och 620, p. 74, "Hornpipe Mr Croft," a4

3 Aire   = Cmc pt-bks., fol. 51, "Slow," a4; Och 620, p. 75, "Aire Mr Croft," a4

4 Slow Aire Round O   = Cmc pt-bks., fol. 50, "Slow," a4; Och 620, p. 76, "Slow Aire Round O Mr Croft," a4

5 Aire   = Cmc pt-bks., fol. 50', a4; Och 620, p. 77, "Aire Mr Croft," a4

6 Trumpett aire   = Och 620, p. 78, "Trumpet Aire Mr Croft," a4

7 Minuet Round O   = Cmc pt-bks., fol. 50, a4; Och 620, p. 79, "Minuet Round O Mr Croft," a4; *Ladys Banquet*, II (1706), p. 8, "Bath Minuet," keyb.

8 Chacone   = Och 620, p. 80, "Chacone . . . Mr Croft," a4

Songs: II.i [Here the Song is perform'd to a Spinet] "Thou soft Machines"

          III.i [SONG, by Mr. Leveridge.] "Venus has left her Grecian Isles"

          V.iii [Song. By Mr. LEVERIDGE.] "The rolling Years the Joys restore"

DO *Macbeth* [William Davenant, LIF, 1664]

? Dance: *Musick's Delight on the Cithren* (1666), No. 65, "A Jig called Macbeth," a1 = *Musicks Recreation on the Viol* (1669), p. 7, "A Dance in Mackbeth," a1; *Pleasant Companion* (1672), No. 7, "Mackbeth M.[atthew] L.[ocke]," a1; *Apollo's Banquet* (1678), No. 13, "The Dance in the Play of Mackbeth," a1

For music to later alterations of this play, see Ckc MS 213, Cfm Mus MS 87, Lbm Add. 12219, and Lbm Add. 29378. For a discussion of the music in 17th-century versions of *Macbeth*, see Roger Fiske, "The 'Macbeth' Music," *M&L*, XLV (1964), 114-125, and Robert E. Moore, "The Music to *Macbeth*," *MQ*, XXVII (1961), 22-40.

DO The Mad Lover, P. A. Motteux (?), LIF [1701]

Act music: Walsh, *Harmonia Anglicana*, II [1701], "Ayres in ye Opera call'd ye Mad Lover Composed by M.ʳ Iohn Eccles," copies in Lbm d.24 (first treble and bass), Dc C.37 (a4), Lgc G.Mus. 153 (second treble), Lcm XXIX.A.11 (a4), Lcm XXIX.A.12 (second treble, tenor, bass)

1 Overture

2 Aire   = Cmc pt-bks., fol. 114, a4

3 Aire   = Cmc pt-bks., fol. 114', a4

4 Slow Aire   = Cmc pt-bks., fol. 5', a4

5 Aire   = Cmc pt-bks., fol. 5', a4; *Select Lessons* (1702), sig. m, "Prelude by M.ʳ Eccles," a1

6 Iigg   = Cmc pt-bks., fol. 50, a4; Eccles, *A Collection of Lessons* [1702], p. 4, "Iigg," keyb.

7 Aire   = Cmc pt-bks., fol. 123', a4

8 Aire

9 Aire   =   Cmc pt-bks., fol. 50', a4

Note: This operatic alteration of Fletcher's play was apparently never published. For the songs in this work, see D&M 13, 55, 182, 497, 719, 1911, 1952, 2088, 2235, 2441, 2507, 3807; also see BUCEM, I, 309.

The Maiden Queen (see *Secret-Love*)

T *The Maid's Tragedy*, Beaumont and Fletcher (1619)

   Act music (for revival in July 1698?): Lcm 1144, fol. 3 "[five tunes by Lewis] Grabu for ye Maids Tragedy," a2

      [1]

      [2]

      [3]

      [4] Prelude

      [5] Retternello

   Song: "Gentle night befriend a Lover" (D&M 1113), apparently for a revival.

The Man-Hater (see *The History of Timon of Athens*)

C *The Man of Mode, or, Sr Fopling Flutter*, George Etherege, DG (1676)

   ? Miscellaneous music: *Dancing Master*, II (1686), No. 15, "Sir Foplin," a1

                             Dancing-Master (1718), p. 330, "Sir Foplin's Airs," a1

C *The Marriage-Hater Match'd*, Thomas Durfey, DL (1692)

   Dance: *Apollo's Banquet*, III (1693), No. 95, "A New dance in the Play of The Marriage-Hater match'd," a1

   ? Miscellaneous music: *Dancing Master* (1695), p. 183, "Marriage-Hater," a1

C *The Married Beau: or, The Curious Impertinent*, John Crowne, DL (1694)

   Act music: Henry Purcell, *A Collection of Ayres for the Theatre* (1697), pp. 21-24. See Z 603.

1 Overture   = LA Finney pt-bks., p. 79, "Overture," a4

2 Slow Aire   = LA Finney pt-bks., p. 80, a4

3 Hornpipe

4 Aire

5 Hornpipe

6 Jjgg

7 Trumpet Aire

8 March   = Lcm [*Apollo's Banquet*, c. 1705], No. 109, "Ayre," a1

9 Hornpipe
   on a ground

Songs: II.i [Thornebacke Sings.]   "Oh fie!   What mean I, foolish maid"
            (D&M 2464, and BUCEM, I, 309; an a4 arrangement is in Lbm Add.
            24889, fol. 22')

            V.i [The song.] "See! Where repenting Celia lyes" (D&M 2887 *m*H.
            Purcell *s*Mrs. Ayliff)

Mary Queen of Scotts (see *The Albion Queens*)

? Matchles [Maids?]

   ? Act music: Lcm 1172, fols. 17-18', airs by "Morgan in Matchles," a4

      [1] Overture   = LA Finney pt-bks., p. 18, "Mr Morgan Overture," a4;
                          Lbm Add. 39565, fol. 39', "Morgan overture," a4

      [2] Gavott   = LA Finney pt-bks., p. 18, a4

      [3] Hornpipe   = LA Finney pt-bks., p. 19, a4; Lbm Add. 39565, fol. 39',
                          "Morgan Hornpipe," a4; *Self-Instructor*, I (1700) [No.
                          29], "Hornpipe," a1

      [4]   = LA Finney pt-bks., p. 19, a4; Lbm Add. 39565, fol. 40,
                          a4; *Self-Instructor*, I (1700) [No. 30], "Ayre," a1

      [5] Round [o]   = LA Finney pt-bks., p. 20, a4; Lbm Add. 39565, fol. 40,
                          "Morgan Rondeau," a4

[6]

[7]

Comment: This is perhaps a fragment of the title of a lost play. See Price, "Eight 'Lost' Restoration Plays," p. 301.

C *Measure for Measure: Or, Beauty the Best Advocate* [Charles Gildon], LIF (1700)

Miscellaneous music: *Apollo's Banquet* (1701), No. 20, "A Scotch Tune in Measure for Measure," a1

24 New Country Dances (1716), p.20, "Measure for Measure," a1 = *Dancing-Master* (1718), p. 323, "Measure for Measure," a1

TC *The Mistakes, or, The False Report,* Joseph Harris, DL (1691)

Act music: Lbm Add. 35043, fols. 88-88', "Mr Ormes Tunes in The Mistakes," a1

[4 Overture]

2

3

1

Song: IV.ii [A Song]

C *The Mock-Marriage,* Thomas Scott, DL (1696)

Act music: Lbm Add. 35043, fols. 45'-46', "Mr Morgans Tunes in Ye Mock Marriage," a1

2 [first music, 1]   = LA Finney pt-bks., p. 25, a4; Ckc 122, fol. 6, a2; Cmc pt-bks., fol. 124', a4; Ob c.73, p. 14, "Morgan," a3

3 [first music, 2]   = LA Finney pt-bks., p.25, a4; Ckc 122, fol. 6', a2; *Apollo's Banquet* (1701), No. 86, "Hornpipe by Mr. Morgan," a1

4 [second music, 1]   = LA Finney pt-bks., p. 26, a4; Ckc 122, fol. 6', "Prelude," a2; Ob c.73, p. 15, "Morgan," a3; *Apollo's Banquet* (1701), No. 84, "Ayre by Mr. Morgan," a1

5 [second music, 2] = LA Finney pt-pks., p. 26, a4; Ckc 122, fol. 6',
"Gigue," a2; Ob c.73, p. 15, "Morgan", a3;
Apollo's Banquet (1701), No. 85, "A Tune by
Mr. Morgan," a1

1 Overture = LA Finney pt-bks., p. 24, "Mr. Morgan
Overtur," a4; Ckc 122, fol. 6', a2; Ob c. 73, p.
13, "Morgan Overture," a3

6 [first act tune] = LA Finney pt-bks., p. 26, a4; Ckc 122, fol. 7, a2

7 [second act tune] = LA Finney pt-bks., p. 27, a4; Ckc 122, fol. 7,
a2; Ob c.73, p. 16, "Morgan," a3

9 [fourth act tune] = LA Finney pt-bks., p. 19, a4; Ckc 122, fol. 7',
"Scots Tune," a2; Ob c.73, p. 23, a3; Lbm
Add. 39565, fol. 40, "Morgan," a4; Lcm 1172,
fol. 10, "Morgan Scotch tune in Mock
Marriage," a4; *Apollo's Banquet* (1701), No. 89,
"Scotch Tune by Mr Morgan," a1

10 [fifth act tune?] = Ckc 122, fol. 7', a2; Ob c.73, p. 23, a3; Lcm
1172, fol. 10, "4th [tune] in Mock Marriage,"
a4

8 [third act tune] = LA Finney pt-bks., p. 27, a4; Ob c.73, fol. 10
"Morgan Cibell," a3; Lbm Add. 35043, fol. 43,
"Round O Cibell," a1; Lbm Add. 39565, fol.
44, "Morgan's sibelle," a4

Songs: II.ii [A SONG, in the Second Act, sung by Mrs. Knight (who plays
Lady Barter)] "O how you protest" (D&M 2479 *m*H. Purcell *s*Mrs.
Knight)

III.ii [SONG Written by Mr. D'Urfey.] "Twas within a Furlong"
(D&M 3500)

IV.iii [A Roundelau by Mr. Motteux.] "Man is for Woman made"
(D&M 2168 *m*H. Purcell *s*Miss Cross)

Monsr Raggou (see *The Old Troop*)

The Mother in Fashion (see *The Disappointment*)

The Moor of Venice (see *Venice Preserv'd*)

The Moor's Revenge (see *Abdelazer*)

Most Votes carry it (see *Love at a Loss*)

T *The Mourning Bride*, William Congreve, LIF (1697)

Act music: LEp MS Q784.21 L969, pp. 16-18 "[Godfrey] Finger['s music] in ye Mourning Bride," a4

[1 Overture] = LA Finney pt-bks., p. 108, "Overture," a4

2 = LA Finney pt-bks., p. 109, a4; *Self-Instructor*, II (1700) [No. 19], "Borre," a1

3 = LA Finney pt-bks.,.p. 109, a4

4 = LA Finney pt-bks., p. 110, a4

5 = LA Finney pt-bks., p. 110, a4; *Self-Instructor*, II (1700) [No. 18], "Aire," a1

6 [a5]

7 = LA Finney pt-bks., p. 111, a4; Lcm 1172, fol. 30, "Finger an act tune in Mourning Bride," a4; *Self-Instructor*, II (1700) [No. 22], "Aire," a1

8 = LA Finney pt-bks., p. 111, a4; Lcm 1172, fol. 30, "Finger Act tune in Mourning Bride," a4

9 = LA Finney pt-bks., p. 112, a4; Lcm 1172, fol. 30', "Finger an act tune in Mourning Bride," a4; *40 Airs Anglois*, II [c. 1701], p. 26, "Gavott Mr Finger," a2

10 = LA Finney pt-bks., p. 112, a4; Cmc pt-bks., fol. 96, "Slow," a4; Lcm 1172, fol. 30', "Finger act tune in Mourning Bride," a4; *Self-Instructor*, II (1700) [No. 23], a1

Miscellaneous music: I.i [The Curtain rising slowly to soft Music, discovers Almeria in mourning . . .]

I.ii [Symphony of Warlike music]

T *Mustapha, Son of Solyman the Magnificent*, Roger Boyle, LIF (1665)

Act music (for a revival in 1686?): Lbm Add. 24889, fols. 7-7', "Mustapha," a4

Overture

1st [tune] Slow

2^d [tune]

3^d [tune] Slow

4th [tune]

5 Slow

6 Slow

P   *Neglected Virtue: or, The Unhappy Conqueror*, Hildebrand Horden, DL (1696)

    ? Act music: Lbm Add. 35043, fols. 63'-64', "Tunes to Mr Hordens Play by Mr. P.[aisible]," a1

        1 Lesson   = Lbm Add. 39565, fol. 47', "Paisible," a4

        2^d Lesson   = Lbm Add. 39565, fol. 47', "Paisible," a4

        3^d Lesson   = Lbm Add. 39565, fol. 47', "Paisible," a4

        [4]

        [Overture]

        1: Act [tune]   = Lbm Add. 39565, fol. 47, "Paisible," a4

        2: Act [tune]

        [third act tune?] = Lbm Add. 39565, fol. 47, "Paisible," a4

        Very Slow. Symp[hony]

    Song: II.ii [. . . A Symphony of Warlike Musick and then a Song.] (see BUCEM, II, 857)

DO   *A New Opera, call'd Cinthia and Endimion: or, The Loves of the Deities*, Thomas Durfey, DL (1697)

    ? Act music: Lcm 1172, fol. 31', three pieces in "Cynthia & Endymion by D.[aniel?] P[urcell?]", a2 and a4

        1st [act tune?]

        [2]

        [3]

Four songs from this dramatic opera survive:

> I.i "Musing on Cares" (D&M 2229 *m*H. Purcell)
>
> III.i "'Twas when the Sheep were shearing" (D&M 3499)
>
> IV.i "The Poor Endymion" (D&M 2715 *m*Underwood)
>
> V.i [SONG, by a Druid] "Black and Gloomy" (D&M 373 *m*Leveridge)

Dance: Lcm 1172, fol. 19, "Cupid's dance in Cynthia and Endymion," a4. This is probably for I.i, "A Dance of Cupid's Lovers here."

The Nest of Fools (see *The Northern Lass)*

No Magick like Love (see *The British Enchanters*)

C   *The Northern Lass, or, The Nest of Fools . . . With Prologue, Epilogue, and New Songs,* Richard Brome, DL (1706)

[a slight alteration of Brome's 1632 play]

Act music: Walsh, *Harmonia Anglicana* [collection c, 1705], "Mr D.[aniel] Purcell's Musick in the COMEDY call'd the Northern Lass," copy in Lbm d.24 (first treble and bass)

Note: At the bottom of the title page of the play-book is the following note: "The Musick to this Play is Composed by Mr. D. Purcel; and Printed for J. Walsh at the Harp in S. Catherine street in the Strand."

    1   Overture

    2   Aire

    3   Aire

    4   Iigg   =   Cmc pt-bks., fol. 117, a4; *Flute Master,* V (1706), p. 5, "Iigg," a1

    5   Aire   =   *Flute Master,* V (1706), p. 5, "Aire," a1

    6   Gavot

    7   Scotch Aire

    8   Iigg

Songs: II.iii [SONG. Set by Mr. William Crofts.] "A Bonny Northern Lad"

II.vi [Musick. The Masquers Enter. All in Willow Garland . . . A Dance here.]

Note: In the 1632 play-book is the following stage direction in this scene: "Before the Daunce, Constance sings this Song." The song is "Nor love nor fate do I accuse" (D&M 2360 *m*R. Simson?).

III.ii [SONG.] "A Bonny Bird I had"

III.iii [They all take hands, and dance round, Widgin in the midst sings this Song. They all bear the burden, while she scolds and strives to be amongst 'em. Tridewell holds her off.] "He that marries a Scold"

(III.iii) [Widgin Sings] "He that marries a merry Lass"

IV.iv [SONG.] "Peace wayward Bairn"

(IV.iv) [A SONG, by Mrs. Prince.] "A bonny Lad there was"

Miscellaneous music: V.ii-iii [Soft Musick.]

Apollo's Banquet (1678) [No. 44], "The Northern Lass," a1 = *Pleasant Companion* (1682) [No. 30], "A new Northern Tune," a1

Dancing Master, II (1686) [No.29], "The Scotch-mans Dance, in the Northern Lass," a1 = *Apollo's Banquet* (1687) [No. 103], "The Scotch-man's Dance, in the Northern Lass," a1

T *Oedipus,* John Dryden, DG (1679)

Act music (for a revival, October 1692?):   LEp MS Q784.21 L969, pp. 21-22 "[Lewis] Grabu in Oedipus," a4

[1 overture]

[2]

3

4

[5]

[6]

[7]

Songs: II.i [SONG to APOLLO] "Phoebus, God belov'd"

                (II.i) [Musick first. Then Sing . . .] "Hear, ye sullen Pow'rs below"

                (II.i) "Musick for a while" (D&M 2224 *m*H. Purcell)

See also Z 583.

Miscellaneous music: I.i [Scene Thebes. The Curtain rises to a plaintive Tune, representing the present condition of Thebes . . .]

C *The Old Batchelour*, William Congreve, DL (1693)

    Act music: Henry Purcell, *A Collection of Ayres for the Theatre* (1697), pp. 25-27. See Z 607.

      [1] Overture

       2 Hornpipe

       3 Slow Aire

       4 Hornpipe   = *Self-Instructor*, II (1700) [No. 42], "Well's Humour," a1

       5 Rondeau

       6 Minuet

       7 Boree   = LA Finney pt-bks., p. 87, a4

       8 March   = LA Finney pt-bks., p. 84, a4

       9 Jigg

Songs: II.ii [Gavot Sings] "Thus to a ripe consenting maid" (D&M 3359 *m*H. Purcell)

                III.iv [SONG] "As Amoret and Thyrsis lay" (D&M 195 *m*H. Purcell)

Dances: III.iv [After the Song a Dance of Antics.]

                V [a final dance]

C *The Old Troop: or, Monsieur Raggou*, John Lacy, TR (1672)

    Act music: (for a revival, perhaps October 1705; see *The London Stage*, II:1, 104): Lbm Add. 35043, fols. 39'-41', "Mr Morgan The Tunes in Monsr Raggou or ye old Troop," a1 [first music, a ground]   = Cmc pt-bks., fol. 38', a4; LA Finney pt-bks., p. 16, a4

2ᵈ Musick   = LA Finney pt-bks., p. 13, a4; Lbm Add. 39565, fol. 36', "Morgan," a4; *Compleat Flute=Master* (1695) [fol. 16], "Mʳ Morgan," a1; *Self-Instructor*, I (1700), No. 24, "Mr Morgan," a1

[second music, 2]   = LA Finney pt-bks., p. 14, a4; Lbm Add. 39565, fol. 36', "Morgan," a4

Curtain tune   = LA Finney pt-bks., p. 12, "By Mr. Morgan Overture," a4; Lbm Add. 39565, fol. 35', "Morgan Overture," a4

1ˢᵗ Act tune   = LA Finney pt-bks., p. 13, a4; Lbm Add. 39565, fol. 36, "Morgan Gavotte," a4

2ⁿᵈ Act tune   = LA Finney pt-bks., p. 13, a4; Lbm Add. 39565, fol. 36, "Morgan gigue," a4

3ᵈ act Tune   = LA Finney pt-bks., p. 15, a4

4th Act Tune   = LA Finney pt-bks., p. 14, a4; Lbm Add. 39565, fol. 36', "Morgan hornpipe," a4

Dance: V.i [A Dance of two hobby Horses in Armours and a Jigg.]

T *Oroonoko*, Thomas Southerne, DL (1696)

Act music: Lcm 1172, fols. 1-2', "Mr. [James] Peacable [Paisible] in Oronoca," a4

[1] Overture   = Lbm Add. 35043, fol. 59, "Overture," a1; Lbm Add. 39565, fol. 53', "Paisible overture," a4

1ˢᵗ Act Tune   = Lbm Add. 35043, fol. 59', "First Act [tune]," a1; Lbm Add. 39565, fol. 54, a4

3ᵈAct Tune   = Lbm Add. 35043, fol. 59', "3ᵈ Act [tune]," a1

2ᵈ Act Tune hornpipe   = Lbm Add. 35043, fol. 59, "6th Lesson--2ᵈ Act [tune]," a1

4ᵗʰ Act Tune   = Cmc pt-bks., fol. 137, "Slow," a4; Lbm Add. 35043, fol. 59', "4th Act [tune]," a1; Lbm Add. 39565, fol. 54, "Paisible," a4

For the probable preliminary music for this play, see Lbm Add. 35043, fol. 58':

1st Lesson   =   Cmc pt-bks., fol. 88'

2 Lesson Slow   =   Cmc pt-bks., fol. 110'

3 Lesson [a ground]

Songs: II.iii [the Scene draws shews the Slaves, Men, Women, and Children
               upon the Ground, some rise and dance, others sing the following
               Songs. A SONG By an unknown hand. Sett by Mr. Courtevill, and
               sung by the Boy to Miss Cross.] "A Lass there lives upon the Green"
               (D&M 1925 mR. Courteville s"the boy")

               (II.iii) [A SONG, by Mr. Cheek. Sett by Mr. Courtevill, and sung by
               Mr. Leveridge] "Bright Cynthia's Pow'r" (D&M 418 mR. Courteville)

               not printed in the play-book: "Celemene pray tell me" (D&M 507
               mH. Purcell s"boy and girl")

Past. *Pastor Fido,* Elkanah Settle, DG (1676)

? Act music: US NYp MS Drexel 3849, pp. 39-41, "M^r [William?] Turner['s music]
             To Pastor ffido 1676," a3

    [1]

    [2]

       4 = [3]

       5 = [4]

    [5]

       6

Songs: III.i "Why does the foolish World mistake" (D&M 3925 mTurner)
               [sung by Mrs. Napier who acted Celia]

               III.i "Let us use time whilst we may"

               IV.iii "Oh glorious Youth, true Child of Hercules"

               IV.iii [The Shepherds Song] "Thank Conquer to thee"

               V.i "Sols Sister, Daughter of great Jupiter"

V.i "Where's artless Innocence"

Dance: III.i [The Song ended, they dance, which done, they go off singing]

Miscellaneous music: I.i [After a sound of Horns, and cry of Hunts-Men, enter Silvio and Lynco]

T *The Patriot, or the Italian Conspiracy,* Charles Gildon, DL (1703)

Act music: Walsh, *Harmonia Anglicana* [V, 1702], "Mr D.[aniel] Purcells Aires in the Tragedy call'd the Patriot or the Itallian Conspiracy," copies in Lbm b.29.a (first treble), Lbm d.24 (first treble and bass), Lgc G.Mus. 153 (second treble), Lcm XXIX.A.12 (second treble, tenor, bass)

[1] Overture

2 Chacconne

3 Aire

4 Aire   = Cmc pt-bks., fol. 58', a4

5 Round O

6 Aire

7 Boree

8 Aire Slow

T *Perolla and Izadora,* Colley Cibber, DL (1706)

See Smith, *Walsh I,* No. 314, and advertisement in Smith, No. 331: "Musick in Perolla and Izadora." This music is not extant.

C *The Perplex'd Lovers,* Susannah Centlivre, DL (1712)

See Smith, *Walsh I,* No. 416, an advertisement in *The Post Man* 19-21 February 1712: "A Set of Tunes in 3 parts for Violins and Hoboys, in the last new Comedy call'd the Perplex'd Lovers, Composed by Mr. John Barret." This music is not extant.

T *Phaedra and Hippolitus,* Edmund Smith, QT [1707]

Act music: Walsh [Act Music of the Queens Theatre, 1708], "Mr John Allnots Musick Made for ye Play call'd Phaedra & Hyppolitus," copy in Lbm g.15 (a4)

1 Overture

2 Prelude

3 Trumpet Aire

4 Minuet

5 Gavott

6 Slow

7 March

8 Minuet Round O

9 Iigg

C *The Pilgrim,* John Vanbrugh, DL (1700)

Act music (for a revival?):   Walsh, *Harmonia Anglicana* [IV, 1702], "M^r [John] Barretts Aires in the Comedy call'd the Pilgrim," copies in Lbm b.29.a (first treble), Lbm d.24 (first treble and bass), Lgc G.Mus. 153 (second treble), Lcm XXIX.A.12 (second treble, tenor, bass)

[1] Overture   = Cmc pt-bks., fol. 121', "Ouverture," a4; LEp MS Q784.21 L969, p. 32, a4

2 Allmand   = Cmc pt-bks., fol. 122, a4; LEp MS Q784.21 L969, p. 33, a4

3 Corant   = Cmc pt-bks., fol. 122', a4; LEp MS Q784.21 L969, p. 33, a4

4 Aire   = Cmc pt-bks., fol. 122', a4; LEp MS Q784.21 L969, p. 33, a4

5 Gavot   = Cmc pt-bks., fol. 122', a4; LEp MS Q784.21 L969, p. 34, a4

6 Allmand   = Cmc pt-bks., fol. 123, a4; LEp MS Q784.21 L969, p. 34, a4

7 Corant   = LEp MS Q784.21 L969, p. 34, a4

8 Round O   = Cmc pt-bks., fol. 123, "Slow," a4; LEp MS Q784.21 L969, p. 35, a4; CDp 1.39 (H), No. 3, "Happy Groves," a1; Lbm Add. 22099, fol 5', "Oh happy groves Mr. Barrett," keyb.; Ob c.95, p. 66, a1; *Apollo's Banquet* (1701), No. 17, "Round O," a1

This is an instrumental arrangement of "Oh happy groves witness of our tender loves" (D&M 2470 *m*Barrett).

9 Minuet	=	Cmc pt-bks., fol. 123, a4; LEp MS Q784.21 L969, p. 35, a4; CDp 1.39 (H) [No. 2], a1; Ob e.397, p. 41, "Minuet in ye Pilgrim," keyb.; Lbm Add. 22099, fol. 6, "Min: Mr B.^{t}," keyb.; *Apollo's Banquet* (1701), No. 18, "Minuett," a1; *Harpsichord Master,* III (1702), p. 8, "Minuett," keyb.

Ob e.397, p. 40, "The Pilgrim," a1

Lcm [*Apollo's Banquet,* c. 1705], No. 24, "A Rigadoon [Trumpet tune the Pilgrim a Country dance]," a1 = *Self-Instructor,* III (1700) [fol. 16], "Hornpipe by Mr Finger Iigg," a1; *Dancing Master* (1701), p. 272, "The Pillgrim," a1; *Apollo's Banquet* (1701), No. 24, "Rigadoon," a1; *Compleat Instructor to the Flute,* II (1700), p. 10, "A Jigg by Mr Finger," a1

Apollo's Banquet (1701), No. 61, "Song Tune in the Pillgrim," a1

Miscellaneous music: III.iii [Musick]

V.v [An Altar, Solemn Musick]

Performed with this play was John Dryden's *The Secular Masque* (1700). For the music in this see D&M 566, 1215, 2948, and 3994.

C *The Plain-Dealer,* William Wycherley, DL (1677)

See Smith, *Walsh I,* No. 516, an advertisement in *The Post Boy* 18-20 July 1717: "A Set of Airs or Tunes; in four Parts, for Violins and Hautboys, with a Trumpet-Part; perform'd in the reviv'd Comedy, call'd The Plain Dealer: Compos'd by Mr. [William] Turner." This music is not extant.

? Pleasure

? Act music: Lcm 1172, fols. 41-42', "Mr. [James] Peasable [Paisible] in Pleasure," a3

[1] Overture

[2] Prelude

[3] Air

4 Round O

[5] Gavot	=	*Vade Mecum* (1679), p. 27, "Mr. Peasible," a1

[6] Allemande

7	=	*Self-Instructor,* III (1700) [fol. 12], "Aire," a1

8

9

[10]   =   Lcm 1172, fol. 43, a3; *Vade Mecum* (1679), p. 27, "Mr.
                            Peasible," a1

A Plot Discover'd (see *Venice Preserv'd)*

The Plotting Sisters (see *A Fond Husband)*

The Pretenders (see *Kensington-Gardens)*

C   *The Pretenders: or, The Town Unmaskt,* Thomas Dilke, LIF (1698)

Act music: US NH Filmer MS 9 [pp. 66-68], "M:^{r} [John] Lenton in the Pretenders," a3

1   =   Cmc pt-bks, fol. 78, a4; *Apollo's Banquet* (1701), No. 15,
                            "Ayre . . . Danc'd by Mr. Eaglesfield at the Theatre,"
                            a1; [*Apollo's Banquet,* c. 1705], No. 15, "Ayre," a1

2   =   Cmc pt-bks, fol. 102', a4

3

4   =   Cmc pt-bks, fol. 17, a4; *Apollo's Banquet* (1701), No. 16,
                            "Jigg . . . Danc'd by Mr. Eaglesfield at the Theatre," a1;
                            [*Apollo's Banquet,* c. 1705], No. 16, "A Jigg," a1

[5] Overture

[6]   =   Cmc pt-bks, fol. 78, "Scoth [sic] Tune," a4

[7]

8

9   =   Cmc pt-bks, fol. 63', a4; *Theater Musick,* I [1689], p. 5,
                            "Iigg," a1

T   *The Princess of Cleve,* Nathaniel Lee, DG (1689), first performed between September
     1680 and December 1682

     Act music: Lbm Add. 29283-5, fols. 62'-65 "[Thomas] Farmers tunes in ye play
                   called Ye Princess of Cleve," a3.   See Milhous and Hume, "Dating
                   Play Premières from Publication Data, 1660-1700," *Harvard Library
                   Bulletin,* XXII (1974), 393, who use Farmer's music to help date the
                   première of this play.

1   = NYp MS Drexel 3849, p. 22, "Farmer," a3

2 Round O

3

4   = NYp MS Drexel 3849, p. 22, "Farmer," a3

5 [Overture]

6   = NYp MS Drexel 3849, p. 23, a3

7 Round O   = NYp MS Drexel 3849, p. 24, a3

8   = NYp MS Drexel 3849, p. 24, a3

9   = NYp MS Drexel 3849, p. 25, a3

10   = NYp MS Drexel 3849, p. 25, a3

11   = NYp MS Drexel 3849, p. 25, a3

Songs: I.i [SONG.] "All other Blessings are but Toyes" (D&M 124 *m*Turner)

            I.iii [The Prince of Cleve's Palace. Musick. Song.] "In a Room for Delight, The Landship of Love"

            IV[iv] [Scene the Bower, Light Song. The Princess of Cleve, Irene. SONG.] "Lovely Selina, Innocent & Free" (D&M 2131 *m*Blow)

            V.iii [The Princess of Cleve, Irene in Mourning, Song, as the Princess kneels at the Stake.] "Weep all ye Nymphs" (D&M 3589 *m*Blow)

Dance: IV.i [Dance.]

The Princess of Persia (see *Distress'd Innocence*)

DO *The Prophetess: or, the History of Dioclesian*, Thomas Betterton (?), DG (1690)

Act music: Henry Purcell, *A Collection of Ayres for the Theatre* (1697), pp. 1-3. See Z 627.

     [1] Overture   = LA Finney pt-bks., p. 118, "Mr Purcell Overture," a4

     2 Prelude

     3 Song tune

4 Trumpet Tune

5 Country Dance = LA Finney pt-bks., p. 107, a4; LA Finney pt-bks., p. 119, a4

6 Aire = LA Finney pt-bks., p. 122, a4

7 Hornpipe = LA Finney pt-bks., p. 122, a4

8 Aire

9 Canaries = LA Finney pt-bks., p. 123, a4

DO *Psyche*, Thomas Shadwell, DG (1675)

? Act music (for a revival 9 June 1704?): Lcm 1172, fol. 11', "Mr. Morgan Airs in Psyche," a4

3^d act [tune]

4th act [tune]

For music associated with the original production, see Matthew Locke, *The English Opera; or The Vocal Musick in Psyche* (1675).

Queen of Brittain (see *Boadicea*)

The Rape of Lavinia (see *Titus Andronicus*)

C *The Recruiting Officer*, George Farquhar, DL (1706)

See Smith, *Walsh I*, No. 210, an advertisement in *The Daily Courant* 5 June 1706: "The Overture and Aires in Four parts perform'd in the Comedy call'd the Recruiting Officer." This music is not extant.

The Rediculous Lover (see *The Generous Enemies*)

C *The Rehearsal*, George Villiers, TR (1672)

? Dance: Lcm 1172, fol. 19', "A Dance in the Rehearsal," a1

C *The Relapse: or, Virtue in Danger*, John Vanbrugh, DL (1697)

Act music (for a revival?): Walsh [Act Music of the Queens Theatre, 1707], "Mr Dan^1. Purcells Musick in ye reviv'd Play call'd Vertue in Danger," copy in Lbm g.15 (a4)

1 Overture

2 Slow aire

3 Hornpipe   =   Cmc pt-bks., fol. 42, a4

4 Aire

5 Brisk aire   =   Cmc pt-bks., fol. 41', a4

6 Slow aire

7 Brisk aire

8 Slow aire

9 Gavott

Song: IV.ii [Loveless's Lodgings.   Enter Amanda and Berinthia.   A SONG.]
               "I smile at love, and all its Arts"

Miscellaneous music: V.v [A Mask.]

C *The Richmond Heiress: or, A Woman Once in the Right,* Thomas Durfey, DL (1693)

? Act music: Lcm 1172, fols. 36-37', music in "A Woman" [Once in the Right], a4

[1] Overture

2

[4] Dance   =   *Compleat Flute=Master* (1695), fol. 11, "Dances by M^r
                     Prince and Mrs Bignell," a1

3

5

6   =   Dtc 413, fol. 15, "Baptist [Draghi?]," a4

7

Songs: II [SONG, by way of Dialogue between a Madman and Madwoman.
               In ACT II.]   "Behold the Man that With Gigantick" (D&M 345 *m*H.
               Purcell *s*Reading and Mrs. Ayliff)

               II.ii [Fulvia Sings] "How vile are the sordid" (D&M 1469 *m*H. Purcell)

(II.ii) [There's a Song in parts, between a mad Man and a mad Woman . . .] "By those Pignies" (D&M 453 mJ. Eccles sDogget and Bracegirdle)

IV [SHINKEN's Song to the Harp. In the Fourth ACT.] "Of Noble Race was Shinken" (D&M 2579)

IV.i [Here a Catch in three parts, in praise of Punch]

V.v [SONG here.]

not printed in the play-book: "Fie Jocky never prattle" (D&M 992)

"Maiden fresh as a rose" (D&M 2153 sPack)

"Stubborn church division" (D&M 3092 mJ. Eccles)

Dances: II.ii [Dance]

V.v [Enter Mummers . . . They Dance.]

Ridiculous Lovers (see *The Generous Enemies*)

T *Rinaldo and Armida,* John Dennis, LIF (1699)

Most of the music for the entertainments (by John Eccles) is found in Lbm Add. 29378. This does not include the act music. In *Theater Musick,* I [1698], 21-27, are the following seven dances "in ye Opera of Armida," only one of which, the "Chacone," is also found in Lbm Add. 29378. See also BUCEM, I, 309.

[1] Country Dance

2 Minuet   = *Apollo's Banquet* (1701), No. 48, "Minuet by Mr. Eccles," a1; *Harpsichord Master,* III (1702) [No. 3], "Minuett," keyb.

3 Chacone   = Lcm 1172, fol. 44, "Chacone Armida," a2; Lbm Add. 29378, fol. 28', "John Eccles, Chacone for flutes and violins in Act III of Rinaldo," a6

4 Rigadon   = Lcm 1172, fol. 45', "Rigadon," a2

5 Rigadon   = Lcm 1172, fol. 45, "Rigadon," a2

6 Paspe

7 Paspe   = Lcm 1172, fol. 44', "W. C[roft?], "Paspe," a2

24 New Country Dances (1714), p. 17, "Rinaldo," a1

DO *The Rival Queens, or the Death of Alexander the Great*, Nathaniel Lee (1677), an operatic version at DL, February 1701

> ? Act music: Walsh, *Harmonia Anglicana*, II [1701], "M.^{r} [Godfrey] Fingers Ayres in the Opera of Alexander the Great," copies in Dc C.37 (a4), Lgc G.Mus. 153 (second treble)

> [1] Overture

> 2 Aire

> 3 Gavott

> 4 Iigg

> 5 Entry

> 6 Bore

> 7 Minuett

> 8 Aire

> 9 Round O Chacone

Lbm Add. 35043, fol. 36', "A Symphony for Alexander ye Great," a1

The "complete" score (lacking the act music), composed by Godfrey Finger and Daniel Purcell, is in Cfm Mus MS 87. For a discussion of "Alexander the Great," see Price, "Eight 'Lost' Restoration Plays," pp. 297-299.

T *The Rival Sisters: or, The Violence of Love*, Robert Gould, DL (1696)

> Act music: Henry Purcell (see Z 609). The present study has located no concordances for Purcell's act music other than those listed by Zimmerman.

? Robin Crusoe

> Dance: Lbm Add. 29371, fol. 110', "The Savages Dance in Robin Crusoe," a1

? The Royall Captive

> Act music: Walsh, *Harmonia Anglicana* [IV, 1702], "Aires in the Play call'd the Royall Captive Composed by M^r [John] Lenton," copies in Lbm d.24 (first treble and bass), Lgc G.Mus. 153 (second treble)

1 Overture

2 Iigg

3 Minuett

4 Aire Slow

5 Aire

6 Aire Slow

7 Aire

8 Hornpipe

9 Iigg

10 Chacone

Note: The tenor part of this set of act music is lacking.   See Price, "Eight 'Lost'
        Restoration Plays," p. 302.

T *The Royal Convert,* Nicholas Rowe, QT (1708)

See Smith, *Walsh I,* No. 264, an advertisement in *The Daily Courant* 22 December
1707: "Mr. [John] Isom's new Musick, in 4 Parts, for Violins made for the Tragedy
call'd the Royal Convert."   This music is not extant.

T *Saint Cecily or The Converted Twins,* Matthew Medbourne (1666)

? Act music (for a revival?):   Lbm Add. 30839, fols. 33'-34', "[tunes by] Talette
        [Thomas Tollet?] in St. Sisile," a1

[1] Overture

2

3

4

5

6

7

C *Sauny the Scott: or, The Taming of the Shrew*, John Lacy, TR (1667)

Act music (for a revival, c. 1698? at DL): Lbm Add. 35043, fols. 104-104', "The Musick in the Play call'd Sawney the Scot or ye Temeing ye Shrew," a1

1		
2		
3		
4		
5		
6	=	*Theater Musick,* I [1698], p. 8, "Bore," a1
7	=	*Theater Musick,* I [1698], p. 9, "Minuet," a1
8	=	*Theater Musick,* I [1698], p. 8, "The Granadears exercise," a1

TC *Secret-Love, or the Maiden Queen,* John Dryden, TR (1668)

Act music (for a revival, c. 1689?): Lbm Add. 35043, fols. 89-90, "Mr Morgans First Trebles in ye Maiden Queen," a1

[1] Overture	=	Ob c.73, p. 19, "Morgan overture in the Mayden Queen," a3
2 Prelude		
3	=	Ob c.73, p. 20, a3
4	=	Ob c.73, p. 21, a3
5	=	Ob c.73, p. 22, a3
6		
7		
[9]	=	Ob c.73, p. 21, "A Cibell in Mayden Queen," a3
8 Hornpipe	=	Ob c.73, p. 22, a3

Note: Ob c.73, p. 19, "2 in Mayden Queen," is not found in the Lbm Add. 35043 set of act music.

Song: IV.ii [SONG.] "I feed a flame within"

Dance: V.I [Dance.]

The Sham Doctor (see *The Anatomist)*

C *The She-Gallants,* George Granville, LIF (1696)

Act music: Lbm Add. 35043, fols. 77'-78', "M^r [Godfrey] Fingers 1st Trebles in
               Ye She Gallants," a1

   [1] Overture   = LA Finney pt-bks., p. 43, "Mr Finger Overtur," a4; Lbm
                       Add. 39565, fol. 48', "Finger ouverture," a4; Lcm 1144,
                       fol. 26, "Finger Overture," a2

   2   = LA Finney pt-bks., p. 44, a4; Lbm Add. 39565, fol. 49,
                       "2^d," a4; Lcm 1144, fol. 26', "2^d tune," a2; *40 Airs
                       Anglois,* II [c. 1701], p. 17, "Minuet Mr G. Finger," a2

   3   = LA Finney pt-bks., p. 44, a4; Lbm Add. 39565, fol. 49,
                       a4; Lcm 1144, fol. 26', a2

   4   = LA Finney pt-bks., p. 45, a4; Lbm Add. 39565, fol. 49',
                       a4; Lcm 1144, fol. 26', a2

   5   = Cmc pt-bks., fol. 114, a4; LA Finney pt-bks., p. 45, a4;
                       Lbm Add. 39565, fol. 49, a4; Lcm 1144, fol. 27, "2^d act
                       [tune]," a2

   6   = Cmc pt-bks., fol. 94, a4; LA Finney pt-bks., p. 46, a4;
                       Lbm Add. 38189, fol. 19, "hornpipe," a1; Lbm Add.
                       39565, fol. 49', a4; Lcm 1144, fol. 30', "1st musick," a2;
                       40 Airs Anglois, II [c. 1701], p. 16, "Air Mr Finger," a2

   7   = LA Finney pt-bks., p. 46, a4; Lbm Add 39565, fol. 50,
                       a4; Lcm 1144, fol. 30', "a 1st musick [second tune]," a2

   8   = LA Finney pt-bks., p. 46, a4; Lbm Add. 39565, fol. 49',
                       a4; Lcm 1144, fol. 30', "Second Musick," a2

   9   = LA Finney pt-bks., p. 47, a4; Lbm Add. 39565, fol. 50, a4

Songs: III.i [Song in Dialogue, between Thirsis and Delia.] "Delia, how long
               must I despair"

               (III.i) [Song.] "So well Corinna likes the joy" (D&M 3014 sLaroche,
               and John Eccles, *A song in the She Gallants . . .* Sung by a little boy,
               London, c. 1697)

IV.i [Song] "While Phyliss is drinking" (D&M 3864 *m*J. Eccles
*s*Cooper, and see BUCEM, I, 310)

Dance: III.i [Dance]

C *She wou'd and She wou'd not: or, The Kind Imposter,* Colley Cibber, DL (1703)

Act music: Walsh, *Harmonia Anglicana* [V, 1702], "M^r [James] Peasables [Paisible]
              Aires in the Comedy call'd She wou'd and She wou'd not," copies in
              Lgc G.Mus. 153 (second treble), Lcm XXIX.A.11 (a4), Lcm XXIX.A.12
              (second treble, tenor, bass)

   1 Overture   = Cmc pt-bks., fol. 111', "Ouverture," a4

   2 Almand

   3 Minuett   = Cmc pt-bks., fol. 112, a4

   4 Aire   = Cmc pt-bks., fol. 112, a4

   5 Iigg   = Cmc pt-bks., fol. 112, a4

   6 Gavott   = Cmc pt-bks., fol. 113, a4

   7 Saraband   = Cmc pt-bks., fol. 132', "Slow," a4

   8 Corrant   = Cmc pt-bks., fol. 112', "Slow," a4

Song not printed in play-book: "Celia my heart has often ranged" (D&M 514
          *m*Weldon *s*Mrs. Campion) (see Lbm Add. 22099, fol. 13', for a
          keyboard arrangement by "R. Courteveil" of this song.)

Miscellaneous music: V.i [An Entertainment]

C *She wou'd and She wou'd not; or, The Kind Impostor,* Colley Cibber, a 1714 revival

See Smith, *Walsh I,* No. 448, an advertisement in *The Post Boy* 24-26 June 1714:
"A Set of Tunes in 3 parts, with a Trumpet, containing an Overture, Symphony and
Aires, as they were performed in the reviv'd Comedy, call'd She Wou'd and She
Wou'd Not."   This music is not extant.

C *She wou'd if she cou'd,* George Etherege, LIF (1668)

Act music (for a revival, 15 March 1705, DL):   Walsh, *Harmonia Anglicana*
              [collection b, 1705], "Music in the COMEDY call'd She Wou'd if She
              Cou'd Composed by a Person of Quallity [William Lord Byron?],"
              copy in Lbm d.24 (first treble and bass)

1 Overture

2 Prelude

3 Aire

4 Aire

5 Iigg   = *Flute Master,* V (1706), p. 6, "Iigg," a1

6 Aire   = Cmc pt-bks., fol. 3, "Slow," a4

7 Gavot   = Cmc pt-bks., fol. 114', a4

8 Scotch aire   = *Flute Master,* V (1706), p. 6, "Scotch Aire Slow," a1

9 Aire

Songs: II.ii [Noise of Musick without . . . Enter the Musick playing, Sir Oliver strutting, and swaggering, Sir Joslin singing, and dancing . . . Enter Sir Joslin, with Ariana and Gatty in each hand, dancing and singing. CATCH.]   "This is sly and pretty"

IV.ii [. . . enter Sir Joslin, Sir Oliver, and Rake-hell, all drunk, with Musick.   They sing.]   "She's no Mistress of mine"

V.i. "To little or no purpose I spent many days"

This song is in Eccles, *A Collection of Songs for One two and Three Voices* [1704], p. 73, "A Song in She wou'd if She cou'd Sung by Mrs Bracegirdle," a2

(V.i) [Enter Sir Joslin with Musick . . . Dance. Sings.] "A Catch and a Glass"

Dances: II.ii [Gatty dances a Jig.]

III.iii [Enter Musick and the Ladies in an Antick, and then they take out, my Lady Cockwood Sir Oliver, the young Ladies Courtal and Freeman, and Sentry Sir Joslin, and dance a set Dance.]

V.i (a final dance)

Dancing-Master (1718), p. 338, "She wou'd if she cou'd," a1

The Silent Woman (see *Epicoene*)

Sir Fopling Flutter (see *The Man of Mode*)

C *Sir Harry Wildair: Being the Sequel of the Trip to the Jubilee,* George Farquhar, DL (1701)

Act music: Walsh, *Harmonia Anglicana,* II [1701], "M.ʳ [Godfrey] Fingers Ayres in the Comedye of S.ʳ Hary Wild Hair," copies in Lbm b.29.a (first treble), Lbm d.24 (first treble and bass), Dc C.37 (a4), Lgc G.Mus. 153 (second treble), Lcm XXIX.A.11 (a4)

    [1] Overture

    2 Round O   = *40 Airs Anglois,* II [c. 1701], p. 11, "Air Mr. Finger," a2; *Select Lessons* (1702), sig. f, "Round O by M.ʳ Finger," al

    3 Iigg   = *40 Airs Anglois,* II [c. 1701], p. 13, "jigg M.ʳ Finger," a2; *Select Lessons* (1702), sig. f, "Iigg," al

    4 Slow Aire   = *40 Airs Anglois,* II [c. 1701], p. 12, "Air M.ʳ Finger," a2; *Select Lessons* (1702), sig. g, "Saraband by Mʳ Finger," al

    5 Round O

    6 Corrant   = *40 Airs Anglois,* II [c. 1701], p. 25, "Allegro Mʳ. Finger," a2

    7 Gavott   = *Select Lessons* (1702), sig. h, "Gavott by Mr. Finger," al; *40 Airs Anglois,* III, p. 13, "Air," a2

    8 Hornpipe   = *Select Lessons* (1702), sig. h, "Hornpipe," al

Dance: V.vi [A Dance here.]

Sir Martin Mar-all (see *Sʳ Martin Mar-all*)

Sir Timothy Treat-all (see *The City-Heiress*)

C *The Spanish Fryar, or, The Double Discovery,* John Dryden, DG (1681)

Act music (for a revival c. 1690?): Lbm Add. 35043, fols. 41'-42, "Mʳ [Robert] Kings Tune [sic] to Ye Spanish Fryar," al

    [1]   = Cmc pt-bks., fol. 118, a4

    [2]   = Cmc pt-bks., fol. 118', a4

    [3]   = Cmc pt-bks., fol. 118', a4

    [4]   = Cmc pt-bks., fol. 118, a4; *Apollo's Banquet* (1691), No. 42, "An Ayre of Mr. King's," al

[5 Overture]   = *40 Airs Anglois,* II [c. 1701], p. 1, "Overture Mr. Robt. King," al

[6]   = Cmc pt-bks., fol. 136, a4

Songs: I.i [A Procession of Priests and Choristers in white, with Tapers, follow'd by the Queen and Ladies, goes over the Stage; the Choristers singing.] "Look down, ye bless'd above" (in Lbm Add. 29378, fols. 138-138')

V.i [A SONG.] "Farewell ungratefull Traytor" (D&M 974 *m*Pack)

F *The Spanish Wives,* Mary Pix, DL (1696)

? Miscellaneous music: Lcm 1172, fols. 39-39', "Mr. Peasable [James Paisible] Spanish Wives," a4

[1]

[2]

[3]   = Cmc pt-bks., fol. 136, a4; Lbm Add. 39565, fol. 55, "Paisible menuet," a4

[4] Trum[pet]
Hautboy Funerall
March   = Cmc pt-bks., fol. 96', a4

Dance: Lcm 1172, fol. 19', "a Dance in the Spanish Wives," al. See also BUCEM, II, 857.

The Spartan Heroe (see *Cleomenes*)

Sr Fopling Flutter (see *The Man of Mode*)

C *Sr Martin Mar-all, or the Feign'd Innocence,* John Dryden, LIF (1668)

? Dances: *Pleasant Companion* (1672), No. 29, "Sr Martin Maralls Jigg by M^r. I.[ohn] B.[anister]," al = *Apollo's Banquet* (1678), No. 7, "Mr. Banisters Jigg," al; *Apollo's Banquet* (1687), No. 4, "Mr. Banisters Jigg," al

Apollo's Banquet (1678), No. 18, "Sir Martin's Jigg," al = *Apollo's Banquet* (1687), No. 17, "Sir Martins Jigg," al

Apollo's Banquet (1678), No. 87, "The Grand Dance in Sir Martin Marall," al

The Stock Jobbers (see *The Volunteers*)

The Stratagem (see *The Beaux Stratagem*)

The Tameing of the Shrew (see *Sauny the Scott*)

T *Tamerlane*, Nicholas Rowe, LIF (1701)

    Act music: Walsh, *Harmonia Anglicana*, III [1702], "M.[r] [John] Lentons Aires in the Tragedy called TAMBERLAIN," copies in Lbm b.29.a (first treble), Lgc G.Mus. 153 (second treble), Lcm XXIX.A.11 (a4)

      [1] Symphony

      2 Trumpet Round O

      3 Slow Aire

      4 March

      5 Slow Aire

      6 Slow Aire

      7 Gavot

      8 Bore

      9 Iigg

Taming of the Shrew (see *Sauny the Scott*)

DO *The Tempest, or the Enchanted Island* [Thomas Shadwell], DG (1674)

    Act music: Matthew Lock[e], *The English Opera; or the Vocal Musick in Psyche . . . To which is Adjoyned The Instrumental Musick in The Tempest* (1675), pp. 62-[76], a4

      [1] Introduction. The First musick

      2 Second Galliard

      3 Gavot

      4 The Second Musick, Sarabrand

      5 LILK

      6 Curtain Tune

7   The First Act Tune. Rustick Air

8   The Second Act Tune, Minoit

9   The Third Act Tune. Corant

10   The Fourth Act Tune, A Martial Jigge

11   The Conclusion, A Canon 4 in 2

For the locations of the rest of the extant music for this dramatic opera, see William Barclay Squire, "The Music of Shadwell's 'Tempest'," *MQ*, VII (1921), 565-578, and John Buttrey, "The Evolution of English Opera Between 1656 and 1695: A Re-investigation," Diss. Cambridge 1967, pp. 96-113.

C   *The Tender Husband: Or, The Accomplish'd Fools*, Richard Steele, DL (1705)

See Smith, *Walsh I*, No. 175, an advertisement in *The Post Man* 5-8 May 1705: "Mr. [John] Barret's new Musick, in 4 parts, perform'd in the Comedy call'd The Tender Husband."   This music is not extant.   See also BUCEM, II, 857.

The Timely Discovery (see *The Generous Conquerour*)

Timon of Athens (see *The History of Timon of Athens*)

T   *Titus Andronicus, or the Rape of Lavinia*, Edward Ravenscroft, DL (1687)

? Act music: Lcm 1172, fol. 10', "M. C[larke or Croft?] in Titus Andronicus," a4

[1]   Overture to Titus
    Andronicus   =   Cmc pt-bks., fol. 95', "Ouverture," a4

[2]   =   Cmc pt-bks., fol. 117, "Slow," a4

The Town Unmaskt (see *The Pretenders*)

A Trip to the Jubilee (see *The Constant Couple* and *Sir Harry Wildair*)

C   *Tunbridge-Walks: Or, The Yeoman of Kent* [Thomas Baker], DL (1703)

Act music: Walsh, *Harmonia Anglicana* [V, 1703], "M^r [John] Barretts Musick in the Comedy call'd Tunbridg walks or the Yeoman of Kent," copies in Lbm b.29.a (first treble), Lbm d.24 (first treble and bass), Lgc G.Mus. 153 (second treble), Lcm XXIX.A.11 (a4), Lcm XXIX.A.12 (second treble, tenor, bass)

[1]   Overture

2   Allmand

3 Corrant

4 Aire   = Cmc pt-bks., fol. 133, a4; *Ladys Banquet,* II (1706), fol. 13, "Aire Barret," keyb.

5 Jigg   = *Dancing Master* (1703), p. 352, "Tunbridge Walks," al; *Ladys Banquet,* II (1706), fol. 13, "Jigg Barret," keyb.

6 Trumpett aire

7 Round O   = CDp 1.39 (J), fol. 51, "Round o," keyb.

8 Round O   = *Ladys Banquet,* II (1706), fol. 13, "Gavott Round O Barret," keyb.

9 Minuett   = *Ladys Banquet,* II (1706), fol. 14, "Minuet," keyb.

See also *Ladys Banquet,* II (1706), fol. 10, "Tunbridge Minuet," keyb. = Cmc pt-bks., fol. 4, "Slow," a4

Songs: II.i [SONG.] "If moving softness can subdue"

             IV.i [Reynard Sings.] "I'll tell you a Story"

Dance: IV.i [Loveworth Sings and dances a Minuet]

Miscellaneous music: V.i [An Entertainment]

C   *The Twin-Rivals,* George Farquhar, DL (1703)

Act music: Walsh, *Harmonia Anglicana* [V, 1703], "M[r] [William] Croft's Aires in the Comedy call'd the Twinn Rivals," copies in Lgc G.Mus. 153 (second treble), Lcm XXIX.A.11 (a4), Lcm XXIX.A.12 (second treble, tenor, bass)

1 Overture

2 Allmand

3 Trumpet Aire   = Cmc pt-bks., fol. 23, a4

4 March

5 Hornpipe   = *Ladys Banquet,* II (1706), fol. 11, "Hornpipe," keyb.

6 March

7 Aire   = Cmc pt-bks., fol. 58, "Slow," a4

8 Scotch Aire

9 Farwell

T *Ulysses*, Nicholas Rowe, QT (1706)

See *The Post Man*, 21-23 March 1706: "New Musick just published . . . The Musick in the Play called Ulysses by Mr [John] Eccles Master of her Majesty's Musick . . . printed by J. Walsh. . . ." This advertisement is not recorded by Smith in *Walsh I*, and the music is not extant.

The Unhappy Conqueror (see *Neglected Virtue*)

T *The Unhappy Penitent*, Catharine Trotter, DL (1701)

Act music: Walsh, *Harmonia Anglicana*, I [1701], "M.^{r} D:[aniel] Purcells Ayrs in the Tragedy of the unhappy Penitent," copies in Lbm d.24 (first treble and bass), Dc C.37 (a4), Lgc G.Mus. 153 (second treble), Lcm XXIX.A.11 (a4), and Lcm XXIX.A.12 (second treble, tenor, bass)

1 Overture

2 Aire

3 Aire

4 Bore

5 Slow aire

6 Aire

7 Hornpipe

8 Chacone   = *Division Violin*, II (1693), p. 40, "Chacone by M^r D Purcell," a2

Miscellaneous music: I.i [An Entertainment]

III.i [They sit, Musick then all rise.]

T *Venice Preserv'd; or, A Plot Discover'd*, Thomas Otway, DG (1682)

Act music: Lbm Add. 29283-5, fols. 15'-19', "Mr Sol:[omon] Egle's [Eccles] tunes in ye play call'd Venice praeserved or A plot discovered," a3

1 = NYp MS Drexel 3849, p. 57, "Ground," a3; US NH Filmer MS 6, p. 26, a3

2 = NYp MS Drexel 3849, p. 55, "Egles," a3; US NH Filmer MS 6, p. 25, a3

3 = NYp MS Drexel 3849, p. 55, a3; US NH Filmer MS 6, p. 28, a3

4 = NYp MS Drexel 3849, p. 55, a3; US NH Filmer MS 6, p. 28, a3

5 = NYp MS Drexel 3849, p. 56, a3; US NY Filmer MS 6, p. 29, a3

6 = NYp MS Drexel 3849, p. 58, a3

7 = NYp MS Drexel 3849, p. 58, a3; US NH Filmer MS 6, p. 23, a3

8 = NYp MS Drexel 3849, p. 56, a3; US NH Filmer MS 6, p. 24, a3

9 = NYp MS Drexel 3849, p. 56, a3; US NH Filmer MS 6, p. 24, a3

10 = NYp MS Drexel 3849, p. 59, a3; US NH Filmer MS 6, p. 29, a3

Miscellaneous music: V.ii [Soft Musick. Enter Belvidera distracted . . .]

T *Venice Preserv'd; or, A Plot Discover'd*, Thomas Otway, DG (1682)

Act music (for a revival c. 1696): Lcm 1144, fols. 4-4', music by [John] Lenton in Venice preserv'd," a2

[1] Overture = Lbm Add. 24889, fol. 6, "Overture in the Moor of Venice," a4; Ob c.72, p. 4, "Lenton Overture," a3

2 = Lbm Add. 24889, fol. 6, "1st tune," a4; Cmc pt-bks., fol. 96', a4; Ob c.72, p. 4, a3

3 = Lbm Add. 24889, fol 6, "2^{d} tune," a4; Cmc pt-bks., fol. 96', a4; Ob c.72, p. 4, a3; *Compleat Flute=Master* (1695) [fol. 26], "Ayre Mr Lenton," a1

4 = Lbm Add. 24889, fol. 6', "3^{d}," a4; Cmc pt-bks., fol. 8', a4; Ob c.72, p. 5, a3

5 = Lbm Add. 24889, fol. 6' "4th tune," a4; Cmc pt-bks., fol. 8', a4; Ob c.72, p. 5, "Hornpipe," a3

6 = Cmc pt-bks., fol. 9, a4

7 = Lbm Add. 24889, fol. 6', "6th tune," a4; *Apollo's Banquet* (1701), No. 125, "Scotch Tune by Mr. Lenton," a1

8   = Lbm Add. 24889, fol. 6', "5th tune," a4; Cmc pt-bks.,
                        fol. 8', a4; Ob c.72, p. 5, a3

9   = Lbm Add. 24889, fol. 6', "8th tune," a4; Cmc pt-bks.,
                        fol. 7, "Slow," a4; Ob c.72, p. 5, a3

T *The Vestal-Virgin: or, The Roman Ladies,* Robert Howard [1664]

See Smith, *Walsh I,* No. 38 and Pl. 7, "Ayres in the Vestal Virgins by M^r. O[rm?]."
This act music, which does not survive, was apparently associated with a revival, c.
1701.

T *The Villain,* Thomas Porter, LIF (1663)

? Dance: Lbm Add. 38189, fol. 30', "In the Villain 4th Act quikly," a1

Comment: This is apparently "The Dance" interrupted by a sword fight in Act IV.

The Violence of Love (see *The Rival Sisters*)

DO *The Virgin Prophetess: or, The Fate of Troy,* Elkanah Settle, DL (1701)

Act music: Walsh, *Harmonia Anglicana,* II [1701], "M^r. [Godrey] Finger's Ayres in
                 the Opera call'd the Virgin Prophetess or the Fate of Troy," copies in
                 Lbm d.24 (first treble and bass), Dc C.37 (a4), Lgc. G.Mus. 153
                 (second treble), Lcm XXIX.A.11 (a4), Lcm XXIX.A.12 (second treble,
                 tenor, bass)

     1 Overture   = Cmc pt-bks., fol. 28', "Ouverture," a4

     2 Iigg   = *40 Airs Anglois,* III, p. 4, "Allegro Jigg," a2

     3 Aire   = Cmc pt-bks., fol. 73, a4

     4 Slow Aire   = *40 Airs Anglois,* III, p. 13, "Air," a2

     5 Hornpipe   = *40 Airs Anglois,* II [c. 1701], p. 22, "Allegro Air Mr.
                        Finger," a2

     6 Prelude   = Cmc pt-bks., fol. 80', a4

     7 Round O   = *Select Lessons* (1702), sig. l, "Round O," a1

     8 Ground

Two scores of Finger's dramatic opera (both lacking the act music listed above) are
found in Lcm 862 and Cfm Mus MS 87.

Virtue in Danger (see *The Relapse*)

C   *The Virtuous Wife; or, Good Luck at last,* Thomas Durfey, DG (1680)

Act music (for a revival?):   Henry Purcell, *A Collection of Ayres for the Theatre* (1697), pp. 45-48.   See Z 611.

    1   Overture   =   LA Finney pt-bks., p. 103, "M^r. Purcell Overture," a4

    2   Song Tune   =   *Compleat Flute=Master* (1695) [fol. 26], "Ah how Sweet it is to Love [by] M^r. Purcell," a1 (D&M 59 *m*H. Purcell, taken from *Tyrannick Love,* John Dryden, 1670)

    3   Slow Aire

    4   Aire

    5   Preludio   =   LA Finney pt-bks., p. 86, a4

    6   Hornpipe   =   LA Finney pt-bks., p. 86, a4; Lcm [*Apollo's Banquet,* c. 1705], No. 110, "Ayre [M^r. Purcell in Tyran. love]," a1

    7   Minuett   =   LA Finney pt-bks., p. 82, a4

    8   Minuett

See also Lbm Add. 35043, fol. 38, "[first act tune?]," a1 = Lcm 1172, fol. 3', "1st act tune in Vertuous Wife," a4; LEp MS Q784.21 L969, p. 1, a4

Songs: I.i [SONG] "Let the Traitors plot on" (D&M 2005 *m*Farmer)

               III.i [Letitia sings . . . SCOTCH SONG.] "Sawney was tall and of noble Race" (D&M 2850)

               not printed in play: "The Sages of old" (D&M 2844 *m*Tollet, also a later version by J. Eccles)

C   *The Volunteers: or The Stock Jobbers,* Thomas Shadwell, DL (1693)

Act music: US NH Filmer MS 9 [pp. 34-36], "M^r. [Thomas?] Tollet in ye Volunteers," a3

    16 [=1]

    17 [=2]

    18 [=3]

19 [=4]

20 [=5 Overture]   = Cmc pt-bks, fol. 113', "Ouverture," a4

21 [=6]   = Cmc pt-bks, fol. 115, a4

22 [=7]

23 [=8]

24 [=9]   = *Apollo's Banquet* (1701), No. 73, "Ayre," a1; [*Apollo's Banquet*, c. 1705], No. 73, "Ayre"

C *The Way of the World*, William Congreve, LIF (1700)

  ? Dances: *Theater Musick*, III (1700), sig. i, "A Country Dance in ye way of the World," a1

            Dancing-Master (1718), p. 143, "The way of the World," a1

The Way to Win him (see *The Inconstant*)

F A Wife for Any Man, Thomas Durfey [lost]

  Act music: Lbm Add. 35043, fols. 71-72, "M^r [Jeremiah] Clarkes 1st Treble in ye Farce Called A Wife for Any Man," a1

    [1] Overture

    2

    3

    4

    5

    6

    7   = Lcm 1172, fol. 16, "Clarke 1st act tune in A Wife for Any Man," a4

    8   = Lcm 1172, fol. 16, "2^d Act tune," a4

    9   = Lcm 1172, fol. 16', "4th act tune," a4

See Cyrus L. Day, "A Lost Play by D'Urfey," *Modern Language Notes*, XLIX (1934), 332-334.

The Wife's Excuse (see *The Wives Excuse*)

C *The Wife's Relief: or, The Husband's Cure*, Charles Johnson, DL (1712)

> See Smith, *Walsh I*, No. 397, an advertisement in *The Post Man* 11-13 December 1711: "A new set of Tunes in 4 Parts, for Violins and Hoboys; Compos'd by Mr. J.[ohn] Barrett, performed in the last New Play, called The Wife's Relief." This music is not extant.

The Wife's Resentment (see *The Lady's Last Stake*)

C *The Wives Excuse: or, Cuckolds make themselves*, Thomas Southerne, DL (1692)

> ? Miscellaneous music: *Apollo's Banquet*, II (1691), No. 10, "New Scotch Tune in the Wife's Excuse," a1

? Wives Victory

> Act music: Lbm Add. 24889, fols. 4-5' "[music in] Wives Victory Mr [Godfrey] Finger," a4

> First Musick [1]

> > [2]

> 2^{d} Musick   [1]

> > [2]

> Overture

> 1[st act tune]

> 2[nd act tune]

> 3[rd act tune]

> 4[th act tune]

> 5[th act tune]

See also Lcm 1172, fol. 46', "J.[ohn] Lenton tune in Wives Victory," a2 = Cmc pt-bks., fol. 73, a4; Lcm 1144, fol. 11', "Sol[omon] Eccles tune," a2; *40 Airs Anglois,* II [c. 1701], p. 28, "jigg," a2; US NH Filmer MS 9 [p. 42], a3.   For more about "Wives Victory," see Price, "Eight 'Lost' Restoration Plays," p. 302.

A Woman Once in the Right (see *The Richmond Heiress*)

C *Womans Wit: or, The Lady in Fashion*, Colley Cibber, DL (1697)

Act music: Lbm Add. 35043, fols. 85-86, "The [William] Lord Birons 1.st Trebles in ye play call'd Woman's Witt or ye Lady in fashion," al

1

2

3

4

5 Overture

6   = *Self-Instructor*, II (1700) [No. 7], al

7   = Lbm Add. 34204, fol. 1', "A Scots Tune," al; *Self-Instructor*, II (1700) [No. 6], "Scotch Tune," al; *Dancing Master* (1713), p. 239, "My Lord Baron's Delight," al

8

9   = Cmc pt-bks., fol. 84', a4

Song: III.i [Olivia plays the harpsichord and then sings.]   "Tell me Belinda, prithee do" (D&M 3155 mLeveridge?)

DO *Wonders in the Sun: or, The Kingdom of the Birds*, Thomas Durfey, QT (1706)

Act music: Walsh [Act Music of the Queens Theatre, 1706], Mr In.^o Smiths Musick in the Opera call'd the Kingdom of the Birds," copy in Lbm g.15 (a4)

1 Overture

2 Allemand

3 Minuet

4 Slow aire

5 Gavott

6 Very slow

7 Iigg

8 Round O

9 Hornpipe

For many of the songs in this dramatic opera, see D&M 1212, 1772, 1891, 2223, 2499, 2742, 2950, 3478, 3622, 3735, and 3872.

The Yeoman of Kent (see *Tunbridge Walks*)

C *The Younger Brother: or, The Amorous Jilt*, Aphra Behn, DL (1696)

Act music: Lcm 1172, fols. 7-9, "Mr. Morgan['s music] in the Younger Brother," a4

    [1] Overture

    [2] Slow Mr. H. Purcells Farewell = Lbm Add. 35043, fol. 62', "Slow Mr. H. Purcells Farewell," a1

    [3] Round O   = Lbm Add. 35043, fol. 63', "Round O," a1

    [4] Chacone   = Lbm Add. 35043, fol. 63, "Chacone," a1

    [5]   = Lbm Add. 35043, fol. 62', a1

Songs: I.ii [A Song of the Town Rake, written by Mr. Motteux] "What lye can compare with the jolly Town Rakes" (D&M 3649 *m*D. Purcell *s*Edwards, and BUCEM, II, 858)

    II.ii "No Delia, no; what man can range"

    (II) [A Song by Sir Rowland in the Second Act to Teresia] "Tho the young prize cupid's fire"

    V.ii [The Dressing Room, Discovers the Prince at his toilet dressing. Musick and a Song.]

Dances: I.ii [Here the Dance, representing the Rakehells]

    III.i [The Spanish Dance]

    (III.i) [Sir Rowland and Lady Youthly dance]

    IV [Dance]

    V (a final dance)

The Younger the Wiser (see *Farewel Folly*)

APPENDIX II

A LIST OF SETS OF ACT MUSIC
PUBLISHED BY JOHN WALSH 1701-1710

In the first decade of the 18th century, John Walsh published more than 50 sets of act music for plays and dramatic operas. Most of these were issued as separate numbers in a series entitled *Harmonia Anglicana or the Musick of the English Stage*, the music being associated principally with dramatic productions of the Theatre Royal, Drury Lane. Only the title-pages of the first two collections survive (the first in Lbm b.29.a and Dc C.37, the second in Lgc G. Mus. 153), and the remaining seven collections, the individual sets of which were probably issued separately as they became available, must be reconstructed from advertisements and the performance dates of the plays. In early 1705 Walsh began publication of another collection of act music, distinguishable from *Harmonia Anglicana* in that it was apparently designed to print act music composed for plays produced at the new Queen's Theatre in the Haymarket. No title-page for this fragmentary collection survives, and one was probably never engraved, as Walsh again issued the music on separate sheets when it became available. The Queen's Theatre collection may be further distinguished from *Harmonia Anglicana* in that the former is printed in folio format and the latter in oblong folio.

The following table lists all sets of act music published by Walsh during the years 1701 to 1710. In the first column is found the number of the individual sets in each collection. The second column provides the number given to the publication in William C. Smith, *A Bibliography of the Musical Works Published by John Walsh during the Years 1695-1720* (London, 1948). The next shows the date of the earliest advertisement for the set of music in contemporary newspapers and other Walsh prints. After the column giving the composer's name is that containing an abbreviation of the type of play for which the music was written (see the List of Abbreviations in Appendix I). The next column provides the title, date of publication, and author of the play. If the ascription in the music is ambiguous or is for a play which has not been traced, the ascription is produced exactly as it appears in the print. The next two columns provide the date of the first production of the play (when known) and an indication of the theatre where the work was first mounted; both data are taken from *The London Stage*. Finally, the state of completeness of the music is shown by the letters A through I, each letter referring to an extant copy of Walsh's publications.

HARMONIA ANGLICANA

A = British Library b.29.a (1st treble)
B = British Library d.24 (1st treble and bass)
C = Durham Cathedral Library C.37 (a4)
D = London, Guildhall Library G.Mus.153 (2nd treble)
E = Royal College of Music XXIX.A.11 (a4)
F = Royal College of Music XXIX.A.12 (2nd treble, tenor, bass)
G = Los Angeles, Clark Library: First Collection (1st treble, 2nd treble, bass); Second Collection (a4)

Set no.	Smith no.	Earliest Walsh advert.	Composer	Type	Title of play / Date of publication / Author	Date of first production	Play-house	Sources
First Collection								
I	42	c. 1701	[Mr. Orm]	–	"A New Set of Ayres for the Consorts of the Musicall Society,"[1]	–	–	A C D E F G
II	43	c. 1701	James Paisible	C	"Mr. Peasable Ayres in the Comedy of Loves Stratagem"	?	?	A C D E G
III	44	c. 1701	William Croft	C	Courtship A-la-Mode (1700), David Crauford	9 Jul 00	DL	C D E F G
IV	45	c. 1701	Godfrey Finger	C	Love at a Loss; or, Most Votes carry it (1701), Catharine Trotter	23 Nov 00	DL	A C D E F G
V[2]	46	8-11 Feb 01	John Lenton	T	The Ambitious Step-Mother (1701), Nicholas Rowe	Dec 00	LIF	B C D E G
VI	47	20-22 Feb 01	Daniel Purcell	T	The Unhappy Penitent (1701), Catharine Trotter	4 Feb 01	DL	B C D E F G
Second Collection								
I	49	27-29 Mar 01	John Eccles	?	"Ayres in ye Opera call'd ye Mad Lover Compos'd by Mr. Iohn Eccles"	?	?	B C D E F G
II[3]	54	27-29 May 01	Godfrey Finger	DO	The Virgin Prophetess: or, The Fate of Troy (1701), Elkanah Settle	12 May 01	DL	B C D E F G

								A	B	C	D	E	F	G
III	58	24-26 Jul 01	Godfrey Finger	C	*Love Makes a Man; or, The Fop's Fortune* (1701), Colley Cibber	9 Dec 00	DL	A	B	C	D	E	F	G
IV	61	13-16 Sep 01	Godfrey Finger	C	*Sir Harry Wildair: Being the Sequel of the Trip to the Jubilee* (1701), George Farquhar	Apr 01	DL	A	B	C	D	E		G
V	62	c. 1701	Godfrey Finger	C	*The Humour of the Age* (1701), Thomas Baker	1 Mar 01	DL			C	D	E		G
VI	66	28-30 Oct 01	Godfrey Finger	DO?	"Mr Fingers Ayres in the Opera of Alexander the Great" [an operatic version of *The Rival Queens, or the Death of Alexander the Great* (1677), Nathaniel Lee]	Feb 01	DL			C	D			G
[Third Collection]														
I	73	11-13 Dec 01	James Paisible	TC?	"Mr Peasable's Ayre's in the Comedy call'd the Humors of Sr Iohn Falsstaf" [?K. *Henry IV with the Humours of Sir John Falstaff* (1700), Thomas Betterton]	?	LIF?	A			D	E		
II	74	16-18 Dec 01	William Croft	C	*The Funeral; or, Grief A-la-mode* (1702), Richard Steele	Dec 01	DL	A	B		D	E	F	
III	78	22-24 Jan 02	John Barrett	T	*The Generous Conqueror: or, The Timely Discovery* (1702), Bevil Higgons	Dec 01	DL	A	B		D		F	
IV	79	10-12 Feb 02	John Lenton	T	*Tamerlane* (1701), Nicholas Rowe	Dec 01	LIF	A			D	E		
V	80	10-12 Feb 02	[William Byron]	C	*The False Friend* (1702), John Vanbrugh	Feb 02	DL	A	B		D	E		
VI	81	3-5 Mar 02	Daniel Purcell	C	*The Inconstant: or, The Way to Win Him* (1702), George Farquhar	Feb 02	DL				D	E	F	

[Fourth Collection]

	No.	Date	Composer	Type	Title	Theatre	Date	A	B	D	E	F
I	86	c. 1702	James Paisible	P	"Mr Peasables Aires in the Play call'd King Edward the Third" [? a revival of King Edward the Third, with the Fall of Mortimer Earl of March (1691), John Bancroft]	?	?			D	E	
II	87	c. 1702	John Lenton	?	"Aires in the Play call'd the Royall Captive Composed by Mr Lenton"	?	?		B	D		
III	88	6-9 Jun 02	John Eccles	—	"A Sett of Aires Made for the Queen's Coronation by Mr J. Eccles Master of Her Majesty's Musick"	—	Apr 02	A		D		F
IV	96	c. 1702	John Barrett	C	The Pilgrim (1700), John Vanbrugh [for a revival?]	? DL	? Oct 00	A	B	D		F
V	97	25-27 Aug 02	Daniel Purcell	P	The Faithful Bride of Granada (1704) [William Taverner]	DL	? May 04[4]	A	B	D		F[5]
VI	100	24-27 Oct 02	Jeremiah Clarke	C	All for the Better: Or, The Infallible Cure (1703), Francis Manning	DL	? Nov 02	A	B	D[6]		

[Fifth Collection]

	No.	Date	Composer	Type	Title	Theatre	Date	A	B	D	E	F
I	105	28 Nov-1 Dec 02	Daniel Purcell	T	The Patriot, or the Italian Conspiracy (1703), Charles Gildon	DL	? Dec 02	A	B	D		F
II	110	15-17 Dec 02	James Paisible	C	She Wou'd and She Wou'd Not; or, the Kind Impostor (1703), Colley Cibber	DL	26 Nov 02			D	E	F
III	111	7-9 Jan 03	William Croft	C	The Twin-Rivals (1703), George Farquhar	DL	14 Dec 02			D	E	F
IV	115	9-11 Feb 03	John Barrett	C	Tunbridge-Walks: Or, The Yeoman of Kent (1703) [Thomas Baker]	DL	27 Jan 03	A	B	D	E	F
V	118	23-25 Feb 03	William Corbett	C	Love Betray'd; or, The Agreable Disapointment (1703) [William Burnaby]	LIF	Feb 03			D	E	F

VI	120	30 Mar–1 Apr 03	John Lenton	T	*The Fair Penitent* (1703), Nicholas Rowe	? May 03	LIF		D E
[Sixth Collection]									
I	122	4–6 May 03	William Corbett	C	*As You Find It* (1703), Charles Boyle	28 Apr 03	LIF	B	D E F
II	132	21–24 Aug 03	William Corbett	C	"Mr Corbet's Musick in the Comedy call'd Henr the 4th Play'd all the time of the Bublick [sic] Act in Oxford".7	?	?	B	D E F
III	141	21–23 Dec 03	William Croft	C	*The Lying Lover: or, The Ladies Friendship* (1704), Richard Steele	2 Dec 03	DL	B	D E F
IV	152	5–7 Sep 04	John Lenton	T	*Abra-Mule: or, Love and Empire* (1704), Joseph Trapp	13 Jan 04	LIF		D E F
V	147	c. 1704	John Lenton	T	*Liberty Asserted* (1704), John Dennis	24 Feb 04	LIF	B	D E
VI	—	—	—	—	—	—	—	—	—
[Collection a]									
III	154	17–19 Oct 04	James Paisible	—	"Mr Paisibles Musick Perform'd before her Majesty and the new King of Spain".8	30 Dec 03	—		D E
IV	146	c. 1704	John Barrett	T	*The Albion Queens: or the Death of Mary Queen of Scotland* [1704], John Banks	6 Mar 04	DL	A B	D E F
[Collection b]									
II	171	17–20 Mar 05	[William Byron]	C	*She wou'd if she cou'd* (1668), George Etherege, a revival	15 Mar 05	DL	B	
-	175	5–8 May 05	John Barrett	C	*The Tender Husband: Or, the Accomplished Fools* (1705), Richard Steele	23 Apr 05	DL		NOT EXTANT

[Collection c]								
II	180	15-18 Sep 05	Daniel Purcell	C	The Northern Lass (1632), Richard Brome, a revival	?26 Jun 05	DL	B
–	191	20-22 Dec 05	John Barrett	C	Hampstead Heath (1706) [Thomas Baker]	30 Oct 05	DL	NOT EXTANT
–	194	22-24 Jan 06	Daniel Purcell	C	The Basset Table (1706), Susanna Centlivre	20 Nov 05	DL	NOT EXTANT
IV	199	21-23 Mar 06	William Corbett	DO	The British Enchanters: or, No Magick like Love (1706) [George Granville]	21 Feb 06	QT	B
–	210	5 Jun 06	–	C	The Recruiting Officer (1705), George Farquhar	8 Apr 06	DL	NOT EXTANT

ACT MUSIC OF THE QUEEN'S THEATRE

H = British Library g.15 (a4)
I = Gerald Coke Collection (a4)

	No.	Date	Composer		Title	(22 Feb 05)	(LIF)	
I	169	30 Jan–1 Feb 05	John Lenton	C	*The Gamester* (1705), Susanna Centlivre	27 Apr 05	QT	H
–	189	20–22 Dec 05	John Eccles	C	*The Confederacy* (1705), John Vanbrugh	30 Oct 05	QT	NOT EXTANT
I	215	27–29 Aug 06	John Smith	DO	*Wonders in the Sun: or, The Kingdom of the Birds* (1706), Thomas Durfey	5 Apr 06	QT	H
I	229	16 Dec 06	Jean-Claude Gillier	–	"Mr Gilliers Musick Made for the Queens Theatre"	–	QT	H
I	239	22 Mar 07	Daniel Purcell	C	*The Relapse: or, Virtue in Danger* (1697), John Vanbrugh, a revival	2 Nov 06	DG	H
II	261	18–20 Nov 07	Jean-Claude Gillier	C	"Mr Gilliers Musick in the Play call'd the Stratagem" [*The Beaux Stratagem* (1707), George Farquhar]	8 Mar 07	QT	H
II	277b	12 Nov 08	John Allnot	T	*Phaedra and Hippolitus* [1707], Edmund Smith	21 Apr 07	QT	H
V	285a	8 Dec 08	William Corbett	–	"A new Set of Tunes Compos'd by Mr Corbett for the Theatre"	–	–	H
I	312	c. 1709	John Barrett	C	"Mr Barretts Musick in the Comedy calld the Ladys fine Aires for Violins and Hoboys" [*The Fine Lady's Airs: Or, an Equipage of Lovers*, 1709, Thomas Baker]	14 Dec 08	DL	H
I	357	8–11 Jul 10	[G. F. Handel]	C	*The Alchymist* (1612), Ben Jonson, a revival[9]	14 Jan 10	QT	I

NOTES

INTRODUCTION

[1]Some of these, of course, are adaptations of earlier plays but were not, strictly speaking, revivals. That is, they so alter their prototypes as to be in approximately the same relationship as, for example, Shakespeare's *Othello* and its latest musical version, *Catch my Soul*, "structured by" Sid Levin.

[2]*A History of English Drama, 1660-1900*, I (Cambridge, 1967), 8.

[3]For a summary of the audience debate, see Robert D. Hume, *The Development of English Drama in the late Seventeenth Century* (Oxford, 1976), pp. 23-28.

[4]The standard work is Nicoll, I. Hume's *The Development of English Drama in the late Seventeenth Century* is the best and most recent, being staggeringly complete and refreshing to read. Among the others, the most useful are Montague Summers, *The Restoration Theatre* (London, 1934), Eleanore Boswell, *The Restoration Court Stage 1660-1702. With a Particular Account of the Production of Calisto* (London, 1932), and Robert E. Moore, *Henry Purcell and the Restoration Theatre* (London, 1961). In a different category because it is absolutely indispensable is Emmett L. Avery's monumental work *The London Stage 1660-1800. A Calendar of Plays, Entertainments & Afterpieces*, Part I, 1660-1700, ed. William Van Lennep; Part 2, Vol. I, 1700-1717, ed. Avery (Carbondale, Illinois, 1960).

[5]The most convenient hand-list of these is in Nicoll, I, 2, n. 2. One might add to that list, which is rapidly becoming obsolete, the currently available volumes of the fine new Dryden, *The Works*, ed. H. T. Swedenberg, VIII (Berkeley and Los Angeles, 1962), IX (Berkeley and Los Angeles, 1966), and X (Berkeley, Los Angeles, and London, 1970); *The Dramatic Works of Roger Boyle*, ed. William Smith Clark, II, 2 Vols. (Cambridge, Mass., 1937); *The Works of Nathaniel Lee*, ed. Thomas B. Stroup and Arthur L. Cooke (New Brunswick, N.J., 1954-1955); and *The Complete Plays of William Wycherley*, ed. Gerald Weales (New York, 1966).

[6]*Foundations of English Opera* (Cambridge, 1928), p. 3. Dent is prying into the dark area of distinction between play and opera, the latter the most elusive of Restoration dramatic types; but as will be shown below, the comparison might well be extended to include the Restoration play which contained considerable music. Dent's assessment of Restoration musical practices is on the whole carefully considered. One statement, however, is misleading (p. 4): "From the Restoration to the end of the century a quantity of plays were produced in which music was a very important feature; but in almost all cases the music was confined to those episodes in which supernatural or quasi-supernatural characters appeared." This remark might apply to many dramatic operas but not to plays; one can sympathize with the Professor's reluctance to discuss the latter; his main concern, after all, is opera.

[7]The latter have, of course, centered mostly on the works of Henry Purcell. The most successful study of Purcell's theatre music as it relates to Restoration drama in general is A. Margaret Laurie's "Purcell's Stage Works," Diss. Cambridge 1962.

[8]A noteworthy exception is Robert Gale Noyes's article, "Conventions of Song in Restoration Tragedy," *PMLA*, LIII (1938), 162-188.

[9]Dramatic operas are not discussed at length in this study, although many of their musical features which are indistinguishable from those of plays are considered in detail.   The most important works on Restoration dramatic opera are Dent, *Foundations of English Opera* and John Buttrey, "The Evolution of English Opera Between 1656 and 1695: A Re-investigation," Diss. Cambridge 1967, neither of which should be relied upon without the other. Moore's *Henry Purcell and the Restoration Theatre* considers only Purcell's dramatic operas. See also Eugene Haun, *But Hark! More Harmony: The Libretti of Restoration Opera in English* (Ypsilanti, Mich., 1971), which does not discuss the music of these works.

[10]The hand-lists on which this project was based are Nicoll, I, Appendix C, "Hand-list of Restoration Plays" [1660-1700] [386]-447, and Nicoll, II, Appendix C, "Hand-list of Plays, 1700-1750" [293]-407.   These lists were supplemented by Gertrude L. Woodward and James G. McManaway, *A Check List of English Plays 1641-1700* (Chicago, 1945) and the main catalogues of the British Library (formerly the British Museum) and the Harvard College Libraries, where most of the reading was done.

[11]Noyes's "Conventions of Song in Restoration Tragedy," for example.

[12]The approach used, for instance, by J. S. Manifold in *The Music in English Drama From Shakespeare to Purcell* (London, 1956), pp. 195-196, would seem unsatisfactory: "Where minor dramatists were concerned, my method was to read a selection of the plays sufficiently wide to give me a feeling of the author's musical sense. Only if this musical sense was evident did I take the further step of reading the complete works. . . . I particularly regret the omission of Southerne, none of whose works are to be had in Queensland."

[13]For a contemporary remark about alterations made in plays during production, see the dedication to Thomas Durfey's *The Banditti* (1686). Durfey is defending his comedy against the criticism it apparently received:

> . . . tho' my Play might be too long, which is a general fault amongst us, and not to be remedy'd 'till the first day is over, and tho' some Scenes might seem Tedious 'till it was shorten'd, which is allways the Second Days work, yet I had the Confidence to think, that the Variety of a pretty Tale, a good Plot, not very ungratefull Characters, and I am sure very good Musick, both Vocal and Instrumental, with Vaulting, Dancing, and all that I cou'd think of to please, might have oblig'd 'em to a Civil Sufferance, tho' not a liking. . . .

In late 17th-century English play-books, deleted passages are sometimes braced with inverted commas at the left margin, but this is certainly not a consistent practice. For example, in the preface to another play by Durfey, *The Comical History of Don Quixote*, II (1694), he similarly admits that "I have Printed some Scenes both in the first and second part which were left out in the Acting--the Play and the Musick being too long. . . ."   But there is nothing in the play-books to indicate what was deleted. Compare this, for example, with P. A. Motteux's frank admission in the preface to *The Loves of Mars and Venus* (1696): "By reason of the Symphonies and Repetitions some Lines are left out in the Singing, which may easily be known by the Marks prefix'd, and past over, when the Music is performing."

[14]In a review of John H. Long, *Shakespeare's Use of Music: The Histories and the Tragedies* (Gainesville, Florida, 1971), in *MQ*, LIX (1973), 311.

[15]The "Superior Order" which prevented *Irene* from including musical scenes is discussed below in Chapter Five.

[16]Compare *King Saul* and this perhaps satirical remark with a far more famous school dramatic presentation, Nahum Tate's and Henry Purcell's *Dido and Aeneas* [1689], prepared for Josias Priest's Chelsea school for girls.

[17]In several instances printers or publishers took what would seem to be authorial control over plays they were trying to sell. In the preface to Katherine Philips's *Pompey* (1663), headed "The Printer to the Reader," an anonymous agent of the author states in rather unflattering terms "that Pompey being a Translation out of the French of Monsieur Corneille, the hand that did it is responsible for nothing but the English, and the Songs between the Acts, which were added only to lengthen the Play, and make it fitter for the Stage. . . ." (For more about this revealing remark, see pp. 62-64). In another instance an author apparently abandoned an unsuccessful play and the bookseller has written one of the most refreshingly witty prefaces to any Restoration play. Gone is panegyric and apology in this preface to Thomas Porter's *The French Conjurer* (1678):

> As Prefaces are commonly nothing to the purpose, even so little an Author as a Bookseller may venture to write one. And to shew you that this is as modish an Epistle as most are, I do assure you, it has as little in it as any you ever read. In the first place I have nothing to say about the Play: for as the Author stood upon no Reputation in the Acting of it, so he has none to defend in the Publication. Nor has he any thing to say about the Critiques: for as he never intends to trouble the Stage agen, he has no occasion of begging their Favours in Reversion, and securing of Votes before hand. And for his Brother Poets, he has nothing to say to them neither; no, not so much as to rail at them. And last of all, the Author has nothing to say for himself, nor I for him; and so I am

> Your Humble Servant.

[18]One song, however, "One hand [All hands] up aloft" from IV.ii, was printed (D&M 113 *m*Berenclow), and the play-book gives indications that others were also sung. Perhaps Higden's remark that the songs were never set "by omission or combination" means that some of his apparent plethora of songs originally inserted in the play were left out altogether or in some cases consolidated.

[19]There are, of course, plays that would never have been printed and thus probably lost forever if it had not been for the music written for them. One such is Thomas Dilke's *The City Lady; or, Folly Reclaim'd* (1697), a distinctly undistinguished comedy, apparently saved from oblivion by its music. As Dilke explains in his dedication to his brother (testimony perhaps to its quality is his temerity in not offering it to some distinguished member of the gentry), one of the reasons he wants his play to be printed is because "the Music being so finely composed by Mr. John Eccles, I was loath it should be wholly lost to the town." There is no doubt that the music of the play was considered important at the time, as the best professional singers, Mrs.

Bowman, Mrs. Prince, and Mr. Harris, are carefully recorded in the play-book as the executants of the songs and dialogues. It is ironic that of all the music which is indicated for this work in the play-book only one song survives (at least in the printed sources), "There lately was a maiden Fair" (D&M 3218), in IV.ii, and even this is published anonymously. The overture and act music, found in two sources (Ob MS Mus. Sch. c.72, pp. 24ff and Lbm Add. 35043, fols. 79ff), is clearly ascribed to "Mr. Finger," not to John Eccles. (Eccles was, most likely, responsible for the banquet entertainment of III.ii, which stage directions indicate, in that oft-used catch-all, contains "singing and dancing.") Current tastes and theatrical applause are soon forgotten, and in most cases only chance is responsible for the preservation of such ephemeral delights.

CHAPTER 1

[1]Perhaps the only limitation of Noyes's fine article, "Conventions of Song in Restoration Tragedy," is that it only considers songs. In the discussion of the use of entertainments and masques, he feels this constraint most acutely. Noyes's study (referred to numerous times below) is, however, concerned only with lyrics; music is not at all considered.

[2]The dialogue is "Hark, you, Madam, can't I move you" (D&M 1271 mJ. Eccles sBoman and Mrs. Bracegirdle).

[3]A similar situation is found in Dryden's *An Evenings Love, or the Mock-Astrologer* (1671), V.i. Jacinta tells her lover, Wildblood, that "I have been retrieving an old Song of a Lover that was ever quarrelling with his Mistress: I think it will fit our amour so well . . . and you shall sing it." The song is vaguely appropriate, but Wildblood declares that "I never sung in all my life; nor ever durst trie when I was alone, for fear of braying. . . ." But the dialogue, "Celimena, of my heart," is sung, although it is not known if it was sung by the pair of lovers or their attendants.

[4]Not only are they listed in the *dramatis personae* as having portrayed Airy and Christina, but also *Deliciae Musicae: Being, A Collection of the newest and best Songs, With the Dialogues in the last New Play call'd (Love's a Jest) Sett by Mr. John Eccles* (1696) records them as singing this dialogue. Note also that Eccles, who wrote many of the songs that Boman and Bracegirdle sang on the stage, was very likely their "Master." In fact, Stoddard M. Lincoln, in "John Eccles: the Last of a Tradition," Diss. Oxford 1963-1964, p. 13, suggests that the lutenist accompanying Mrs. Bracegirdle in the frontispiece of *Deliciae Musicae* (1695) might be Eccles. See also Lucyle Hook, "Portraits of Elizabeth Barry and Anne Bracegirdle," *Theatre Notebook*, XV (1961), 129-137.

[5]Mrs. Bracegirdle's other duets include "By those pigsneyes that stars do seem" (D&M 453 mJ. Eccles sDogget and Bracegirdle) in II.ii of Durfey's *The Richmond Heiress: or, A Woman Once in the Right* (1693), and "When will Stella kind tender Recompense Fidele amour" (D&M 3822) in Pix's *The Deceiver Deceived* (1698), "A Dialogue in the fourth Act, between Mr. Bowman and Mrs. Bracegirdle: The Words by Mr. Durfey and set by Mr. Eccles." Note that D&M do not associate these singers with Durfey's song. Besides this dialogue, Boman sang "Hark, my Damilcar, we are call'd below" (D&M 1261 mH. Purcell sBoman and Mrs. Ayliff) in IV.i of a 1694 or 1695 revival of Dryden's *Tyranick Love, or, the Royal Martyr* (1670), and "No more sir no more I'll

e'en give it o're" (D&M 2339 *m*H. Purcell *s*Boman and Mrs. Butler) in IV.ii of Southerne's *Sir Anthony Love: or, The Rambling Lady* (1691).

[6]In "Conventions of Song," Noyes identifies nearly 30 uses of song in tragedies alone. Some of these, such as songs for scenic effect (p. 174), songs in masques (p. 175), serenades (pp. 176-178), weddings (p. 178), processionals (p. 176), songs for mad characters (pp. 185, 187), for opening tableaux (pp. 165-166), supernatural events (pp. 167, 175, 180), and love songs (p. 169), are found in equal abundance in comedies. Furthermore, Noyes discusses the use of songs between acts and scenes (pp. 172-173), which, by his own admission, lie quite outside the drama. Lincoln (in "John Eccles: the Last of a Tradition," p. 177) divides songs in comedies into two general categories: true comic songs in a popular style, usually in triple meter, and parody songs, meant to satirize the art songs of tragedy and which require the considerable vocal abilities of a trained singer. This categorization might accommodate a few songs written in the last decade of the 17th century but is inadequate to deal with the wide range of song types found in comedies throughout the entire period. Lincoln's second category is particularly nebulous.

[7]"Conventions of Song," p. 171.

[8]Songs placed in this location probably often functioned as act music, that is, the song most likely began before the act or scene got underway, before the curtain went up, or before the character came onto the stage.

[9]The songs are "Imperial Sultan, Hail, To whom Great Kingdoms bow," and "A Dialogue Song. Suppos'd to be between an Eunuch Boy and a Virgin. Made for Boyn and Mrs. Crosse. Written by Mr. D'Urfey," entitled "Fly from my Sight, fly far away" (D&M 1022 *m*D. Purcell *s*Bowen and Mrs. Cross). See Noyes, p. 185.

[10]"Let business no longer usurp your high mind" (D&M 1960 *m*Staggins).

[11]"Some happy soul come down and tell" (D&M 3025 *m*R. Smith).

[12]These include Lee, *The Tragedy of Nero, Emperour of Rome* (1675), III.i, "Weep you Muses, drain the Springs" (sung to Britannicus whose sister Octavia has just been killed by Nero); Oldmixon, *The Governour of Cyprus* (1703), I.i, "When Sylvia runs to Woods and Groves" (sung to a sad Lucinda); Powell, *Alphonso King of Naples* (1691), IV[ii], "Long time, alas! our Mournful Swains" ("The King discover'd melancholy, some Attendants standing by him"); Powell, *The Treacherous Brothers* (1690), III.iv, "Were I with my Orinda bless'd" ("The Scene drawn discovers Marcelia sitting Melancholy"); Charles Saunders, *Tamerlane the Great* (1681), IV[iii], "Behold ye Sylvans frequent" ("Arsanes sitting melancholly on a Green Bank"); Settle, *The Ambitious Slave; or, a Generous Revenge* (1694), III.i, "Why do's the Idle World mistake," D&M 3938 *m*J. Eccles *s*Mrs. Hudson ("Herminia discover'd Sleeping on a couch attended by Marvan and Amorin"); Tate, *The History of King Richard the Second* (1681), V.iv, an unspecified song (Richard, alone in a prison, "A Table and Provisions shewn . . . the Table sinks down").

[13]The second scene of Act IV begins similarly: "The King discover'd melancholy, some Attendants standing by him, and Symphony of Musick within."

[14]For example, in the middle of III.ii of *Valentinian* (1685), by John Wilmot (the Earl of Rochester), Lucina commands her lady, Marcellina, to "fetch your Lute, and sing that Song / My Lord calls his: I'll try to wear away / The melancholy Thoughts his Absence breeds!" After the song ("Where would coy Aminta run," D&M 3852) she sleeps, and then comes an entry dance of Satyrs. Both the song and the dance have very little to do with the dramatic situation. Rochester probably felt this sagging third act was a convenient place in which to inject a little sugary diversion to sustain the audience until the fifth-act gore would recapture their attention.

[15]This image of man in nature is common in Dryden's plays. It was he who six years earlier writes in *The Conquest of Granada by the Spaniards*, Part I (1672), I.i,

> I am as free as Nature first made man,
> 'Ere the base Laws of Servitude began
> When wild in woods the noble Savage ran.

See Dryden, *Works*, ed. Swedenberg, X, 331, for a discussion of this poet's naturalistic images.

[16]The song, "Ah cruel bloody fate" (D&M 35), is one of Henry Purcell's earliest for the London stage.

[17]"Cloris we see the offended God." Phillocles and Selindra sit within the scene, probably to conceal the fact that this main character's song was sung by someone else.

[18]Other instances of this use of music include Crowne, *Darius King of Persia* (1688), II.iii ("Scene, a Room in the Palace, Barzana sate melancholy, attending to a song. Sometimes weeping"); Dryden, *The Duke of Guise* (1683), V.i, "Tell me Thirsis, tell your Anguish," D&M 3172 mPack (". . . a sudden damp, I know not why, / Has seiz'd my spirits. . . ."); Mountfort, *The Successfull Straingers* (1690), IV.iv, "Come, come, ye Inhabitants of Heaven, Conduct me to my Love" (Bianca, played by Mrs. Bracegirdle, sings her own song of grief); Payne, *The Fatal Jealousie* (1673), IV.i, "Ah Choridon, in vain you boast," D&M 33 mR. Smith (Caelia says ". . . prethee sing that Song I love so well, / That harmony, perhaps, will Charm my cares, / And give my senses Rest"); William Phillips, *The Revengeful Queen* (1698), V.i, "Oh Love how mighty are thy Joys" ("*Rosamund.* These sad thoughts, Musick and Love shall banish, / Retire with me to my Alcove, and try their Force. . . ."); Pix, *The False Friend: or, The Fate of Disobedience* (1699), III.ii ("*Appamia.* . . . let the Italian Eunuch Sing; and softest Musick turn her Griefs"); Pordage, *The Siege of Babylon* (1677), IV.iii, "What are all the Joys, of life" ("*Statira.* . . . Bid Charmion sing-- / In her sweet Voice, I oft have pleasures found, / Musick, like Balm, eases grief's smarting wound"); Ravenscroft, *The Italian Husband* (1698), II.i, "Nymphs that now are in your prime" ("*Dutchess.* A Song to lull my troubled thoughts asleep"); Catherine Trotter, *Agnes de Castro* (1696), IV.i ("*Agnes.* . . . I've heard soft Musick Charms a troubled Mind / Luls Cares asleep, and calms the roughest Passions: / Who waits there? sing me some mournful Song"); Francis Manning, *All for the Better* (1703), IV.ii, "Oft have I heard our Poets sing" ("*Alphonso.* . . . Let me have Musick, Boy; I am melancholy, perhaps 'twill mitigate my Pain"); Crowne, *Regulus* (1694), II.iii, "Ah me! to many deaths decreed," D&M 65 mH. Purcell ("*Fulvia.* Go, bid the music cease, I find it vain. . . ."); Powell, *Bonduca: or, The British Heroine* (1696), V.i, "Oh lead me to some peaceful gloom," D&M 2486 mH. Purcell sMiss Cross ("*Bonvica.* Where shall the wretched Off-Spring of Bonduca fly, / To escape those dismal

Screams of Horror . . . I'd have the Song you taught me last. / I fear, I do resemble now the Swan, / That Sings before its Death"; note that Bonvica, played by Miss Cross, sings her own song); Lee, *Mithridates* (1678), IV.i, "One night when all the village slept," D&M 2633 *m*Grabu (a song to comfort Ziphares); Southerne, *Oroonoko* (1696), II.iii, "A Lass there lives upon the green," D&M 1925 *m*R. Courteville, and "Bright Cynthia's power divinely great," D&M 418 *m*R. Courteville (note Noyes, p. 184, misreads the title of the latter) (both songs divert Imoinda's sadness at her husband's absence); Tate, *Brutus of Alba* (1678), V[ii], "Bid the sad forsaken Grove," D&M 370 *m*Farmer ("*Amarante*. Soft Musick, and complaining Songs may calm / This Rage, I've known it a successful Charm").

[19]See Nicoll, I, 389.

[20]"Underneath a Gloomy Shade" (D&M 3514 *m*D. Purcell *s*Mrs. Shaw) and "Happy ever happy we" (D&M 1237 *m*D. Purcell *s*"the boy").

[21]A fuller discussion of incidental music is found in Chapter Two.

[22]One of the characteristics of Restoration dramatic opera that distinguishes it from the ordinary play is, of course, an abundance of scenic spectacle (see, e.g., the famous opening of the operatic *Tempest* of 1674). The opening scenes of many tragedies, however, differ little from those of the more operatic stage representations, save perhaps in degree of magnificence. Both are apt to involve extended musical scenes. Generally, what distinguishes the two dramatic types is the presence of masques (often with a unified theme) after each of the five acts in the more operatic form. As a result, a dramatic opera rarely has a tragic end, although the spoken part may closely resemble a tragedy.

[23]See, e.g., Nicoll, I, 82-83. Summers, however, in *The Restoration Theatre*, pp. 94-152, presents an admirable discussion of the use of the curtain, although he is not specifically concerned with music.

[24]Davenant apparently anticipated not only the reopening of the theatres but the kind of music his soon-to-be-restored king would prefer to hear in them.

[25]See Nicoll, I, 401.

[26]In his article "Corpses, Concealments, and Curtains on the Restoration Stage," in *Review of English Studies*, XIII (1937), 438-448, William S. Clark discusses the former. He is concerned principally with the small traverse or draw curtain, which concealed a portion of the upstage area. For the most part, however, Clark fails to associate music with discoveries; and the function of the traverse is no different from that of the more usual draw scene whose opening and closing might also be accompanied by music. See, e.g., Lee's *Caesar Borgia: the Son of Pope Alexander the Sixth* (1680), V.iii: "Scene draws, and discovers a Chair of state under a Canopy . . . The Indian Boys Dance."

[27]Other examples include Behn, *The Second Part of the Rover* (1681), I.i ("Scene draws and discovers a Church, a great many people at Devotion, soft Musick playing"), R. Carleton, "The Martial Queen" [1675], IV.i ("A curtain opens and discovers Apollo on a Throne . . . Loud Musick and scene shuts"), Crowne, *The Destruction of Jerusalem* (1677), I.i ("The curtain draws, the brazen gates of the Temple appear; music is heard

within . . . Queen Bernice and Clarona at their devotion"), Lee, *Theodosius* (1680), I.i
("A stately Temple . . . Instruments are heard, and many Attendants . . . A Chorus
heard at distance"), Saunders, *Tamerlane the Great* (1681), I.i ("The Curtain being
drawn up discovers the Temple of Mahomet," a hymn is sung).

[28]Other banquets or entertainments discovered in progress in tragedies include Centlivre,
The Perjur'd Husband, or, The Adventures of Venice (1700), I.i ("The Curtains fly up,
and discover a Mask in Pizalto's House . . . A Spanish Entry"), Crowne, *Thyestes*
(1681), I.i ("The Song at Atreus his Banquet"), Lee, *Caesar Borgia* (1680), V.iii
("Scene draws, and discovers a Chair of state under a Canopy, a large Table, with a
rich Banquet . . . The Indian Boys Dance"), Lee, *Gloriana* (1676), I.i.

[29]This is a reference to the custom of opening the upper gallery to footmen, link boys,
etc., at the end of the fourth act.

[30]See, e.g., Pix, *The Czar of Muscovy* (1701), I.i ("Scene draws, and discovers Demetrius
and Marina coming from the altar, as just marry'd . . . The Priest sings the following
Song set to Solemn Musick," "Blessed are they who Heaven Obey"), and Howard,
The Surprisal (1665), III.i (Emilia's bridegroom salutes her with Musick: "As soon as
the Masque begins the Curtain draws and Emilia appears. . . .").

[31]In Restoration plays scenes were generally demarcated only by the absence of any
character on the stage.

[32]See Farquhar, "A Discourse upon Comedy, In Reference to the English Stage," in
The Works Of the late Ingenious Mr. George Farquhar, II (1760), 105-106, for a
mention of the value of fiddles to connect the scenes of a hypothetical comedy that
are separated by time and place.

[33]Noyes, in "Conventions of Song," p. 167, sees certain lyrics as being employed in
breaking episodes within a scene and creating the illusion of the passage of time.

[34]Serenades, to be considered below, are more often organic rather than atmospheric to
the dramatic situation.

[35]The song is "That devine form which the deluden thy sense." See Noyes,
"Conventions of Song," pp. 169-170 for this and other examples of love songs.

[36]See also pp. 6-7, above, for a song accompanying Athenais's suicide in Lee's
Theodosius (1680), V.i.

[37]For example, in Dennis's *Rinaldo and Armida* (1699), a scene (III.i) of an enchanted
wilderness is made quite hellish by "The Serpent and basses softly [playing] under the
Stage." Urania exclaims:

> In Frantick haste ev'n now the Furies Arm,
> Th'Infernal Trumpet thro' the Abiss profound,
> Horribly Rumbles with its dreary Sound.

[38]As in Davenant's *The Rivals* (1668), IV.i: "A hunt in Musick. The Call at distance
representing the sound of Horns by instrumental Musick . . . Musick expresses the
Chase by Voices and Instruments like Hollaing and Winding of Horns."

[39]See p. 168 of "Conventions of Song." He cites the casket song in *The Merchant of Venice* as being among the finest examples.

[40]"Love shot himself into my breast like flame."

[41]See Noyes, "Conventions of Song," pp. 168-169. In addition to Gabriel's lyric he considers the following songs to be structural: "In vain dear Cassander in vain you employ," in Banks, *The Rival Kings* (1677), III.i; "Venus chanced to love a boy," in Payne, *Siege of Constantinople* (1675), III.v; and "Fair and soft and gay and young," in Gould, *Rival Sisters* (1696), III.i.

[42]Also known as "Marriage a la Mode." See Nicoll, II, 310. Cibber's play is an adaptation of the comic scenes from Dryden's tragi-comedy *Secret-Love, or the Maiden Queen* (1668) and his comedy *Marriage A-la-Mode* (1673).

[43]Mrs. [Mary] Porter, who played Doralice, is unusual in that she appears never to have sung on the stage. The song was probably rendered by Beliza, whose portrayer is not listed in the *dramatis personae*, the role being a small one.

[44]The following section is taken largely from my article "'. . . to make amends for One ill Dance': Conventions for Dancing in Restoration Plays," *Dance Research Journal*, X (1977-1978), 1-6.

[45]Eric Rothstein would disagree; see his defense of these plays in *Restoration Tragedy* (Madison, Wisconsin, 1967), p. vii: "The neglect of Restoration tragedy . . . seems to me indefensible, explicable only because serious study of the Restoration is comparatively recent."

[46]D&M 3172. The song is reprinted in *Dryden: The Dramatic Works*, ed. Montague Summers (London, 1932), V, 293-295.

[47]Lbm Sloane MS 1828.

[48]Music to enhance the supernatural is a common dramatic convention in the plays (see Noyes, "Conventions of Song," p. 180). Other instances of music accompanying supernatural happenings (not mentioned above) include Behn, *The Forc'd Marriage* (1671), V.ii: Erminia speaks "in a tone like a spirit and points to a chair, soft music begins to play, which continues all this Scene"; Crowne, *Juliana or the Princess of Poland* (1671), V[i]: "Enter 2 Queens followed by 2 ghosts, they pass slowly over the stage. Soft Musick"; Crowne, *The Misery of Civil-War* (1680), V.iv: "Scene, a Room in the Tower, Henry Sleeping. Enter the Ghost of Richard the Second . . . The Ghost goes out, and enters with soft Musick [i.e., recorder players] one clad in white Robe. . ."; Dryden, *Oedipus* (1679), II.i: an extended scene of music and hauntings which includes the song "Music for awhile shall all your cares beguile" (set for a revival as D&M 2224 *m*H. Purcell); Dryden, *Indian Emperour* (1667), II.i: Montezuma in the magical cave, "Kalib ascends all in White in the shape of a Woman, and Sings" the song "I looked and saw within the Book of Fate" (set for a later revival as D&M 1550 *m*H. Purcell *s*Pate); Dryden, *Tyrannick Love* (1670), IV.i: an elaborate scene in an "Indian Cave," where spirits prophesy emperor Maximin's future; *The Unnatural Mother* (1698), I.ii: a scene involving another airy spirit;

Shipman, *Henry the Third of France* (1678), II.ii: "The Cave in the Wood . . .
Musick far off.   Spirit descending leasurely"; Banks, *Cyrus the Great* (1696), I.i: a
scene of a haunted battlefield.

[49]Later is heard "Sing all ye Muses your lutes strike around," D&M 2973 *m*H. Purcell.

[50]*The Comical History of Don Quixote, Part the second* (1694) and *The Comical History
of Don Quixote.   The Third Part.   With the Marriage of Mary the Buxome* (1696).

[51]Noyes, in "Conventions of Song," p. 186, cites the song in Lyly's *The Woman in the
Moone* (1597), V, as the first song of a lunatic in English drama.

[52]Other instances in tragedies of mad songs or songs to ease madness are found in the
anonymous *Romulus and Hersilia* (1683), IV.ii: Feliciana sings a bit of "White as the
Lilly will she lye," and later she is sung to sleep by "Where art thou God of dreams"
(D&M 3841 *m*Draghi); and in Payne, *The Siege of Constantinople* (1675), V.i:
Thomaso, mad, sings "In caves full of sculls, and rotten old Bones." For a similar
scene in a comedy, see Powell, *Imposture Defeated* (1698), I[ii]:   ("A SIMPHONY.
Sforsa Comes forward Softly in a Mad Posture and Sings."), "Peace no Noise, you'l
wake my Love." ("A Symphony of soft Musick here.   Mean time Sforza stands fixt as
if he Look'd on some Body").

[53]See, e.g., *A Fool's Preferment, or, The Three Dukes of Dunstable* (1688), V.i: "Enter
Lyonel in a mad posture . . . Lyonel sings" (no music is specified, but at the end of
the play-book is found "A Song sung in the Fifth Act, by Mr. Monfort" [who played
Lyonel], "If thou wilt give me back my Love" (D&M 1710 *m*H. Purcell); and *The
Richmond Heiress* (1693), II.ii: "There's a Song in parts, between a mad Man, and a
mad Woman," entitled "By those Pigsneyes that stars do seem" (D&M 453 *m*J. Eccles
*s*Dogget and Mrs. Bracegirdle).   Giuacum says, "She makes up to him now, the
Distemper works now, they are curing one another, the two mad Men rise and dance
with 'em."

[54]The song is "Royal and Fair, great Willy's dear Blessing" (D&M 2835).

[55]Music is occasionally used for erotic effect.   In Otway's comedy *The Atheist: or, The
Second Part of the Souldiers Fortune* (1684), III.ii, the scene changes "to the inside of
a very fair House, adorned with rich Furniture and Lights."   As its occupant,
Beaugard, is undressing, "Enter two Black Women," who perform a sensuous dance
before him.   In Dryden's tragedy *The Conquest of Granada* (1672), III, Almahide
presents an erotic song ("Beneath a Myrtle shade," D&M 3577 *m*Banister) and a
Moorish dance to try to still the factious Zegrys and Abencerrages with "soft
pleasures."   In Gould's *Rival Sisters* (1696), IV.i, a lecherous old man in love with
Ansilva sings "Take not a woman's anger ill" (D&M 3145 *m*H. Purcell *s*Leveridge).

[56]See "Eccles and Congreve: Music and Drama on the Restoration Stage," *Theatre
Notebook*, XVIII (1963), 11-12, for a lengthy discussion of this scene.   Lincoln
includes an. analysis of how the music of the song reflects the battle of facial
expressions (e.g., "Millamant's glory is given a little march").   The song, by Eccles,
was sung by Mrs. Hodgson and was issued as a single sheet, copies of which are in
Ckc, Eu, and Lbm.

[57]See, e.g., Scott's *The Mock-Marriage* (1696), IV.iii: Sir Arthur, who is preparing a serenade, addresses his musicians: ". . . be sure keep your Countenances.   You Fidlers generally make worse Faces than Sir Martin."

[58]Some examples of serenades in tragedies are Dryden, *The Conquest of Granada* (1672), IV.ii: Lyndaraxa exclaims: "Musique! and I, believe, addresst to me."   The song, "Wherever I am or whatever I do" (D&M 3853 *m*Marsh) is ordered by Abdalla; Gildon, *The Roman Bride's Revenge* (1697), IV.i: the emperor orders the musicians to go beneath Portia's window to "charm my Goddes with your humble Lays. / The Force of Musick, and the Pow'r of Numbers, / May break the Icy spell that chills her Heart, / Against the pressing Beams of warmer Love."   The diverting song "If Celia you had youth at will" (D&M 1670 *m*Leveridge?) follows; Settle, *Ibrahim the Illustrious Bassa* (1677), III: the song, "No Art Loves Influence can destroy" is sung to Isabella.   See also Noyes, "Conventions of Song," pp. 176-178.

[59]For humorous serenades in tragedies and tragi-comedies, see below.   The earliest serenade in a Restoration tragedy (a comic one) is in Porter's *The Villain* (1663), I.i: Officers of Brisac's regiment are on a drunken midnight ramble.   They hire some passing fiddlers but are dissatisfied with their "newest Ayrs."   They ask the musicians to accompany their singing, the mere volume of which finally gets the attention of the ladies above.

[60]See Ravenscroft, *The Wrangling Lovers; or, The Invisible Mistress* (1677), III.ii; Scott, *The Mock-Marriage* (1696), III.ii; and Shadwell, *The Libertine* (1676), I.i, for scenes similar to this one.

[61]Motteux's serenade is unusual in that it contains no song.   This is in keeping with a promise he makes in the preface to the play.

[62]See Dryden, *The Dramatic Works*, ed. Summers, V (1932), 425:   "There is a naughty jest here.   'Moon' is a slang term for the *pudendum muliebre.*"

[63]*Milton and the Miltonic Dryden* (Cambridge, Mass., 1968), p. 91.

[64]The practice of reading songs in Restoration plays has troubled two writers.   W. J. Lawrence, in "Music and Song in the Eighteenth Century Theatre," *MQ*, II (1916), 71, states that this problem "has eluded all my attempts at a solution."   Frederick Hatch Teahan, in "The Literary Criticism of Music in England, 1660-1789," Diss. Trinity College, Dublin (1957), p. 76, offers an explanation: "Notwithstanding Purcell's immortalizing many a commonplace couplet, the playwright wanted his audience to judge his songs for their literary merit."   He lists three examples (taken from Lawrence's article):   Field, *Amends for Ladies* (1610), IV.i, Brome, *The Novella* (1632), III.i, and Etherege, *The Man of Mode* (1676), IV.i, and adds four more of his own: Crowne, *Sir Courtly Nice* (1685), V.ii, Southerne, *The Maid's Last Prayer* (1692), III.ii (see below), Steele, *The Tender Husband* (1705), III.i, and C. Cibber, *The Refusal* (1721), IV.   In light of the Restoration examples of this use of song, one finds his explanation for this convention weak.   Most of the songs he cites are either purposefully of poor quality, intended to show the foolishness of their authors or are read simply to make their subsequent singing less incongruous to the action of the scenes in which they appear.   The following examples of the practice of reading songs may be added to Teahan's list: Steele, *The Funeral, Or, Grief A-la-mode* (1702), II.ii: Lady Sharlot reads "Let not Love on me bestow" (D&M 1982 *m*D. Purcell *s*Mrs.

Harris) before it is sung; Steele, *The Lying Lover: or, The Ladies Friendship* (1704),
II.i: Penelope reads "Thou soft Machines" before it is "perform'd to a Spinet"; C.
Boyle, *As You Find it* (1703), I.ii (see below); Burnaby, *The Reform'd Wife* (1700),
I.ii: Cleremont reads the song "Corinna with a graceful Air" which is not sung;
Henry Higden, *The Wary Widdow: or, Sir Noisy Parrat* (1693), II.ii: Sir Noisy reads
"with great admiration" "an air of my composing and setting," entitled "Thou life of
all the sun," which "the Musick" later sings; Matthew Medbourne, *Saint Cecily or the
Converted Twins* (1666), I.i: Angusta reads a song ("If each have, of swarming bees")
which Cecilie later sings.

[65]The song, "Set by Mr. John Eccles," is entitled "Sabina's Haughty as she's Fair."

[66]The following is a list of plays (published 1663-1703) with masques. (T) = tragedy,
(C) = comedy, and (TC) = tragi-comedy: K. Philips (T), *Pompey* (1663), V;
Stapylton (C), *The Slighted Maid* (1663), V[ii]; Dryden (TC), *The Rival Ladies* (1664),
III.i; Stapylton (TC), *The Step-Mother* (1664), III[ii], IV.i; Robert Howard (C), *The
Surprisal* (1665), III.i; Medbourne (T), *Saint Cecily or the Converted Twins* (1666), V.i;
W. Davenant (C), *The Rivals* (1668), IV.i; Dryden (C), *Sir Martin Mar-all* (1668), V.ii:
see J. Downes, *Roscius Anglicanus*, ed. Montague Summers (London, 1927), p. 28; W.
Killigrew (T), *The Imperial Tragedy* (1669), II.i, III.i; Frances Boothby (TC), *Marcelia*
(1670), III.vii; Settle (T), *Cambyses* (1671), II.v; John Caryll (C), *Sir Salomon: or, the
Cautious Coxcomb* (1671), III; E. Howard (TC), *The Womens Conquest* (1671), I.ii;
Crowne (T), *The History of Charles the Eighth of France* (1672), V.ii; Ravenscroft (C),
The Citizen Turn'd Gentleman (1672), V.i; Settle (T), *The Empress of Morocco* (1673),
IV.iii; Peter Bellon (C), *The Mock-Duellist* (1675), IV.iii; Payne (T), *The Siege of
Constantinople* (1675), II.i; Behn (C), *The Rover* (1677), IV.iii; William Cavendish (C),
The Humorous Lovers (1677), III[ii]; (C) *The Counterfeit Bridegroom* (1677), IV.i;
Rymer (T), *Edgar, or the English Monarch* (1678), IV[i]; Shadwell (T), *The History of
Timon of Athens, The Man-Hater* (1678), II.i; Tate (T), *Brutus of Alba: or, The
Enchanted Lovers* (1678), III.i; Behn (TC), *The Young King* (1683), III.i; Lee (T), *The
Princess of Cleve* (1689), IV.i; Antony Rivers (T), *The Traytor* (1692), III.i; Cibber (C),
Love's Last Shift (1696), V; Motteux (C), *The Novelty* (1697), III; T. Scott (T), *The
Unhappy Kindness* (1697), II.i; Vanbrugh (C), *The Relapse or Virtue in Danger* (1697),
V.v; (T), *The Discovery: or, Love in Ruines* (1698), II.i; W. Phillips (T), *The
Revengeful Queen* (1698), III.i; Powell (C), *Imposture Defeated* (1698), V.ii; Ravenscroft
(T), *The Italian Husband* (1698), III.i; Cibber (T), *Xerxes* (1699), II.i; Durfey (T), *The
Famous History and Fall of Massaniello*, Part II (1699), V.iv; Harris (C), *Love's a
Lottery, and a Woman the Prize* (1699), III.iii; Centlivre (T), *The Perjur'd Husband*
(1700), I.i, V.i; Gildon (C), *Measure for Measure, or, Beauty The Best Advocate* (1700),
I.i, II.ii, III.ii; Vanbrugh (C), *The Pilgrim* (1700), V.iii; Granville (C), *The Jew of
Venice* (1701), II[ii]; Dennis (C), *The Comical Gallant: or The Amours of Sir John
Falstaffe* (1702), V.i; C. Boyle (C), *As You Find it* (1703), with Motteux's masque,
"Acis and Galletea" (see *The London Stage*, II.1, 34-35); Burnaby (C), *Love Betray'd*
(1703), V.i.

[67]Matthew Locke's music survives in Och Mus. MS 692.

[68]The fourth act became the traditional location for musical entertainments in plays.
See, for example, Charles Sedley's prologue to his comedy, *Bellamira, or the Mistress*
(1687):

When our two houses did divide the Town,
Each Faction zealously maintain'd their own,
We liv'd on those that came to cry us down,
Our Emulation did improve your sport:
Now you come hither but to make your Court:
Or from adjacent Coffee Houses throng
At our fourth Act for a new Dance or Song. . . .

This was written when the two companies (the King's and the Duke's) had united under one roof at the Theatre Royal.

[69]The song is "To love and all its sweets adieu."

[70]Play-books were published within a month or two or longer after the production of a play. In addition to whatever desire both poet and theatre company had to preserve these works for posterity, they were principally made up as mementos or souvenirs.

[71]The song is "Many I've lik'd and some enjoy'd." Unlike act music, which was written specifically for each new play, it is rarely possible to determine what music was played at such entertainments.

[72]See Noyes, "Conventions of Song," p. 173, for a further discussion of this scene.

[73]Other instances (all from the first 15 years of the Restoration) are found in Crowne, *Calisto* (1675), prologue: "Here the Princesses and the other Ladies dance several Sarabands with Castanets," see E. Boswell, *The Restoration Court Stage*, pp. [177] ff; W. Davenant, *The Law Against Lovers* (1673), IV.i: "Enter Viola dancing a Saraband awhile with Castanietos"; W. Davenant, *The Play-House to be Lett* (1673), V (4th entry): ". . . a Saraband is play'd whilst two Spaniards enter . . ."; Porter, *The Carnival* (1664), II.i: "*Felice*. . . . wee'll give the Donzellas A Serenade first: Sirrah, have ye no Castinets? *Sancho*. Yes Sir, here. . . . [but no dance follows]; Shadwell, *The Royal Shepherdess* (1669), II.i: "Dance with Gittars and Castanietta's." The popularity of this exotic instrument is reflected in a contemporary advertisement in *Melothesia: or, certain general rules for playing upon a continued-bass*, I (1673): "All sorts of Books, and Ruled Paper for Musick; Songs and Airs Vocal and Instrumental ready Prick't; Lutes, Viols, Violins, Gittars, Flagelets, Castinets, Strings; and all sorts of Musical Instruments, are Sold by John Carr, at his Shop in the Middle-Temple, London."

[74]Much of what follows is extracted from "'. . . to make amends for One ill Dance': Conventions for Dancing in Restoration Plays," pp. 3-4.

[75]A good source for such pieces is John Walsh's *The Compleat Flute=Master* (1695) (only copy in Lbm).

[76]*The First Modern Comedies* (Cambridge, Mass., 1959), pp. 182-183.

[77]*The Diary of Samuel Pepys*, ed. Robert Latham and William Matthews (Berkeley, 1976), IX, 183-184, 2 May 1668.

[78]Cibber's *She wou'd and She wou'd not, or the Kind Imposter* (1703), is such a play. The only required music (besides the act tunes) is a final entertainment. Only the

song "Celia my heart has often ranged" (D&M 514 *m*Weldon *s*Mrs. Campion), which is not printed in the play-book, survives.

[79]As is shown in Chapter Three, later play-books usually give quite complete lists of actors and singers in the *dramatis personae*, and often the songs (published separately) name the singer.

[80]The song is "How unhappy a Lover am I" (D&M 1466 *m*Staggins).

[81]See Lewis Maidwell, *The Loving Enemies* (1680), IV.i: "Lucinda [played by Mrs. Shadwell] sings in the Window."

[82]See Rawlins, *Tom Essence* (1677), IV.i: Betty [Mrs. Napper] enters with a song in her hand. Old Monylove asks her to sing it. She sings "Ah Sacred Boy desist"; Settle, *Pastor Fido* (1677), III.i: Celia [Mrs. Napper] sings "Let us use time whilst we may."

[83]The song is "In vain, Cruel Nymph" (D&M 2331?).

[84]Goring, *Irene* (1708), II.i.

[85]It is "When Phillis watch'd her harmless Sheep" (D&M 3783), one of the earliest surviving songs from a Restoration play.

[86]The song is "Restless in thoughts" (D&M 2800 *m*J. Eccles *s*Mrs. Hodgson).

[87]See also IV.ii of Shipman's *Henry the Third of France* (1678), in which a grove figures prominently in the development of the plot.

[88]That is, dances were often performed to instrumental arrangements of the songs they precede or follow, or singing and dancing occur simultaneously.

[89]By Mr. [John] Oldmixon.

[90]See Eric Walter White, "New Light on 'Dido and Aeneas'," in *Henry Purcell, 1659-1695, Essays on His Music*, ed. Imogen Holst (London, 1959), pp. [14]-34, for a further discussion of Gildon's play and *Dido*.

CHAPTER 2

[1]For a catalogue of instrumental music in the plays, see Appendix I.

[2]See Robert Gale Noyes, "A Manuscript Restoration Prologue for *Volpone*," *Modern Language Notes*, XLII (1937), 198-200.

[3]These include Settle's *The Empress of Morocco* (première, 3 July 1673), with music by Locke (in Och Mus. MS. 692); a satire with the same title by Thomas Duffett (première, December 1673); an unidentified "Italian Opera in musique" mentioned by John Evelyn (see *Diary*, 5 January 1674); Pierre Perrin's opera *Ariadne; or, The Marriage of Bacchus* (première, 30 March 1674), music by Louis Grabu; Thomas Shadwell's operatic alteration of *The Tempest* (première, 30 April 1674) (for the music, see discussion below); Duffett's parody called *The Mock-Tempest* (première, 19

November 1674); and Shadwell's semi-opera *Psyche* (première, 27 February 1675), with music by Locke and G. B. Draghi.

[4]He appears to have invented "Fivyion" and "Peripatic." "Exode" is a farce in one act (*OED*) and "Epopeeia" means the making of epics (*OED*).

[5]Trans. in Samuel de Sorbière, *A Voyage to England*, ed. Thomas Sprat (London, 1709), p. 69: "The Musick with which you are entertained diverts your time till the Play begins, and People chuse to go in betimes to hear it." See also L. Magalotti, *Travels of Cos[i]mo the Third, Grand Duke of Tuscany* (London, 1821), p. 191: "Before the Comedy begins, that the audience may not be tired with waiting, the most delightful symphonies are played; on which account many persons come early to enjoy this agreeable amusement." The Duke visited England in 1669, but Magalotti may have combined de Sorbière's account with that of the Duke. See Michael Tilmouth, "Chamber Music in England, 1675-1720," Diss. Cambridge (1960), p. 74.

[6]See, for example, the account of the playgoing of James Brydges (later the first Duke of Chandos) in C. H. Collins Baker and Muriel I. Baker, *The Life and Circumstances of James Brydges First Duke of Chandos* (Oxford, 1949), pp. 30 ff. Brydges did not regularly attend the theatre, but when he did, he nearly always called at both the Theatre Royal and the Lincoln's Inn Fields Theatre on the same afternoon, rarely staying for the play at either house. See also Lucyle Hook, "James Brydges Drops in at the Theatre," *The Huntington Library Quarterly*, VII (1945), 303-311.

[7]E.g., the program piece that prepares Prospero's magical storm in the operatic version of *The Tempest* (1674) is called "overture" in the play-book ("While the Overture is playing, the Curtain rises . . ."), but in *The English Opera; or the Vocal Musick in Psyche . . . to which is Adjoyned the Instrumental Musick in the Tempest* (1675), p. 68, Locke's extraordinary music is entitled "Curtain Tune in the TEMPEST."

[8]Perhaps this explains Locke's choice of title for the piece mentioned in n. 7: it is not a French overture.

[9]Not all Restoration plays open with the ascent of the curtain, as is explained in Chapter One, above. Normally the curtain did not fall again until the epilogue was ended and the stage empty.

[10]This set appears to be lacking a piece, perhaps one of the act tunes, which may have been replaced by one of the songs printed with the play-book.

[11]It is so labelled in a manuscript note. *Ayres for the Theatre* does not specify the performance order of Purcell's theatre tunes.

[12]I am grateful to Dr. A. Margaret Laurie for bringing this to my attention.

[13]Apparently the manuscript lacks only the "mournfull Musick" played while the curtain rises at the beginning of Act V and the song discussed below.

[14]D&M 4118 *ms*Leveridge.

[15]Dennis, *The Musical Entertainments in the Tragedy of Rinaldo and Armida* (1699) (copy in Worcester College Library), rpt. in *Theatre Miscellany*, ed. C. H. Wilkinson (Oxford, 1953), p. 107.

[16]In Lbm Add. MS 29378 is contained John Eccles's music for the entertainments in this tragedy, including on fols. 5'-6' an overture in G minor for strings in four parts (no trumpets are indicated or appropriate); this is probably the introductory music to a musical episode within the first act. Additional dances for the tragedy are found in *Theater Musick Being A Collection of the newest Ayers . . . perform'd by Both Theaters*, I [1698], 21-27 (only copy in Dc), also by Eccles.

[17]Lincoln, "Eccles and Congreve: Music and Drama on the Restoration Stage," *Theatre Notebook*, XVIII (1963) [7], erroneously implies that the curtain fell to music at the ends of acts: "Each act ended with a curtain tune which began during the final couplets of the closing speech, and each act opened with Act music." There is no evidence that the descent of the curtain (at the end of the play) was accompanied by music.

[18]As is shown below, a few plays apparently had fifth-act tunes, and the prompt notes for Edward Howard's *The Change of Crownes* [1667] include the direction "Act Ready" a few dozen lines before the end of the last act, thus suggesting a fifth-act tune (see n. 19 below).

[19]For example, in *The Change of Crownes*, "Act Ready" is found about 30 or 40 lines before the end of each act. And a copy of James Shirley's *The Sisters* (1652), apparently used for a post-1660 production (see *The Poetical and Dramatic Works of Sir Charles Sedley*, ed. V. de Sola Pinto, I [London, 1928], 300), has the handwritten stage direction "Act Ready" or "Ring" about 20 or 30 lines before the end of each act. "Ring" is apparently directed to the musicians, as no special stage effects follow nor do forthcoming entrances need to be prepared. "Act" refers either to the act tune or to the interval between two acts. This double meaning is made clear in, for instance, "A Lampoon on the Greenwich Strowlers," in *Covent Garden Drollery* (1672), p. 24, a satire on travelling companies, in which the story teller, in a reference to the troupe's embarrassingly small orchestra and slowness in changing the scene, says, "I ordered the Drummer to beat a long Act."

[20]The first three act tunes may not be by Locke; concordances for these pieces in Yale University Filmer MS 7, fols. 23'-24, are ascribed in part to "Mr Robt Smyth." Furthermore, in the Yale copy of Locke's printed score, each piece has been carefully marked in a contemporary hand with an "X." I am grateful to Mr. Robert Ford for this information.

[21]Brisk's remark in V.i of Shadwell's *The Humorists* (1671) is typical of the dozens of allusions to the inter-act behavior of certain members of the audience: ". . . no man appears better upon a Bench in the Play house, when I stand up to expose my person between the Acts, I take out my Comb and with a bonne mien combe my Periwig to the tune the Fiddles play."

[22]In *The Works Of the late Ingenious Mr. George Farquhar*, II, 105-106.

[23]An act tune is rarely used more than once in a play. Besides the third act tune in *Rinaldo*, there are two other instances of borrowing: in Dryden and Grabu's *Albion*

and Albanius: An Opera or, Representation in Musick (1687), p. 93. At the end of the first act is this note: "Take for the Entract the AYRE play'd in page 78." Therefore the "AYRE for the four Parts of the World" is used as the act tune. Also in the same score on p. 230 at the end of Act II is the following note: "The AYRE for the Gods of the Floods is to be play'd betwixt the Act[s], Page 167."

[24]In *The Musical Entertainments in the Tragedy of Rinaldo and Armida*, p. 113. Dennis also states that the "Musick betwixt the First and Second Acts, begins with a Trumpet Tune, suppos'd to be play'd by the same Spirits who play'd the Overture, but changes with the Scene to soft Musick, and falls gradually to softer, and at last Drowzy Musick, which continues very softly the first Ten or Twelve Lines of the Second Act."

[25]Purcell only rarely failed to observe this "restriction." See, for example, *Ayres for the Theatre*, p. 47, "Slow Aire" in C minor in his act music for a revival of Durfey's *The Virtuous Wife* (published 1680).

[26]Act music was performed at public concerts and other music meetings. See Tilmouth, "Chamber Music in England, 1675-1720," pp. 13-67. See also Appendix II, *Harmonia Anglicana*, First Collection, Set I: "A New Set of Ayres [by Mr. Orm] for the Consorts of the Musicall Society."

[27]Cf. Estcourt's definition of act music in the dedication to *The Fair Example*, discussed above, in which he states that the preliminary music consists of an "Air" and a "Chacone."

[28]Only the following additional play-books from the period contain songs: Durfey's *The Fool Turn'd Critick* (1678), Dryden and Lee's *The Duke of Guise* (1683), Tate's *A Duke and no Duke* (1685), Durfey's *A Fool's Preferment* (1688), and Dryden's *Amphitryon* (1690).

[29]Roy Lamson, Jr., in "Henry Purcell's Dramatic Songs and the English Broadside Ballad," *PMLA*, LIII (1938), 150, assumes that these songs replaced the instrumental tunes, as does Zimmerman, in *Henry Purcell 1659-1695: An analytical catalogue of his music* (London, 1963), pp. 282-283. Although no act tunes survive for *Theodosius*, this does not preclude instrumental pieces also being played between the acts, as may have happened between Acts IV and V of Rowe's *The Fair Penitent* (1703) and several other plays.

[30]Otway's *The Souldiers Fortune* (1681), after Act IV; Tate's *Cuckold's-Haven* (1685), after Act II; Dryden's *Love Triumphant* (1694), after Act II; Norton's *Pausanias* (1696), after Act II; and Rowe's *The Biter* (1705), after Act I.

[31]By [John] Barret[t] in Lcm 1144, fol. 15 ff, entitled "The Fool in Fashion" (this is the second title of the comedy).

[32]"Go home unhappy wretch and mourn" (D&M 1141 *m*Frank *s*Mrs. Cross and "the boy") and "What ungrateful devil moves you" (D&M 3668 *m*D. Purcell).

[33]See Appendix I. *The London Stage*, II:1, 37, records that Steele's *The Funeral* (1702) had considerable entr'acte music accompanying its performance on 28 May 1703. This might account for the diminished amount of act music for the play. The incidental

music to Ravenscroft's tragedy *The Italian Husband* (1698) is not surprisingly missing the third and fourth act tunes, as this play consists of three instead of the usual five acts.

[34]Published in *Letters from Orinda to Poliarchus* (London, 1705). Although the original letters (written some 40 years before their publication) are not extant, their authenticity is beyond doubt. See Philip Webster Souers, *The Matchless Orinda* (Cambridge, Mass., 1931), esp. pp. 180-187, for an account of the correspondence between Mrs. Philips and Cotterell.

[35]10 January 1663; *Letters*, pp. 110-111.

[36]D&M 2370. The song-book, John Playford's *Choice Ayres, Songs, and Dialogues* (1675), does not reveal Philaster's identity.

[37]Not extant, but Mrs. Philips states that it was composed by "a Frenchman of my Lord Orrery's" (see *Letters*, p. 120).

[38]2 May 1663; *Letters*, p. [142].

[39]The music survives in Och Mus. MS 350, pp. 93-94, where it is ascribed to "Mr Banister," presumably the musician who was a member of the King's Violins at the time. That he could have been in Ireland in May 1663 is shown by a gap in the payments made to him as court musician between 15 April and 10 July of that year when he performed at Windsor. See Henry Cart de Lafontaine, ed., *The King's Musick* (London, 1909), pp. 156 and 159.

[40]3 June 1663; *Letters*, p. 157.

[41]In Och Mus. MS 350, p. 98, unascribed. According to Mrs. Philips (31 January 1663; *Letters*, p. 120), it was set by "one Le Grand a Frenchman, belonging to the Dutchess of Ormond."

[42]In Och Mus. MS 350, p. 100. The stage directions state that the masque was "made (as well as the other Dances and the Tunes to them) by M. John Ogilby." This is the first mention of a dancing master in a Restoration play.

[43]*Letters*, p. 120.

[44]Consider, for example, the show that Dryden planned for the first entr'acte of his dramatic opera *The State of Innocence* (1677):

> Betwixt the first Act and the second, which the Chiefs sit in the Palace may be expressed the Sports of the Devils: as Flights and Dancing in Grotesque Figures; and a Song expressing the change of their Condition. . . .

CHAPTER 3

[1]Some authorities on Restoration drama hold the unfortunate notion that actresses never sang songs specifically required of them in the play-books. See, for instance,

Lincoln, "Eccles and Congreve," p. 9: ". . . it must be realized that actresses during the Restoration never sang. If a song was called for, a professional singer rendered it and then the play continued."

[2]That she sang is also confirmed by Durfey's preface, which remarks that the song was "incomparably well sung, and acted by Mrs. Brac_girdle, that the envious do allow. . . that 'tis the best that [was] ever done before. . . ."

[3]See Dryden, *The Assignation* (1673), III.ii: *Lucretia*. . . . I am resolv'd we'll make our selves as remarkable as we can: I'll exercise my tallent of Dancing. *Hippolita* [played by Mrs. Knepp]. And I mine of Singing. . . (a "SONG and Dance" follow; the song is "Long betwixt Love and fear," D&M 2057 *m*R. Smith); Dryden, *An Evening's Love* (1671), IV.i: "Beatrix [played by Mrs. Knepp] sings. SONG" ("Calm was the Even," D&M 468 *m*Marsh); Dryden, *Secret-Love* (1668), IV.ii: *Asteria* [played by Mrs. Knepp]. Shall I sing the Song you made of Philocles, And call'd it Secret-Love? *Queen.* Do, for that's all kindness: and while thou sing'st it. I can think nothing but what pleases me . . . (the song, "I feed a flame within," follows); Durfey, *Trick for Trick* (1678), II.i: *Sabina*. . . . Come, prithee sing us a Scotch Song, I know thou art good at it . . . (Dorothy, played by Mrs. Knepp, sings "A Broad as I was Walking," D&M 5); Wycherley, *The Country-Wife* (1675), V.iv: "Lady Fidget [played by Mrs. Knepp] sings" ("Why should our damn'd Tyrants oblige us to live"); Wycherley, *Love in a Wood, or, St James's Park* (1672), I.ii: *Lady Flippant* [played by Mrs. Knepp]. Stay, Sir, because you hate marriage, I'll sing you a new Song against it ("A Spouse I do hate," D&M 3965 *m*Humphrey). See also Boyle, *The Black Prince* (1669), I.ii, in which Sevina (played by "Mrs. Napp," i.e., Knepp?) "plays upon the Lute."

[4]His first name, like those of many of the early Restoration players, is not known.

[5]See *Diary* (25 February 1669): "[*The Royal Shepherdess* was] the silliest for words and design, and everything, that ever I saw in my whole life, there being nothing in the world pleasing in it, but a good martial dance of pikemen, where Harris and another do handle their pikes to admiration. . . ." Pepys probably refers to IV.ii: "The Scene changes to the Temple. After the Sacrifice, there is a Consort of Martial Musick . . . [then] A Martiall Dance."

[6]See, for example, John Downes, *Roscius Anglicanus* (1708), p. 28: "[Dryden's *Sir Martin Mar-all*] was Crown'd with an Excellent Entry: In the last Act at the Mask, by Mr. Priest (the land-lord) and Madam Davies (Millicent)." See also Flecknoe, *Euterpe Reviv'd* (1675), p. 64:

How I admire thee, Davies!
Who would not say, to see thee dance so light
Thou wert all air, or else all flame and spright--

[7]See II.ii: Gatty (played by "Mrs. Davies") sings in a catch, "This is sly and pretty." And in V.i she sings "To little or no purpose I spent many days."

[8]See D&M, "Index of Singers and Actors," pp. 416-417.

[9]See Farquhar, *The Constant Couple* (1700), III.i: Plume (played by Wilks) sings the song "Come fair one be kind," the musical sources of which mention this actor as its singer (see D&M 626 *m*Leveridge *s*Wilks). See also Southerne, *The Wives Excuse* (1692), IV.i:

> *Mr. Friendall* [played by Mountfort]. Get the cards in the Drawing-room.
>
> *Mrs. Witwoud.* Not till we have the Song; Mr. Friendall, you promis'd us.
>
> *Mr. Friendall.* Why, faith, I was forc'd to set it my self. I don't know how you'll like it with my voice; but faith and troth, I believe the Masters of the Musick-meeting, may set their own words, for any trouble I shall give 'em for the future about mine. . . .

> [Song written by a Man of Quality] "Say cruell Amoret, how long"

For this song, see D&M 2852 *m*H. Purcell *s*Mountfort.

[10]*An Apology for the Life of Colley Cibber, with an Historical View of the Stage during His Own Time* (1740), ed. B. R. S. Fone (Ann Arbor, 1968), p. 76.

[11]That is, Crowne, *Sir Courtly Nice: or, It Cannot Be* (1685).

[12]Cibber's lack of an adequate singing voice is the subject of the epilogue to his comedy *The Lady's last Stake, or, The Wife's Resentment* [1708], which he delivered. After parodying Italian opera recitative, he says,

> My Voice, 'tis true, The Gipsy's but unkind to,
> Tho' that's a Fault you ev'ry Day are blind to,
> But if I change my Name, that half will win ye,
> O! the soft Name of Seignior Cibberini.
> Imagine then, that thus with amorous Air
> I give you Raptures, while I squall Despair.

See *Rare Prologues and Epilogues 1642-1700*, ed. Autrey Nell Wiley (London, 1940), p. 295, for a quotation reprinted from *The Daily Courant* (1 January 1708) probably concerning this epilogue. See also the tongue-in-cheek remark in Cibber's *Apology*, p. 125: ". . . no Italian Eunuch was more applauded than when I sang in *Sir Courtly*."

[13]30 October. See *The London Stage*, II:1, 46 and *passim*.

[14]*Apology*, p. 98.

[15]See, for instance, Durfey, *Don Quixote*, Part III (1696), III.i: Mary the Buxome (played by Mrs. Verbruggen) sings "The old Wife she sent to the miller her daughter" (D&M 2602).

[16]These include Farquhar, *The Constant Couple* (1700), IV.ii: "Wildair [played by Mr. Wilks] sings" ("Thus Damon knocked at Celia's Door," D&M 3351 *m*D. Purcell *s*Pate); Gould, *The Rival Sisters: or, The Violence of Love* (1696), IV.i: "Gerardo

[played by Mr. Johnson] sings" ("Take not a Woman's anger ill," D&M 3145 *m*H. Purcell *s*Leveridge); Southerne, *The Maid's Last Prayer* (1693), IV.ii: "A Song. Set by Mr. H. Purcell and Sung by Mrs. Hodgson" ("Though you make no return," D&M 3331 *m*H. Purcell *s*Mrs. Dyer). Pate's singing of the song ascribed to Wilks in *The Constant Couple* is puzzling, for in III.i of the same play, the song "Come fair one be kind" was sung by Wilks (D&M 626 *m*Leveridge *s*Wilks). Songs first heard in plays were frequently sung elsewhere, and, therefore, the song-books might on occasion record the performer of a song at a concert rather that the actor who first sang it at the theatre.

[17]The child singer also became popular at this time. Jemmy Bowin, Lucretia Bradshaw, Mary Anne Campion, Letitia Cross, and James Laroche are the best known (see D&M, "Index of Singers and Actors," pp. 416-417). But child singers had been heard even in the first years of the period. See, for example, Porter's *The Villain* (1663), V.i: "Song within by the Boy" ("Beyond the malice of abusive fate").

[18]"Shou'd I not lead a happy Life, were but my Bottle like my Wife!" (D&M 2922 *m*J. Eccles *s*Reading and Lee).

[19]"Loud Music" refers either to the "loud" instruments, such as trumpets, kettle-drums, and oboes, or the music that these instruments make.

[20]From Roger Boyle, *Mr Antony* (1690), IV.ii.

[21]The "principal social functions" of late 17th-century fiddlers are discussed by Harold Love in "The fiddlers on the Restoration stage," *Early Music*, VI (1978), 391-399.

[22]"Lesson" can mean any type of instrumental piece.

[23]"Come lay by your cares" (D&M 662 *m*R. Smith).

[24]See Crowne, *The Countrey Wit* (1675), II.i: Rambler tries to retrieve a fleeing lady with music. He tells the fiddlers, "never stay for tuning--she does not come yet--scrape as loud as you can, make your Catguts squeek as loud as a Consort of Catterwaulers would at the Roasting of one. . . ." When he realizes the music is having no effect, he asks them to change the tune: "she's gone to bed, I'm ruined--sing, join all your throats." The song, "A Pox of this impertinent age" follows. Etherege, *The Comical Revenge* (1664), III.ii: Sir Frederick Frollick asks the fiddles to "Sing the Catch I taught you at the Rose [tavern]." They sing "He that will win a Widows heart." Also, see below concerning the singing fiddler in Shadwell's *Epsom-Wells* (1673), III.i.

[25]D&M 2475 *m*R. Smith.

[26]Even in the elaborate scores for dramatic operas, solo songs with more than simply a continuo accompaniment are rare. The best known are Purcell's "When I am laid in earth" from *Dido and Aeneas* and "See even night herself" from *The Fairy Queen*, both of which have four-part string accompaniment.

[27]"Fiddler," besides referring to almost any stage musician, also had a more specific meaning, though not as specific as its present one. A "fiddler" was a person who

played any one of the family of stringed instruments. See, for example, Otway, *Friendship in Fashion* (1678), V.i: Goodvile asks where Malagene is, and Victoria answers:

> Below with Sir Noble. Whilst the Butler was asleep they stole the Key from him: And there they are with the Fat-Red-Fac'd-Fidler that plays upon the Base, sitting Cross-leg'd upon the Floor, stript to their Shirts, and Drinking Bawdy-Healths.

Fiddlers were also probably skilled on wind instruments. See, for instance, Shadwell, *The Squire of Alsatia* (1688), II.i: a foolish character has been made a "compleat Gentleman" by learning music, and Sir William Belfond asks, "But among all things, how came you to make him a Fidler, always Fluting or Scraping?" One should not assume that dance music was performed only by a group of strings.

[28]See, for example, Durfey, *The Campaigners* (1698), V.iii:

> *King.* Sir, Musick shall be my task to procure, for but half an hour ago, I saw a whole Band of them Practising at a Tavern over the way, from this Window here I can beaken 'em.

[29]See *Dido and Aeneas An Opera*, ed. Margaret Laurie and Thurston Dart (London, n.d.), pp. iii-iv.

[30]"Come all away, come and sing" (D&M 586 *m*D. Purcell *s*Freeman). Also see *Dido and Aeneas*, Act I, in which the chorus to "Fear no danger to ensue" serves as a dance. Stage directions do not always provide reliable records of the playing of music in a scene, however. In Dryden's *An Evening's Love* (1671), III.i, for example, a servant announces that "the Ladies have commanded me to tell you that they are willing, before they Play, to present you with a Dance; and to give you an Essay of their Guittars." A stage direction states simply, "A DANCE," but afterwards, Wildblood says to Jacinta, one of the dancers, "While you have been Singing, Lady, I have been Praying. . . ." Perhaps she sang as well as danced.

[31]Laurie, in "Purcell's Stage Works," p. 188, remarks that this piece suffers from poor workmanship in the inner parts and suggests that Purcell probably had no hand in its arrangement. He apparently contributed only the song to this play (no act music survives).

[32]See Henry Cary, *The Mariage Night* (1664), IV.i: "Loud Musick. Enter the King, Cardinall . . . Voices, Lutes . . ."; Dryden, *Sir Martin Mar-all*, V.i: a lute accompanies Sir Martin's mouthed song in this scene; Porter, *The Carnival* (1664), II.i: "*Elvira.* . . . go touch thy Lute; / For Musick is best Physick for a mind / So out of Tune as Mine. *Bianca.* Madam, I will obey in All . . ."; John Wilson, *The Cheats* (1664), V.i: "The Lute Playes. . . ."

[33]It is probably played onstage in the following tragedies: Powell, *Bonduca* (1696), V.i: "*Bonvica.* . . . call Lucius, and bid him bring his Lute; / Fain would I leave this dire consuming Melancholy." [Enter Lucius with a Lute]; W. Killigrew, *The Imperial Tragedy* (1669), II.i: a musician plays an air and sings a song to Longinus; Dover,

The Roman Generalls (1667), II.i: "Caesar is discovered asleep in his Pavillion, a Page playing on a Lute . . ."; Otway, *Alcibiades* (1671), V.i: "*King*. Boy take thy Lute, and with a pleasing ayr / Appease my sorrows, and delude my care."

[34]See, for example, Tate's comedy, *A Duke and no Duke* . . . *With The several Songs set to Music, With Thorow Basses for the Theorbo, or Basse Viol* (1685).

[35]Also see Porter, *The Carnival* (1664), II.i: "Enter Antonio with a Guittar playing. . ."; Shadwell, *The Royal Shepherdess* (1669), II.i: "Dance with Guittars and Castanietta's."

[36]The only other mention of the harpsichord in stage directions is in Behn's farce *The Emperor of the Moon* (1687), II.iii: "Here is a song in Dialogue with Fleut Deux and Harpsicals."

[37]Reproduced in Love, "The fiddlers on the Restoration stage," p. 397.

[38]See *L'Evrope vivante, ov relation novvelle* (Paris, 1667), p. 215:

> Il faut ájoûter . . . Que la Musique y est excellente & les Ballets magnifiques; Qu'elles n'ont pas moins de douze violons chacune pour les Preludes & pour les Entr'acts. . . .

(It should be added . . . that the music [at the Theatre Royal] is excellent and the dancing marvelous; there are no fewer than 12 violins to play both the preludes and the entr'actes.) See also *Le Théâtre françois* (Paris, 1674), p. 240, by the same author: "Les Violons sont ordinairement au nombre de six, & on les choisit des plus capables." (There are usually six violins [in the French theatres], selected on their merits.)

[39]Nicoll, I, reproduces many of these documents. See esp. 353, 355, 358, 359, 365, and 379.

[40]Even Noyes, in "Conventions of Song in Restoration Tragedy," p. 171, suggests that a song in V.i of Otway's tragedy, *The Orphan* (1680), was sung by a singer "placed without doubt in the music-room above the proscenium arch."

[41]See also the *Diary* for 23 March 1661, when Pepys attended the Red-Bull theatre in Clerkenwell to see a revival of William Rowley's tragedy *All's Lost by Lust* (1619). He reports that there were several moments of confusion during the performance, "among others, that in the Musique-room, the boy that was to sing a song not singing it right, his master fell about his eares and beat him so, that put the whole house into an uprore."

[42]See Nicoll, I, 323, and Hamilton Bell, "Contributions to the History of the English Playhouse," *Architectural Record*, XXXIII (1913), 359-368, esp. 367. The most thorough study of the Theatre Royal section is Edward A. Langhans, "Wren's Restoration Playhouse," *Theatre Notebook*, XVIII (1963-64), 91-100.

[43]See Lawrence, "The English Theatre Orchestra," *Musical Quarterly*, III (1917), 20.

[44]Defined in the *OED* (s.v. "against," 1) as "facing, in front of, in full view of."

[45]If Pepys had referred to a music room over the middle of the stage, he probably would not have used the expression "over against" to describe its location, since he states that he sat in the side balcony. To be facing the room shown in *The Empress of Morocco* engravings, one would have to have been in the center of the balcony.

[46]Compare the use of this expression with Pepys's, above.

[47]In Congreve, *The Complete Works*, ed. Summers, I (London, 1923), 71-72. This is a letter written to his friend, Joseph Keally, of Dublin. See also *William Congreve Letters & Documents*, ed. John C. Hodges (London, 1964), pp. 20-21.

[48]For a detailed account of this contest, see Lincoln, "John Eccles: the Last of a Tradition," pp. 332-380.

[49]See Buttrey, "Dating Purcell's Dido and Aeneas," *PRMA*, 94 (1967-1968), 51. Also see his "The Evolution of English Opera Between 1656 and 1695," pp. 87-95, for a detailed examination of *Ariane*.

[50]See Nicoll, I, 323, and Bell, p. 367.

[51]See Summers, *The Restoration Stage*, p. 95. Bell ("Contributions to the History of the English Playhouse") believes that Wren's section shows "a 3 feet space for the orchestra" in front of the stage. But Langhans ("Wren's Restoration Playhouse," n. 1) points out that the dotted line illustrates "the curve of the apron, not an orchestra pit."

[52]See Chappuzeau, *Le Théâtre françois*, p. 240, for an account of how musicians in the French theatre were similarly moved about from place to place:

> Cy-deuant on les plaçoit, ou derriere le Theâtre, ou sur les ailes, ou dans vn retranchement entre le Theâtre et le Parterre, comme en vne forme de Parquet. Depuis peu on les met dans vne des Loges du fond, d'où ils font plus de bruit que de tout autre lieu où on les pourroit placer.

(Formerly, they were located either at the back of the stage, or in the wings, or in a pit between the stage and the auditorium, in a small enclosure. Recently, they have been situated in one of the lower boxes, where their sound carries better than from any other place in the theatre.)

CHAPTER 4

[1]Printed in *Court and Society from Elizabeth to Anne. Edited from the Papers at Kimbolten*, ed. W. D. Montagu, Seventh Duke of Manchester, II (London, 1864), 55.

[2]But see Hume, "A Revival of *The Way of the World* in December 1701 or January 1702," *Theatre Notebook*, XXVI (1971), 30-36.

[3]In the preface to *Brutus of Alba* (1678).

[4]See Noyes, "A Manuscript Restoration Prologue for *Volpone,*" *Modern Language Notes,* XLII (1937), 198-200.

[5]*Tragedies of the Last Age Consider'd and Examin'd* [1678], p. 6.

[6]*A Short View,* pp. 1-2. Collier's effectiveness as a critic must certainly be due in part to the undeniably low state to which drama had sunk at the time when he attacked it. His tepid remarks about music in plays suggest that he did not consider it capable of expressing gross immorality, which, after all, was his principal target.

[7]*Apology,* pp. 66-67.

[8]That is, John Fountain, from whose play *The Revvards of Vertue* (1661) Shadwell took much of *The Royal Shepherdess.*

[9]See Jonson, *The Alchemist* (1612), "To the Reader . . ."

> If thou art one that tak'st up, and but a Pretender, beware at what hands thou receiv'st thy commoditie; for thou wert never more fair in the way to be cos'ned (then in this Age) in Poetry, espcially in Playes: wherein, now, the Concupiscence of Daunces, and Antickes so raigneth, as to runne away from Nature, and be afraid of her, is the onely point of art that tickles the Spectators.

Also see *Bartholomew Fayre* (1614), "The Induction":

> Hee is loth to make Nature afraid in his Playes, like those that beget Tales, Tempests, and such like Drolleries, to mixe his head with other mens heeles, let the concupisence of Iigges and Dances, raigne as strong as it will amongst you. . . .

[10]A similar sentiment is expressed contemporaneously by Aphra Behn in the prologue to *The Debauchee* (1677):

> From France you bring us Noise [i.e., music], instead of Sence:
> Instead of Courage, saucy Confidence. . . .

[11]*The Man of Mode* (1676), prologue.

[12]*Love and Revenge* (1675), prologue.

[13]Of comedy, he says later, "Your true English and my way is to write your Plays with double sense and brisk meaning songs."

[14]In "Of Heroique Playes An Essay," published with *The Conquest of Granada by the Spaniards,* Part I (1670).

[15]"Why so cruel to your Lover?" a dialogue between a man and a woman.

[16]The song, sung by Sir John himself (played by Mr. Boman) is "Delia tir'd Strephon" (D&M 835 *m*J. Eccles *s*Boman).

[17]The song "O how you Protest" (D&M 2479 mH. Purcell) was sung by Mrs. Knight, who played Lady Barter.

[18]The song is "Ah Sacred Boy desist," sung by Betty (played by Mrs. Napper). The music does not survive in the printed sources.

[19]"A Nymph and a Swain to Apollo once prayed" (D&M 2443 mJ. Eccles sPate).

[20]The first such songs are probably those by Katherine Philips for the intervals of her translation of *Pompey* (1663).

[21]Sometimes "modesty" prevented the person's name from appearing, but the play-books make the person's rank clear. For instance, in Tate's *A Duke and no Duke* (1685) are three songs printed at the end of the play-book, with no indication of where they are to be sung in the play: "A SONG written by a Lady, and set to Music by Mr. King" ("Ah poor Olinda! never boast," D&M 74 mKing), "A SONG written by a Person of Quality, and set to Music by Signior Baptist" ("Who can resist my Celia's charms," D&M 3905 mDraghi), and the last, by an author who had no reason to dissemble, being "A SONG written by Sir George Etheridge, and set to Music by Signior Baptist" ("Tell me no more I am deceiv'd," D&M 3162 mDraghi).

[22]"A wig that's Full" (D&M 3966 mRamondon).

[23]To ensure the latter, nonautonomous masques were frequently a collaborative effort by two or three composers. For example, John Eccles and Godfrey Finger collaborated on the music for Motteux's masque, "The Loves of Mars and Venus," attached to Ravenscroft's *The Anatomist: or, The Sham Doctor* (1697).

[24]In V.ii is the masque "Endimion; The Man in the Moon."

[25]Will Mountfort, Will Pinkethman, Thomas Dogget, Joe Haines, Cave Underhill, Cibber, and Powell are just a few of the actor-playwrights of the Restoration.

[26]From *The Comical History of Don Quixote. The Third Part. With the Marriage of Mary the Buxome* (1696), preface.

[27]"A Letter to Mr. D'Urfey, occasioned by his Play called the Marriage-Hater Match'd [from Charles Gildon]," printed in *The Marriage-Hater Match'd* (1692).

[28]Beginning in the 1690s, a playwright received the box office receipts of the third, sixth, ninth, etc., performances as payment for his services.

[29]His highest praise for a composer is expressed in the famous preface to his dramatic opera, *Psyche* (1675):

> And by his excellent Composition, that long known able and approved Master of Music, Mr. Lock, (Composer to His Majesty, and Organist to the Queen) has done me a great deal of right. . . .

Shadwell was also pleased to have his play saved by a singer or dancer. For example, in the preface to *The Humorists* (1671), is the incredible remark that his play would have

fall'n beyond Redemption, had it not been revived, after the second
day, by her kindness (which I can never enough acknowledge) who,
for four days together, beautified it with the most excellent Dancings
that ever has been seen upon the Stage.

The dancer was probably Mrs. Johnson.

[30]Purcell's song "In these delightful pleasant [fragrant] groves" (D&M 1782) was used in
a 1691 or 1692 revival of *The Libertine* (1676), IV.ii. See *The London Stage*, I, 399.

[31]See, e.g., *The Squire of Alsatia* (1688), II.i, where this comedian and musician (who
acted the role of Belfond Junior) probably played one of the two accompanying flutes
in "Still wilt thou sigh and still in vain" (D&M 3076), the music for which was
written by Shadwell himself.

[32]See William Bowden, *The English Dramatic Lyric, 1603-42* (New Haven, 1951), pp.
87-94, for a study of "blank songs" in Jacobean drama, and F. W. Sternfeld, *Music in
Shakespearean Tragedy* (London, 1967), p. 21-22. Sternfeld's suggestion that "the
frequent absence of the texts of the songs [in the Elizabethan era] is probably
connected with the difficulties of musical notation which is legible only to theatre
musicians and a few actor-singers . . ." does not explain the Restoration phenomenon.

[33]See Michael Tilmouth, "A Calendar of References to Music in Newspapers Published
in London and the Provinces (1660-1719)," *R. M. A. Research Chronicle*, No. 1.
(1961), *passim*. This calendar, more than Avery's *The London Stage*, provides the
clearest and most comprehensible view of extra-theatrical musical life in London
during the Restoration.

[34]For another reference to these famous concerts, see Charles Boyle's comedy *As You
Find it* (1703), II.iii. Sir Pert reminds Bevil that the little concert they have just heard
is as fine or finer than the real thing:

> *Sir Pert.* This is a noble Entertainment . . . and much beyond any
>   thing I ever heard in York-Buildings.
> *Bevil.* I believe they are most of 'em the same Hands that play
>   there.

Bevil's comment does not dampen Sir Pert's pride, as he counters: "So far
from that, that there are Three Faces I never saw before."

[35]The most complete and accurate account of Britton's activities is found in Sir John
Hawkins, *A General History of the Science and Practice of Music*, II (London, 1875),
788-793. Britton is honored elsewhere in Restoration dramatic literature: the
prologue to Boyle's *The Tragedy of King Saul* (1703) is critical of the quality of
English poets and their metrical translations of the Psalms and declares that

> Musick succeeds your Inharmonious Songs,
> And Brittain does atone for Brittain's Wrongs,
> As David's Pleasures, David's Pains Requite,
> And makes him Sing a Poem he would write.

The reference is obscure, to be sure, but is almost certainly to the "small-coal man," for this prologue plays with the dual meanings of pairs of words.

[36]The following songs are used in at least two plays: "How vile are the Sordid Intregues" (D&M 1469 mH. Purcell) in Durfey's *The Marriage-Hater Match'd* (1692), II.i, sung by Berenice [?] (who was played by Mrs. Lassells), which is also in Durfey's *The Richmond Heiress: or, a Woman Once in the Right* (1693), II.ii, sung by Fulvia (played by Mrs. Bracegirdle); "Whilst wretched fools" (D&M 3895 mD. Purcell) in Durfey's *The Famous History of the Rise and Fall of Massaniello*, I (1700) (the act in which it is sung is not specified), sung by Messrs. Pate and Leveridge, is also in Durfey's *The Famous History and Fall of Massainello: or, A Fisherman a Prince*, II (1699), II.i, as "A Dialogue between a Town-Sharper and his Hostess"; "Since we poor slavish Women know" (D&M 2971 mBanister) in William Wycherley's *The Gentleman Dancing-Master* (1673), II.ii, is also in Reuben Bourne's *The Contented Cuckold, or the Womans Advocate* (1692), V.i. Songs which appear in plays but which were first published elsewhere include "Come thou glorious object of my sight" (D&M 714 mH. Lawes) in Sir William Killigrew's *Selindra* (1665), III.i, published first in Henry Lawes, *Ayres and Dialogues, For one, Two, and Three Voyces*, I (1653); "Love thou art best of Human Joys" (D&M 2115 mH. Purcell), in Thomas Wright's *The Female Vertuoso's* (1693), V.i, text published in *The Gentleman's Journal: or The Monthly Miscellany*, II (October, 1693), 330, attributed to "a Lady of Quality"; note that D&M fails to associate Purcell's song (2115) with this play; "Phylliss [Phyllis] for shame let us improve" (D&M 2682 mHumphrey), in Bourne, *Contented Cuckold* (1692), III.i, published first in *Choice Songs and Ayres for One Voyce* (1673); "Since we poor slavish women know" (D&M 2971 mBanister), from the same play, V.i, first published in *Choice Ayres*. Again, D&M fails to associate either song with this play.

[37]See, for example, the notice in *The Daily Courant* for 6 July 1702 announcing that the Theatre Royal would present the next day Southerne's *Oroonoko* "with new Musick set to Flutes; and to be perform'd by Mr. Banister and his Son, and others, and some of Mr. Weldon's new Songs, perform'd in his last Consort." One might think that this new music was to be heard between the acts or before or after the play. But see below.

[38]See Tilmouth, "Calendar," *passim.*

[39]Quoted in Tilmouth, p. 52.

[40]Trumpet sonatas are found elsewhere in Restoration drama as interludes in masques; Henry Purcell's "Sonata while the sun rises" in the fourth-act masque in *The Fairy Queen* (1692) (Z 629) is perhaps the most noteworthy. *Love's Last Shift*, III.ii, is, however, the only appearance of a "trumpet sonata" in a standard five-act comedy.

CHAPTER 5

[1]The letter is printed without date in Percy Fitzgerald, *A New History of the English Stage* (London, 1882), I, 240. The "Italian woman" is perhaps Margarita de l'Epine.

[2]Much of the rest of this chapter is drawn from my article, "The Critical Decade for English Music Drama, 1700-1710," *Harvard Library Bulletin*, XXVI (1978), 38-76, to which the reader should refer for more detailed documentation.

[3]See Jack A. Westrup, *Purcell* (New York, 1962), pp. 75, 82, 114-115, 241, and 319.

[4]See, e.g., Shadwell's *Bury-Fair* (1689), III.i ("They Sing an Italian Song of two parts") and this playwright's earlier comedy *The Lancashire-Witches* (1682), III.i, where an Italian song is preceded by a discussion of how the English gentry "are so much poysoned with Forreign Vanities. . . ."

[5]The singer is generally identified without documentation as Margarita de l'Epine; see, e.g., Tilmouth, "A Calendar," p. 13. However, Margarita is first recorded as singing in London at the Lincoln's Inn Fields Theatre in 1703 (see *The London Stage*, II:1, 37 ff.), having sung in Venice around 1700 (see Ursula Kirkendale, *Antonio Caldara, sein Leben und seine venezianisch-römischen Oratorien* [Graz, 1966], p. 29, n. 3). The details of the unknown 1693 singer's visit to London are recorded by John Baynard, an amateur musician, in a letter of 7 January of that year to William Holder (in Lbm Sloane MS 1388, fols. 78-78').

[6]Evidence that singers performed before plays began is found in a letter dated 18 April 1706 from Nicola Haym to the Vice Chamberlain, in which Haym apologizes that the two singers he had agreed to supply that night are unable to attend before the play ends; he suggests that his pupil, the Baroness, "begin with her Songs . . ." (in US CAh Thr 464.4.15*, fol. [35], copy in Lbm Add. 38607, fol. 97). See also the proposals submitted to the Lord Chamberlain on 28 January 17[06] regarding Katherine Tofts's fee for singing "each time . . . before the Curtaine is drawn up" (rpt. in Nicoll, *A History of English Drama*, II, 290).

[7]See Lowell Lindgren, "A Bibliographic Scrutiny of Dramatic Works Set by Giovanni and His Brother Antonio Maria Bononcini," Diss. Harvard (1972), pp. 166-167. The aria was "S'envola il dio d'amore," published in *The Monthly Mask of Vocal Music ... for December 1703.*

[8]This group of actors, headed by Betterton, had since the secession occupied a theatre in Lincoln's Inn Fields. For an account of disputes between Betterton and the Theatre Royal, see Nicoll, *A History of English Drama*, I, 336-342, and Shirley Strum Kenny, "Theatrical Warfare, 1695-1710," *Theatre Notebook*, XXVII (1972-73), 130-145.

[9]See Cibber, *An Apology*, p. 172.

[10]For an account of the establishment of this theatre, see Judith Milhous, "New Light on Vanbrugh's Haymarket Theatre Project," *Theatre Survey*, XVII (1976), 143-161. Professor Milhous shows convincingly that from the beginning of the project Vanbrugh intended to accommodate operas and "Entertainments by Musick" in his new theatre.

[11]For a detailed description of this opera, see Lindgren, "A Bibliographic Scrutiny," pp. 172-175.

[12]Appended to François Raguenet's *A Comparison of the French and Italian Musick and Opera's* (1709, rpt. Farnborough, Hants., 1968), p. 65.

[13]Copy in US Wc. The wide disagreement between these nearly contemporaneous accounts, while striking, is partly explained by the fact that Nicola Haym, the adaptor of Bononcini's *Camilla* and an occasional enemy of the English musician, is probably

the author of "A Critical Discourse on Opera's and Musick in England." This important discovery is made by Lindgren in "Parisian Patronage of Performers from the Royal Academy of Music (1719-28)," *Music & Letters*, LVIII (1977), 7. Cf. Stoddard Lincoln's conjecture that John Ernest Galliard penned this work, in "J. E. Galliard and *A Critical Discourse*," *Musical Quarterly*, LIII (1967), 347-352.

[14]Lindgren, "A Bibliographic Scrutiny," p. 174.

[15]18 December 1705. See *The London Stage*, II:1, 110.

[16]This is the only act in any of Congreve's comedies which could conceivably stand alone as a piece of bedroom farce. Its featured characters, Mr. and Mrs. Fondlewife, do not appear in any of the other four acts; it is an interlude of low humor in the middle of Congreve's complex plot.

[17]Rpt. in *William Congreve Letters & Documents*, p. 35.

[18]See Milhous, "New Light on Vanbrugh's Haymarket Theatre Project," p. 156.

[19]*English Theatre Music in the Eighteenth Century* (Oxford, 1973), p. 34.

[20]*Roscius Anglicanus*, p. 48. Hume, in a review of Fiske's book (*Philological Quarterly*, LIII [1974], 565-567), also doubts that *Ergasto* was sung in English.

[21]See the 25 November-2 December 1704 advertisement in *The Diverting Post*, which states that "*Segniora Sconiance*, a Famous *Italian* Singer, who lately came from those Parts. . . ," sang at the inaugural concert for the Haymarket, more than four months before the April 1705 opening (rpt. in Milhous, "New Light on Vanbrugh's Haymarket Theatre Project," pp. 152-153).

[22]The work was announced in *The Diverting Post* on 4 November 1704: "An Opera in French, Set to Musick by Baptista de Lully, and translated into English by the Honorable G. Granville, Esq.; now set to Musick by Mr. Eccles; the Parts are all disposed, and will speedily be perform'd at the New Theatre in Little Lincoln's-Inn-Fields." See Lincoln, "The Anglicization of *Amadis de Gaul*," *On Stage and Off: Eight Essays in English Literature* (Washington State Univ. Press, 1968), pp. 46-52.

[23]The last new dramatic operas to be mounted were Daniel Purcell and Godfrey Finger's "Alexander the Great," an operatic version of Lee's tragedy *The Rival Queens, or the Death of Alexander the Great* (1677), performed on 20 February 1701 at Drury Lane, and Finger and Settle's *The Virgin Prophetess: or, The Fate of Troy*, performed on 12 May 1701, also at Drury Lane. For more information on "Alexander the Great," see my "Eight 'Lost' Restoration Plays 'Found' in Musical Sources," *Music & Letters*, LVIII (1977), 297-299.

[24]Downes, *Roscius Anglicanus*, p. 49.

[25]G[iles] J[acob], in *The Poetical Register; or, the Lives and Characters of All the English Poets* (1723), I, 124-125, gives an account of *The British Enchanters*:

> My Lord [Granville was later made Lord Lansdowne] had taken an early Dislike to the French and Italian Operas, consisting meerly of

Dancing, Singing, and Decorations, without the least Entertainment for any other Sense but the Eye or the Ear. His Lordship therefore in his Attempt, seems to have applied himself to reconcile the variety and Magnificence essential to Opera, to a more reasonable Mode, by introducing something more substantial. . . . The Success in the Representation every way answer'd; but all future Entertainments of this kind were at once prevented, by the Division of the Theatre. . . .

26Of Eccles's music, only the song in Act III, "Plague us not with idle stories," appears to survive (D&M 2702). For Corbett's complete incidental music, see Appendix I. Cf. Elizabeth Handasyde, *Granville the Polite: The Life of George Granville Lord Lansdowne, 1666-1735* (London, 1933), p. 91: "Unfortunately no record of the music remains, not even the composer's name." Lincoln states ("The Anglicization of *Amadis de Gaul*," p. 46) that this is the only known collaboration between Granville and Eccles, but see the former's *The She-Gallants* (1696), IV.i, where the song "While Phyliss is drinking" is by Eccles (D&M 3864).

27The prologues and epilogues to *Camilla* are reprinted and discussed in Avery, "Some New Prologues and Epilogues, 1704-1708," *Studies in English Literature 1500-1900*, V (1965), 461, and in Henry L. Snyder, "The Prologues and Epilogues of Arthur Maynwaring," *Philological Quarterly*, L (1971), 615 and 624-625.

28For a selection of these attacks found in prologues, epilogues, and prefaces to contemporary plays, see Nicoll, *A History of English Drama*, II, 225-232.

29His contract with Nicola Haym for the production is partially printed in Nicoll, *A History of English Drama*, II [274]-275.

30This especially bitter attack on behalf of the shareholders (for a list of them see Lbm Add. 20726, fols. 22-23, rpt. in Fitzgerald, *A New History of the English Stage*, I, 271) is in Lbm Add. 38607, fols. 59-60. The undated document states that Rich had been manager for 12 years (since 1693; see Nicoll, *A History of English Drama*, I, 334-335), and therefore it probably dates from the summer of 1706, when rumors of an imminent change in the organization of the theatres were spreading.

31See, e.g., Mrs. Tofts's demands submitted to Rich on 28 January 1706, summarized in Nicoll, *A History of English Drama*, II, 290-291, and discussed in Mollie Sands, "Mrs. Tofts, 1685?-1756," *Theatre Notebook*, XX (1965-66), 105. See also Cibber, *An Apology*, p. 184: ". . . the Patentee of *Drury-Lane* [i.e., Rich] went on in his usual Method of Paying extraordinary Prices to Singers, Dancers, and other exotick Performers, which were as constantly deducted out of the sinking Sallaries of his Actors. . . ."

32For a discussion of the powers of the Lord Chamberlain, see Cibber, *An Apology*, pp. 186-194.

33See the copy of a 13 September 1709 letter addressed to the actor Barton Booth, in Lbm Add. 20726, fol. 33.

34In an 11 May 1708 letter, quoted in John Barnard, "Sir John Vanbrugh: Two Unpublished Letters," *The Huntington Library Quarterly*, XXIX (1965-66), 349.

[35]The documents are found principally in four locations: (1) the A. M. Broadley Collection ("The Annals of the Haymarket") in the City of Westminster Public Library, London; see Ronald C. Kern, "Documents Relating to Company Management, 1705-1711," *Theatre Notebook*, XIV (1959-60), 60-65; (2) in MS Thr 464.4.15* of the Harvard Theatre Collection at Houghton Library, Cambridge, Mass.; the largest source of Vice Chamberlain papers, this manuscript, which Sands ("Mrs. Tofts, 1685?-1736," p. 100) thought to be lost, once belong'd to W. H. Cummings, who published selected documents from it in "The Lord Chamberlain and Opera in London, 1700-1740," *Proceedings of the Musical Association*, XL (1913-14) [37]-72; (3) in Lbm Add. 38607, "The Winston Theatrical Collection"; this volume, little noticed by musicologists and drama historians, is in an early 19th-century hand and contains copies of many of the original documents in both US CAh Thr 464.4.15* and the Broadley Collection, as well as several pseudo-facsimiles of early 18th-century theatrical papers which have not been traced; (4) in US NYp MS Drexel 1986, which is similar to Lbm Add. 38607, although more corrupt in its readings of the original documents.

[36]US CAh Thr 464.4.15*, fol. [36] (copy in Lbm Add. 38607, fol. 83).

[37]In a petition submitted by Haym on 12 January 1708, the musician demands that ". . . I have a power to comand all the Musick . . ." and "that I be not considered Less, or made second to any other person of ye Musick, neither as to ye profit, nor any other matter, beliving my self perhaps, not of inferiour merit to any of my Profession now in England, particulary [sic] of ye Foreigners. . ." (US CAh Thr 464.4.15*, fol. [38'], copy in Lbm Add. 38607, fols. 98-99).

[38]See Lindgren, "A Bibliographic Scrutiny," p. 169, and Gladys Scott Thomson, *The Russells in Bloomsbury, 1669-1771* (London, 1940), pp. 123-128. Haym came to London by 1702.

[39]Halifax also owned a copy of the score of *Camilla*; see Lindgren, ibid.

[40]One of the conditions of the *Camilla* contract between Haym and Rich is that the musician be allowed to accompany his pupil Joanna Maria (the Baroness) at the rival Haymarket theatre (see Nicoll, *A History of English Drama*, II, 275). And a complaint made by the Baroness against Vanbrugh and Congreve reveals that the joint managers had struck an oral bargain with Haym that the Baroness should sing ten times for 100 guineas "either in the Pastoral [i.e., *The Loves of Ergasto*] with which the house was to be open'd, or in other playes between the Acts. . . ." But by the end of the season, the Baroness had sung only five times (the number of times *The Loves of Ergasto* was performed), and Haym complained. Congreve then offered to pay the singer 50 guineas for what she had done and to consider the bargain closed, with which Haym and his pupil agreed. But then Congreve backed down on his agreement, which occasioned the 1 March 1706 complaint (printed in Hodges, *William Congreve Letters & Documents*, pp. 113-114).

[41]Rpt. in Hodges, p. 38.

[42]*An Apology*, p. 176.

[43]Both of these documents are printed in *The Post-Boy Robb'd of his Mail* (London, 1706), pp. 342-347.

[44]The petition is in Lbm Burney 938.a.4. There is some question about the date of this important broadside. It is bound in a 1704-05 volume of the Burney newspaper collection, and Fitzgerald (*A New History of the English Stage*, I, 258-259) implies that it dates from 1708. The list of persons given on the handbill and its subject, however, place it most likely in June 1705. A copy in US NYp MS Drexel 1986, fol. 30, dates it "June 1706" in a hand and ink different from the document itself.

[45]Hodges, p. 40.

[46]See US NYp MS Drexel 1986, fols. 10-10', a 19th-century copy of a 26 April 1706 letter from the Duke of Montague to the Lord Halifax. Montague names the Duchess of Marlborough as his source for this information. Further advance warning of the Lord Chamberlain's plan is provided by "A Prologue on the propos'd Union of the two Play-Houses," in *The Poetical Courant*, No. 21 (Lbm Burney 938.a.4), dated in ink in a contemporary hand, 22 June 1706:

> Two different States, Ambitious both, and bold,
> All Free-born Souls, the New House [Haymarket] and
> the Old [Drury Lane],
> Have long contended, and made stout Essays,
> Which shou'd be Monarch, Absolute in Plays.
> . . . .
> But now (as busie Heads love something new)
> They wou'd propose an *Union*--Oh! *Mort-dieu.*
> . . . .
> If we grow one, then Slavery must ensue
> To Poets, Players, and, my Friends, to you.
> For to one House confin'd, you then must Praise
> Both cursed Actors, and confounded Plays. . . .

[47]The date of the reorganization is ascertained from Congreve's 10 September 1706 letter quoted below. The official Lord Chamberlain order does not survive (if there ever was an "official" order), but an undated, unsigned "Play house Order of Separation" is found in the Vice Chamberlain papers (US CAh Thr 464.4.15*, fols. [15-16], with a 19th-century copy in Lbm Add. 38607, fols. 45-46); this is perhaps a draft or an office copy, but it clearly pertains to this season. Since the Drury Lane company, now the only theatre permitted to produce opera, continued to act plays during the 1706-07 season, the key clause forbidding Rich's company "to represent any comedies Tragedies or other Theatrical Entertainm[ts] that are not sett to Musick" might seem to contradict the theatrical records for this season. However, the phrase "sett to Musick" did not refer just to operas but also to spoken plays with songs, masques, dances, and entr'actes--in other words, the kind of heterogeneous entertainments that Rich exploited during this period.

[48]*An Apology*, p. 178.

[49]See Lindgren, "A Bibliographic Scrutiny," p. 172.

[50]*An Apology*, pp. 177-179.

[51]Ibid.

[52]Lbm Add. 38607, fol. 60.

[53]*An Apology*, pp. 177-179.

[54]Hodges, p. 43.

[55]Cibber, *An Apology*, pp. 181-182.

[56]See Appendix I. Further evidence that the Haymarket maintained musicians is offered by a report written by Swiney for the Lord Chamberlain to explain that he had refused to let a young musician into the theatre orchestra because he was utterly unqualified (see Nicoll, *A History of English Drama*, II, 291).

[57]See *The London Stage*, II:1, 134.

[58]Lbm Add. 38607, fol. 51. The letter, superscribed "Cockpit Monday Night," is undated; since the dramatic opera was advertised for the following evening, then canceled and replaced with a standard repertory piece (*Hamlet*), this is the most likely date for Granville's complaint.

[59]See *The London Stage*, II:1, 143 and 145. There is no evidence that these last performances contained any music.

[60]See *The Muses Mercury* (January 1707), p. 11.

[61]See *The Muses Mercury* (September and December 1707), pp. 218 and 288.

[62]Lcm MS 183. For a discussion of *Semele*, see Lincoln, "The First Setting of Congreve's 'Semele'," *Music & Letters*, XLIV (1963), 103-117, and Winton Dean's response to the article, same journal, p. 417.

[63]E.g., ibid., pp. 105-106, and W. Barclay Squire, "Handel's 'Semele'," *The Musical Times*, LXVI (1925), 138.

[64]Pp. 10-11: "The Opera of *Semelé*, for which we are Indebted to Mr. C--------e is Set by Mr. *Eccles*, and ready to be Practic'd, and from the Excellence of those two Masters, in their several Kinds, the Town may very well expect to be Charm'd, as much as Poetry and Musick can Charm them." Lincoln ("The First Setting of Congreve's 'Semele'," p. 105) incorrectly ascribes this passage to the December 1707 issue, an error which weakens his speculation about the fate of this opera.

[65]US CAh Thr 464.4.15*, fols. [68-69'], with a copy in Lbm Add. 38607, fols. 51-53. This important document, written in February or March 1707, attempts to clarify several agreements between Rich and his various pasticcio makers. Its date is ascertained from internal evidence ("M[r] Claytons opera call'd Rosamond is finished & in all Probability may be perform'd in 3 Weeks time, the parts being getting up by M[r] Rich his performers"; it was first performed on 4 March 1707). The last paragraph pertains to *Semele*:

> Besides my Lord Chamberlain knows that M[r] Rich was in a manner
> Engag'd in the presence of himselfe & my Lord Hallyfax to perform

an Opera written by Mr Congreve & sett by Mr Eccles before ever Mr Headacre [i.e., Heidegger] offered his Opera [*Thomyris*] to Mr Rich, who thinks himselfe hardly used to putt by other good Bargains meerly for Mr Headacres Interest & profitt.

[66]See Lindgren, "A Bibliographic Scrutiny," pp. 228 ff.

[67]Cibber, *An Apology*, pp. 181-183.

[68]See Cibber, op. cit., and *The Muses Mercury* (January 1707), p. 12: *Julius Caesar*, e.g., "was Play'd at the Desire of some persons of Quality, who have contributed 400 l. by a *Subscription* to Support the Dramatick Muse. . . ."

[69]See, e.g., her complaint against Rich summarized in Nicoll, *A History of English Drama*, II, 290, and Kern, "Documents Relating to Company Management, 1705-1711," p. 63.

[70]This bitter petition against Rich is in US CAh Thr 464.4.15*, fols. [77-78], and in Lbm Add. 38607, fols. 77-80; Cummings prints it in "The Lord Chamberlain and Opera," pp. 42-44. Earlier in the same year (5 March 1707) Rich had been temporarily silenced by the Lord Chamberlain for disobeying an order regarding the speaking of a banned prologue. See Nicoll, *A History of English Drama*, II, 282.

[71]A report in *The Post-Boy* of 13-15 November 1707 (rpt. in *The London Stage*, II:1, 158) states that the women will not perform because there are "no Articles of Agreement between them and the Managers. . . ."

[72]See pp. 218 and 288. This opera does not appear to survive. The editor reports that "'Tis entirely Scarlati's" and that it was adapted by Leveridge, the singer, who "has the good Fortune to be an *Englishman*. . . ."

[73]Printed in Nicoll, *A History of English Drama*, II, 285.

[74]See *The Daily Courant*, 8 December 1707 (rpt. in *The London Stage*, II:1, 160).

[75]See the petition mentioned in n. 70 above.

[76]The last Drury Lane opera of the season was given on 18 December 1707 (see *The London Stage*, II:1, 161).

[77]In Lbm Add. 20726, fols. 36-36', printed in Philip Olleson, "Vanbrugh and Opera at the Queen's Theatre, Haymarket," *Theatre Notebook*, XXVI (1971-72), 95-96. The wording of this document is similar to the 1706 Lord Chamberlain "order" described in n. 47 above.

[78]*An Apology*, p. 212: "*Swiney* their sole Director was prosperous. . . ."

[79]See Olleson, "Vanbrugh and Opera," pp. 96-98, and various documents in Lbm Add. 38607, e.g., fol. 3 (proposes alternative ways of paying Valentini, Tofts, Margarita, Dieupart, Haym, and Pepusch); fol. 58 (a letter of 14 May [1708] concerning the salaries of various opera singers); Vanbrugh's original letter is in the Huntington Library, MS 6833.

[80]Rpt. in Olleson, "Vanbrugh and Opera," p. 96.

[81]In New York, Carl H. Pforzheimer Library, MS 117, printed in Arthur R. Huseboe, "Vanbrugh: Additions to the Correspondence," *Philological Quarterly*, LIII (1974), 136-137. Apparently unknown to Huseboe is the copy in Lbm Add. 38607, fols. 55-56.

[82]This is convincingly shown by Huseboe, p. 137.

[83]*An Apology*, pp. 199-208. According to a document printed in Fitzgerald, *A New History of the English Stage*, II [443], the transfer was made on 6 October 1707.

[84]*An Apology*, p. 207.

[85]See Cibber, *An Apology*, pp. 212-214, and Fitzgerald, *A New History of the English Stage*, II, 444-445.

[86]On 31 March 1708. For a discussion of this appointment, see *An Apology for the Life of Mr. Colley Cibber*, ed. Robert W. Lowe (London, 1889), II, 56, n. 1.

[87]See Nicoll, *A History of English Drama*, II, 284.

[88]Quoted in Olleson, p. 99, and in Barnard, "Sir John Vanbrugh: Two Unpublished Letters," p. 349.

[89]See Lbm Add. 38607, fols. 40-41 and 56-57.

[90]In *The Poetical Register*, I, 125.

[91]Drury Lane apparently retained only a small orchestra, as the Haymarket had done when Rich's theatre held the opera monopoly. Musicians would have been needed, for instance, when Baker's comedy *The Fine Lady's Airs: Or, an Equipage of Lovers* (1709) opened at Drury Lane on 14 December 1708, with incidental music composed by John Barrett (see Appendix I).

[92]This was not, however, the last dramatic opera to have a première. Durfey's *Wonders in the Sun, or, The Kingdom of the Birds; a Comick Opera*, "With great Variety of Songs in all kinds, set to Musick by several of the most Eminent Masters of the Age" (1706), opened at the Haymarket on 5 April 1706 and had five performances before closing on 10 April. For many of the songs in this unsuccessful work, see D&M 1212, 1772, 1891, 2223, 2499, 2742, 2950, 3478, 3622, 3735, and 3872. The incidental music is by John Smith (see Appendix I). One more dramatic opera was published in 1709: *Alarbas*, "Written by a Gentleman of Quality." Apparently it was never performed.

[93]Reproduced in Sands, "Mrs. Tofts, 1685?-1756," Pl. 2.

[94]These disagreements are summarized in Cibber, *An Apology*, pp. 214-223. For another account, told from Rich's point of view, see Lbm Add. 20726, fols. 29-29'.

[95]E.g., Swiney made a contract with the actress Mary Porter before Rich was silenced and before actors were allowed to return to the Haymarket (see Nicoll, *A History of English Drama*, II, 286).

[96]Rpt. and discussed in Avery, "Some New Prologues and Epilogues, 1704-1708," pp. 464-466.

[97]*An Apology*, p. 139.

[98]The Lord Chamberlain's succinct order is partially quoted in Nicoll, *A History of English Drama*, II, 282.

[99]The personnel of the Haymarket company and their duties appear in a document issued on 24 December 1709, although the troupe began acting in September of the 1709-10 season (see Nicoll, ibid., pp. 278-279). The Drury Lane company, temporarily without a manager, did not open until November.

[100]See Lbm Add. 20726, fols. 29'-33'.

[101]See Lbm Add. 38607, fols. 24-25, and the Lord Chamberlain's response in Nicoll, *A History of English Drama*, II, 292.

[102]See Lbm. Add. 20726, fols. 31'-33.

[103]*An Apology*, esp. p. 173. The location of the new theatre was probably equally responsible for its being selected as the opera house. *The Muses Mercury* for December 1707 (pp. 287-288) explains that plays were attended largely by a middle-class audience from the City, whereas opera was the court's favorite pastime. Since Drury Lane was farther east than the Haymarket (therefore closer to the City), it was more convenient to "the Scene of Business," while the opera company, situated closer to St. James's, was "nearer than ever to their Protectors."

[104]For the date of his arrival in England, see Olleson, "Vanbrugh and Opera," p. 100. The letter is in US CAh Thr 464.4.15*, fols. [97-98'].

[105]Nicoll, *A History of English Drama*, II, 275-276.

[106]See *The London Stage*, II:1, 203 and 206.

[107]See his complaint in Lbm 1879.c.3, fol. 58.

[108]A Lord Chamberlain's order of 17 April 1712 requires that "The Undertakers and Managers of the Comedy shall not be pmitted to represent any Musical Entertain.ᵗ or to have any Dancing pform'd but by the Actors" (Nicoll, *A History of English Drama*, II, 281).

[109]3 April 1711. *The Spectator*, ed. Donald F. Bond, I (Oxford, 1965), 119-120.

[110]See *The London Stage*, II:1, 246.

[111]From the prologue to Edmund Smith's tragedy *Phaedra and Hippolitus* [1707].

APPENDIX II

[1] In Source D is the rubric "M.ʳ Orm's Musick for Mʳ Banisters Consort."

[2] This is labelled as "I" in Source B.

[3] This is labelled as "VI" in Source B.

[4] This date, suggested by *The London Stage*, II:1, 66, is probably too late.

[5] No printed first-treble part for this suite survives; it can be supplied from US Wc M1515.A11 Case, pp. 232-245. This manuscript is compiled mostly from *Harmonia Anglicana*.

[6] A complete four-part setting of this set of act music is found in Och MS 3, fols. 41'-44.

[7] It is not certain to which "Henry the Fourth" Corbett's music belongs; perhaps this is one of the plays that the Lincoln's Inn Fields company acted while in Oxford during the summer of 1703. See *The London Stage*, II:1, 25.

[8] This is probably some of the music played at a concert in honor of Queen Anne and Archduke Charles (later King of Spain) at Windsor Castle on 30 December 1703, being repeated at the Theatre Royal, Drury Lane, on 4 January 1704. For a discussion of this event see Henry L. Snyder, "The Prologues and Epilogues of Arthur Maynwaring," *Philological Quarterly*, L (1971), 613, and n. 11.

[9] See Price, "Handel and the Alchemist," *The Musical Times*, CXVI (1975), 787-788.

GENERAL INDEX OF NAMES, TOPICS, AND COLLECTIONS OF MUSIC

Titles of critical works are omitted, although authors' names are included. Entries under playwrights, librettists, and composers refer only to general discussions rather than to specific works. Manuscripts are listed by city and library, but the locations of unique copies of printed editions are not indexed. Principal discussions are shown in bold-face type.

INDEX OF SONG TITLES

INDEX OF STAGE WORKS

For a more complete listing of second titles, lost titles, abbreviations, and other corruptions, see Appendix I.

DATE DUE

HIGHSMITH 45-220